S0-EHG-271

Atlantic Ocean

N

W   S

Yours in Christ!

Joseph A. Maier

Rom. 8, 37.

Victory Through Christ

BX
8066
·M25
V5

82481

Victory
Through Christ

RADIO MESSAGES BROADCAST IN
THE TENTH LUTHERAN HOUR

By WALTER A. MAIER, PH. D.

Professor of the Old Testament
Concordia Theological Seminary
SAINT LOUIS, MISSOURI

*"O earth, earth, earth,
hear the Word of the
Lord!"* —Jeremiah 22:29

CONCORDIA COLLEGE LIBRARY
BRONXVILLE, NY 10708

CONCORDIA PUBLISHING HOUSE
ST. LOUIS, MO. :: 1943

Copyright 1943
by
CONCORDIA PUBLISHING HOUSE
St. Louis, Mo.

PRINTED IN U. S. A.

To

Mr. and Mrs. Charles G. Lang

"My fellow workers unto the kingdom of God"

Colossians 4:11

Foreword

Our 1942–1943 radio season was notable because it brought the tenth anniversary of our mission of the air. The opening announcement on every program during this period proclaimed: "Bringing Christ to the Nations! The Tenth Anniversary Lutheran Hour!" We felt that attention should be called to the remarkable fact that during a decade of peace and war God had permitted us to broadcast the Gospel of Jesus Christ with its pledge of salvation and its divine help for our distracted age.

For ten years the Holy Spirit touched the hearts of our listeners, and in an increasing degree prayers ascended to heaven beseeching divine benediction on our work. For ten years the broadcast promises of peace and pardon through faith in the Savior's atonement led tens of thousands in our country and many beyond its borders to contribute the large sums required for our broadcast (we pay for every moment of our network time at the full commercial rate). For ten years our appeal for repentance and faith in Christ has led multitudes from sin to salvation. We thus have overabundant reason to thank our Triune God for the benediction and direction without which our efforts would have failed. I praise the goodness of the Lord because He gave me health and strength to speak in every regular broadcast.

During a period as long as this, personalities inevitably come to the forefront. Lest too much recognition be given the human side of our radio endeavors, I tell our readers emphatically — as I have stated in gatherings from coast to coast — that no credit whatever should be given me personally. All honor to God and to Him alone! In my own eyes it is a marvel of divine grace that this mighty missionary enterprise, begun with hesitation and executed as only a part of my busy seminary life, has enjoyed such startling success. Humbly and reverently we who have witnessed God's glorious guidance in this happy work declare that the Lutheran Hour should be classified as one of the mighty miracles of missionary history, a twentieth-century wonder, in which the Savior demonstrated the unfailing truth of His promise, "All things are possible to him that believeth."

The aspect of our radio mission which fills me with constant awe is the fact that these years have recorded an unmistakable increase in the listening audience. For the first half of the tenth season (the period from October 25, 1942, to Palm Sunday, April 18, 1943, represented by the messages in this volume) about 275,000 letters came to radio headquarters and to my office. These communications, the largest number ever received during a similar period, furnish definite evidence that the American people are not tired of the Gospel. Despite war and its disturbances, restrictions, and counterattractions our broadcast has gone forward in amazing strides.

During the ten seasons a total of more than 1,500,000 letters were sent to the Lutheran Hour. If the ratio of advertising men is correct in its claim that we should figure 1,000 listeners for every letter, the radio has certainly demonstrated its remarkable power in spreading the Savior's Gospel.

The tenth-anniversary season was appropriately marked by farsighted action on the part of the Lutheran Laymen's League when it adopted the long-discussed and earnestly desired resolution to broadcast continually each Sunday throughout the year. If it be God's will, may our mission of the air now be maintained uninterrupted until Christ returns in His second coming! The new fifty-two-Sundays-a-year program entails almost double the previous expense, but with unlimited confidence in the Lord's power to help us, we have adopted these concise statements as the expression of our purpose:

> Through the whole year — Now!
> Through the whole world — Soon!
> Through the whole Gospel — Always!

The international character of the Lutheran Hour was strikingly emphasized again by the truth that, although the war prevented us from maintaining our broadcast in the Philippine Islands and China or from using scheduled outlets in Australia, New Zealand, India, and Portuguese West Africa, we were able to maintain about 450 stations in the United States, Canada, and the following countries and territories:

Alaska	Costa Rica	Iceland
Argentina	Cuba	Nicaragua
Bolivia	Dominican Republic	Panama
Brazil	Dutch Guiana	Paraguay
British Guiana	Ecuador	Peru
British West Indies	Haiti	Puerto Rico
Chile	Hawaii	Uruguay
Colombia	Honduras	Venezuela

Our messages were transmitted from these stations either in English, Spanish, or Portuguese, and the Gospel reached far beyond the confines of their countries.

It was indeed gratifying, for example, to read reception reports like these:

A missionary from Tarma, *Peru*, writes:

It has been my good pleasure to listen to your broadcasts over Station WLWO, Cincinnati, for some time. I am happy to report the messages are bringing special blessings both in English and in Spanish. You will be interested in the enclosed picture showing this missionary in the midst of a group of Indians. Far in the interior, where few civilized men penetrate, the Red Men gather around the portable radio to hear about the living God. Unconscious of the fact, through the interpreter, you occasionally speak to Indians in the remote regions of the Amazon jungle. The radio messages, true to the Gospel, bring much personal encouragement to me when I am alone in the hinterland among the semi-civilized and savage tribes, sometimes a week's journey or more beyond the bounds of civilization.

A convert in Jamaica, *British West Indies*, says:

I listen in to your program and enjoy it very much. I'm sure that all who hear it must derive some spiritual benefit. I am a new convert who accepted the Lord through hearing your broadcasts over Station HCJB, from Quito, Ecuador. I want to live as full a life for God as I possibly can.

From *Colombia* a young inquirer writes thankfully:

With intense spiritual blessing I listen to the Lutheran Hour each Sunday. I will appreciate receiving literature and all available publications. I am a medical student and receive spiritual strengthening from the Christian truth and Gospel grace explained on your broadcast. I shall continue to listen regularly and tell my friends.

A *Dominican Republic* resident pleads:

I write you in Spanish, but by nationality I am a Chinese and, of course, born a Buddhist. With all sincerity I want you to know that I have felt a great desire to hear God's Word since listening to your broadcast. I hope to receive from you the necessary help toward my salvation in Christ.

A Maracaibo, *Venezuela*, woman says:

I do enjoy your teachings. For almost fifteen years I have not heard Gospel messages like yours. Thank God for His Word, which has brought me back to the path I once walked, the path of light!

A grateful listener in *Costa Rica* reports:

I congratulate you, and I hope that your work will prosper greatly. My mother has now become a true believer in Christ. There are twelve in our family, but my older brothers love the world and its pleasures very much. We hope the Lord may sooner or later touch their hearts.

A pastor in Mexico City, *Mexico*, sends this interesting account:

I rejoice over the fact that our Lutheran Hour is being translated into the Aztec or Nahuatl language at Milpa Alta, D. F., Mexico. We used an extension and placed the radio out in the *patio*, or yard, so that as many persons as possible could listen to the Lutheran Hour without having them crowded and uncomfortable.

The results of our broadcasts in each of these countries and in many others, could they be catalogued in detail, would fill a good-sized volume. As we survey the whole Latin-American situation, places and incidents like this flash across our minds: In a Dominican Republic village the one family that owns a large loud-speaker, every Sunday invites scores of people to hear the Lutheran Hour. The villagers bring their lunch and assemble as at our out-door mission services. When the broadcasting time arrives, they all listen carefully. After the program they try to sing as many of the songs as they can.

Despite military restrictions which have eliminated our short-wave transmission from this country, we are able to reach Great Britain and other English-speaking countries, especially through station HCJB in Quito, Ecuador. The international program sponsored by the British Broadcasting Company literally reached around the world. We were startled to receive letters like these:

Bebington, Cheshire, England — Sunday's international program was truly unique. For was it not a most rare occasion in the history of English broadcasting when the true Gospel of Jesus Christ was fearlessly and unashamedly proclaimed, without any frills, by the American professor? I wonder whether he would have been allowed to preach so full of fire in this country. Compared with the polite, dead, political droning of the majority of our broadcasters, it was truly refreshing. It was a trumpet call to the sleeping Church to proclaim the truth of the Gospel story in its simplicity and wonder, and not as we get it, so dressed up in church organization that it lulls people into smug, half-doped complacency. Surely, if such truth is proclaimed, the people of Britain will realize how Christ loathed the Laodicean church, and return to their first love and serve the Savior of the world in great humility. Our people need the Gospel of Christ's redeeming love. That and that alone can save our beloved land of England and the world.

Barking, Essex, England — I thoroughly enjoyed the speech. If only the British preachers would preach to the English public like that, I am sure more people would attend church.

Brigus, Newfoundland — I am an Englishman who has given forty years to the preaching of the Gospel in Newfoundland. This morning I had the pleasure of hearing your truly wonderful address over the radio. Yours is a message that I would like to see written across the sky, where everyone who runs might read. In all you said I am entirely with you. Long may you be spared to give such shining messages as the one we heard this morning!

Marine Parade, Bluff, New Zealand — You voiced exactly what I myself believe, and I do hope that you will be able to carry on the good work.

England — I feel I must write to thank you for the many times you have encouraged and comforted me and many of my friends over Station HCJB. (We have an excellent reception here.) For the duration of the war I am doing part-time transport work and arrive home in time to catch your 1:15 A. M. English program. Many is the time when we have had to leave our beds during a raid, and after the all-clear we have tuned in and picked you up. On one occasion in particular during a severe *Blitz* on my home town, after the all-clear we tuned in. I cannot tell you in words what it meant to us at that time. It has been just like the voice of almighty God encouraging me.

I sincerely hope that the British Broadcasting Company will permit us to send regular transatlantic messages after the war is over. The results from one effort up to date have convinced us that England, Ireland, and Scotland need the Gospel at least as much as our own country. Pray for a regular broadcast to Britain!

The department of our mission which received the most emphasis during the past season was the work among our military men and women. We thank God that we were able to increase our station list on two vital fronts, Hawaii and Alaska. The Hawaiian broadcast is significant because at first some, expressing sincere doubt as to the results on that distant island, urged us to move cautiously. What a loving rebuke of weak faith God has given us in a large and responsive Hawaiian audience! One grateful woman in Honolulu alone contributed generous gifts, which exceed the total broadcasting costs of the two stations KGMB in Honolulu and KHBC in Hilo. In Alaska the station at Anchorage, KFQD, has helped to bring Christ's courage and comfort not only to the isolated inhabitants of this section but also to our soldiers in the Arctic regions. A chaplain one Sunday, after services, writes that his men on the Aleutians voluntarily contributed $150 to help maintain and expand our Gospel network.

Special efforts were devoted to reaching our fighting forces. Here, too, we were under the evident guidance of God. Censored soldier mail from abroad brought us letters like these:

Somewhere in the Pacific — Here on the battle front God has permitted me to listen to your broadcast. In these perilous times, when I can see so much sin around me, it does my heart good to listen to a Gospel message. God is still on His throne and still cares for His own, no matter where they are.

Aleutians — I just heard the Lutheran Hour. We surely should be thankful to have such a great and convincing broadcast. I get more good out of one of your sermons than all these modernistic preachers preach in a year. A couple of boys here also listened to the Lutheran Hour sermon with me. One said the sermon made him feel very cheap because he hasn't gone to church in so long a time.

On an Atlantic Island — I am a boy in the service. For eight months I have been stationed where there are no churches. Recently I turned on your broadcast. When I started to listen to it, the fellows turned it off. When I turned it back on and told them to listen, they got mad. But after your broadcast they felt ashamed of themselves. We are stationed on an island forty miles from the

Atlantic Seaboard; the only way to hear the news from the main-
land is by radio.

Somewhere in Hawaii — I have had the opportunity to hear
Dr. Maier's message Bringing Christ to the Nations for the past
three Sundays, and I can assure you that the importance of the
Lutheran Hour was impressed on me as I sat listening here in
Hawaii, thousands of miles from its origin.

Somewhere in the Pacific — We heard the Lutheran Hour this
morning. We are Seabees; some of my mates here expressed the
desire to have a copy of your sermon. It was very touching to
one of my mates in particular, whose wife had just lost a baby
at birth. Your broadcasts are doing a wonderful work in bringing
others to Christ.

In Southern Waters — I tuned in yesterday to your Sunday
broadcast and enjoyed it very much. Where I am, under the
Southern Cross, I, too, would like the small gold cross to wear
to serve as a personal inspiration and to encourage the boys
whom I, as a surgeon, am treating.

On the Atlantic — I am a captain in the Navy and move ships
in and out the convoy fleet at sea. The submarines and foreign
warships never bother me. Please pray for me! Your Sunday broadcasts mean much to me, whether I am on land or sea.

With the Pacific Fleet — A sailor of the U. S. S. —— requested
my used transcriptions of the Lutheran Hour in order that his
shipmates might hear them. They have a chaplain aboard who is
glad to cooperate. The sailors went to considerable trouble and
expense in preparing a turntable.

Somewhere in the Pacific — If it is possible, I would like to
receive copies of as many of your addresses as possible. We have
Bible-class meetings on this ship, and I'm sure that your messages,
especially on Scripture, prayer, and the sure plan of salvation,
will be of great help.

The response from soldiers still in our country and Canada
was, of course, far larger, and the help which the Lutheran
Hour offered these men and women in the service can hardly
be estimated. If during our entire broadcasting season we had
been able to accomplish nothing more than to bring our
military youth the Savior's promise of forgiveness, strength,
companionship, and guidance, all the money spent for this
mission of the air would have been well expended. We have
received many revealing letters like these:

Iowa — I am a soldier in the Army Air Corps and have been
in service for six and a half months. I haven't missed one of your

programs since you started this season. I don't know of anything that I have experienced in my entire life that gives me the same satisfaction, peace, comfort, and assurance that I get when I can sit before my radio here in the barracks and listen to your inspiring words of how to receive eternal life through Christ. Quite a number of boys in my barracks do not believe in Christ, but this does not stop me from tuning in your program. One of the boys got so "brave" that he turned off the current this afternoon, but I have a portable radio, which is a plug-in or battery set. I just turned it on the battery with very little time lost, and your program went on just the same. I am mocked for my belief, but this doesn't stop me from letting people know what I am. I pray to Christ, our Savior, to give you and me strength to carry on the work of bringing Christ to the world.

Ontario — I brought a radio down to our canteen and tuned in to the Lutheran Hour. I was very much impressed by the sermon and also the music.

Kansas — I have recently joined the Army Air Corps. I haven't missed a Lutheran Hour since I am here, and every Sunday I get a few more together around my radio to listen in. The sermon today was especially commented on, even by boys who do not ordinarily go to church. I am sure that before long the entire barracks will be listening to your Bringing Christ to the Nations.

Maryland — I enclose a small contribution to aid your splendid work in spreading the Gospel of our Lord. I am a Roman Catholic and an Army officer who recognizes the great work you are doing.

Oregon — Scene: Portland Army Air Base. The telephone rings. My commanding officer is calling. He wants me, his chaplain, to come to his room to listen with him to the Lutheran Hour. We sit in an unfinished room of the officers' barracks and hear the Lutheran Hour over his auto radio. He tells me that he has listened faithfully for years. He is a flying officer, a devoutly Christian officer.

A particularly impressive part of our work among the soldiers was the Lutheran Hour transcription service, which, as part of our war service, brought our message to more than sixty United States Army camps. By special arrangement with the local chaplains the Lutheran Hour was reproduced for the men, usually as the regular Sunday evening service. Typical reactions to these programs may be seen in this tribute:

Camp Roberts, California — It might interest you to know we began reproducing the Lutheran Hour last Sunday evening with marked success. It is to be a regular feature.

The transcriptions were also used on Pacific troop transports and in remote military outposts.

Once more the radio proved its unique power of penetration, by bringing the Gospel to those who live in remote districts, on islands, in forests, beyond the range of the Church, or to those people who were kept from church by gasoline rationing, storm, sickness, or occupation. Besides, our messages reached homes and listeners who ordinarily could not be induced to enter a Lutheran church. Notable again were the increasing number of letters from Roman Catholic listeners. Here are a few:

Immaculate Conception Convent — I have been quite a frequent listener to your Sunday program. I was so happy over last Sunday's. It was new life to me. The manner in which you can explain God's Word is marvelous. Please accept this small token to help further your message! Would you be so kind as to send me the sermon? Please pray for me! I, too, am praying for you that God in His own goodness and mercy may help you to carry on this broadcast. You are doing wonderful work. God bless you!

Saint Mary's Seminary — May I thank you for the pleasure and inspiration which you, by the help of God, brought to me this afternoon? I liked your conviction and your sincerity. I am not a Lutheran. In fact, I am about as far removed from Lutheranism as I could be. I am soon to be ordained to the Catholic priesthood.

Rhode Island — In a recent conversation with Father —— of Saint Mary's Church of this city he expressed great admiration for the way that you preach the Gospel in its pure and unadulterated form.

New Jersey — I was born and brought up a Catholic in Switzerland. However, through a friend, who has interested herself in me, I listen to the Lutheran Hour every Sunday and also attend a Lutheran church here in Paterson quite regularly. I seem to get so much more comfort and strength from the Lutheran faith than I do from my own. God willing — I hope to become a Lutheran some day.

Ontario — We are a Roman Catholic family and seldom listen to religious programs on the air. But for some reason we cannot dial you off. Your sermons are good and to the point. We would like to know more about your faith. You preach Christ and His works.

Virgin Islands — I want to assure you that it is now of more interest and satisfaction to me to turn on the radio, not only by my bed but also in the parlor (so that the family can hear your words), than it is to go to Mass.

Pennsylvania — I am a Roman Catholic, but I am dissatisfied with my religion. After hearing your recent broadcasts, I desire to know more about the Lutheran faith and doctrines.

Minnesota — My husband and I listen to your program every Sunday and are glad to have such wonderful church service on the air, especially with the tire and gas rationing. My husband was a Catholic when I married him, but his listening to your program has helped me to convert him to the Lutheran faith. Our pastor instructed him and confirmed him.

North Carolina — It has been my pleasure, and an enjoyable one, to listen to your broadcasts for several Sundays, when not engaged in my own official duties as priest. I want to say to you how much I get out of them. I am helped so very much by them that I frequently call others' attention to the time and station, hoping they, too, will find comfort and strength in them. I have wondered if those sermons preached for the current quarter could be had for personal reading, help, and inspiration. Because of my work, I have missed hearing one or two of these. But I should like to have a chance to read them all. May God strengthen you to continue such broadcasts to the world that man may be converted, for certainly this is one great need of the world today!

By divine blessing we are permitted to establish contact with many of the neglected and misunderstood racial groups in our country. For instance, Japanese Christians in the relocation centers write letters like these:

Hunt, Idaho — Your program reaches us through the radio station in Twin Falls, Idaho, every Sunday, and you can be sure that our dials are turned that way every Sabbath afternoon.

Minidoka, Idaho — I have been an ardent listener of the Lutheran Hour for about three months, ever since the time we have been sent to this war relocation center. I am an American citizen of Japanese ancestry. We have been evacuated from the vital coastal area. I know that in a time like this nothing is more important than our faith in God. I enjoy your Lutheran Hour program immensely, and each Sunday it has brought me new inspiration and a deeper reverence for God.

The Lutheran Hour has a large and growing audience among Negroes at home and abroad as well as among other racial groups. Communications like this are ample reward for all our efforts:

Pittsburgh, Pennsylvania — I am a Negro. In my twenty-six years of life in the world I have endured the hatred and abuse that most of white America feels for its colored citizens. I have observed and read colored newspaper accounts of the incredible viciousness of color prejudice in the South. Through it all I grew to hate white people indiscriminately. I became more and more bitter with each new incident of social, economic, or political injustice. I have stated this in order to give you an idea of how deeply I felt and what a great change your program, Bringing Christ to the Nations, has brought about in me. Today the same conditions exist in regard to the Negro, but I no longer feel bitter about it because I have learned from your sermon about the love of Christ for everyone, His enemies, unbelievers, as well as those who love Him.

Missouri — I, an American Indian, am praying for you and hope you are in good health. I love your sermons more than those of any other preacher. God bless you! Let me hear from you please!

Particularly gratifying was the response from pastors of practically all Protestant denominations. Literally thousands of letters have poured in with sentiments like these, which show a new appreciation for Scripture truth:

Maryland — No words can express the gratefulness we feel and the joy we have in hearing the Lord Jesus Christ proclaimed and glorified. We are workers in the Methodist Church, humble believers.

Illinois — I have been enjoying your services on the radio and I would like very much to have some of your addresses if you have copies available. I am pastor of a Baptist Church and have used some of your material in my sermons. I am heartily in accord with your emphasis on a Christ-centered ministry and pray that the Lord will mightily use you in the future.

Pennsylvania — I, a Congregational minister, listen to your weekly broadcasts. I announce them from my pulpit. I have been sending contributions.

New Jersey — I greatly appreciate your positive faith in the Gospel of our Lord and Savior Jesus Christ. We also appreciate the fact that you speak fearlessly about sin and the one way of salvation. May God continue to bless you in your work! I am the pastor of a Holland Reformed church.

Pennsylvania — We at Westminster Seminary join in the work of your radio broadcast. We share in the thoroughly Biblical and militant Christianity which you preach. We pray the Lord to bless both the message and the beautiful Christian music to the hearts of men.

Florida — Here is a check for $25.00 to be used as you deem best to the spread of the Gospel. I am able to send you a little

Tenth Lutheran Hour

more than I had planned since the income tax proved to be less than I had saved for. I am a volunteer church worker here in this little place under a young priest of the Episcopal Church. He is really a missionary priest, with about ten small missions to care for.

California — I have listened to your hour on Sunday afternoon both this year and last and have enjoyed it very much. I believe that is what this country needs. I am a minister in the Church of the Nazarene and wish you much success in your work.

The tenth-anniversary broadcast continued to fulfill one of its most important functions by helping our missionaries find open doors in their house-to-house calls. Our pastors continue to write us letters like these:

Pennsylvania — When I left Concordia Seminary I became "missionary at large" and spent five months canvassing from house to house in various cities and towns of New York and Pennsylvania. My partner and I always identified ourselves with the Lutheran Hour. It was indeed gratifying to see how many people listened to you regularly and to experience the many warm receptions we received when the people learned we were connected with the Lutheran Hour and had attended your classes at the Seminary.

Ohio — Recently I received a list of several Lutheran Hour contact names. The day before yesterday I completed the pleasant task, requiring three days and nearly 250 miles of driving. In every instance the meeting with these folks was a most cordial one. What a remarkable change was registered in their faces as soon as the Lutheran Hour was mentioned! These follow-up calls for the Lutheran Hour were among the most interesting and fascinating that the undersigned has experienced during his nine brief years in the ministry. God bless you and your co-workers for your efforts in behalf of Bringing Christ to the Nations!

Michigan — I want to express again my deepest appreciation and thanks for the boundless inspiration you have given me with your marvelous soul-saving message Sunday after Sunday. They have helped me wonderfully to carry on and improve my work here in the Christian day school, the congregation, and the community. Your powerful influence has helped greatly in building up our school inwardly and numerically, which by the first week of February had already grown from thirty pupils to seventy-three pupils.

Texas — The Lutheran Hour is doing much to open the door to us down here on the southern tip of Texas. When I came here several years ago as a missionary, people sometimes looked at me rather askance when I told them that I was a Lutheran, but now

I get many a greeting like this: "Oh, yes, come in! I have been hearing your Lutheran Hour."

Oklahoma — The large number of adult members whom we have been privileged to instruct and add to our roster during the past year were induced to attend the instruction classes partly because of the knowledge of our Church which they gained from listening to the Lutheran Hour.

Once again in this tenth season we were visibly reminded that God keeps His word and that His Gospel does not return void. Although the radio speaker is under the obvious disadvantage of not being able to see his hearers and meet them after the sermon, the power of the Holy Spirit once more recorded remarkable victories for Christ by calling men and women from the darkness of sin into the glorious light of salvation. We thank the Lord especially for the letters from which excerpts like these have been taken:

Minnesota — I was saved through you. When I was about to resort to self-destruction, I heard your voice, and now I am a member of your faith here in St. Paul. The pastor visits me regularly and is of great help to me.

Pennsylvania — I am writing you to say I listened to your broadcast last Sunday. A load was lifted off my shoulder, and I accepted the Lord Jesus Christ. I am now happy to think you have opened a way for me, and I hope you will keep on praying for me, as I am not so strong yet in the Lord. I attend church and feel like a different person as I know I am one of His now.

Alabama — I am so grateful to my precious Savior for all He has done for me through the last four years. It was through you that I found my Lord all the way. Of course, as I have already told you, I loved Him; but I have never realized what Jesus did for me until I listened to the Lutheran Hour. The first time I ever heard you, you told me more about my Savior than all the preachers I had ever heard before.

Michigan — We listen to your sermons on Sunday, and we surely get food for our souls. We appreciate your straight-from-the-shoulder delivery of Bible facts. I don't want to find fault, but we don't get that kind of preaching in the churches here. We were converted at home through your broadcast and reading the Bible. Neither of us had even been in church for twenty years before that. We were terrible people — drank, swore, and fought, in fact, did about anything we or anyone else could think of.

California — I am writing to tell you that today I was received into full communion with Grace Lutheran Church by confirmation.

I am also glad to say that your sermons have helped me to see the light. I was formerly a member of the Roman Catholic Church.

Pennsylvania — I came to know Christ through the Lutheran Hour only a few years ago. Since then I am not only a listener but have advertised the broadcast in the daily paper, told many individuals of it, and had our minister ask the congregation to tune in regularly.

Ohio — I want to thank you very much for the soul-stirring sermon you preached today. It filled me with such a longing for Christ that I cried all through the message. I've never had a definite religion, but I want you to know that your sermon has come to me in an hour of need. I was disgusted with life and ready to end it; but, oh, how wonderful I feel now! I believe I have the strength to carry on. This is the first time I have heard your program. I shall endeavor to lead a righteous life in future. Oh, there are no words to express the wonderful things that happened to me during that program! My one hope is that it reached the hearts of others as it did mine.

Colorado — I received Mrs. ——'s name through the Lutheran Hour about two years ago and ministered to her regularly until the day of her death. I officiated at her funeral several weeks ago and was privileged to state that she departed this life trusting in Him who alone is able to save. She listened to every Lutheran Hour broadcast and voiced a genuine appreciation. May God continue to bless your broadcast!

Ohio — I listened to your program, and it has helped me. I am going to join the catechism class in the Lutheran church in my city.

Ohio — I wrote you one year ago as an unchurched listener. Today I am a member of the Lutheran Church, baptized and confirmed.

Missouri — A student mission activity at Venice, Illinois, bears testimony to the results of the Lutheran Hour. A large percentage of the Christians attending our services there praise God for the Lutheran Hour, for it was through this radio program that they first made contact with the Lutheran Church. There is, for instance, Mrs. ——, eighty years old. For seven years she listened regularly to the broadcasts. Then one day she sent her son to the city library for some biographies of Luther. She read them, with the result that she asked the nearest Lutheran pastor for instruction. Two years ago she was confirmed. Then there is Mrs. C——, who has searched long for the Church with the truth. She found the truth in the message of the Lutheran Hour and expressed her joy over the fact by tithing to this radio program.

When later she was visited by one of our canvassers, she soon began to take instructions and has now become a very zealous church worker.

California — Thanks to the Lutheran Hour, my husband is now a Lutheran. I cannot thank God enough for all His blessings and rejoice that the Lutheran Hour has made our family all of one faith.

Nebraska — If it weren't for the Lutheran Hour on Sunday, I don't know what I would do. I have listened to it for years, and it has brought my husband to church with me every Sunday. If it weren't for the Lutheran Hour, I could never get him there. Now he can't miss a Sunday, and if something should happen that we don't get to church, my husband says the day is not right. I was baptized and confirmed and surely do get a lot of good out of the broadcast.

Not only were many thus saved, but others who had denied the Savior were reclaimed by the Spirit through the Lutheran Hour message. Those won again for Christ send us grateful acknowledgments like these:

California — I trust you will remember me in your prayers. Through you I have just recently gotten back to the Lord. I had backslidden and fallen deep into sin. I have prayed sincerely for forgiveness. We have such a gracious God, or He would never have heard my prayers.

North Dakota — This summer I was home alone one Sunday and listened to your broadcast. I was deeply thrilled. It made me realize that we shouldn't live our lives as a daily routine but that we should live for our Lord. After your broadcast I knelt down beside the radio and prayed. I had for a time almost lost my faith because none of my prayers was answered. But your sermon brought me back, and I now know that there is no one to whom we can really take our prayers but our precious Lord Jesus.

Texas — About two years ago I found in Paris a Lutheran Hour fan in an old man who has been reared in the shadow of the old Seminary in St. Louis, instructed and confirmed by Dr. Stoeckhardt, and had drifted for twenty-five years or more, but found his way back to his God and Church through the Lutheran Hour.

As in previous years, God has moved friends throughout the country to supply the funds required to defray the costs of our radio crusade for Christ, for the transcriptions at home and abroad, and for the maintenance of a large office staff which during the peak of the broadcasting season lists about fifty employees. No salary was paid the speaker, the announcer, the Seminary students' Lutheran Hour Chorus, nor a group of voluntary workers. In reviewing the financial help, we recall these instances of remarkable stewardship:

A $7,000 check from a Baltimore business man (the largest single gift ever received) who regards this broadcast as one of the Church's greatest missionary endeavors.

A $1,500 check from a Chardon, Ohio, listener, not a member of our Church, who appreciates the interest the Lutheran Hour has shown in our nation's soldiers.

A letter from Worcester, Massachusetts, declares: "We are poor boys and earn our money by shining shoes on the streets. We enclose two dollars of our shoe-shine money to help you in your glorious work."

A crippled child asks that his Christmas gift of money be sent to the Lutheran Hour.

A widow forwards $1.25, found in her deceased husband's pocket.

A California man sends his life's savings in coin.

A Pittsburgh industrialist encloses a $100 check with a note stating that he thinks this will do more good than a contribution to his modernistic church.

A Decatur, Illinois, couple contributed $102, a dollar for each man in the nation's service from their congregation.

Another Decatur congregation contributes $2.50 for each member in the armed forces from its midst.

From Iowa a woman writes: "I am enclosing a small contribution, seventy-one cents. Of it, twenty-one cents were left in our little son's bank when he died.

A listener gives $20 which he had received for two blood transfusions.

An Addison, Illinois, congregation sells its unused school building and devotes a part of the proceeds for the Lutheran Hour.

Besides giving thanks to God for His constant help, I must express my gratitude to many co-workers and friends whose interest, efforts, prayers, and gifts have been of inestimable help to me. Particularly am I grateful to:

All listeners who have prayed, worked, and given for these international broadcasts;

All pastors who have co-operated in following up missionary opportunities and gaining support for our cause;

All teachers who have encouraged the school children to publicize and promote the Lutheran Hour;

Dr. Miller McClintock, president of the Mutual Broadcasting System, for his sympathetic and co-operative spirit;

All members of the Lutheran Laymen's League, which has sponsored nine of the ten seasons of broadcasts, especially their president, E. J. Gallmeyer, for his personal kindness to me in connection with the tenth anniversay;

Homer J. Fitzpatrick, chairman of the Lutheran Laymen's League Radio Committee, for his constant counsel and his friendship;

Dr. Eugene R. Bertermann, for his tireless assistance in every broadcasting problem and his entire disregard of self;

Eugene Bernald, president of the Pan-American Broadcasting Company, for his initiative and sincere co-operation in extending the field of our foreign broadcasts;

Reinhold W. Janetzke, for his regular announcing during the past seven years;

The Lutheran Hour Chorus, under the direction of Martin Werfelmann, all the other choruses and their directors, for providing the hymns;

Alfredo Saez, Manuel Morales, the Rev. Andrew Melendez, and Richard Narvaez, for their help in the production of Spanish recordings;

The members of the Lutheran Business and Professional Women's Association, for offering clerical help without any charge.

_____

We pray that these messages, now in book form, will carry on the testimony to Christ for which they were broadcast. They are printed as originally written, considerably longer than the radio version. It has been of great encouragement to note that some of the previous sermons have been translated into Spanish, Slovak, Arabic, Portuguese, French, Finnish, and reproduced for the blind in Braille or other systems of raised lettering. May the Holy Spirit again bless these pages and use them for the one purpose for which they were written: to exalt Christ, the Son of God and Savior of the world, by calling sinners to repentance and faith in His full, free, final mercies!

I wish to recognize publicly the help I received in the preparation of this volume. Prof. William Arndt, D. D., Ph. D., head of the New Testament Department at Concordia Seminary, for ten consecutive seasons has now read these broadcast messages in their original form, as in proof, and offered stimulating counsel. Miss Harriet E. Schwenk likewise has read the pages in manuscript and given deeply appreciated help in their preparation for print. Miss Lucille Biehl and Miss Bertha Wernsing have contributed stenographic help. For all this generous assistance, by which the appearance of this book has been improved and expedited, as well as for the co-operation of Concordia Publishing House, its editorial staff and management, through which many wartime problems were solved, I offer my sincere thanks.

In particular do I express publicly my gratitude to my wife for her constant companionship, her practical suggestions, and her unswerving encouragement during the entire broadcasting season.

Victory Through Christ is not only the title of this volume, but the summary of the prayer which has accompanied each of these messages. I have besought God that through the preaching of His Word heavily burdened souls might experience the blessed conviction that in Christ, and in Him alone, the believer can defeat sin, death, and hell. At the same time we who love the Lord Jesus Christ know that there can be "a victory through Christ" even in a warring world. He is our God. He can intervene to stop the horror of this struggle soon. May we learn the full lesson of repentance and faith! Whatever the months ahead may bring, let "Victory through Christ" be the resolute watchword of our personal faith and of our determination to lead others to the truth triumphant, the Savior's glorious Gospel!

WALTER ARTHUR MAIER

Concordia Theological Seminary
Saint Louis, Missouri
The Festival of Pentecost, 1943

*"Go ye into all the world and
preach the Gospel to every creature!"*

Saint Mark 16:15

Contents

XXVI   CONTENTS

Our Eyes Are Upon Thee, O Christ!

> Jehoshaphat said, "'Our eyes are upon Thee.' And all Judah stood before the Lord, with their little ones, their wives, and their children."
> 2 CHRONICLES 20:12, 13

God of Truth, Mercy, and Might:

We begin our broadcasts in Thy name, to the glory of Thy Son, Jesus Christ, our only Savior, and by the power of Thy Holy Spirit. Use this mission of the air mightily to call sinners everywhere to repentance, to comfort the sorrowful, strengthen the tempted, and convince the doubting, all through faith in the glorious Gospel of pardon and peace in Christ's cleansing blood and atoning death! Humbly we thank Thee that Thou hast preserved for us Thy sustaining Word, and we beseech Thee by Thy Spirit: Help us keep Scripture's promise in our hearts and households as Thy sacred comfort, guide, and assurance during these overshadowed days! Look mercifully on our embattled nation and, according to Thy will, grant us soon a blessed peace with the victory of righteousness and truth! Guard the young men in our armed forces who have left Christian homes to fight for our cause and bring them back to us safe in body and sound in soul! We ask it in Jesus' precious name. Amen.

RECENTLY I came across the story of an old downtown church in St. Paul, Minnesota. Years ago it had been a popular house of worship, but when the neighborhood changed, the congregation disbanded, and the building was sold. Then suddenly, on a bitter cold night, fire broke out, swept the structure and destroyed

1

everything except an eight-foot marble statue of Jesus. Entirely unharmed, it was brought to the street and placed before the smoldering wreckage. For days that figure of Christ stood in the black ruins, and multitudes, many for the first time, saw the Savior with His arms outstretched in invitation, *"Come unto Me, all ye that labor and are heavy laden, and I will give you rest!"*

In a much higher degree the whole world should see the Redeemer, not in the lifelessness of cold marble but in the living power of His love, as He rises against today's background of bloodshed, devastation, and ruin. Much that we cherish throughout the world is being consumed by the flames of fiery hatred; yet Jesus — praise His holy name! — towers victoriously, eternally, over the charred ruins of human failures. That indestructible Son of God, the Christ of endless compassion, we must bring out to the highways of humanity, so that men lift their eyes to Him in His helping, holding power. The strongest assurance for our beloved country, the immovable pledge for our churches, the unshakable promise for our homes, the holiest benediction for our souls and lives, come from beholding the Lord with eyes of faith, acclaiming Him our God, worshiping Him as our own Redeemer. His appeal *"Look unto Me, and be ye saved!"* re-echoes with heavenly comfort over the toil and tears, anguish and blood of the world's turmoil today. As we begin our tenth season of broadcasting His glorious Gospel over the largest network we have ever employed, we plead with you in His name, Behold the Lord Jesus, your Savior! In rededicating our entire broadcast to His cross, join us across the United States and Canada, beyond our borders, and out on the high seas, as we pledge:

OUR EYES ARE UPON THEE, O CHRIST!

These words are taken from Second Chronicles (chapter twenty, verses twelve and thirteen): Jehoshaphat said, " 'Our eyes are upon Thee.' And all Judah stood before the Lord, with their little ones, their wives, and their children." Though this text takes us to a far-off land and an ancient age, it offers—and may God's Holy Spirit mightily prove this now in your hearts — strength in our embattled world; it grants Heaven's joy for all earth's sorrows.

I

THE NATION'S EYES SHOULD BE UPON CHRIST

Bitter, heart-breaking days of war and bloodshed had dawned for Judah when King Jehoshaphat spoke this prayer. His country had been treacherously assailed by a powerful enemy axis: Moabites, Ammonites, and Seirites. Greatly outnumbered, God's people did what every nation should do in a crisis: they gathered to pray the Almighty for help. With heroic trust Jehoshaphat arose in the Temple courtyard at Jerusalem and in a memorable plea asked: *"O Lord God of our fathers, art not Thou God in heaven? And rulest not Thou over all the kingdoms? . . . And in Thine hand is there not power and might, so that none is able to withstand Thee? . . . O our God . . . we have no might against this great company that cometh against us; neither know we what to do."* Then he concluded with triumphant trust, *"But our eyes are upon Thee"*; that is, "we look to Thee, O Lord; we put our whole confidence in Thy power and love."

What firmness of faith that prayer showed! What a challenging example it gives us when our beloved land likewise wages a bitter, stubbornly contested war against formidable enemies! On the whole the battle has not gone well with us during the past months, and who knows what

the future can bring? In this uncertainty we should follow Jehoshaphat in training our eyes on the Lord and
pleading: "O God, *all things are possible*' for Thee. If it
be Thy will — and we pray that it may be — stop this war!
Give to our nation victory with a righteous peace for all
men and the defeat of every evil force throughout the
world!" Instead of relying only on our own strength, our
airplanes, tanks, cruisers, guns, and military organization,
we should be aware, as was this godly king of old, that
victory is finally in God's hand. He can grant or withhold it according to His purpose. Courage, sacrifice, patriotism — these and other high national virtues are necessary, but they are not enough. We need the faith that
cries, "*Our eyes are upon Thee,*' O Christ!"

If we would thus see Jesus, we must approach Him
humbly, with a penitent spirit. When Jehoshaphat and
his subjects prayed to the Almighty, they fell on their
knees before Him; and we can discern Christ's mercy
only when we sincerely humble ourselves, confess our
sins, and then receive the assurance of His blood-bought
pardon. The prayer front is as essential as any military
front, repentance as vital as any naval strategy, faith as
necessary as any aerial equipment.

How distressing, then, to realize that millions within
our borders, despite war's sorrows, have not turned to
God in His Son! At a time when America should be
moved by the greatest revival of faith in the Savior this
country has ever seen, we witness, to the contrary, an
alarming upswing of atheism, worldliness, spiritual indifference. Are the Christian churches overcrowded with
eager worshipers? Do they list sweeping numbers of con-
versions? Is the war helping to bring masses of our
countrymen to Jesus? The glaring fact remains that multitudes have turned completely from Him, that the denial

of the Almighty is often applauded, the abuse and misuse of His holy name regarded as smart and sophisticated. Magazines with circulations of several millions — not to mention the cheap gutter publications — have become notorious for their printed endorsements of cursing and swearing. One play, a record-breaking success on the American stage, permits a single character to abuse God's name forty times within two and one-half hours, while overflow audiences clap their hands. George Washington had to fight against profanity. In 1776, when the American cause seemed most difficult, he asked his officers to check this evil by their example and influence, adding, "We can have little hope of the blessings of Heaven on our arms if we insult it by our impiety and folly." Increased profanity, increased crime, increased adultery, increase of atheism, increase of unbelief, can surely mean increased struggle, more and longer battles; for, according to Holy Scripture, all war, even the most necessary and justified, comes as a visitation, the penalty for sin and ingratitude. If, then, we would see the Father as the Lord of mercy who can forgive, heal, and strengthen, you and I must come to Him with repentant sorrow for our national sins, but in the trust without which no one can see Him — the personal faith in the Lord Jesus by whom and through whom alone we are granted forgiveness and blessing. If only throughout the wide areas of our land our Christless fellow countrymen would accept the Savior, they would not only find redemption, life, light, the joy of salvation for themselves; they would also contribute to the righteousness which more than any other force can make America spiritually strong and exalted in God's sight! Oh, that it could be said in truth, "The *'eyes'* of all America *'are upon Thee,'* O Christ!"

II

THE CHURCHES' EYES SHOULD BE UPON CHRIST

It is, therefore, of double importance during these trying days that the churches with all their power help men behold the Lord. When Jehoshaphat spoke his victorious prayer, he was gathered with his people before the Temple. And where can the 135,000,000 Americans find light and guidance if not likewise in the Savior's true churches? The agonies of this hour should remind us that Christian congregations have been established, not to discuss war policies, preach hatreds, incite passions, but to proclaim Christ's sure mercies, God's whole counsel for our salvation. The preacher is not to train our eyes on men, but to direct our gaze upward to the cross and the crucified Savior of mankind, so that we find in Him pardon and peace, redemption and rest. With American young men on the six continents and the seven seas daily facing death; with the minds of the populace restless and disturbed; with our country's future now being weighed in the balance, this is not the time for pulpit attacks on the Christian faith, for Modernist denials of the Lord's atonement, for skeptical ridicule of our Holy Bible. It is the time for the churches to proclaim the full, free, final Gospel of salvation from sin, hell, death, with the promise of deliverance from fear, worry, and doubt. This is the time, high time, for the churches to follow their charter instruction, *"Comfort ye, comfort ye My people!"* by pouring the soothing, healing balm of the divine, errorless Word into the soul wounds of this suffering age. In truth this is God's time for His ministers to tell all classes and castes of men, soldiers and civilians, that Jesus is the one Hope of our age; but more: He is the sole Source of salvation, the one Answer to every personal problem, the only Friend who never fails. If in war's aftermath, when the world may be gripped by social convulsions such as we have never seen before, the churches would escape the terror of destruction that overtook religious work in Europe, let them prepare now by turning the eyes of men toward God in Christ, by serving the sorrowful, downtrodden, underprivileged, poor, neglected, among whom Jesus worked and who may easily be won for anti-God, anti-Bible movements unless they are convinced that the Church is vital, necessary, and blessed as it proclaims the message of the cross and the blood! Remember that, clergymen of America, as you also recall why the Government wisely exempts you from military service. You are spared the danger of actual conflict — not to conduct parish teas and socials, not even for soldiers and sailors. Theological training is not required for that. You have been left on the home front, not to organize scrap drives, issue rationing cards, and perform other community services, as necessary as they are. A million able-bodied women can fill such positions. You remain in your parish, rather than march to battle, not so that you can sow doubt and distrust in your hearers' hearts; the devil will take care of that. You are exempt because you are to strengthen the nation spiritually. History combines with God's Word to testify that this can be done effectively only when you lead your hearers to say, " 'Our eyes are upon Thee' O Christ!"

You who Sunday after Sunday occupy the pews of our churches, are you doing anything to help men see Jesus? Are you raising your hands or your voices to stop the treacherous assaults on your Savior that too often originate in the pulpits? Oh, may God grant that in this emergency American Christians will not be weighed and found wanting, but that by the Spirit's guidance they may stand up for Jesus and rally to His cross as never before in this plain but powerful self-dedication, " 'Our eyes,' O Christ, 'are upon Thee!' "

III

THE EYES OF ALL THE FAMILY SHOULD BE ON CHRIST

When King Jehoshaphat went to the Temple, as our text puts it, "all Judah stood," with him, "before the Lord, with their little ones, their wives, and their children." Every family and the whole family—husbands and wives, sons and daughters — turned to God. Today, too, if there is to be a deepening of our reliance on Jesus; if we are to face tomorrow's toils with assurance, then, under God, we should build Christian homes. These are trying days for our households, with many fathers preoccupied, mothers at work, and therefore children neglected. Juvenile crimes, unhappy marriages, broken households are on the increase. If the home base is weakened or destroyed; if the forces of impurity and lust gain the upper hand; if in States like Massachusetts the citizens permit the enactment of anti-Scriptural and anti-American birth-control laws; if the education of boys and girls becomes paganized, with no time left for God and things spiritual, we shall have sustained a loss a hundred times greater than all reverses on Bataan. During the months before us our households will face rationing in heat, meat, and many other commodities; yet we can survive this restriction. A house burned to the ground can be rebuilt. A family separated can be reunited; but the home that rejects Christ is built on sand; and, as the Savior warns, it will collapse when the winds of affliction blow and the floods of adversity come. How vital, then, that you fathers and husbands stand before the Lord and resolve as the head of your families: " 'As for me and my *house, we will serve the Lord.'* We will worship Him in our households"! How necessary that you wives and mothers, whom God has given an important position in human affairs, accept and follow Christ, consider your marriage vows as holy, regard the children whom God puts into your arms as sacred trusts, make your home an abiding place for His Son! How gladly you boys and girls, sons and daughters, should pray for His help and joyfully welcome Him!

If this message is now directed to families torn by misunderstanding, cruelty, abuse, selfishness, then may their members give the Redeemer His way in their hearts as they declare: " '*Our eyes are upon Thee!*' Forgive us our sins! Remove this strife! Banish all self-seeking!" That prayer will be answered. If death has snatched a loved one, focus your attention on Christ; and the same Savior who in the days of His flesh and through His Easter victory proved His power over the grave, declaring, *"I am the Resurrection and the Life; he that believeth in Me, though he were dead, yet shall he live,"* can strengthen you with the divine comfort, *"Blessed are the dead which die in the Lord."* If God lets me address families burdened by worry and uncertainty over a son in the far-off Solomons, on the high seas, with an African air corps, again I tell them: "Lift up your eyes to Christ! Accept the promise of His Word, '*casting all your care upon Him; for He careth for you!*' Entrust your faith-filled son to Him, and you need worry no longer! For whatever happens to your Christian boy is for his soul's salvation and his eternal happiness!" Let me put it all in one summarized plea: Fathers, mothers, children, families of America, stand before the Savior! Repeating this ancient prayer, *"Our eyes are upon Thee,"* you will see light behind the dark clouds, joy beyond sorrow, life victorious over death.

IV

YOUR EYES SHOULD BE UPON CHRIST

In all this, however, the appeal to you individually asks you to stand beneath the cross and declare, "My *'eyes are upon Thee,'* O Christ!" During these moments when many of you have been led before your radio for the express purpose of being turned from your sins and sorrows to the all-merciful Savior, direct your thoughts and glances away from everything else on earth! Shut out from your vision everything that would disturb or distract your mind and prevent you from concentrating on Jesus: all the fears and sorrows, the sins and vices, the griefs and burdens, the temptations and lusts! Raise your eyes to see Him alone whom angels adore, whom the mighty heroes of God rejoiced to behold, the beautiful Savior, fairer than the children of men, more glorious and radiant than cherubim and seraphim — the Son of God and the world's Redeemer. As you rivet your eyes on Him, whom do you see, and what is this Christ to you? Oh, may this truth abide deeply and irremovably in your soul! This Jesus is first of all the Lord of lords, the Sovereign of sovereigns, together with the Father and the Spirit the very God of very God. He can help you. No besetting sin, no oppressing sorrow, is too grievous or heavy for Him to remove. When everything else collapses and the last human support on which you lean breaks, kneel before Jesus, declaring, *"My Lord and my God!" "With God nothing shall be impossible."*

Who is this Christ, and what does He mean to you? Oh, hear, believe, and trust the holiest message human lips have ever spoken or mortal ears ever heard! He is your Savior, your Redeemer, your Ransom, your Atonement! If you have never known this truth before, you are now to learn the glorious fact for which our sin-corroded world still stands. This Jesus, with a love immeasurably surpassing the highest human devotion, went the way of the cross for you, because He loved you before you were born, loved you even when you rejected Him, hated Him, cursed Him. He gave Himself, His own sinless, stainless, holy, divine self into death as your Substitute, to suffer in His own body, mind, soul, and spirit the consequences of your iniquity, the punishment of your sin, the sentence of doom, death, damnation, which divine justice pronounced on you, as on every sinner. Because your eternal soul was worth more in His sight than the whole world with its glitter and glory — O wondrous love! — He shed His blood for you and on the cross endured the immeasurable, inconceivable agonies of paying for all human sin. Because He died in your stead, in payment for your transgressions, you have no iniquity in the Lord's sight. Once you acclaim your Redeemer, you have become a child of God, an heir of eternal salvation. You have a title to your prepared place in the many mansions of your Father's eternal home. All this is granted you without exemption and limitation and restriction; granted fully and freely, assuredly, eternally, by faith through the mercy of Christ. Directing your eyes upon Him, learn to say,

> My faith looks up to Thee,
> Thou Lamb of Calvary,
> Savior divine!

and He who looked at backsliding Peter with a glance of grace, who beheld the dying, penitent thief at His side and promised him paradise, will take you, just as you are, though you have turned your back on Him and lived your whole life in rebellion against Him.

Who is this Christ, and what is He to you? Here is

the promise for which millions of strife-torn men and women yearn with fervent desire: He is your Helper in every need, your Guide on each earthly path, your Comfort in all sorrow. Because He has taken away your sins and thus removed the greater obstacle to your happiness, He can banish fear and doubt, pain and heartache. He can do even more: He can change life's trials and tribulations into triumphs of His grace and have you come forth from your suffering purified, refined, stronger in your faith. Are you oppressed by an overpowering sense of your own helplessness and weakness? Look to Jesus! Train your eyes on Christ! His promise, *"My strength is made perfect in weakness,"* will give you new courage, new determination, new resistance to evil! Are you afraid of some ordeal before you? Do you face a serious operation tomorrow? Look to Jesus, and as He says, *"I will never leave thee nor forsake thee,"* you have the assurance that in the operating room He will be close by you to help you face any trial! Are you lonely, homesick? Raise your eyes to Christ! Meet Him in His Word! Hear His Gospel truth! And as during the days of His suffering He was *"alone, yet not alone,"* so He will prove Himself a soul Companion for the heavy paths you must tread. Are you distracted because hatred seeks to take possession of your heart and you find so much of godlessness in your life, so much selfish fear for the future, and even the dread of death? If, as you read the Psalmist's words, *"Unto Thee lift I up mine eyes, O Thou that dwellest in the heavens,"* if you give the Savior the control of your heart and soul; if you go all the way with Him, then the joy of an achieving, victorious life can be yours. — Over in Holland the Nazis shot a Dutch boy who had plotted against them. On the last night of his life, with only a few more hours on earth, he wrote these lines to his parents:

"I have been able to pray much and have the firm conviction that I may look forward to a death in Christ. . . . God knows that our cause was a just one. . . . I have confessed all my sins to Him and have become very quiet. . . . Therefore do not mourn, but trust in God and pray for strength. . . . Thank God that we may have the certainty of His grace. . . . We are courageous. Be the same! They can take only our bodies. Our souls are in God's hand. That should be sufficient consolation. Have no hate! I die without hatred. God rules everything."

You can have the faith by which to live, the trust by which to conquer, the love by which to forgive, the strength to face death itself, if with all your heart you turn away from the world, from self, from sin, fears, failures, and in humble contrition, yet with triumphant assurance, stand beneath the cross to say, "My *eyes are upon Thee,* O Christ!" God grant you that vision of victory for Jesus' sake! Amen.

America, Don't be Ashamed of Jesus!

> *"I am not ashamed of the Gospel of Christ; for it is the power of God unto salvation to everyone that believeth."*
> ROMANS 1:16

God of All Grace and Glory:

Humbly we bow before Thee in gratitude for the Reformation blessings, especially for the open Bible and the message of free grace through faith in the shed blood of the Lord Jesus Christ, our only Savior. For His sake forgive us our indifference toward His atoning death, our coldness in confessing Him our Redeemer, our hesitancy in proclaiming His name! Bring us all humbly yet triumphantly to the cross of His compassion! Mercifully guard our country, embattled as it is in this world-wide struggle! Give us a deep sense of personal repentance for our individual and national transgressions! Increase our trust in Christ! Protect our fighting men! Comfort the prisoners, heal the wounded, sustain the dying with the promise of eternity through their Savior, and, O Father of mercy, grant us by Thy will a just and lasting peace! We implore Thee for this benediction in Jesus' saving name. Amen.

A FEW months before Charles Darwin, often called "the Father of Evolution," died, he was visited by Lady Hope. In a signed statement this titled English woman tells how she found the scientist, who had flatly denied Scripture, propped up in his bed, reading the very Book he had attacked — the Bible. Calmly, yet forcefully he spoke on the guidance offered by the sacred Volume. He bemoaned the fact that people had accepted

14

his theories regarding man's origin as assured truth. Then he suddenly asked Lady Hope: "I have a summer house in the garden which holds almost thirty people. . . . Tomorrow afternoon I should like the servants on the place, some tenants, and a few of the neighbors to gather there. Will you speak to them?" "What shall I speak about?" Lady Hope inquired. Clearly, emphatically he replied, "Jesus Christ and His salvation," adding in a lower tone, "Is not that the best theme?" Thus, with death approaching, did Charles Darwin, evolutionist and denier of the Bible, acclaim the Lord Jesus.

This same eleventh-hour seeking refuge in Christ occurs every day along the far-flung battle lines of the Second World War. Why is it that a sailor from a torpedoed ship, rescued after floating eighteen days off Australia, cries out, "You can't be an atheist on a rubber raft!"? Why was it that when the Japanese bombardment began, soldiers on Corregidor, even those otherwise irreligious, fell on their knees before God? Why, during a recent blackout, did New York hotel guests telephone the desk for Bibles? Must we not conclude that, as danger and death approach, men usually banish their boasting ridicule of religion and humble themselves before their Maker?

How tragic, then, that even the disasters of war have not thus shocked all our people into a sense of utter dependence on Christ! Masses are crowding bars, night clubs, and places of sinful amusement, while across the Pacific American soldiers daily lay down their lives. Millions, with fatter pay envelopes than they have ever received before, are drinking, gambling, and carousing, while the sea daily takes its toll in the flower of American youth. We dare not permit pleasure to go on as usual. In this critical hour we need serious thought and especially a humble, prayerful return to the Lord. Therefore, though unbelievers reject Christ, skeptics question His Gospel, paganized thinkers ridicule His promises, atheists deride His holy name, proud sinners spurn His mercy, the cry must be:

AMERICA, DON'T BE ASHAMED OF JESUS!

Glory in His Gospel! Confess Him courageously! That loyalty to the Savior marked the mightiest of all apostles, Saint Paul, who exclaimed (Romans, chapter one, verse sixteen), *"I am not ashamed of the Gospel of Christ; for it is the power of God unto salvation to everyone that believeth"* — heroic words which I give you not only as the text but also as the motto for a Christ-centered life.

I

WE HAVE EVERY REASON TO GLORIFY HIS GOSPEL

It took magnificent courage for Saint Paul to write the first Christians in the ghettoes and slums of Rome, *"I am not ashamed of the Gospel of Christ!"* and it required marvelous strength of faith for the apostles and those early disciples, surrounded by the pomp and display of imperial Rome, to stand up for Jesus and confess publicly that they were followers of a lowly Nazarene, who in distant, despised Galilee had died on the cross as a criminal. The declaration "I am a Christian" often meant the death sentence, even as Saint Paul paid for his loyalty with his life.

How much easier it is for us to champion the crucified Savior! Thank God, we live in a country, founded by believers, that still grants full religious liberty! Thank God, we can read the records of nineteen centuries during which the Gospel has mightily changed men's hearts, just as it has lifted nations from the depths of vice and degradation, transformed cannibals into humble believers, and, in short, enriched the world with its highest, noblest blessings.

Despite all this the very word "gospel" is misunderstood, misapplied, and misinterpreted. A Minnesota architect maintains that, though most people in our country repeatedly use the word "gospel," they actually do not have a personal understanding of its meaning. Glibly men mention "the gospel of Communism," "the gospel of hatred," "the gospel of internationalism," and a hundred other "gospels." Pointedly Saint Paul warned, *"Though we or an angel from heaven preach any other gospel unto you than that which we have preached unto you, let him be accursed!"* Yet false gospels have crept into churches: political gospels, social gospels, ethical gospels — all as far from our Lord's saving Gospel as blackest night is from brightest noon. Why do we not stop such misuse? Why do we not restrict this precious word "gospel" to its original, true, and sacred sense? In the same way, we believe, many hear the names "Jesus" and "Christ," the words "redemption," "atonement," "salvation," and fail to grasp their full, deep, true wealth of comfort.

So that on the great day of our Lord's reappearing you cannot say, "You preached, but you never showed me the way to life," let me tell you just what His Gospel is! It took six weeks for the bad news of the Solomon Islands naval encounters to reach our people, but in less than six seconds this glorious message can be heard around the world. It is the "good news" (that is the original meaning of "Gospel"), the best news anyone can ever receive, the assurance that Jesus Christ, the Son of the Almighty and the Son of the Virgin, moved by unmeasurable love, came into this sin-saturated world, lived His life among sin-bound men and died on the sin-cursed cross, all to remove your transgressions and grant you pardon, eternal salvation, and heaven itself! Though blinded, willful enemies of the faith try to change or alter, add or detract, question or quibble, this is how the Scripture explains the Gospel: *"God so loved the world that He gave His only-begotten Son, that whosoever believeth in Him should not perish but have everlasting life."*

Never since Saint Paul's day has the Gospel been proclaimed with the clarity and conviction shown by that mighty spiritual leader whose work millions commemorate this Sunday — Martin Luther, reformer of the Church and restorer of New Testament Christianity. Just four and one quarter centuries ago yesterday he started the titanic task of restoring the Gospel. While time restrictions prevent us from broadcasting his immortal Ninety-five Theses, or religious truths, by which that earth-shaking Reformation began, we can present nine and five theses reemphasizing the glorious truths which Luther rediscovered and courageously restated. Here they are: First, the nine theses, or facts, which explain our redemption:

1. *"All have sinned and come short of the glory of God,"* that is, lost the holiness with which the Lord created them. This is Bible truth.

2. Unforgiven sin is punished by eternal death in hell. Scripture, which has never made a mistake and never will, warns, *"The wages of sin is death."*

3. No man can remove his own transgressions, make himself pure and spotless in Heaven's sight. *"Can . . . the leopard"* change *"his spots?"* Holy Writ demands, to show how utterly impossible it is for us to cleanse our stained souls.

4. Nor can even saints or angels take away our transgressions. Revealed truth assures us that no man can *"redeem his brother nor give to God a ransom for him."*

5. Only the Almighty can remove sin's curse. If there is to be hope for men and women burdened with many and terrifying transgressions, they must find it in the God who cries out to a world of anguish and evil, *"In Me is thine help!"*

6. God not only *can* save us; He *has* saved us. He sent His Son to fulfill the Law we had broken, to assume the punishment of our iniquity, as our Substitute to pay the death penalty of all our guilt, so that, beholding the cross, we know, He *"was delivered for our offenses."*

7. Through faith in the Crucified — and through faith alone — we know that our sins are removed forever. The Bible promises, *"There is, therefore, now no condemnation to them which are in Christ Jesus."*

8. By accepting the Savior we who were *"children of wrath"* have become *"children of God,"* who live under divine love, guidance, and protection.

9. By believing this glorious Gospel heaven is ours; for if we remain faithful to the end, God has promised us the *"crown of life"* eternal amid the indescribable radiance of our celestial homeland.

These are nine facts of the Gospel. As I repeat them I am sure some of my Modernist friends are shaking their heads either in protest or in condescending wonder. I can hear them call these Gospel truths "old-fashioned," "out of date," "narrow," "bigoted." Yet the only message which can turn souls from hell to heaven is this old but ever new Gospel, of which proud, self-sufficient men are ashamed, but for which the contrite can never thank God sufficiently.

There is more to Christ's Gospel, however. Here are five additional theses, divine truths, showing its glorious grace:

1. The blood-bought, cross-gained salvation is for *you*, each one of you individually. Our text offers its blessing *"to everyone that believeth."* You may be on the lowest rungs of human society, cut off from your fellow men because of your misdeeds. (I am now thinking of the triple murderess in the Ohio penitentiary at St. Mary's, who every Sunday urges the women convicts to hear our radio message. I have in mind a young man in the Jefferson City, Missouri penitentiary, serving his second sentence, who recently wrote me that he had altogether forgotten Jesus until he heard our broadcast, when he pledged himself never to reject his Savior again.) You may be soldiers or civilians, rich or poor, white or black, yellow or red; yet each of you can say, "This is *my* Gospel, *my* Christ, *my* Savior."

2. You can approach Christ despite the multiplied misdeeds in your past life. You can come just as you are, unclean, impure, unworthy, to learn, *"Though your sins be as scarlet, they shall be white as snow; though they be red like crimson, they shall be as wool."*

3. Your redemption is free. You cannot buy your salvation, for Christ has paid everything. One drop of His precious blood can outbalance all your transgressions, for here is the unbreakable promise: *"The blood of Jesus Christ, His Son, cleanseth us from all sin."*

4. To receive the full Gospel blessing you need only believe, only approach God as a poor, miserable sinner who accepts the Savior's grace. Divine truth assures us, *"By grace are ye saved, through faith."*

5. Your forgiveness is unquestioned and positive. Our

text calls the Gospel *"the power of God"* — not of man. *"Heaven"* itself *"and earth shall pass away"* before this supreme pledge is violated.

These five theses present to you the most sacred and sublime love which even God Almighty can give. For your souls' salvation I ask you to study their life-and-death certainty. Wherever you are, let me direct to your home one of the thousands of pastors who work together with me for this same glorious Gospel and who can help you declare in the fervor of sincere faith, *"I am not ashamed of the Gospel of Christ"!*

II

WE HAVE NO REASON TO BE ASHAMED OF HIS GOSPEL

Now, with all the pardon and perfect peace Jesus can speak into sorrowing, aching hearts; with all the light His Gospel offers for life's darkest hours, should we not expect that every person on earth would accept His message as the highest good and the greatest blessing? Did you ever hear of anyone being ashamed of the friend who rescued him from death? Have you ever met a Negro whose heart is not moved by gratitude toward Abraham Lincoln, a true American who does not honor Washington's heroic work? Have you ever read of a nation which does not pay tribute to those who fought and fell in its defense? Why, then, with Christ offering deliverance from death's grip, sin's slavery, hell's tyranny, do millions blasphemously reject Him? How does it happen that some theological seminaries in the United States have not one man on their faculties who believes in the inerrancy of the Scriptures or in Jesus' atoning death and life-giving resurrection? How can we account for the fact that Christ is pushed aside in many modern churches

which ban all hymns concerning the cross and the blood?
Why do we sometimes behold, even in Gospel churches,
lukewarmness and indifference toward the Savior? Why
does a nation as wealthy as ours rob God? (If our people
gave only 10 per cent of their income for religious purposes, the churches would have $4,000,000,000 annually
for the extension of the Kingdom. Actually they receive
only a fraction of that amount.) Why is it that a country
founded by Christian pioneers, settled by Christian colonists, developed by Christian frontiersmen, richly endowed as no other nation in any other part of the world
or in any previous age, now has more unbelievers, more
public enemies of Jesus, than ever before?

Ask the large group of those who, despite the appeals
of this "Go to Church Sunday," have kept their distance
from every place of worship, why they are ashamed of
the Gospel, and they will answer, "Christianity has failed
because it has not prevented this World War." Nothing
could be more unfair than to cry out, "The churches have
been tried and failed in this crisis." Rather should we admit that our age suffers its sorrows because it has failed
to try Christianity. The postman recently brought a letter
with one-cent postage due to a Duxbury, Massachusetts,
man, who refused to accept it and pay the penny. Back
it went to the Dead Letter Office, where it was found
to contain $450. Does any one charge the United States
postal system with failure when the fault lay entirely
with the man who would not accept the letter? Why,
then, blame Jesus for the war when multitudes within
our boundaries spurn the free offer of His help and mention His name only in foul-mouthed profanity? Recently
we read that the chaplain of the United States Senate
died because a druggist had mistakenly compounded a
prescription with fifteen times as much narcotic as the

doctor had ordered. Does any sound-minded person hold the doctor responsible for that pharmacist's mistake? Is it fair, then, to charge the Gospel with failure in this world of war, when many, ordained to preach the whole Bible, offer an erroneous substitute, a destructive counterfeit? If Jesus' Gospel were universally accepted and His teachings followed, there would have been no Second World War. But because men hate Christ and love sin; because selfishness, carnal ambition, avarice, lust, love of power, and worship of money make them trample the rights of their fellow men, the world has been turned into bloody shambles. Jesus pleads, *"Love one another!"* but willful unbelievers insist, "Hate one another!" Jesus gave the Golden Rule, but dictators lay down the rule of steel and blood and iron.

Ask philosophical minds why they are ashamed of Christ, and they will demand in counterquestion: "How do you expect us to accept a religion in which a God permits war's terrors and agony? How can we harmonize the existence of pain and evil with the Christian faith?" Some of you likewise refuse to acclaim Jesus your Redeemer because you think that the Lord has dealt too cruelly with you. A dear one has been snatched from your side, and in stubborn resentment you demand: "How can there be a God if I must suffer this way? How can there be a Savior if I am plunged into this agony?" You have tried to settle these issues apart from the Word. If only you would realize that Jesus has the key and explanation of human suffering! Those who come to Him in faith know that each affliction is laid upon them, as the Lord's redeemed, by divine mercy instead of His anger, that trials which seem beyond analysis are the Almighty's way of purifying faith and strengthening trust.

Again, ask proud enemies of our faith why they are hostile to the Gospel, and they will sneer: "Well, hasn't Christianity been rejected by outstanding scientists? Isn't it true that all great thinkers have discarded the Bible?" To both questions we answer with an emphatic "No!" Not only have leaders in every branch of learning been humble followers of the Lord Jesus, but today, during the heyday of unbelief and atheism, recognized teachers and intellectual leaders have come out strongly for Christ. Listen to these testimonies offered by men on the faculties of great American universities: From the University of Wisconsin: "In the Bible we find . . . our Savior, and eternal life through faith in Him"! From Ohio State University: "The Bible has shown me my sin with its terrifying consequences; but it has also brought me the direct comfort of the Savior who died for me on Calvary"! From Michigan State College: "The Bible reveals Christ and His vicarious atonement for the sins of mankind"! From Johns Hopkins University: "I believe that . . . the Son of God Himself came down to earth and by the shedding of His blood on the cross paid the infinite penalty of the guilt of the whole world"! From Temple University: "I have praised the Lord that as a physician He has given me the privilege of testifying to Christ's saving grace"! From the University of Illinois: "In Jesus Christ I have found my Savior and Lord, my Helper along the way. Without Him life would be empty and worthless, the load of sin . . . still separating me from God"! — If these and hundreds of other present-day scientists, far from being ashamed of Christ, acclaim Him the Savior, should you refuse to accept Him? Many who attack the Bible have never reverently studied His Word, and many who assail His Word are led by blind and willful ignorance. Popular magazines this month bring the confession of a physician under the title "I Was an Atheist — Until" — until that doctor took time to examine the human body and study the miracles which led him to conclude that there must be a divine Creator. — If you who place question marks behind the glorious truth of the Savior's atonement would only stop locking the Holy Spirit out of your heart and take time to consider the *"many infallible proofs"* of His forgiving, sustaining love, you, too, could write a glorious chapter in your life's story entitled, "'I Was an Atheist—Until'—until I studied God's Word and the evidences of Christianity." Do not be troubled by the fact that men with headline names often attempt to discredit our Lord! I remind you that before Pearl Harbor some of the enemies of the faith publicly urged our people under no circumstances to take arms in behalf of this nation. Of course, they have changed their advice now; but the point I wish to emphasize is this: if these false prophets in academic garb could be so utterly mistaken in matters of human life, dare you follow them in their poisonous, destructive teachings concerning the heavenly life? Rather — and I am pleading particularly with you college men and women — join those scientific leaders who with inner joy and spiritual conviction exulted, *"I am not ashamed of the Gospel of Christ!"*

As men reject Jesus, they advance one excuse after the other. Many of their claims are dishonest; all of them are mistaken and destructive. Behind every refusal to accept the Gospel lies the love of sin, the unwillingness to serve God, the stubborn pride that will not repent. Christ is spurned and the appeal of His cross set aside because men love evil; because they want to serve the flesh; because the Savior is too lowly and humble, the Bible too stern and unbending in its denunciation of all wrong. Jesus says, *"If any man will come after Me, let him . . . take up his cross";* He insists, The *"first shall be last";* He warns, "Ye *'must through much tribulation enter into the kingdom of God'";* and since men prefer greatness, power, glamour, money, applause, the glorious Gospel of grace is contemptuously cast away. The consequence of that rejection, Jesus declares, is this: *"Whosoever shall deny Me before men, him will I also deny before My Father which is in heaven." "He that believeth not shall be damned."*

Thus once more I have laid before you this inescapable issue: Are you ashamed of Christ, or do you glory in His Gospel? I know that across the United States and Canada millions of you cling to the Savior as your only Salvation. God grant you continued loyalty and the determination to remain faithful always and everywhere! The Lord give you the courage to speak up in clarion voices, rebuking the enemies of the Cross, but testifying valiantly to the hope that is in you! Stand by us, my fellow redeemed, in this radio crusade dedicated to spread the message of Christ's atoning love! England, Scotland, and Ireland are literally pleading for this Gospel. Our Sunday evening short-wave transmissions to these countries bring us a flow of letters which urgently ask that we maintain and increase our trans-Atlantic mission of the air. Help us reach the young men in the American fighting forces, who are ready to give themselves for our cause! Last week a corporal at an Ohio airfield wrote me that he had been on the verge of taking his life, when he heard our appeal to behold Christ and to trust Him. That changed everything, he said, and he has promised with God's help to follow in the Savior's footsteps. Give us the means for reaching *all* our young soldiers!

Some of you had not accepted Jesus as your Savior,

were still ashamed of Him, when this broadcast began. Now that you have heard the message of His love for you; now that you have beheld the crucified Son of God, wounded, bleeding, nail-pierced, blood-streaked, death-marked, can you say, "I am ashamed of Him"? May the Holy Spirit mercifully keep you from that terrifying denial! May He rather lead you (and I have prayed especially for those who once knew the Lord, but who followed the path of sin; for you who until this hour have neglected your soul and steadfastly turned from Christ), if necessary, through suffering, sorrow, and pain, but always from cross to crown! May He bring you, humble, repentant, yet trusting, joyful, to Calvary, where, your sins forgiven, your cares cast on Him, your hope strengthened by His unfailing promise, your faith exults: "Blessed Savior, how could I be ashamed of Thee and Thy Gospel, the promise of my forgiveness, life, salvation? O Jesus, precious Jesus, grant me constantly more of Thy love, as I give myself in soul and body, mind and spirit, to Thee now and forever!" For heaven is yours when Christ thus becomes your Savior. God give you this unashamed, unhesitating, unending faith in the blessed Redeemer! Amen.

The Greatest Faith: Firm Trust in Christ

> *"I say unto you, I have not found so great faith, no, not in Israel."*
> SAINT LUKE 7:9

Jesus, Our Sure Hope and Salvation:

Grant us the humble, contrite spirit by which we confess our utter unworthiness of Thy mercy! Enrich us with a firm, triumphant faith, which takes Thee at Thy Word and trusts confidently in Thy repeated pledge of personal grace! O Jesus, Thou art our God, and with Thine almighty power nothing shall be impossible for Thee; but Thou art also our Savior, and in Thy love for sinners Thou didst not only redeem us on the cross from hell and death, but Thou dost also watch over us now, so that no harm can draw near our souls. Help us understand that through Thee our afflictions become our advantages! For Thy believers turn war's sorrows into spiritual blessings! Protect our country and its fighting men! By Thy mercy grant the world a peace with truth and justice! We ask it all, precious Savior, in Thy name, by Thy will, and with Thy promise. Amen.

ONE of the bravest chapters in the war has been the struggle of our gallant troops on Bataan Peninsula. For weeks these besieged soldiers were constantly buoyed up by the hope that somehow help would arrive from America. Days of bloody battle gave way to nights of dark terror, yet exhausted, sleep-robbed, half-starved, our men, fighting against overwhelming odds, were cheered by radio rumors that relief was approaching. So confident were they of their escape that in an almost superhuman effort they cleared a wide jungle stretch and made a runway on which rescue planes might land. Despite these frenzied preparations, no reinforcements came. The encircled troops were finally forced to surrender. With all our billions of dollars and numerous military experts; with our large armies, proud navies, and mighty airplane squadrons, we could not aid that brave band.

If money, power, intelligence, the resources of a wealthy government, are not always able to rescue men from dangers, they are even less capable of establishing true, lasting peace. As the Armistice anniversary approaches, we recall the past promises of a warless world. Twenty-one short years ago President Warren Harding, standing before the tomb of America's unknown soldier, declared: "The sacrifice of these millions of dead shall not be in vain. . . . This Armistice Day shall mark the beginning of a new and lasting era of peace on earth." Yet today the world is gripped by the horror of history's most destructive struggle. The first World War cost us 233,000 killed and wounded; but for this second war a general prophesies, "Our losses may be a million or two million or conceivably three million men," and a rear admiral estimates five million casualties. Pray God once more that these predictions may be put to naught as He who has all power, the rightful King of men, swiftly intervenes in His mercy and might to stop this devastating slaughter, rebuke greed and aggression, grant triumph to truth and righteousness! If God's eternal principles are barred from the peace table, we may face World War III, which can be vastly more terrifying even than the present conflict.

You can understand, therefore, that, if men cannot solve the problems of a nation's war and peace, perplexities dealing with facts and factors which can be seen, felt, measured, tabulated, then certainly the soul's afflictions, the heart's anguish, the mind's agonies, which cannot be examined in laboratories nor computed by statistical experts, will not be removed by any human agency, powerful and resourceful though it be. You may have endured crushing blows, and in the difficult years ahead you will doubtless be called upon to bear unaccustomed burdens. You may be restless, confused, distressed, conscience-lashed, gripped by worry and terror — fear for your sons, brothers, husbands in service; anxiety about your home; sorrows brought on by ill health, accident, disappointments in love. To all of us and for every dark moment comes this message of sustaining comfort: "Don't give up! Don't surrender to indifference or despair! Don't try to drink or play your grief away! Don't turn, as millions of your fellow men do, to superstition and new but false religions!" Instead, ask God for

THE GREATEST FAITH: FIRM TRUST IN CHRIST!

Strive for this immovable reliance on Jesus, which our Savior Himself exalts in the Scripture for this Sunday (Saint Luke, chapter seven, verse nine), *"I say unto you, I have not found so great faith, no, not in Israel."*

I

WE MUST TURN TO THE DIVINE CHRIST
FOR THIS FAITH

If you think that the person who is thus praised for having the greatest faith was a priest, a scribe, a learned rabbi in the higher circles of Jerusalem, you are completely mistaken. Jesus spoke these words in Capernaum, one of those half-breed cities in the North, from which all self-respecting Jews kept their distance. But our Lord,

with His marvelous love particularly for the neglected, oppressed, underprivileged, overburdened, deliberately and in fulfillment of ancient prophecy sought out that Galilean center to bring its people comfort, help, and hope. Take heart and study the geography of our Savior's grace! As you write me from isolated, unimportant places, from settlements without even a name, from the dingy, run-down sections of the city, even from prisons and penitentiaries, remember that you are just as precious in the Savior's sight as the country's outstanding citizens! Though men may rarely find the way to your home, Jesus now speaks to you personally.

This man whose faith Christ held up for our example was not one of Capernaum's leading Jewish citizens. Listen to this, and thank God: he was a Gentile, outside the boundaries of the Old Testament Church! Thank God, I say, because through Jesus we are in the New Testament, with His grace freely granted, regardless of rank or reputation, color, clime, or condition. Today in a world cursed by caste and privilege, slavery and dictatorship, with the claims of racial superiority and the practice of financial superiority, we can never sufficiently express our gratitude to the Almighty for the mercy that salvation is offered all men with the same marvelous love, no matter how differently they may be classified by false human standards. Because it is Scriptural truth that Jesus *"died for all"*; because it is His own command, *"Go ye into* ALL *the world and preach the Gospel to every creature,"* we must, more than ever before, extend the invitation to accept Christ, and with Him, joy for life, strength for death, and the assurance of heaven to many more millions who have never heard a syllable of the saving Gospel. Our Bringing Christ to the Nations messages are now transmitted by stations in twenty-four

countries outside the United States and heard in many
more lands. Those who love the Lord Jesus will praise
God with us because a committee has been appointed to
expand our foreign broadcasting into additional countries. Ultimately we hope that your prayers and your
gifts will help us realize this glorious objective: to use
every available and suitable radio station throughout the
entire world in the service of the Savior's Gospel. The
results of our foreign broadcasting have been astonishing.
Outside Mexico City a group of Aztec Indians regularly
meets to hear this message and have difficult Spanish
words explained by a young Aztec brought to Christ
through our mission of the air. One of the most encouraging letters I have ever received came only a few days ago
from a South American missionary to tell me that far in
the interior of Peru, where few white men ever penetrate,
the Indians, descendants of the Incas, crouch around a
portable radio to hear the Lutheran Hour and have the
interpreter explain the Redeemer's message. There, in
the remote Amazon jungles, among semicivilized and
savage tribes, a week's journey and more beyond the
bounds of civilization, these broadcasts bring the Savior's
comfort and strength. Does that not make your heart
beat a little faster in grateful joy? Yet all this need be
only the beginning of our most far-reaching radio mission; and I promise you that if you will stand by us with
your prayers, the Lord helping us, we will leave nothing
untried or undone in bringing Christ's hope to the ends
of the earth.

Note especially that the man whose faith is praised
by Jesus was a soldier, a centurion, the leader of one
hundred troops, actually the captain of the Roman garrison in Capernaum. In those days military men were
generally held in contempt. For that matter some people

today have only a low regard for our fighting men. With much consternation I read a high military authority's description of the American soldier, which said, "He plods and groans, sweats and toils; he growls and curses." How tragic to publicize profanity in that way! How unfortunate, too, that overcrowded night clubs and road houses re-echo with the blaring strains of "Praise the Lord and Pass the Ammunition," while masses, far away from the dangers of conflict, making more money in war than they ever could in peace, sing this melody without a flicker of reverence in their hearts, often in the same breath with heavy curses! Remember the Bible's warning: *"Out of the same mouth proceedeth blessing and cursing. My brethren, these things ought not so to be!"*

Jesus was ready to help the centurion by healing his servant. We, too, must be prepared to help sustain our youth under colors. Bringing Christ to the Soldiers is the Church's greatest missionary opportunity and obligation. Washington now reports that 4,000 chaplains will be needed. Again I promise you fathers and mothers, worried because your sons are far removed from home, that we will do everything possible to broadcast the messages of the crucified Christ to all our American fighting men. If you want us to mail your boy uplifting, strengthening literature, write us today, and we shall consider it a Christian and patriotic privilege thus to serve him.

Speaking directly to you in the armed forces, I remind you that some of the most stalwart military men have been outstanding Christians. Soldiers, think of General Sir William Dobbie, former governor of Malta! Above the din of a thousand bombings his testimony rings clear: "I cannot attempt to describe what I owe to the Lord Jesus Christ nor what He has meant to me throughout my army career (and longer). The knowledge that it is

to Him I owe my eternal salvation has given me a peace which nothing has been able to disturb!"

Sailors, recall Captain Mahan, author of several standard volumes on naval warfare, who declared: "In the Word of God I have found . . . not merely comfort and strength, but intense intellectual satisfaction. I rejoice that . . . I am able publicly to lay at His feet the confession that all I have, all that I am, all that I know has come from Him and through Him"!

Air men, remember that when Colin Kelly, the first outstanding American hero of World War II, began his dangerous flight, he said, "I am ready to go, ready to meet my Savior"!

Fighting men of America, take these outstanding leaders as your example! With the military captain of our text, turn to Christ!

The shadow of sorrow had overtaken the centurion when he approached Jesus. His servant, really his slave, lay deathly sick with the dread palsy. Instead of trying to heal him merely because he represented a certain money value; instead of turning away in utter unconcern, as many slaveholders would have done in those harsh days, this centurion was moved by love in the effort to save the life of his faithful servant. Where could he secure help, now that his attendant was at death's door and apparently all medical resources had failed? Where, indeed, if not in the same Savior through whom every one of you can always find courage? He had heard of Jesus. He was convinced of His power and, therefore, he went straight to the Redeemer with his appeal. It is my glorious, if undeserved, privilege to assure you that in every dark hour you, too, can turn to our Lord for light and hope. No earthly friend or human aid can begin to offer the comfort and strength you have in Christ as soon as

you say, "He is my Savior!" Then you know that, if Jesus performed the immeasurably greater task of removing and canceling your guilt forever, so that you are saved for heaven, He certainly can do the far smaller work of guiding, guarding, and protecting you, according to His will, on earth. If He loved you even when you hated Him; if He called you when you rejected Him; if He pleaded with you at the moment you forsook Him; if He stretched out His arms to you even though you turned your back on Him; if He shed His blood at Calvary and died for you while you were yet in your sins, will you not believe that He who rules the universe, keeps the stars in their courses, directs the affairs of nations, gives life and breath to all creatures, can mightily sustain you *after* you have come to Him, *after* you have knelt before Him to say, "O precious Savior, Thou art mine, and I am Thine"? As Saint Paul cries out, *"He that spared not His own Son but delivered Him up for us all, how shall He not with Him also freely give us all things?"* — all things for this body, this existence and this earth.

In every uncertainty of life as we live it today, with the avalanche of afflictions that may hurl itself down upon us, we, too, should turn to Christ. Not nearly enough believers are on their knees before their Savior. Not nearly enough Americans have recognized that Jesus is the only and last Hope for our dying world. Not nearly enough soldiers and defense workers understand how necessary faith in the Redeemer is during this emergency. On the contrary, a proud, boastful spirit stalks abroad throughout the land. A religious leader confidently predicted that he would live to be 120 years, only to die a few weeks ago, forty-eight years short of that mark. Many churches, forsaking the purpose and reason of their existence — the preaching of the holy Gospel — continually speak of this new order or that new order. They forget that real newness comes only when men are born again *"of water and of the Spirit."* More than ever before we need courageous, consecrated leaders who, without counting cost or consequence, will direct men to the true Christ, the atoning and redeeming Christ, the divine and eternal Christ, the comforting and sustaining Christ, the Christ for every sin and sinner, for every need and afflic-tion, for every doubt and disaster — the Christ for your transgressions, your problems, your afflictions.

II

WE MUST TURN TO CHRIST HUMBLY, YET CONFIDENTLY

The centurion not only comes to Jesus with his sor-row, he turns to Him with remarkable humility. Realiz-ing his own sinfulness, but acknowledging the Savior's complete holiness, that captain of the Capernaum troops tells the Redeemer, *"I am not worthy that Thou shouldst enter under my roof."* He regards Christ as so exalted that even his dwelling, which could have been one of the larger, more attractive houses in the city, was far too small, his family and household altogether too lowly and unworthy, to receive the sinless, stainless Son of God.

Today the situation is often completely reversed: proud, conceited people think themselves too good for Christ, and the Savior too unworthy to enter their home. How can we account for the tragic fact that half of America's households maintain no connection with any congregation, that even most of the church members' families have no desire to welcome Jesus into their midst through Scripture reading and prayer? How does it hap-pen that religious groups which a generation or two ago

were founded by consecrated believers in Christ now
have no room for the Redeemer, no love for the Gospel
of the cross and the blood? One reason explains this, as
well as the widespread rejection of Jesus today by masses
who have the time, the money, and above all the need
to receive and acclaim the Savior; and that reason is to
be found in the stubborn unwillingness to bow humbly
before the Lord, to say: "He is everything, but we are
nothing. He is the spotless Lamb of God, but we are
stained with iniquity, false and full of sin." The lesson
for every one of us is clear and personal: We, too,
must humble ourselves before Christ. The direction to
the masses in our beloved country is equally emphatic:
"America, on your knees in contrite confession!" The appeal to our world is similarly unmistakable: "'O earth,
earth, earth, hear the Word of the Lord' and submit
humbly to His good and gracious will!"

Like the centurion, truly great believers have always
been humble. While small, dirty, negative minds ridicule and blaspheme Christ, mighty intellects have bowed
low before Him. Ambroise Paré, the Huguenot scientist
in the sixteenth century, who more than any other person
of his age helped to make surgery a science, performed
such remarkable curative work that during the massacre
of Saint Bartholemew's Day he was hidden by the French
king, who himself had ordered the bloody massacre. With
a humility that all professional men may well copy, Paré
used to declare, after operations, "I dressed him [the pa-
tient], but God cured him." And today Dr. D. M. Blair,
regius professor of anatomy at Glasgow University, with
the same humble faith confesses: "Since God is the
Author of good and the Source of all truth, the discoveries of physical science are due to Him in spirit and
letter, whether or not the physical instrument of dis-

covery realizes and acknowledges that fact. Science . . .
cannot . . . hold man to a right direction. Only the Gospel
of Jesus Christ can point the way."

Those who have the centurion's humility also know
more of faith's joy and blessing than those who critically
question and suspiciously examine the Savior's truth.
A few days ago the *St. Louis Post-Dispatch* brought an
interesting account of the tin mining in Durango, Mexico.
Searching desperately for this metal, vital for war purposes, geologists, metallurgists, surveyors, and other experts, after considerable investigation, issued a report
stating that the tin at Durango was too poor in quality
and too small in quantity to be mined successfully. Yet
soon after their survey was submitted, attention was
called to the fact that the natives, operating without the
advantages of modern equipment, sometimes working on
their hands and knees, produced 2,000 tons of high-grade
tin annually. The experts had failed, but the humble folk
had succeeded. So it is in the quest for the joy of salvation. The proud and self-confident often lose the treasures of the Kingdom, while those who turn contritely
to Christ, fall humbly on their knees, and trust the
simple assurance of faith find Heaven's hidden riches in
abundance.

Therefore may the Spirit give everyone of you the
centurion's humility to approach the blessed Savior and
cry out: "O Christ of all compassion, I am not worthy
that Thou shouldst come to me or even consider me.
I am not worthy even to speak to Thee, let alone hope
for Thy mercy or forgiveness. Yet I take Thee at Thy
Word, *'Him that cometh to Me I will in no wise cast out.'*
And now, blessed Redeemer, I come in full reliance on
Thine unbreakable mercy."

Such firmness of trust made the centurion's faith the

greatest Jesus had found. So convinced was this Gentile soldier that our Lord could restore his servant; so assured was he that Christ was more than man, yes, the mighty God Himself, that he told the Savior, "*Speak the word only, and my servant shall be healed!*" If he, as a military official, could command his soldiers and they would carry out his purposes, certainly Jesus, divine and all-powerful, could on that very spot say to the victim of the palsy, "Be restored to health!" and he would recover. No wonder, with the Jews questioning and quibbling over Christ's truth, demanding signs and miracles, He could say of this Gentile centurion's trust, "*I have not found so great faith, no, not in Israel.*"

Today, too, many question marks are placed behind the Savior's promises. Many of you are not satisfied with His pledge of salvation and help. You want to experience something. You want your own emotions to be the seal and assurance that Christ is with you and for you. Don't rely on your feelings! They have never brought anyone to glory, but they have often tried to keep people out. Some of you insist on seeing signs and miracles before you believe; yet you have the cross, the mightiest of all signs, and history, changed by the Gospel, as a startling miracle. You demand earth-shaking upheavals, while the Almighty often speaks in the "*still, small voice*" that can move heaven and earth. You want the Bible plus some human book, God's Word supplemented by man's. However, if Scripture alone cannot give you positive assurance, certainly nothing puny men have ever penned will move your heart.

In these decisive days we need the centurion's immovable firmness of faith. We, too, must say: "O Jesus, '*speak the word only,*' and the horrors of this war will cease! O Jesus, '*speak the word only,*' and the burdens that crush us can be removed! O Jesus, *'speak the word only,'* and all our afflictions, sickness, pain, injury, loss of contentment, happiness, life itself, family trouble, finan-cial trouble, spiritual trouble, can vanish!"

In this firmness of faith we know that Christ can intervene when everything seems hopeless. An Associated Press dispatch tells us of a British submarine disabled on the ocean floor. For two days the crew worked ceaselessly in the effort to raise the craft. Finally all hope was aban-doned. The officer in command explained to the men that they did not have long to live, since no help whatever could come from the outside. In preparation for ap-proaching death the seamen sang "Abide with Me!" and then each took a sedative to quiet his nerves. One sailor, however, fainted soon after he had received the narcotic. He fell with all his weight against the submarine's ma-chinery, with the result that somehow he set the jammed surfacing equipment into motion, and the submarine was eventually brought to the top. Have not similar startling deliverances come to every one of you in automobile ac-cidents and a hundred other calamities that would have proved fatal, had not God intervened in some utterly un-expected and unexplainable way to save your life?

If you, too, will say to Jesus, "Abide with me!" His presence will constantly protect and bless your lives. He may not always deliver you from earthly dangers. Some of our Christian soldiers now on distant shores will never return, not because the Savior cannot bring them back safely, but because He wants them with Him in heaven now. Many of you will continue to endure a thorn in the flesh, not because our Redeemer cannot remove it, but because He wants to use physical weakness as a means of building spiritual strength. It takes 50,000 flowers to produce an ounce of that costliest of perfumes, attar of roses. They have to be pressed and crushed so that the drops of the fragrant, costly oil may be distilled. In our own lives it often requires a hundred days of sorrow, with all their crushing affliction, to produce the fragrance of a living faith. Yet for every spiritual necessity, for every need of our blood-bought and redeemed soul, you have this positive, unchanging, exceptionless promise by Christ Himself, "*Verily, verily, I say unto you, Whatsoever ye shall ask the Father in My name, He will give it you.*"

Therefore, across the vast expanse of our hemisphere, O Christ, we now take Thee at Thy word. With contrite hearts, but with triumphant trust, we ask Thee: "Give us this greatest faith, this firm reliance on Thy mercy and might! Make us centurions in the marching army of Thy Church here on earth! Grant us '*the victory that over-cometh the world,*' the immovable, heroic, constant faith which looks to Thee in life and death! We ask it, blessed Savior, by the promise of Thine unfailing truth!" Amen.

Victory Through Christ

"Thanks be to God, which giveth us the victory through our Lord Jesus Christ!"
1 Corinthians 15:57

Jesus, Our Only Savior:

How can we ever thank Thee sufficiently that Thou, our mighty God, didst become one of us, yet without sin, that on the cross of shame and agony Thou couldst die the death we had deserved as the punishment of our transgressions? Eternal praise be to Thee for such pure mercy and saving love! Show us that since Thou hast overcome sin and death, all sorrows have likewise been completely defeated for those who believe Thy promises and accept Thee as their Savior! Put this victorious faith into many hearts through our broadcast! Strengthen our fighting men with Thy Gospel grace and stand by them in hours of doubt or danger! In Thine own time — and may it be soon, O Christ — end this war! Grant lasting triumph to truth, righteousness, freedom! We ask this, precious Redeemer, because Thou hast promised to hear us. Amen.

THOSE who love Jesus should steadfastly work for true peace with righteousness and justice for all. Therefore in the present crisis American Christians must not only obey governmental decrees, fulfill their civic duties by giving their scrap, their money, even their bodies; they should also constantly strive to become peacemakers in this world of war. They should say:

1. We must believe and act with the conviction that God is still supreme and that His will must be done. Our country's victory, prosperity, and blessing lie in His hands. He can give, and He can withhold.

2. We who accept the Savior must invoke His divine help by persistent prayer.

3. We who are Christ's should lead humble, God-fearing lives so that the answer to our petitions will not be denied because of our unbelief and obstinate sin.

4. We who know that we have been redeemed by our Lord should strive to counteract rising atheism and to keep the Savior supreme in our churches, homes, religious schools.

5. We who call ourselves Christians must revitalize our religious work, direct our energies especially toward bringing the Gospel to the underprivileged and downtrodden. They may be easily enlisted against Church and country if led to think that Christianity has failed.

6. We, the Savior's followers, in order to help increase the righteousness which alone exalts a nation, must engage in personal and organized missionary work. The more believers our country has, the greater its spiritual resources and inner strength.

7. We who have pledged loyalty to the Cross must rebuke and check crime, public and private profanity, applauded lust, for which the war can be protracted; and we must pray that deep repentance grip the masses who have turned their backs on God.

8. We who bear Christ's name must stand by the Christian young men who risk their lives for our defense, sparing nothing that can help keep them in the faith.

9. Finally, we who know our Lord's grace must proclaim His comforting love, so that in households struck by disaster or bereavement courage in Christ may remove doubt, hatred, and despair.

If Americans from coast to coast would subscribe to this program for a just peace, we could, under God, witness the most spectacular triumph of truth this nation has ever known. My countrymen, in this hour when decisive battles seem much closer than ever before, I commend these Biblical principles to your study as you ask, "What can I as an American Christian do on the spiritual front in the present conflict?"

Yet even in this war against earthly enemies we must never forget the longer, harder, more bitter struggle in which all of us take a personal part on one side or the other — the battle against the unholy impulses, wicked words, and destructive actions; the contest with powerful forces of evil both in our sin-tainted hearts and in a hostile, anti-Christian world. The campaign which our armed forces are waging in North Africa, on the Southern Pacific islands, on the high seas, can destroy lives; but the conflict in which every one of you should daily engage can deliver your souls. For — praise God! — no matter what the final outcome of all military campaigns may be, you can have the assurance of

VICTORY THROUGH CHRIST,

pledged by this song of spiritual triumph in First Corinthians, chapter fifteen, verse fifty-seven, *"Thanks be to God, which giveth us the victory through our Lord Jesus Christ!"*

I

IT IS THE TRIUMPH OVER DEATH, "THE LAST ENEMY"

This exalted cry of victory concludes a most impressive chapter, in which Saint Paul explains the resurrection of the body. Confident that those who fall asleep in Jesus will rise again, the Apostle issues this gripping challenge which has brought heavenly strength to many standing beside newly made graves: *"O Death, where is*

thy sting? O Grave, where is thy victory?" Then, in
one of the mightiest proclamations ever heard, he continues, *"Thanks be to God, which giveth us the victory
through our Lord Jesus Christ!"* Particularly in these uncertain days, with danger and destruction close to hundred thousands of American young men in the nation's
armed forces, words like these should ring with heavenly
reassurance: those who are Christ's have the victory over
death. We cannot stop infidels if in their perversion they
insist that man dies like a beast; that, when his breath
stops, the absolute end has come and all is over forever. We cannot keep atheists from demanding that their
corpses be cremated and their ashes scattered to the four
winds, as they defy God to reassemble these ruined,
widely separated remains. We cannot prevent anti-Christian, skeptical scientists from proclaiming to the world
that, since they discover no evidence whatever for the
soul's immortality, there is none. If they willfully, continually, reject Jesus and insist on opposing His truth,
let them have their drab, dismal, devilish doctrine of
despair, their denial of the resurrection! But as for us
who find in every promise of our Savior's Word Heaven's
own unbreakable truth, we ought daily join the Apostle
in thanking God for the victory over eternal death that
is ours through Jesus.

Do some of you object, "How can you say that the
grave is defeated for those who are the Lord's when the
one assured fact in life is this, that all men must die?"
We answer, "True, death is inevitable, unavoidable; but
all who are Christ's have the triumphant faith that they
will not remain dust and ashes. They will be restored, resurrected." The end from which even the bravest shrink
in fear and horror; the last terrorizing moment, the very
thought of which has turned men's hair white in a single

night and made them lose their senses — this worst of all human sorrows, need be only a passing annoyance to Christians, the quick entrance into the celestial radiance. That is why sincere believers have found joy in leaving this world. When Frances Ridley Havergal, writer of many beloved hymns, came to the last day of a consecrated though pain-ridden life, she whispered to her friends: "God's will is delicious. He makes no mistakes." Bidding one of her physicians farewell, she asked, "Do you really think that I am going today?" and when he replied, "Probably," she answered: "Beautiful! Too good to be true! Splendid to be so near the gates of heaven!" When the moment of her departure came, she folded her hands and exclaimed: "There, it is all over! Blessed rest!" and those who watched at her bedside testify that her face was illumined with the glory dawning in her soul. She appeared to be speaking to her Savior in His resurrected majesty. You, too, can have the same radiant light in death's darkness, the same joy at life's end, the same comfort in the last, lonely hour when the Father calls you, His beloved, faithful child home, provided you know this victory over death which comes through His Son and through Him alone.

To understand this triumphant truth you must first face the bitter fact that all men without exception come under the divine condemnation, *"The soul that sinneth, it shall die."* The All-holy One in His absolute, unapproachable stainlessness has decreed, *"The wages,"* that is, the payment, the consequence, *"of sin is death."* So absolutely flawless and perfect is the Almighty, and so completely does He hate every fracture of His Law, even the wicked desire of a lust-filled, covetous heart, that He has made unending, unrelieved death the terrifying penalty for your sins and mine, the punishment for those transgressions which once seemed attractive and alluring, but which now rise up and haunt you day and night.

Eternal praise, glory, honor be to our Lord Jesus Christ, that in His unfathomable mercy He came to break this tyranny, descending from His heaven to the earth that despised Him, living for those who persecuted Him, teaching those who sought to stone Him, pleading for those who spit upon Him, stretching out His arms toward those who called Him—the Lord of Life—a devil, suffering for those who sneered at Him, dying for the enemies who had hammered heavy nails through the quivering flesh of His hands and feet! — Adore Him everlastingly, the Son of God, because He came to free us from the doom of hell, to take away our sins, their guilt, their punishment, their damning death sentence, and place the whole accursed burden of our transgressions on Himself, to die our death on the cross and then in the glorious Easter marvel, being resurrected into life, to seal our promise of a blessed eternity!

As Christ now offers you this victory, God grant that you will not turn away in protest and unbelief! Consider the hope we extend you in this broadcast through the Lord Jesus: life instead of death; a glorified body, with all the blemishes, the marks and amputations of war and accident, the signs of feebleness and old age, the scars and ravages of sin removed; a heavenly homeland in which — O marvelous truth! — you can be like Jesus, in fulfillment of this superpromise, *"We shall be like Him"!*

If the Spirit has now touched your heart and urges you to ask: "How can I share this *'victory . . . through . . . Christ'?* How can I who was once loyal to the Savior be reassured of this triumph over death?" — let me tell you: you need only the humble, trusting faith which hears Jesus' promise, *"I am the Resurrection and the Life: he that believeth on Me, though he were dead, yet shall he live,"* and answers: "O Christ, the Lord of all the living, I was *'dead in trespasses and sins'* but I take Thee at Thy word; with all my heart I believe that on the cross Thou didst suffer for all the world, and also for all humanity, unquestionably also for me; Thou didst die for me; Thou didst break the power of death and the grave for all men, and that means, God and Savior of grace and truth, even for me." If you have this faith, if you can say and believe: *"'Through Christ'* I can overcome death; *'through Christ'* the grave now holds no terror for me; *'through Christ'* heaven is mine; *'through Christ'* I can hope and pray that my merciful Father will not keep me too long in this sin-saturated world of woe and war," then you have learned the sacred assurance which in the Lord's sight is worth more than any academic distinction universities can grant. Then life everlasting is yours even now.

II

IT IS THE TRIUMPH OVER ALL OTHER ENEMIES

Scripture calls death *"the last enemy"* because it is the final and hardest opposition we face. Because Christ died to give you eternal victory, He can grant you the conquest of every smaller difficulty and obstacle. When an army captures a central fortress, the little trenches surrounding it are easily taken.

Those who have accepted Jesus as their Savior soon find that loyalty to Him brings enmity. The forces of hell work in day and night shifts to break down allegiance to God's Son. Temptations multiply. You young people know the teasing, coaxing, tugging, that tries to tear you from your Savior and seeks to make you regard purity, decency, honest living, the ideal of keeping yourself clean for your life's helpmate, as an outworn superstition, an unnecessary restriction on personal liberty. Despite the fact that war always produces a sag in morals, you can triumph over multiplied temptations if you turn trustfully to the Lord, since He knows your every weakness. Over in England, when the one hundredth anniversary of the birth of George Stephenson, inventor of the steam locomotive, was celebrated, a long parade in Newcastle honored the distinguished engineer. As the procession moved on, the spectators noticed a small band of farmers marching under a homemade banner inscribed with the words "He was one of us." They were the people among whom Stephenson was born, and proudly they acclaimed their closeness to the great inventor. In a much higher degree, whenever you are assailed by the forces of darkness; whenever the love of quick and easy money would make you forget your God — a very real danger for thousands in the United States today; whenever you are urged to indulge in fleshly lusts, to covet that which is not rightfully yours, you can find the strength to resist in the Lord Jesus, for He was one of us. He was tempted, the Scriptures say, *"like as we are,"* and because He understands our infirmities, He knows how to help us. Give Him the leadership in your soul!

If you are troubled by evil habits, the disgrace of drunkenness, the flare-ups of a hot temper, secret transgressions which you blush to mention, remember: no bond of vice is so strong, no slavery of sin so long-standing and powerful, that it cannot be broken by the Savior's almighty power! Members of this audience tell us that through Christ they have mastered their craving for liquor and become sober, God-fearing, loving husbands or wives, who praise God instead of cursing Him and protect their families instead of attacking them in drunken rage. The history of missions shows how complete this victory over evil habits can be. A hundred years ago Tamatoe, a South Sea Island king, was converted, whereupon his heathen subjects conspired to destroy him and all others who had embraced the Gospel. The plot was discovered. All the would-be assassins were captured, and they began to shake in terror of the death which they had rightly earned. Can you imagine their surprise when Tamatoe assured them that because Jesus had commanded him to love his enemies and do good to those who hated him, the plotters would not be harmed? An impressive banquet was prepared, to which the conspirators were invited. They were so amazed at this treatment that some were unable to eat. Finally one of their leaders arose and, after thanking the king for his mercy, declared that this unlooked-for kindness had convinced him of the Savior's power and the utter helplessness of their heathen gods. Soon every idol on the Island of Hushine was broken, and the murderous heathen became humble Christians. If you give Jesus His way in your life, the idols of hatred and lust will likewise crumble away.

Again, you can have victory over your doubts. Even the strongest believer is sometimes assailed by questions, misgivings, uncertainties; but the more steadily you behold Jesus, the more reverently you delve into His Scriptures, the more regularly you hear and apply His Word, the stronger your faith becomes, the more heroic your allegiance to Him. You will not be able to understand Christ's mercies, and you may wonder especially why He chose you, with all your sins and shortcomings; your intellect will be altogether too small to explain the mysteries of faith which even angels cannot fully comprehend, but that will not bother you. You will know the joy of obedience; you will say, "*Speak, Lord; for Thy servant heareth!*" In his last days Daniel Webster told his biographer: "I had intended to prepare a work for the press to bear my testimony to Christianity, but now it is too late. I would like to bear witness to the Gospel before I die." So he propped himself up and began to dictate: "'*Lord, I believe; help Thou mine unbelief!*' Philosophical opposition has often shaken my reason with regard to Christianity, especially the opposition drawn from the magnitude of the universe compared with the littleness of this planet; but my heart has always assured me and reassured me that the Gospel of Christ is a divine reality." In the Savior's name, I promise you, beset by doubts, that if you, too, bow before Him to say, "*Lord, I believe; help Thou mine unbelief!*" many question marks will vanish as the mist flees before the rising sun.

Through Jesus you have victory over your fears. Millions of you are living your hardest years. Beneath life's outward calm and below all glamour and pleasure seeking are heavy heartaches. What will this war bring you before the last shot is fired? Will your sons, now in Africa, come back? Will your eighteen- and nineteen-year-olds, soon to be called to the colors, return safe in body and sound in soul? Fortune tellers make fabulous sums as they give false, fraudulent answers to questions only God can answer. Why not go directly to God in Christ, then, and believe that whatever your heavenly Father ordains is good, because you are His? Why not trust Christ implicitly, beseeching Him for the faith which prays, "Thy will be done!" because it knows His way is best?

In your redeeming Lord you can also gain the victory over all of life's trials and sorrows. Never has a burden been so heavy that He could not share and lift it. Never has a personal perplexity been so crushing that He could not remove it.—He may not always come to your rescue in the moment and manner you desire. I read the other day of a group of airmen whose plane had been forced down on the Atlantic. When all seemed hopeless, a United States destroyer appeared on the horizon. The flyers screamed at the top of their voices, waved their hands frantically; yet the ship continued on its way. Overcome by disappointment, the men collapsed. They were wrong, however, in assuming that the destroyer had not seen them. The captain was trying to bring the raft under his lee side, so that it would be sheltered from the full force of the wind. Only by this maneuver could he hope to effect the rescue at high sea. Sometimes the Almighty has to direct His help slowly and gradually, so that we can really endure it; and it may appear at first that He passes us unnoticed. Yet, be sure of this, our loving Father always chooses the right hour, the right place, the right way, to deliver His children! Remember, too, the marvelous purposes our Lord has in permitting His own to suffer afflictions! These sorrows come to them not from God's wrath but from His unfathomable mercy.

Finally, the redeemed by Christ have the promise of victory over all opposition. It seems inevitable that during the hard reconstruction years following the war Christianity in this country will be tried as never before. We are already witnessing brutal cutthroat assaults on the Gospel. With sinister, foreboding force taunting claims are urged, charging that Christianity is on its way out, that the Gospel of Christ is discredited, that America must look to itself and not to God. If atheism thus preens itself during days of lush prosperity, what will happen when the war is over and multitudes face greater trials than they have yet seen? Even now some of you are

being persecuted because of your faith. You live in homes
where the Church is ridiculed; daily you suffer taunts
because of your allegiance to the Lord. I tell you with
all the promise of divine truth: yours, too, will ultimately
be the victory, if in difficult moments you look to Jesus
for strength. Yesterday I met one of our repatriated missionaries from Ichang, China, where the enemy's bar-
barity has burned practically the entire city. He told me
that under pressure by Japanese invaders a few native
Christians had forsaken the faith; but he also reported
that often when Japanese soldiers, entering the mission,
pointed to a picture of Jesus or the cross and sneeringly
cried: "False God! False God!" Chinese believers, at the
risk of their lives, publicly declared their loyalty to Jesus.
Those experiences alone, he said, made him thank God
for the privilege of serving Christ in China. May the Holy
Spirit constantly build our trust, so that, the longer a
scoffing world blasphemously attacks the Savior of men,
we may rise to His defense with the assurance, "*Whosoever, therefore, shall confess Me before men, him will
I confess also before My Father which is in heaven.*"

I have been trying to tell you in all this that there is
no personal perplexity, no hidden problem in your life
which cannot be solved; no enemies of your soul, however powerful they may appear, which cannot be defeated in this "*victory through . . . Christ.*" I remind you
that for this triumph you yourself must know Jesus, believe Him, trust in Him as *your* God, *your* Redeemer
from ruin. It is not enough that you have some vague,
uncertain ideas about Him. You must welcome Him into
your heart as *your* sin-removing, sin-destroying Lord.
It is not sufficient that you have mildly warm feelings
for Him as a great Benefactor of mankind. You must
rather experience the terror of your own sins, and then

with unshakable trust turn to the Savior as your personal Substitute, on whom God laid each of your transgressions, the guilt of all your iniquities. For this victory you need much more than a family creed. The fact that your parents are Christians, that your husband or wife lives in the Lord, can never save you. You yourself must believe. You cannot rely on your church membership, for some churches lead away from Jesus instead of to Him. Your heavenly Father wants far more than outside connection with the best of churches, far more than lip worship, ritual religion, attendance at services, hymn singing, society membership. He wants you, gripped in heart and soul by the terror of your sins but assured of Christ's greater grace and His blood-bought pardon.

If, when this broadcast began, you were still without this faith, destitute of any desire to accept the Lord Jesus, may the Holy Spirit bring directly to your heart this appeal for victory over sin, doubt, hell, death, all life's sorrows and afflictions! In the ten years of our radio mission, at all the mammoth meetings held from coast to coast, it has probably not been given to me to see as much as 1 per cent of this vast congregation of the air; and I have been able to speak personally, concerning their soul's salvation, to only a fraction of that fraction. Try to think, however, that these words now leap over space particularly to you who have never declared Christ your Savior or who, having known His grace, left Him to serve sin and heap up condemnation for the day of divine wrath! Believe it when I tell you: This conquest of sin and death was a costly triumph, because it could be won only by the agony your Savior suffered! Not long ago we read that, when the United States aircraft carrier *Yorktown* was sunk, the Navy spent $500,000 to save five sailors from that burning craft, in what has been called "history's most costly rescue." As you thank God for that deliverance, realize also how immeasurably much more it cost Jesus to save you! He, your God and Lord, had to lay down His own life in payment for your freedom; yet by the marvel of His mercy your salvation costs you nothing. You need only believe Christ's grace, and the eternal rescue is yours.

It is a complete victory. The Savior left nothing undone, nothing that you, any saint, or hero of the faith has to finish in this world or the next. His invitation to you is, "*All things are ready: come!*"

Our Lord offers a sure, lasting victory. Many of us, sadly disappointed by the failure of diplomacy to prevent history's two greatest conflicts in a single generation, are troubled by the thought that World War II may, after a period of recuperation, give way to World War III unless the principles of everlasting truth, justice, and righteousness are followed at the peace conference. Yet listen to the Savior's promise: "*The mountains shall depart and the hills be removed; but My kindness shall not depart from thee, neither shall the covenant of My peace be removed*"! Such pledges are not mere wishful thinking. Nor are we asking you to accept His Gospel as something which may or may not be right but which at least deserves a trial. We are not dealing with possibilities, but with heaven's and earth's greatest reality — the assured, unbreakable, eternal truth that through Christ victory is yours now and forever. Jesus never makes a mistake.

In no other way can the enemies of your soul be defeated. Your good intentions to conquer sin will collapse quickly. Your own strength will prove utter weakness. The triumph song still is, "*Thanks be to God, which giveth us the victory through our Lord Jesus Christ!*" — not through anyone else; for the Savior Himself declares:

"I am the Way, the Truth, and the Life: no man cometh unto the Father but by Me"; "There is none other name under heaven given among men, whereby we must be saved" but the name of our God and Redeemer. Every once in a while, of course, infidels rise up to contradict this claim. In 1905 Aristide Briand, French statesman, revealed the true colors of his atheism when he cried out: "We have driven Jesus Christ out of the army, the navy, the schools, the hospitals, the lunatic asylums, and the orphanages! We must now drive Him out of the state altogether!" Many Frenchmen tried to follow this program, with the result that today their unfortunate nation lies prostrate in one of history's most tragic defeats. Some of you have sought to banish the Savior, but even now you are paying the fearful consequences. Before it is too late, ask the Holy Spirit for the repentant faith required to approach the Redeemer and to learn for yourself that *"this is the victory that overcometh the world, even our faith"*!

Many of you, however — and I thank God for your reliance on Christ — have witnessed the blessed results of this triumph in your own lives. To you the Apostle says in the words following our text, *"Therefore, my beloved brethren, be ye steadfast, unmovable, always abounding in the work of the Lord, forasmuch as ye know that your labor is not in vain in the Lord."* In His name and on behalf of the hundreds of millions all over the face of the earth who are still overshadowed by sin's darkness, I plead with you to present yourselves as firm, unyielding defenders of His cause and to rededicate yourselves to spreading the victory message throughout the world. In last week's unusually heavy mail, with all the small silver contributions to this mission of the air, came the largest gift I have ever received in ten years of broadcasting, a check for $7,000, contributed by an earnest follower of the Lord Jesus, who wants the Gospel sent to the far corners of the earth. If other leaders in business and industry, men and women of wealth and influence, will stand by us in a similar generous way, while the masses of our hearers continue to hold up our hands by their prayers, interest, and gifts, we shall be able, under God, to proclaim the Savior's grace to the ends of the world. By extending our broadcast, Bringing Christ to All the Nations (now heard in English, Spanish, and Portuguese throughout the Western Hemisphere from Alaska to the Argentine), you will help multitudes in various countries and climes join us in many languages and different dialects in this hymn of triumph, *"Thanks be to God, which giveth us the victory through our Lord Jesus Christ!"* Especially on the great day of heavenly assembly before the throne will their voices blend with ours in exalted, celestial strains to sing — O God, may every one in this radio audience be there! — heaven's victory song: *"Thine, O Lord, is the greatness and the power and the glory and the victory and the majesty; for all that is in the heaven and in the earth is Thine; Thine is the kingdom, O Lord, and Thou art exalted as Head above all. Both riches and honor come of Thee, and Thou reignest over all; and in Thine hand is power and might; and in Thine hand it is to make great and to give strength unto all. Now, therefore, our God, we thank Thee, and praise Thy glorious name,"* through Jesus Christ, our only Savior, our Lord of victory. Amen.

The Lord Jesus Is
My Shepherd

> *"I am the Good Shepherd; the Good Shepherd
> giveth His life for the sheep."*
> SAINT JOHN 10:11

Jesus, Good and Gracious Shepherd of our Souls:

Without Thee we are hopelessly lost both in this world and
the next. Therefore we come before Thee humbly to ask
pardon for our sins, peace for our souls, blessings for our
lives, and guidance for the darkness and distress of these
heavy days. "All we, like sheep, have gone astray," but in the
marvel of Thy mercy Thou art indeed the Good Shepherd,
who dost lay down Thy life for the flock! Guard us against
hirelings who seek to destroy us! Teach us that if we have
but Thee, we shall not want! May Thy rod and Thy staff
comfort those who labor under sorrows of soul or stagger
under burdens of increasing afflictions! O blessed Savior,
protect especially our youth as it goes forth to war! Keep
our sons and daughters in the faith though they be called
to distant battle fronts — and, O Christ of endless compassion, send them home to us soon, uninjured in body, mind,
and soul! Stop this war, if it be Thy will, and grant us true
peace that pleases Thee! Help us, blessed Redeemer, for
besides Thee we have no hope! Thou alone art our Savior!
Amen.

TWELVE years ago a Swarthmore College
professor told a religious conference that the Bible has
outlived much of its usefulness, that it must be modern-
ized, rewritten. "Take the Twenty-third Psalm, for example," he said, selecting the most frequently memorized
verses of Scripture. "People who live in the city simply

do not know the meaning of *'The Lord is my Shepherd.'*"
Therefore, he concluded bluntly, "we must scrap the
Twenty-third Psalm and put its thought in a modern
language." This is the substitute he suggested: "The
Lord is my automobile's low gear to help me in climbing
hard hills. The Lord is my antiseptic in times of dangerous epidemics. The Lord is sunlight in my room, bringing
me the health of ultraviolet rays." I shall not bother you
with his other emendations; instead I remind you that
atheists, godless Communists, sneering infidels before and
after him have pompously boasted that the Bible, including this Shepherd Psalm, must be discarded by all thinking people. Remarkably, however, this radical changing
of the Twenty-third Psalm, proposed in 1930, has boom-
eranged and been utterly discredited only a dozen years
later by the agonies of war. A few days ago newspapers
told the story of Vern Haugland, noted Associated Press
foreign correspondent, who was forced to bail out of
a crippled bomber over the New Guinea jungles. During
forty-three days of groping through the trackless wilderness, over steep, jagged cliffs, through foodless weeks,
in which he lost half his weight and developed arm
sores and leg ulcers, what sustained him with unshakable
courage? No atheistic boasting that *he* was the master
of his fate, that, though his head was bloody, it was un-
bowed! The intrepid reporter, after receiving the Silver
Star from General MacArthur, wrote his family: "I'd
never have made it but for God's care and the prayers
I know were being said for me. I often repeated the passage, *'The Lord is my Shepherd; I shall not want.'* It was
marvelous how it worked; I would be unable to go one
step further, and then I would remember, *'I shall not
want,'* and sure enough, there would be some berries or
chewable grass or a creek with good water just ahead."

About the same time the daily press also reported, Secretary of the Navy Knox was so concerned about the secret movements of our troops to North Africa that for several nights he could hardly sleep. What finally gave him rest and assurance? Not a detective story — apparently the favorite reading material of many public figures — not his own Chicago newspaper, but, as Secretary Knox told an American Legion audience, the Twenty-third Psalm read to him by his wife from the Bible he carried through the first World War! He said, "I finally dozed off with the words . . . echoing in my ears, *'The Lord is my Shepherd; I shall not want.'* "

Again, President Roosevelt has just issued a proclamation calling for two days of prayer to God, and in the climax of his appeal he asks the American people to keep a certain passage in mind. What is it — a quotation from the Atlantic Charter? A new promise of victory? A startling, new social change? No! Instead, the President proclaims, "I recommend that all of us bear in mind this great psalm, *'The Lord is my Shepherd; I shall not want.'* " Thus a war correspondent, the man entrusted with the destiny of hundred thousands of American men at sea, the chief executive of the nation found rest despite the present-day crisis in the very psalm ruthlessly rejected a dozen years ago by a Modernist professor.

No matter who you are, regardless of where you are, irrespective of what you are, this glorious Shepherd Psalm can similarly bring you guiding strength and send you out into a world of war and woe with peace in your heart, provided — and this is often overlooked — you understand its deathless words as they have been explained by that holy, perfect, sinless, errorless Teacher of all teachers, Jesus Christ. In the tenth chapter of Saint John's Gospel and its eleventh verse that blessed Savior, referring to the words, *"The Lord is my Shepherd,"* assures us in our text, *"I am the Good Shepherd; the Good Shepherd giveth His life for the sheep."* May we (every one of us, O Holy Spirit) look to our royal Redeemer, and as we declare in firm faith,

"THE LORD JESUS IS MY SHEPHERD,"

find rich, eternal blessings in this infallible promise of grace and glory!

I

EVERY ONE OF US NEEDS DIVINE GUIDANCE

To measure fully the meaning and comfort of Scripture's many shepherd passages, we must understand how clearly the weaknesses of the sheep suggest men's frailties. First of all, sheep are easily misguided. Many stockyards employ a ram or goat — in East Saint Louis they call him "Judas" — which stands at the foot of the runway whenever a shipment of sheep arrives. These new animals, fresh from prairie farms, accept his leadership and follow him into the killing pens. But as soon as the gates of the pens are closed, "Judas" is not to be found among those assembled for slaughter. Is this not a striking picture of humanity as it is often misled? Every century of history is marked by deep sorrows which have come from blind obedience to selfish leaders. War lords who delight in slaughter, industrialists who profiteer by the shedding of human blood, dictators who play fast and loose with human lives, have repeatedly incited the masses to hurl themselves into brutal conflict. Lying teachers of religion have directed multitudes from heaven to hell. False prophets and false Christs have repeatedly made their victims suffer anguish, despair, excruciating death. Many of you are following destructive direction. In swift, blind affection you married someone whose heart was estranged from God, and as a consequence your own faith is weakening, your life is being buried beneath misery. Some of you trusted associates in financial matters, only to be cheated; you shared your confidences with friends, only to be betrayed. You have been lured by the lust of the flesh and are now distressed in your conscience to find yourselves on the road to moral ruin. Others, once firm in the faith, listened to the deniers of Jesus, enemies of His Bible, who have coaxed you away from church (perhaps because it was no longer large and fashionable enough) into Christless creeds that have no confession of sin and therefore no room for the Redeemer from sin. Every one of us — and God grant that we realize this humbly, penitently, personally — has too often followed Satan instead of the Savior, sought mammon instead of mercy, practiced folly instead of faith. This is Humiliation and Prayer Sunday, the day on which, according to ancient custom, Christians should bow penitently before the Almighty to admit their guilt. Let us make this a nationwide humiliation and prayer service, as everyone — and I make no exceptions — kneels in spirit before the just God to confess with the ancient prophet: "'All we like sheep have gone astray,' away from our heavenly Father and the Word of His truth, away from the cross of His Christ and the promise of His pardon, away from heaven and its glories, away from our salvation! O God, have mercy upon us! O Christ, have mercy upon us! O Holy Spirit, have mercy upon us!"

Not only do sheep readily accept false leadership, but of all domesticated animals they have the poorest sense of direction. In heavy snow-storms they have been known to hurl themselves blindly over cliffs. Most of our world today has also lost its way. God, who has spoken twice to this generation in the sorrow of history's bloodiest wars, is still not recognized and obeyed. We have more atheists in the United States than ever before. Jesus, who says, *"I am the Way, the Truth, and the Life; no man cometh unto the Father but by Me,"* is still rejected by masses, just as blasphemously as He was when they crucified Him on the first Good Friday. Without realizing that the world is at war, that American lives are being lost every day on battle fronts, people drink and gamble, spend and waste, debauch and debase themselves, losing all sense of moral and spiritual direction. Even some who have pledged their loyalty to Christ and His Church have been caught in the careless, carnal carousal of these trying times, when they ought to stop and ask themselves: "Where am I? Am I on the pathway to God or on the highway to hell?" As we confess that, like wandering sheep, we have repeatedly lost the way, what better can we do than turn to God in Christ and, begging for pardon, plead: "O heavenly Father, have mercy upon us! Guide us aright and teach us to walk in Thy ways!"

Sheep are pitiful creatures also because they often deliberately return to the very dangers from which they have been saved. If the barn in which they are kept catches fire, the flock can be led out to safety only with the utmost difficulty; and usually the sheep try to run back into the flames. As hard as it is to explain this, it is a hundred times harder to account for the fact that human beings, gifted with reason and intelligence, are guilty of a far more serious folly. Recall what has happened within twenty-one years! One war was concluded that cost 37,000,000 lives in slaughter, starvation, and disease — not to mention the financial loss of $350,000,-000,000. Yet before another generation arose, humanity

with all its culture and scientific achievement, led itself
back into even more destructive flames of fiery conflict. The principle of this world tragedy is re-enacted
in individual lives. Christ's Gospel is preached to multitudes who contemptuously turn from His outstretched
arms and wilfully reject the message of His surpassing
love. Why? Simply because they insist on continuing
in their transgressions. They do not want to be rescued
from the flames of their passions, their illicit affairs, their
hatreds, their evil ways. After they have confessed and
renounced their sins, after they have known the grace
of Christ, they deliberately hurl themselves back into
the ruin of their old, death-dealing vices! This message
comes with a personal appeal and a prayer to the Spirit
that you humble yourselves before the Almighty and
plead: "O God, I have fallen back into unbelief and
heavy sin. I have broken my promise of allegiance to
Thy truth. O Father, forgive me! May the Good Shepherd lead me, a lamb strayed from the fold, to mercy,
salvation, and life eternal!"

Again, sheep are easily frightened. A clap of thunder
can throw a flock into terror. Even a fluttering piece of
paper may produce panic among them. How similarly
people are agonized into unfounded fright! Beneath the
glamor of this pleasure-seeking age, fears gnaw at our
peace and composure. For masses these are the years of
deep worry and disquieting uncertainty. Nervous breakdowns, mental disorders, suicides, all poisonous fruits of
fear, have cursed our age. While Jesus repeatedly seeks
to sustain us with His comforting promises: *"Be not
afraid"; "My peace I give unto you"; "Let not your heart
be troubled,"* too many, spurning His mercy, are endangering their souls, injuring their bodies, reducing the
power of their minds by vicious fear.

Besides, we, like sheep, are powerless to defend ourselves, too weak properly to direct our own lives. With all our colleges and universities, our resources and material advances, we of ourselves are still unable to secure the simplest and most basic of life's blessings. How, for example, can we establish peace on earth and stop men from killing one another by the millions as they have in recent years? By diplomacy? In 1939, Edouard Daladier, French statesman, asserted that his country and Great Britain were "inseparably united even beyond victory." Less than three years later, however, France is at virtual war with England. Can we establish peace by international law, if this is completely cast aside whenever selfish interests wish? By a League of Nations, when its headquarters are closed and barred during a world conflict? By peace movements, when we realize that every endeavor of this kind has failed in the past? By Esperanto, or a universal language? No; it takes more than a common speech to make people live and act in harmony. By education? The world's worst war is being fought when culture has reached its highest level. Can we ban bloodshed by force, completely crushing our enemies? We ought to admit by now that force begets force. Now, if men of and by themselves are too weak and powerless to maintain outward peace, how can they establish the inner harmony with God and their consciences, for which we yearn with unsatisfied longing? If some of you cannot get right with your fellow men, how can you get right with the Almighty?

No lengthy argument should be required to show that, in this age of unparalleled pride and boasting, men are like wandering sheep, deprived of their sense of direction, lost in their own trespasses and sins. It ought not be hard to convince people, with danger and death lurking on all sides for millions of the nation's young men, that our insistent prayer should be the pointed appeal: "O God, give me the guidance of a divine and heavenly Leader! Give me a Shepherd for my soul, who will lead me along the right path and accompany me especially when I *'walk through the valley of the shadow of death'!*"

II

EVERYONE OF US CAN HAVE CHRIST AS "THE GOOD SHEPHERD"

That plea has been marvelously answered by God's grace in Christ. Jesus is not only *a* shepherd for wandering mankind, He is *the* Shepherd, the *"Good Shepherd,"* as He calls Himself in our text for today.

What a wealth of reassuring love in this statement that He, our great and glorious God, is *"the Good Shepherd"*! There was nothing in our sin-tainted souls and sin-stained lives that could deserve His consideration, nothing that could make Him leave His heavenly glory to live for thirty-three years in this selfish, greed-cursed world. Yet all this and much more Jesus, *"the Good Shepherd,"* did for every one of us, in the most magnificent mercy which even He, God's Son, could offer.

See how the Scriptures repeatedly stress His good and gracious shepherding! He leaves the flock of ninety and nine to go and seek the one stray lamb until He finds it. May that merciful pledge strengthen many who are wandering and lost! We all rejoiced when, after a long search, the United States Navy found Captain Rickenbacker and his companions afloat on a raft in the South Pacific. However, the newspapers make no comment on the far greater rescue, by which the Lord Jesus constantly saves those who without Him are eternally lost. For years He has invited you: Come back to God! Be reconciled with your heavenly Father! He sought you, while you tried to avoid Him. He found you and pleaded with you when you would have hidden from Him. He returned to help you, but you rejected Him. He never let you out of His sight, though in your sins you went as far from Him as you could. Today, through this broadcast, He continues to seek you. Hundreds of stations throughout our country and Canada are united in this mighty network to help bring Christ's Word into your heart with His abiding peace and pardon. How much longer must He plead: *"Come unto Me!" "Follow Me!" "Believe . . . in Me!"?* May many of you whom He has sought from the very first day of your life, in civilian or now in military activity, approach Him and say: "Lord, Thou art my Shepherd, my Savior, my truest Friend. Receive me with all my sins! Accept me! Lead me!"

Again, Jesus is *"the Good Shepherd"* because He leads us aright. What a marvelous assurance to know that in a world of falsehood and error there is an unfailing source of true direction for prosperity and pain, joy and sorrow, life and death itself! No one has ever made a mistake in following Christ; for while the road along which He conducts us may often be hard and steep and stony, it is always the right path. Though it starts with the cross, it always ends with the crown. If you want to rise above the disappointments and failures of a selfish existence; if you want your home to radiate joy and calm, then make His Word your guide! Acclaim Him your only but all-atoning Redeemer! Take time to study His Gospel and apply its saving truth to yourself! Read what Christ has to say to you and your family in His Word! Give Him the leadership in your home! Pray for the strength to obey His instructions loyally and continually!

Jesus is *"the Good Shepherd"* also because He knows our weaknesses and is ready to help bear our burdens. If Old Testament prophecy could foresee Him as One who carried the sick sheep and the little lambs in His arms, then how much more should we, who have seen the New Testament fulfillment of His promised support, believe that in every moment of affliction He is at our side to uphold us! Make the most of this heavenly comfort, you to whom life has been a rough pathway through a wilderness of sorrows! Some of you, as you write me, have been languishing on sickbeds for ten, twenty, thirty years! Not a few are weighted down with the heaviness of unfaithfulness, cruelty, abuse, murder in your own households. Still others suffer from a hundred additional sorrows. Though your burdens are crushing, they are never too heavy for Him; though your afflictions are many, they can never be too numerous for His divine help. Say to Him, "Take Thou my hand and lead me o'er life's rough way!" and you will never need to face difficulty or opposition alone! Put your whole trust in Christ without questions or doubts, and His promise *"Your sorrow shall be turned into joy"* will be proved in your life!

Jesus likewise is *"the Good Shepherd"* because He knows His sheep; and, as the text chapter reveals, *"He calleth"* them . . . *"by name."* In the regimentation and mass production of our age, men often lose their identity and become mere numbers. In armies including millions and in countries populated by many tens of millions the individual may count for little or nothing. Do you complain that nobody pays friendly attention or shows real regard for you? Jesus does! He knew you before you were born. He calls all this world to repentance and to faith, but when you hear that invitation, He is summoning you especially, you individually. Some years ago three American travelers went to the top of Mount Calvary, cut a small piece of wood there and had it made into a walking stick. This they presented to Governor George Briggs of Massachusetts with the words, "We wanted you to know that, when we stood there at Calvary, we thought of you." The Governor thanked them for the gift but added, "I am still more thankful, gentlemen, that there was Another who thought of me there." As Thanksgiving week dawns, have you raised your heart in similar gratitude to Christ? He thought of you when the agonies of Gethsemane almost crushed His soul into death. He thought of you when the scourge cut its bloody stripes in His back. He thought of you when they forced the crown of thorns on His head. He thought of you when they nailed Him to the accursed tree. He thought of you when He pleaded, *"Father, forgive them; for they know not what they do!"* He thought of you when on that cross He died your death. You can take every promise of God in Christ and write your full name into its pledge. He tells you, *"Fear not: . . . I have called thee by thy name; thou art Mine."*

There at Calvary we learn fully that Jesus is *"the Good Shepherd"* because, as He assures us today, He *"giveth His life for the sheep."* His flock will be attacked by ravenous bears, hungry lions, treacherous wolves — foes so powerful that the sheep would be destroyed, were it not for His willingness to protect them even at the cost of His life. I pray God that you see the full mercy this picture offers you. You, too, are beset by enemies of your soul which seek your destruction. Sin and hell are mobilized against you in a death struggle. You yourself can never overcome them. You are doomed to defeat. But Jesus, blessed Savior, enters the battle in your behalf, crushes this opposition completely and forever, though He pays for that triumph with His lifeblood. All this happened when at Calvary the Son of God became our all-embracing Sacrifice for sin, the ever-valid Atonement for every sinner. He died that you might be saved. He was crucified for your victory. He shed His blood for your rescue.

If we reward our heroes in the present war with citations, Congressional medals, and silver stars, purple hearts, distinguished service orders, and oak-leaf awards, should we not gladly give to Christ the faith and trust of our believing hearts? Should we not realize that, while everything else can fail, His grace for our souls and His leadership for our lives can never fail? Don't be impressed when they tell you that it is out of date and out of fashion to say, *"The Lord is my Shepherd!"* This Shepherd Psalm has been the refuge and strength of God's children in every hour of trial. It was prayed by the martyrs in the first Christian Church before they stepped into the Roman arenas to be torn to pieces by wild beasts. It was studied by Bishop John Hooper before he was burned to death in the cruel persecutions under Bloody Mary. It was intoned by Isabel Allison and Marion Narvie, two young girls hanged in 1681 at Edinburgh because of their religion. "Come, Isabel," said Marion, only twenty years old, as they stood on the scaffold, "let us sing the Twenty-third Psalm!" and with *"The Lord is my Shepherd"* on their lips they went to a blessed eternity. Now, this year, you, too, can have every want supplied, *"green pastures"* for rest and refreshment, *"still waters"* after every hot conflict, guidance for the right path from earth to heaven, if with contrite hearts and confident spirit you say, " *'The Lord'* Jesus *'is my Shepherd.'* "

If you are a sheep in the Savior's flock and know what a blessed Guide and Redeemer He is, you will also remember His words, *"Other sheep I have, which are not of this fold; them also I must bring."* That missionary motive was carved into the gravestone which marks the earthly resting place of Livingstone, mighty messenger of God. Does your life show a love for souls, a sacred passion for the redemption of your fellow men? Oh, work and pray that many more, from all corners of the earth, be brought into Christ's fold! Help us, in this far-flung mission of the air, as we plan to dedicate our efforts especially to the most vital of present-day missionary efforts, bringing Christ to the nation's armed forces, to gather the Savior's redeemed into the one eternal flock, the Church of Christ in earth and heaven! O Jesus, Shepherd of our souls, bring us all to Thee and keep us in Thy fold forever! Amen.

Thank God Even in Darkened Days!

> *"He kneeled upon his knees three times a day and prayed and gave thanks before his God."*
> DANIEL 6:10

Our God of Endless Grace:

During another year Thou hast blessed us with overflowing bounty, prospered the yield of our farmlands and orchards, generously supplied us with food and sustenance. For these benedictions and for Thy constant care we owe Thee endless thanks. America, large in its territory, wide in its influence, strong in its power; America, rich in its possessions, wealthy in its vaulted gold, abundant in its prosperity; America, blessed above all other nations in its churches, schools, and homes; America, feasting despite rationing, while other countries starve; America, the land favored by Thee, our God, should be on its knees in penitence and prayer, thanksgiving and recognition of Thy goodness. Forgive us, for Jesus' sake, our ingratitude, our disregard of divine compassion, our indifference to the earnest warnings of Thy Word! If it please Thee, let this be the last wartime Thanksgiving! May we next year on this day praise Thy power and love for having banished bloodshed and restored peace among all nations! Without Thy direction, O God — Father, Son, and Spirit — we are destitute, cursed by conflict, eternally lost. Therefore be with us, O triune Lord, as Thou wast with our fathers! Humbly, thankfully, we beseech Thy guidance in Christ's name and by His merits. Hear us and continue to bless us! Amen.

BACK in November, 1930, when unemployment was high, farm prices low, bread lines long, shelters for the homeless full, the American Association for the Advancement of Atheism sent a petition to the President

72

asking that the annual Thanksgiving proclamation be omitted. How, these deniers of truth argued, can anyone give thanks with so much suffering and want throughout the land? How can people praise a God who permits such widespread anguish?

The A. A. A. A. petition has not been repeated *this* year, for the present-day evidences of outward prosperity are many and striking. From coast to coast Thanksgiving orators have called attention to America's unparalleled blessing even in war time; and today many have applied the Psalmist's words, *"He hath not dealt so with any nation,"* to our unequaled prosperity. Thanks be to God! — ours is the greatest and, in point of habitable, useful territory, the largest country in the world. We have immeasurable natural resources hidden in treasure houses beneath our soil, spreading in almost unlimited extent over its surface in forests, fertile farmlands, bounteous orchards. We now have more gold and silver than the rest of the world. While diseases ravaged large areas in Europe, this country has escaped serious epidemics. Eleven thousand were destroyed by a single typhoon in India, but no such disaster has swept through our States. Millions in China and Greece hover on the very edge of starvation; yet the past year, despite restriction and rationing, has not deprived our people of necessary and wholesome food. We have had bounteous harvests.

Even in war's afflictions God has been good to us. No enemy troops have landed on our shores. No enemy planes have bombed our cities. No enemy invasion has even threatened our borders. True, we have blackouts, but only for practice. With all our casualty lists, we have suffered less than any other country actively engaged in the war.

Add to these material blessings the liberties that are

ours. We have a democratic government, while other peoples are crushed beneath the heel of tyranny. Freedom of thought, freedom of expression, freedom of education — all these, though now necessarily restricted, are still ours in principle, while other nations are regimented by destructive dictatorships. Above all, we still have religious freedom, the personal privilege of worshiping the Almighty according to His Word without state direction. No wonder, with all these material and spiritual advantages, the President of the United States this year has asked for two days of prayer to God instead of one!

Yet despite these reasons for gratitude, many among you are seized with bitterness because of financial reverses, family losses, personal afflictions. You read in the newspapers that a New York department store records a profit five times larger than last year's; that a fur store advertises, "We have sold more mink coats this year than in any previous year," and you know that you will never have even a small piece of mink in your home but must be satisfied with enough fuel and food to keep your family warm and properly fed. You hear of happy Thanksgiving reunions, when soldiers on furlough sit around the holiday table; yet some of you soldiers and civilians are far from your families today, downhearted, inwardly distressed; and some of you parents know that you will never see your sons again. They lie buried at Bataan, in North Africa, on the Solomons, or even unburied in the sea, beneath Alaskan snows, or in a New Guinea jungle. Again, Thanksgiving finds many of you in hospitals, on sickbeds, or in a house divided against itself, with growing fear concerning the things that are to come. Crepe may hang on your door; tomorrow you may stand at the cemetery to pay the tribute of your love to a departed one. Every time you hear the word "thanksgiving," a feeling of resentment may well up within you. Now, I would speak to you, the lonely, distressed, spiritually shaken, destitute, bereaved — but also to you, the satisfied, secure, socially prominent, financially firm with larger incomes than you have ever before received and the heaviest prosperity you have ever enjoyed. To *all* of you I say in the name of Jesus Christ:

THANK GOD EVEN IN DARKENED DAYS!

Take as your example heroic Daniel, of whom it is written in our text (Daniel, chapter six, verse ten), *"He kneeled upon his knees three times a day and prayed and gave thanks before his God."*

I

DANIEL THANKED GOD EVEN IN HIS AFFLICTION AND WAS DELIVERED

Heart-shaking sorrow must have gripped Daniel at the time to which these words refer. He was in exile in Babylon, far from his beloved Judah and Jerusalem, a stranger in a strange, hostile nation. Many of you know the pangs of that loneliness right here in your homeland, separated as you are today from your husband or wife, your parents or children. Keep in mind, however, that Daniel lived among a pagan and perverted people!

Besides, many personal enemies surrounded him. By maintaining strict allegiance to the Lord, he who had come as a captive slave had risen to a high position in the Persian kingdom; and the greater his achievement, the more numerous the jealous opponents who sought to discredit him before King Darius. Many of you have likewise suffered from slander and envy. You know by experience the indescribable agony caused by lying, deceitful individuals who smile when they face you, but who loose foul, slanderous tongues when they leave you.

Yet few, if any, I am sure, have ever felt the brunt of an attack as steady, evil, and systematic as this assault directed against that young Israelite when, as the verses preceding our text declare, "*all the presidents of the kingdom, the governors, and the princes, the counselors, and the captains . . . sought to find occasion against Daniel.*"

Daniel's heaviest burden, however, was imposed by Darius' decree, demanding that all people in his realm pray to him, the king. This meant that, if Daniel continued to kneel before the true God, he would be thrown to hungry lions. Can you imagine how that weighted his heart and mind? He loved his Lord and had consistently prayed to Him; but to continue this loyalty meant public disgrace, the sacrifice of his high office, the loss of any influence he might have wielded in restoring his people to their homeland, and above all, death in the jaws of ravenous beasts. No hope could be held that the royal edict would be changed, for it was officially sealed and signed. Such laws of the Medes and Persians were unalterable. Therefore Daniel had to obey either God or man, do or die. — It takes much less than this to make people renounce their faith today. None of you — except some of our missionaries — has ever been placed before the danger of giving up your life for your religion, but many of you have denied Christ under the slightest pressure. You thought that it would cost you business or popular favor to remain loyal and the price was too high to pay. It meant foregoing sinful pleasure, and you were unprepared to make such sacrifice. It required breaking off destructive friendships, and you did not love the Savior enough for that. Then, when adversities swirled down on you, unfaithful and disloyal, you screamed and shook your fists at God.

What did Daniel do? Knowing that every movement of his was being watched by his enemies, he did not swerve even slightly from his daily prayer habits. He went, as was his custom, before the open window, where official spies could easily see him. As our text tells us, *"He kneeled down upon his knees,"* not in a single hurried gesture, but *"three times a day and prayed."* And now comes the climax — although his public career, his reputation, his happiness, his very life were at stake, he *"gave thanks before his God."* What magnificent courage! And how gloriously it was rewarded by the Lord!

You know the rest of the story. His enemies stealthily watched his house, found him on his knees worshiping God, accused him at the royal court, and insisted that Darius sentence him to death. Unwillingly the monarch obeyed, and before the day closed, Daniel was cast into the lions' den. Yet, instead of being torn to pieces by the bloodthirsty beasts, he was miraculously protected. An angel shut the lions' mouths. The Lord's servant was rescued and returned to his position. His deliverance provoked another decree, directing men throughout the kingdom to bow before Jehovah, since, as King Darius declared, *"He is the living God and steadfast forever."* What a glorious Thanksgiving Day that was for Daniel!

II

WE WILL BE BLESSED IF WE, TOO, PRAISE GOD DESPITE OUR SORROWS

What a blessed Thanksgiving Day this can be for you if with all your heart you follow Daniel by turning to the Almighty in Christ and, despite war's sorrows or personal hardships, thank Him for His marvelous mercies! No matter how hard the past has been, how uncertain the future, if you have accepted the Lord Jesus as your

Savior, the twenty-four hours of Thanksgiving Day will not be long enough to express your gratitude for His mercy in redeeming you from sin and its sentence of eternal death. Can you say and believe sincerely, "Jesus died for me"? Then thank God without ceasing for the greatest gift even His love can give you — this assurance of your salvation! What if you have financial problems? Through the Redeemer heaven is yours. — Are you born again into a new, Christ-centered life? Then join the Psalmist in declaring, *"O give thanks unto the Lord, for He is good, because His mercy endureth forever!"* What if you are seized by worry and fears concerning your Christian son in Tunisia or the South Sea Islands? Praise the Almighty that he is under divine protection, that nothing can happen to him except by Heaven's good and gracious will. Do you own a Bible, the errorless Word of redemption, *"which is able to build you up"?* Thank God for this sacred truth which can direct you safely in every dark hour, along each uncharted path! Even if you have been guilty of many and serious sins, read the promises of Sacred Scripture to learn, *"Though your sins be as scarlet, they shall be white as snow; though they be red like crimson, they shall be as wool"* — all through the complete, assured grace of the Savior who gave Himself for you! Do you know the power of prayer uttered in Jesus' name, accompanied by the confession of all your sins, spoken with grateful acknowledgment of divine mercies? Then, before this day closes, kneel, as Daniel did, before God to glorify Him with all your heart and soul for this privilege of communion with Him. What if doubt of divine goodness tries to invade your heart? Rejoice because you have Christ's promise, *"All things, whatsoever ye shall ask in prayer, believing, ye shall receive"!* That pledge never fails.

Are you tempted to refuse thanking God since your happiness has been small? When the Plymouth Pilgrims observed their first Thanksgiving, they had harvested the yield of only twenty acres of corn, six acres of barley and peas. Their world was but a few square miles surrounded by the perils of pathless wilderness, yet they set aside a special day to praise their Lord. How much more you have for which to sing your gratitude to the heavenly Father! Count your blessings, one by one, and believe that the almighty Creator and Sustainer, with whom *"nothing shall be impossible,"* can, if it be for your eternal good, multiply your earthly benedictions overnight.

Do not think that your voice must be raised in lament instead of praise because you have suffered repeated afflictions! If you have Christ as your Savior, you know the secret of human suffering, for at the cross you understand that the Lord of love, far from punishing His children in His wrath, only corrects them in His mercy. What seems a crushing blow may in reality, through Jesus, prove a marvelous, uplifting power. The other day I read of a shipwrecked man who managed to reach an uninhabited island. There, to protect himself against the elements and to safeguard the few possessions he had salvaged, he painstakingly built a little hut from which he constantly and prayerfully scanned the horizon for the approach of a ship. Returning one evening after a search for food, he was terrified to find the hut completely enveloped in flames. What a crushing disaster that seemed! Yet by divine mercy this hard affliction was changed into a mighty advantage. Early on the following morning he awoke to find a ship anchored off the island. The captain stepped ashore and explained, "We saw your smoke signal and came." Everything the marooned man owned had to be destroyed before he could be rescued.

Some of you have likewise had to face complete loss of your pride, your overconfident self-reliance before you could be saved and realize this glorious comfort, "*All things work together for good to them that love God.*"

Do not be discouraged when you find opposition on all sides! Remember Daniel! When his enemies sought to destroy him, he turned to the Lord in thanksgiving for His mercies. If you show a similar loyalty to your heavenly Father, if with the Apostle Paul you learn to rejoice in your afflictions and thank God for your infirmities, as they reveal Christ's power more clearly, then the Almighty will stand by you, as He supported Daniel. This help may not come in the spectacular deliverance by which that Prophet was rescued from the lions. Indeed, it may often seem that your faith brings you too much of the cross, too little of the crown; but finally, in your Father's good time, in His perfect way, you, too, will be preserved for His celestial kingdom. You will be able to rise over all obstacles and opposition, all trials and temptations, all agonies and afflictions, to challenge, "*If God be for us*" — and He *is* for us, because He gave His only Son to redeem us from sin — then "*who can be against us?*"

Do you not see, therefore, that for full Thanksgiving blessings you should dedicate your souls in unswerving loyalty to Jesus? Acclaim Him your Savior, and He will proclaim you His eternally redeemed. His promise is, "*Be thou faithful unto death, and I will give thee a crown of life.*" If the Holy Spirit now grants me the privilege of speaking into the souls of some of you who up till this Thanksgiving Day have spent your own lives apart from the Lord and against Christ, only to realize that your plans have been battered in the past and your hopes shattered for the future, then may the Spirit help you make this a day of the truest thanksgiving — a time of rejoicing even in heaven — as you stop your rebellion against the Almighty and turn to His Son for pardon, joy, salvation! We read of Saint Paul that in one of his many difficulties *"he thanked God, and took courage."* May you, my fellow redeemed, on this wartime Thanksgiving praise God for the Savior and take courage in Christ for whatever may confront you! In true courage stand beneath the cross and, with your arm raised in the oath of allegiance to the crucified Redeemer, cry out, *"Thanks be to God, which giveth us the victory through our Lord Jesus Christ!"* The Lord grant you that supreme Thanksgiving joy for the Savior's sake! Amen.

CONCORDIA COLLEGE LIBRARY
BRONXVILLE, NY 10708

———————

Jesus Christ, Our God of Grace

> "He [Jesus] said, Young man, I say unto thee, Arise! And he that was dead sat up, and began to speak."
>
> SAINT LUKE 7:14, 15

Enlightening, Comforting Spirit of God:

*T*ake possession of our hearts and lead us to believe with all our souls that because Jesus died on the cross in our stead, atoning for our sins, humble faith in His mercies can strengthen us in weakness, comfort us in sorrow, and sustain us in every trial! Bring the glory of full Gospel grace into many sin-marked lives throughout the land! Show the impenitent that the way of the transgressor is hard, but that the way of the Redeemer is the road, through pardon and peace, to heaven itself! Bless our broadcast everywhere, especially among the men in our military forces! Many of them, we know, are not at peace with Thee. Prove Thy power mightily in their hearts and call them, contrite and trusting, to their Savior! Keep those in the Army and the Navy who are God's children clean amid temptations, and daily show them the courage they can find in Christ! Bring them back to us, O Holy Spirit, and soon grant the world blessed peace in which righteousness and truth prevail! Hear us and help us for Jesus' sake! Amen.

RECENTLY our American troops, trying to land near Buna, New Guinea, were suddenly attacked by a squadron of eighteen Japanese planes. The air bombing became so heavy that two of our generals, their staffs, and most of the men were forced to dive into the water and under constant fire swim a half mile to shore. On board one of these landing trawlers was Captain Wilfred

Schnedler, a graduate of Concordia Seminary, one of our 138 Lutheran pastors now serving the armed forces as chaplains. He stayed on deck as long as he could, tossing over hatch covers and oil drums, by which others might keep afloat and save their lives. Finally he, too, had to leave the ship and make for shore. After thanking God for their deliverance, our troops stopped to take inventory. All their possessions had gone to the bottom. Many of the men were without even clothing. "In fact," Chaplain Schnedler summarized, "We lost everything except our religion," and then, naming the heaviest loss sustained, he concluded, "I could not save even my New Testament."

Why do you suppose that New Testament meant more to the chaplain and to many of his men than anything else? Or, why do many American soldiers, when asked which gift they prefer, not answer, "Cigarettes"; "Cookies"; "Candy," but, "The Bible"? Why do letters come to our desk every day from men with the nation's fighting forces stating that the strongest morale-building agency in their lives is Scripture? All this testifies to the glorious truth that God's Word, as the errorless, complete, inexhaustible truth of Heaven, is man's priceless, peerless possession today because it reveals Jesus as God and Savior, the one and only Answer to our greatest needs in this critical hour. Destroy every copy of Holy Writ, tear the memory of its promises from the human mind, and the world will become an even more brutal battlefield on which the horrors of the Second World War will appear small by comparison! But spread the Bible with its pledge of Christ's cleansing power, give a constantly increasing number of sin-torn human hearts the assurance that Jesus is both Lord of lords and the universal Redeemer, and men will find new hope for the life that now

is and for that which is to come. That is why Chaplain
Schnedler missed his New Testament more than all else,
why thousands of American marines, sailors, airmen appreciate the Scriptures above all other gifts you send
them. That is why — with the New Testament picturing
Christ as our eternal God and Redeemer — you and I
must turn to His Word for the guarantee of pardon and
the pledge of heaven.

In His name, then, and with the Spirit's help, I devote
this broadcast to exalt

JESUS CHRIST, OUR GOD OF GRACE,

choosing as the text Saint Luke's memorable words
(chapter seven, verses fourteen and fifteen): *"He* [Jesus]
*said, Young man, I say unto thee, Arise! And he that was
dead sat up and began to speak."*

I

HIS GRACE IS SHOWN BY HIS SYMPATHETIC COMFORT

This miracle takes us outside the gates of Nain, a small
city in southern Galilee. At first glance its geographical
location may seem of little importance, but as every word
in the Bible is packed with meaning, so these cities where
the Savior lived and worked bring us a special message.
Do you realize what it meant to live in Galilee? That
was the land of mixed races, mixed bloods, mixed languages — the territory from which self-respecting church
leaders and the socially prominent in Judea and Jerusalem kept their distance. It was a country generally of
poor, underprivileged, lower-class people, which according to popular estimate would never produce a great
man of God — a district so despised that the Pharisees
and Sadducees could sneer, *"Out of Galilee ariseth no
prophet!"* Yet in this neglected province Jesus lived. Here

He spent most of His ministry. Here He chose practically all His disciples. — What a vital lesson and present-day challenge in this fact that Christ grew up among the Galileans and performed His miracles for them! His grace is offered all men, but especially those on whom the world pours its self-righteous scorn. His appeal *"Come unto Me"* is addressed to the whole race, but particularly to those who *"labor and are heavy laden."* Priests and Levites might refuse to cross the threshold of a tax-gatherer's home, lest they contaminate themselves, but our Lord sat at table with those social outcasts, lest they be deprived of hearing the promise of eternal life.

Jesus never changes; and today you need not fear that you are too humble and unimportant to be received, welcomed, comforted, saved, by His love. The Gospel we bring you in His name is the pledge of grace for *every* sinner, no matter how spurned he may be; the Christ we preach is the Savior for *all*, for the forgotten and forsaken. Let American churches learn to follow Him in His compassion for the underpaid and underprivileged, the overlooked and overburdened! Sometimes we have too many churches in the suburbs and too few in the slums, imposing granite sanctuaries on the right side of the railroad track and dilapidated structures on the wrong side. Too much time is often spent with the rich and prominent, too little with the poor and ignored. Although we are fighting for democracy, millions of Americans, including many nominal Christians, still speak with contempt of Jews and Negroes, of "okies" and "hillbillies," immigrants and aliens, when in the sight of Him who died for their salvation, their souls are immeasurably precious. Before it is too late and the neglected masses rise up to indict the churches for catering to the rich and throwing only a few crumbs to the poor, the pulpits of the United States should emphasize that, as the Lord spent practically His whole life and more than half of His public ministry among these pushed-aside people of Galilee, so the mission of His kingdom is particularly directed to the Galileans of our twentieth century.

When Jesus stopped outside the Nain gates, He paused to greet a widow. At that time the lot of the woman who had lost her husband was often crushing; and throughout the world, until Christ's principles penetrated heathen strongholds, widows were systematically oppressed and persecuted. In India the bereaved wife was urged to throw herself on the flaming funeral pyre that consumed her lord husband's remains. In sections of New Guinea a widow even now must veil her face and for six months daily crawl on hands and knees to her husband's grave. Papuan widows are compelled by custom to wear the skulls of their departed husbands on a chain around their necks. In China widows are often driven to suicide because relatives seek to force them into a life of shame. In New Britain, even during recent years, widows were still choked to death, so that they might serve their husbands throughout the next life. — Into this maze of cruelty and brutality came the Lord Jesus, to fulfill His promise, *"Behold, I make all things new,"* to change the human heart so that widows would be regarded with charity and compassion, supported in their needs, comforted in their bereavement.

Added to the Nain widow's sorrow was the fresh wound that her son, the only support for her advancing age, had now been taken by death. What doubly crushing heaviness must have burdened her heart, and how she must have yearned for true comfort! Small wonder that a throng of sympathizers followed her in the funeral procession! They meant well, even the professional mourners who probably marched along with the cortege, raising their voices in loud lament. Yet the words of the Psalmist must have run through the bereaved woman's mind, *"I looked for . . . comforters, but I found none."* — Many of you can understand the depth of her anguish: you recall a bereavement in your own family circle and remember that flowers, messages of condolence, visits of sympathetic friends could hardly lessen the aching grief. You were inconsolable, tempted to charge God with cruelty. You, too, had only human comforters.

While the long funeral procession slowly passes through the gates, another column of marchers appears, intent on entering the city. It is the Lord Jesus with His disciples and many of the common people who had followed Him from Capernaum, where He had healed the centurion's servant on the day before. How was it, we may well pause to ask, that these two processions — one of death and the other of life — met on the Nain road? Apparently it was only accidental; but there are no chance happenings in Christ's comforting grace! That morning, when Jesus had set out with His followers, no one except our Lord Himself knew that, before the day closed, He would meet this agonized widow. And this morning many of you arose without realizing that today could be a time of heavenly destiny when Christ would approach you with forgiveness for sin and comfort for affliction. Fifteen or twenty minutes ago many of you were thinking of anything else except the Lord Jesus and His salvation; yet it was not chance which led you to your radio at this particular time to hear Christ's message of grace and truth. Stop everything that may keep you from concentrating on His appeal! Lay your newspaper aside! Let household duties remain unfinished for a few moments! A crisis moment for this life and the next has now come for many of you, just as it came to the grief-stricken widow on the Galilean road. God grant you will not permit the Redeemer to pass without welcoming Him!

When Jesus beheld the sobbing, grief-gripped widow, Saint Luke tells us, *"He had compassion on her."* His heart was moved by deepest sympathy, for His divine gaze penetrated her wounded soul to discover the full extent of her anguish. The same blessed Savior is moved by divine sympathy for you in all your needs of soul and body; yet who can worthily picture His inexhaustible, immeasurable, indescribable love? Every time I come to the heart and center of these messages, the Savior's eternal mercy, I feel keenly and personally the utter weakness of words, the stark limitations of the human mind. All I can do is ask the Spirit's blessing on your soul as I tell you: The Lord Jesus had compassion on you when you had only hatred for Him. He loved you, even when your sins helped crucify Him. He saw you in your iniquities, while your eyes were too blind to behold Him in His forgiving grace. He found you, lost in your transgressions, spiritually dead, completely helpless; then, driven by His limitless devotion, He forsook His majestic heaven and came, as this Advent Sunday recalls, into a world of war and woe, to prove His love for you on the cross. What glorious assurance for sin-burdened souls to know: Christ has compassion on me!

Jesus has the same compassion for the entire race with its crime and endless wickedness. Could you blame Him, holy, stainless, perfect in His purity, if He would reject and destroy an earth in which, from its earliest centuries, men have oppressed and murdered their fellow men; a world that for the last 3,300 years, according to a Union College professor, has known only 227 years of general peace — fifteen sixteenths of all known history being marked by bloodshed and destruction? Were the full facts known, the proportion of war would be even greater. Could you really blame our Lord if — as He searches human hearts, only to find in every one of them, envy and hatred, avarice and greed, lying and falsehood, impurity and lust, unbelief and mockery of God — He would turn completely away from the whole rebellious race and permit men to destroy themselves? Yet — praise His everlasting grace! — He has mercy on us; and though you may doubt it and wonder why He could love you with your wretched hatreds, yet the Christ of the Nain road is the Christ of your life's road with grace for your soul.

He shows the same sacred sympathy for every sorrow endured by those who accept Him. His unbreakable Word assures us that He is *"touched with the feeling of our infirmities."* Some of you parents know by heart-breaking experience what agony that Galilean mother suffered when her son was snatched away in death. Hundreds of you have been saddened by Government notices informing you that your boy was killed in battle, drowned in the sea, or lost in a plane crash. Throughout this deepest anguish learn the strengthening truth that in the Savior you can find heavenly compassion! Turn to Him for consolation! Find sustaining grace for the burdens some of you Christian women bear because of a brutal husband, or the affliction some of you men endure because of an unfaithful wife! See His countenance light in loving sympathy for your agony, you whose health, home, happiness, are gone, but who can never lose Him as long as you remain in the faith! Do not think dark thoughts of vengeance nor waste time and energy pitying yourselves! Look to Jesus for the unmistakable courage He alone can give!

because it gave clear proof that Jesus was more than a Leader, Teacher, Guide; more than a Model, Pattern, Ideal; more than the mightiest Man, the outstanding Hero, the most masterful Mind of the ages. There on a rocky Galilean road Jesus showed that He was God; when by His own authority He declared, "*I say unto thee, Arise!*" and the corpse, infused with new life, obediently rose, He demonstrated that He was the Almighty, the Lord of life and death. Men can stand before caskets and cry: "Arise!" "Arise!" "Arise!" only to learn that the hollow echo of their failure continually mocks them. Scientific experts and medical authorities may devise remarkable, complicated apparatus by which they seek to restore or prolong life, but they cannot add a split second to the allotted life span, let alone return a soul that has entered the valley of death. Multimillionaires and rulers of mighty empires have pleaded on their deathbed for a day, an hour more; but all their money and might could not purchase the slightest extension. When their breath stopped, they were gone beyond recall. Yet here is One who is higher than princes and potentates, scientists and savants; here in Christ we have our God of grace and glory, who has to speak but one word, "Arise!" and death is robbed of its victim. If all Scripture passages testifying to the Savior's deity were to disappear, only the record of the resurrection at Nain remaining, truth alone should convince the most skeptical this of Nazareth was more than man, more than anything less than the very God of very God.

No our history has more desperately needed the acknowledgment of Jesus as the Lord of lords. To escape eternal punishment of sin, to be freed from the grip of everlasting death, and at the same time to have comfort for the heaviest earthly sorrows we need far more than the best human counselors, the most fervent hopes and wishes. We must find the Almighty in Christ! One of the reasons the all-wise and all-knowing God has permitted the horrors of two world wars to overtake this generation may be seen in the supertragedy that our age, more than any similar previous period, has questioned, spurned, ridiculed His deity, one of the pillar truths for the men and women who founded this nation. Read the declarations of the brave colonists who settled our shores, built our earliest towns, established our first colleges, and you will learn that these men and women regularly were moved by the sincere conviction Jesus' deity. Trusting Him, they could, as they did, and a nation of unparalleled wealth and resources on the North American continent! Yet today many have forgotten this keystone creed in our faith, that Jesus, together with the Father and the Spirit, is the only God. Churches by the thousands have denied this climax truth. Theological seminaries, Sunday schools, foreign mission boards, young people's religious groups, in far too many instances have joined unbelievers who insist that Jesus was only another prophet alongside of Moses, Mohammed, Zoroaster, Buddha, Confucius. Then we wonder why Protestantism has so often failed. My fellow redeemed, you bear Christ's name, remember that the Savior expects unshrinking loyalty and faithful testimony from He looks to you for protest every time unbelief seeks to drag Him down to the low level of men. He asks you to come out from those groups in which preachers willfully persistently exalt Him as the most outstanding of the race, yet refuse to kneel before Him and with Thomas call Him *"my Lord and my God!"*

Especially does Jesus desire the loyalty above of those who until this time have never known be-

lieved that He is their Lord; that He can turn eternal
death into everlasting life for them. Let no one now say:
"Miracles can never happen!" "This story of the young
man at Nain can't be true." Why not? Listen to this statement by Daniel Webster and ask yourself whether you
can continue to doubt Christ's miracles and His deity:
"I believe Jesus Christ to be the Son of God! The miracles
which He wrought establish, in my mind, His personal
authority and render it proper for me to believe whatever
He asserts. . . . And I believe there is no other way of salvation than through the merits of His atonement." Or,
considering the commonplaces of everyday life and the
wonders in nature, which you accept every moment you
live, listen to William Jennings Bryan as he speaks of the
radish and declares: "Some skeptics say, 'Oh, the miracles — I can't accept miracles!' One may drop a brown
seed in the black soil, and up comes a green shoot. You
let it grow, and by and by you pull up its root and you
find it red. You cut the red root and find it has a white
heart. Can any one tell how this came about — how brown
cast into black results in green and then in red and white?
Yet you eat your radish without troubling your mind over
miracles. Men are not distressed by miracles in the dining
room; they reserve them all for religion!"

Why doubt, when you can see the evidences of
Christ's divine power in human lives saved from spiritual
death? A visitor to the island of Raiatea in the South
Seas tells of finding 600 children gathered to worship
Jesus. Had the Gospel not been brought to that uncivil-
ized island, many parents would have followed the pagan
perversion and killed their children. As these boys and
girls sang the Savior's praises, a father could be heard to
say, "What mercy it is that we spared our dear girl!"
An old gray-haired chief cried out, "Oh, that I had known

that the Gospel was coming! My children would be here among this happy group! But I destroyed them." Wherever the Gospel of the Savior slain for an evil world is heard and believed, those who have been *"dead in trespasses and sin"* are born again *"of water and of the Spirit."* They die, of course, but death in Christ is only a passing from suffering to glory. Because Jesus Himself bore their *"sins in His own body on the tree,"* He has removed the curse of everlasting death. As He united mother and son outside the Nain gates, so, but in a much higher way, He will re-unite all the faithful in the neverending happiness of the heavenly homeland. For His holy Word leads us to believe that in the celestial radiance, husbands and wives, parents and children, relatives and friends, will not only recognize one another, but will also be together in unspeakable bliss as part of *"the whole family in heaven."* To you, the bereaved who wonder whether in the *"many mansions"* where Christ has prepared your place you will know your loved ones who have gone before you in the faith or who follow after, I say: "The Bible clearly teaches that we do not lose our personal identity in heaven, for Scripture mentions many by name whom we will meet in that better and blessed land." Of course, earthly relationships will be changed and hallowed. For instance, there will be no more marrying or giving in marriage. However, God will supply something so incomparably better that with our restricted reason we simply cannot understand *"the glory which shall be revealed in us."* Rest assured, those who love the Lord Jesus shall meet in the hereafter with the higher knowledge by which *"I shall know even as also I am known."* What an appeal in this to keep the whole family for Christ! A California listener wrote me that two years ago after her godly father had died, our message reminded her that if she was ever to meet him again, she would have to accept the Savior. On that blessed day the Spirit touched her soul; she came to Jesus for pardon, peace, and life. God grant that many of you will understand in a personal, unmistakable manner that, if you are to join your faithful, Christ-dedicated parents; if you are to escape death's doom and hell's terrors; above all this, if you are to see Jesus face to face, then be certain of this: You must acclaim Him your Redeemer! There is no other way.

This is a special appeal to American youth. Jesus speaks to you young men and women in our armed forces and in civilian life, to our high-school students, our college and university men and women, and His cry is still: "'Young man,' young woman, 'I say unto thee, Arise!' 'Arise' from sin and selfishness! 'Arise' from unbelief and doubt! 'Arise' from the low level of sneering and scoffing at Christ! 'Arise' from the gutter philosophy, which urges you, Yield to your passions, follow the lure and lust of the flesh! 'Arise' for Jesus! Exalt Him before the world as Savior! Trust His Word! Build your hope on His promises! Fight temptations in His name! Follow the good, pure, helpful paths with His power and guidance! Meet Jesus daily and prayerfully in His Word, and you will not only give our country what it needs, even above armaments: the exalting righteousness; you will not only be privileged to help save others for Christ, but you yourself will have a new life, new strength, new joy!" Youth of America, arise for Christ — and on the great Day of Judgment Christ will arise for you! Amen.

What Have You in Your Home?

"Tell me, what hast thou in the house?"
2 KINGS 4:2

God, True, Triune, and Eternal:

A year ago our country entered this world war; and today we pause to thank Thee for every act of protecting love by which Thou didst shield the lives of Thy children during the past twelve months, sustaining them amid peril and affliction. We praise Thy mercy that our shores have not been invaded nor our homes blasted by bombs. We have not suffered as the people in other lands. Continue, we beseech Thee, to look mercifully on us! We confess that too often we have been proud, forgetful of Thy grace, heedless of Thy warnings. We have deserved punishment in place of pardon. Forgive us these and all our sins for Jesus', our only Savior's, sake! Bless us according to Thy holy purpose with victory and a triumph of Christian truth! Comfort the wounded, the imprisoned, those under fire of attack! Turn them from war's destruction to the blessed pursuits of peace! Without Christ we can do nothing; but with Him, through firm faith, we can overcome the world. Enrich us with a fuller measure of humble trust! We ask it in the name of Jesus, our Redeemer. Amen.

IN many Midwestern cities civilian defense workers are now making house-to-house calls to learn whether our homes are prepared for air raids and other war emergencies. With splendid and unpaid devotion to their important tasks these volunteers ask one family after the other: "What have you in your home: A blackout room? A first-aid kit? Sand pails to check incendiary

bombs? Fire extinguishers and other useful equipment?"
They want every American household to be fully prepared against danger.

How helpful if the churches could similarly take a
spiritual checkup on all our households, if every family
from coast to coast would honestly answer questions like
this: "What have you in your home — a place where you
regularly pray God for light in these dark days, a Bible
that you daily use as spiritual first aid for domestic difficulties, Christian faith to subdue fiery passions and
quench burning anger?"

If the Government marks with a victory V those
dwellings in which the family limits its needs, saves scrap,
purchases bonds, follows civilian defense instructions,
and is guilty of no careless speech, then certainly we
ought to mark with the Savior's cross those households
which have room for prayer, ban loose, profane talk, contribute to our Lord's kingdom, and follow His Gospel
with its plans for soul defense.

We need such faith-blessed homes not only because
Christian families are a strong part of the country's foundation, because war and its separation are weakening
domestic ties, because the Bible's code of married life is
being attacked as never before, but especially because
the Christian home (which acclaims the Lord Jesus, emphasizes the blessings of wedlock, exalts parenthood and
childhood, denounces divorce, pleads against sinful birth
control, and helps bring parents and children constantly
closer to the Savior) can, under God, be a powerful agent
in helping lead many to eternal salvation.

On the first Sunday of this year's last month, then, as
we pause for spiritual inventory of our family life, I ask
every one of you:

"WHAT HAVE YOU IN YOUR HOME?"

This is not a new question, for 2800 years ago the prophet Elisha (Second Kings, chapter four, verse two) spoke these words of our text, *"Tell me, what hast thou in the house?"*

I

DO YOU HAVE EARTHLY, MATERIAL, PHYSICAL SORROW IN YOUR HOME?

Back in those distant days when Elisha went about teaching and preaching, a widow came to him for relief in her helplessness. She had no money, her debts were mounting, and her creditors were demanding repayment at the usurious rates the loan sharks of those days extorted. When Elisha asked her, *"Tell me, what hast thou in the house?"* the poor soul was forced to reply, not that her cupboard contained meat, bread, wine, figs, honey, and other foods, but that she was on the verge of destitution, since only one pot of olive oil remained. That was usually mixed with meal and baked into bread; but she had no flour, no other food with which the oil could be used.

Her plight recalls the poverty and privation many have suffered even in this richly blessed country. Since the 1929 crash about three and a third million American families have lost their homes, their farms, or real estate through mortgage foreclosures. If you of the comfortably situated middle and upper classes could see 10,000,000 of your countrymen living in dingy, overcrowded, unsanitary slum tenements and ramshackle, rickety huts, you would understand that multitudes across this broad land would have to answer the question, *"What hast thou in the house?"* as did the widow, "We have destitution, want, poverty." I know that these conditions often arise from laziness and destructive sins; but I am just as

certain that too many have been deprived of a real
chance in life for themselves and their children because
they have been cheated, underpaid, and generally defrauded. — Now what are you going to do, you whose
pantries are empty and clothes closets bare, whose husbands or wives are pale and sickly, whose children must
forego the comforts and luxuries other boys and girls
enjoy? Will you join the radical Communists as they cry
out against every form of private property and demand,
"Divide all wealth equally!" Unless God is especially
merciful to our country, the years of the postwar readjustment may tempt many to reject the principles of true
Americanism and the requirements of Christian faith.
God keep you clear from such crash and ruin! Rather
follow the faith of this widow! In her anxiety she made
contact with God through His prophet, and by the miracle of divine power the oil in that pot was multiplied.
All the vessels she had in her home and as many as she
could borrow from her neighbors were filled with such
an abundance of oil that the money derived from its sale
paid her debts and met her needs.

I cannot promise you, in a day of rationing and restriction, that this miracle will be exactly repeated in your
home; but I can give you higher assurance, since we have
One who is greater than Elisha, Jesus, God in His own
right and by His own power. His unbreakable Word
pledges that He, the Christ of limitless might, can grant
all our needs *according to the riches of His glory.* He
who in the days of His flesh looked compassionately on
the hungry masses, multiplying bread and fishes for them;
He who changed water into wine at a humble country
wedding and told Galilean fishermen, disappointed after
a night of unsuccessful toil, how they could catch an unparalleled draught of fishes, has lost neither His provid-

ing love nor His producing strength. If it be His will, and that always means if it be for the eternal good of those who trust Him as their Redeemer, He can enrich you miraculously, if necessary, with everything essential for your happiness. Do not protest, "This is irresponsible talk and wishful thinking!" Many can testify how, just when it seemed there could be no more hope, the Almighty stepped in with heaven's help. May God give all of you the faith to approach Christ for every bodily need!

This widow was also tormented by the thought that her sons would soon be taken from her. She had already borne one crushing bereavement — the loss of her husband. Now her creditors threatened to sell her two boys as slaves. Some of you have personally felt the anguish of similar sorrows. Perhaps your husband, on whom you leaned for love, support, and guidance, has been claimed by death or, even worse, has deserted his family, run away with another woman. Many thousands of you fathers and mothers know what it means to be separated from your children. — I think of families in our Church that have given seven, even eight, sons to the armed forces. What a tremendous sacrifice! — Now, what will you do when, at the end of this month, the Selective Service Act registers 2,000,000 of our eighteen- or nineteen-year-old young men and later on your son is summoned to the colors? Will you drive yourself to the verge of nervous collapse, run to fortunetellers for false assurance? I hope not! Do what this widow did: she turned to God's prophet and found that the oil, miraculously increased, brought enough money to save her sons from slavery for debt. So you can turn to Jesus, your Prophet, Priest, and King, who by the shedding of His blood and His self-sacrifice on the cross freed everyone of us — be sure that you believe it! — from the indebtedness of our sins, from the slavery of hell, and the despair of eternal death. Now He also seeks to liberate us from fear and fill our hearts with the confidence that all His ways, even though far beyond our powers of understanding, are always right and blessed. Commit to Him your sons, on whatever front they may be.

Many when asked, *"What hast thou in the house?"* will answer, "Sickness, pain, injury!" Some of you have been invalids most of your lives. Others have deformed, subnormal children. Oh, treat them tenderly, for Christ loves them just as much as the healthiest and most brilliant child! Not a few among you have been crippled by the carelessness or cruelty of others. What will you do? Continually murmur and grumble? Take recourse to religions which seek to convince you that there is no sickness, that your sufferings are only a state of mind? Do not make this mistake! Rather bring your pain and agony to Jesus in trusting faith! And if this will help your soul, He can heal you even though medical specialists have decreed, "There is no hope!" Scripture records twenty instances where Jesus laid His healing hand on the diseased, and He never departed from sickrooms without leaving aid. What He did then He can do now. Every Christian doctor will tell you that God can start when medicine and surgery stop. If in His far-seeing plan for you He permits you to remain an invalid, deprived of your sight or hearing, your strength wasted, believe, although you now cannot explain it, that all this is divinely scheduled for your good because you love the Lord in Christ.

"What hast thou in the house?" I can hear some of you answer, "Nothing but quarreling, stinginess, jealousy, faultfinding, cursing, nagging, even physical violence, there where above all other places we should find love,

self-sacrifice, companionship." Why is it that some husbands and wives only a few years after their wedding no longer take their helpmates into their arms to say, "O my dearest, how I love you!" Is this not because Jesus, who can bring husbands and wives more closely together, has been banished from their hearts and homes? — If affection is vanishing in your marriage, what will you do about it? Consult a psychiatrist? Try modern theories for a smooth family life? I have just read one of the latest of these volumes, intended to help develop "morale on the home front." It is written by a professor of education at a California school. Significantly, the author does not mention Christ as essential to home happiness. God appears only in absurdly childish rhymes or in repeated profanity, which is indirectly called an aid to democracy. Not a word of Scripture, not a syllable on the necessity of prayer, not a sentence about church, not even a vague reference to spiritual strength! That paganized policy is becoming stronger day by day in the United States. Need we wonder, therefore, why we miss family happiness more frequently than before we heard of psychologists, psychiatrists, and psychoanalysts? They can render excellent services, but they can never take the Savior's place. You must go to Him if you would have quiet instead of quarrel, for He alone can change the human heart, root out selfishness and supplant it with sympathy.

"What hast thou in the house?" Do I hear some of you falter, "Drunkenness and its disgrace!" It brings tears to many eyes, I know, to recall the joyous moment of your marriage, when you stood with your beloved before God's altar, and to contrast with that the brutality and bestiality you now suffer because the demon of drunkenness controls his life. But don't give up! Follow good counsel, but remember, you need superhuman power to

overcome alcoholism, especially in this loose age when the Christmas issue of a magazine features eight full-page color advertisements of whiskey. Implore the Savior's assistance! Again and again in the days of His flesh He drove out demons, and He can repeat that purifying cleansing in those who have become slaves to alcohol and are bound for hell unless they repent! Believe this: *Jesus* can help you! A Minneapolis family, regular listeners to our messages, suffered because the father was a habitual drunkard. One Sunday, as we warned against this destructive sin and pleaded in the Savior's name for recourse to His help, the Spirit touched that man's heart. He arose quietly, went to his wife and said, "From this moment on I will never touch another drop!" She was skeptical, because he had promised before. But this time he implored Christ's help; and for more than two years he has been a total abstainer. The same Savior can deliver you.

"What hast thou in the house?" One of the most distressing replies will be, "Unfaithfulness!" You can stand anything else, you say: poverty, sickness, even bereavement. But a broken marriage vow, disloyalty, deception, a secret affair — this is too much. Do not think of divorce! Sometimes it is far better to forgive and try to forget, to follow Jesus, who says we are to forgive our brother not seven times, but seven times seventy times. Besides, divorce at best is hard and dangerous. The wave of broken marriages flooding our country is a peril to our national morale and strength. Altogether too many world leaders who regulate the affairs of others are divorced because they have not been able to direct their own home. — No, look to Christ! Despite infidelity, your married life can still be happy through Him. Listen to this thankful letter from a Wisconsin woman: "About three years ago I wrote

you my problem, an unfaithful husband. You advised me to stand by him and told me how. I have, and now God and time have changed him completely"! The same Savior can work this change in any marriage.

"What hast thou in the house?" I can almost hear some parents sob as they answer, "Selfish, ungrateful, disobedient children." The cry of alarm goes up from all parts of the country: Juvenile crime is on the increase! You may complain that you have spent thousands of dollars on your children; that you have sacrificed and denied yourself even necessities in their behalf. Nevertheless they turned against you, though you have done everything you could for them. Have you? Is it their fault entirely? Or were they spoiled in their younger years, brought up without discipline? Were they neglected, as many children are today because their parents are too preoccupied with business or the pursuit of pleasure? Have you given your children a Christian training which taught them to love, honor, and obey their parents? Have you set them a good example by attending a true church regularly? Do you know where your children were last night, where they will be tomorrow night? A week ago long lines of panic-stricken parents and relatives waited before morgues in Boston to see whether their sons and daughters, missing from their homes, were among the almost five hundred on whom swift, horrifying death descended in that night-club fire. Parents of America, God holds you responsible for doing everything humanly possible to have your children, your own flesh and blood, grow up into clean, consecrated manhood and womanhood. How will you meet this responsibility? Now that the damage is done, night clubs and drinking places are to be inspected for fire hazards. Curfew laws and other legal remedies are being enacted to keep young people

off the streets. Yet state legislatures could meet day and night to grind out new regulations without solving this problem or changing youthful hearts. We need Christ in the home to give young people both the example and the power of obedience and love for Christian parents. Wherever sons and daughters recall the solicitous love He showed His mother even in His agony on the cross, faith in Him builds a superhuman foundation for the loving regard and generous support of parents. Remember that, you men in the armed services, whose fathers and mothers are continually thinking of you, praying for the Savior's abiding love in your hearts!

"What hast thou in the house?" Some of you will answer, "Well, that widow had at least two sons, and despite my pleading I have no child." You see some who consider children a burden, whose boys and girls grow up unwanted and unloved; yet your arms are empty, and doctors tell you that you will never cuddle a child of your own. Do not surrender to bitterness! The Almighty can overrule medical opinion and lay a precious mite of humanity, His highest human gift, into the arms of an overjoyed mother. Ask God, if it be His will, to bless you, even belatedly, as He enriched Hannah, Sarah, and countless other mothers. However, should it be His will that you are to remain childless, then remember the Church agencies that can still help you! Thousands of couples have found inexpressible joy in receiving one of Christ's little ones from our home-finding societies or orphanages and then bringing them up *"in the nurture and admonition of the Lord."* Perhaps we can help you. If this is your particular problem, write us! It may be that, under God, this broadcast will be the means of opening the door for lasting happiness in your household.

"*What hast thou in the house?*" we ask again, and some of you are beginning to feel, as the years increase, that you may never have a home of your own. Often we cannot understand why splendid Christian girls, who would make devoted wives, have been disappointed in love, had engagement promises broken. If you have suffered in this way, do not let your heart grow hard! Put your life under Christ's control! He can still give you a happy home. Perhaps His mercy has kept you from entering a marriage that would have proved an unrelieved heartache. He may have lofty purposes for you which you can best perform without family ties. As soon as you are the Lord's, you are under divine love and guidance; whatever turn your pathway takes, through Him it always leads to your eternal blessing.

II

DO YOU HAVE SPIRITUAL SORROWS IN YOUR HOME?

Besides all these bodily, material burdens there is a far deeper sorrow in which Jesus can manifest His mercy as your Savior. When I ask you once more, "*What hast thou in the house?*" many thousands of you will be forced to reply, "We have unbelief, the refusal to accept the Redeemer, the rejection of His mercy!" And that is the heaviest load. Therefore this is the most vital question, "Does Christ reign in your heart, and have you brought Him into your home?" Do you answer that you do not need Him; that, since the war began, you have higher incomes, greater crops, better business, larger salaries, than you ever thought possible; that you are living in a more pretentious house; that you and your wife have been buying new rugs, furniture, silverware, and equipment you could not have purchased before; in short, that you are getting along pretty well without worrying about religion! Just how much happiness can you really buy with your increased income? What good is a new dining-room suite if accident knocks at your door or sudden death crosses your threshold? All the money you have heaped up will not secure pardon and forgiveness for the sin you have thought was safely concealed, but is always revealed to God's penetrating eye; the iniquity which once seemed enticing and alluring, but now after twenty, thirty, forty years, as your letters testify, torments your conscience with this warning, *"He that soweth to his flesh shall of the flesh reap corruption."*

Will you not see eye to eye with me when I tell you: The greatest issue before you personally and your home is this, that you stop resisting divine grace and take time, blessed time, to learn what a glorious Deliverer Jesus is! Though your life may have been sinful, sordid, until this moment, if you believe and repent, Jesus is ready to blot out the *"handwriting of ordinances that was against us."* However many you may have misled into wickedness, the Lord is eager to save your soul. Come, then, in repentant faith and with sincere effort to make restitution whenever possible. No matter how unworthy and unclean you may seem to yourself in comparison with the spotless, stainless Savior, you have this assurance, *"The blood of Jesus Christ, His Son, cleanseth us from ALL sin."* O my fellow sinners and my fellow redeemed, let Him reconcile you to your heavenly Father! Let Him, as His Spirit now seeks sacred entrance into your heart, give you the precious promise beyond all question, hesitation or doubt that He alone can cleanse every sin-laden soul, yours especially, if you trust Him as the crucified, yet victoriously risen Son of God and Redeemer of the race!

When you can truly say — and may you make this blessed declaration today! — that Christ is in your home because you are in Him, do everything you can to dedicate your whole household to Him and to let the world know that yours is a Christ-exalting home! Throw out all suggestive, indecent pictures, and adorn your walls with sacred scenes, a motto showing all who cross your threshold that Jesus is the Head of your family! Remove all lust-laden, sex-ridden magazines; they help send souls to hell! Have at least one good religious publication in your home! Put constructive, Christian volumes on your bookshelves! Watch the household conversation! Banish profanity, abuse of God's name, slander, and unworthy talk! Christmas is coming. Begin now to sing its joyful carols! Say grace at table! Set aside at least a few moments each day when the whole family unites to read the Scriptures, to pray God's blessing on the home! Send your children to bed with a heart-spoken prayer! When they arise in the morning, have them commend themselves to the Savior's guidance! Join a true church! Take part earnestly in its work! Have a minister of the Gospel come into your house! In the verses following our text we read that Elisha was graciously received into another home, where a special room was provided for him. His presence there brought blessing. Throughout the United States and Canada thousands of pastors, united with me in the complete fellowship of the faith which this broadcast proclaims, eagerly await an invitation to your home, so that they can instruct you in the saving truth, baptize your household, and bring the whole family to Jesus!

Do you say: "Oh, that my whole family were dedicated to Christ! Instead, my husband has not accepted the Savior. My children are not in the faith. My parents are still unbelievers. Mine is a house religiously divided against itself." That — let there be no mistake about it! — is a serious situation. If the members of your family are to be saved, they must cling to Christ in their own individual faith. You may be married to a person without that trust. You were moved only by good looks or a pleasing personality; you thought that as a follower of the Lord Jesus you could make a convert of your mate. You failed. Years of contact with unbelief have weakened your own allegiance to the Savior. Therefore, I say to Christian young people: "Don't marry an unbeliever, no matter how attractive such a marriage would seem! Don't marry even a member of an opposing Church and bring spiritual disunity into your wedded life!" To my Roman Catholic friends — and your letters show that thousands are regular listeners — I declare further: "Don't marry a Protestant! Choose someone from your own Church, for too often these mixed marriages produce life-long misery. If you question this statement, go to the officials of your Church, and they will repeat essentially what I have just said." If it is too late for some of you to take this counsel, be patient! Realize that nothing is impossible for God and His Spirit! Pray for your unconverted mate! Live a consecrated life! Read the Scriptures in your family circle! It has been our repeated experience that the Holy Spirit has used this radio mission to bring the Savior into unbelieving homes. Listen to these testimonies, only a few of the many the Almighty has graciously given us:

Wisconsin. — "God's grace and your broadcast brought my husband to the faith. He goes to church with me now every Sunday."

Massachusetts. — "My wife and her mother have always been Christians, but the writer is a convert by radio.

The Lutheran Hour was mainly instrumental in my decision at the age of fifty-two to accept Jesus as my own personal Savior."

Illinois. — "My husband was an unbeliever who said all pastors were hypocrites. One day I tuned in your station. When my husband heard of Christ, he was spellbound. The following Sunday he attended our Lutheran service. Last Sunday he was confirmed, although once he had said that he would never consent. His sister and brother-in-law were also confirmed."

Nebraska. — "My parents have been married twenty-five years, and my father never wanted to hear about belonging to the Church; but since he has listened to the Lutheran Hour, he has become a member of our Church."

Illinois. — "My husband joined our Church after we were married. He heard several broadcasts of the Lutheran Hour, and then he had a talk with our minister and started instructions immediately. That is why I feel so grateful toward your messages."

New York. — "We never miss the Lutheran Hour sermons on Sunday; through its help my husband has joined the Church."

When the whole family is won for Jesus and kept in His grace, then, no matter whether you live in a trailer or on a large estate, in furnished rooms near war plants or in a commodious apartment on an élite boulevard, whether your family is still united or separated because husbands, sons, brothers have answered the country's call — as long as you have Jesus, you can answer the Prophet's question with this triumphant declaration of fact and faith: "We have peace in the midst of war; joy, though we may be visited by sorrow; hope, when all seems dark around us; faith, though others may doubt; love, even in a world of hatred. We have all we need for time and eternity! We have the seal and pledge of our salvation. We have the title to our prepared place in the celestial mansions. We have the radiant foregleam of *the whole family in heaven.* We have this and more, because — oh, blessed assurance! — first, last, and forever uppermost we have — in our homes as in our hearts — Jesus Christ, God's Son and our Savior. Eternal praise be to Him for His blood-bought mercies!" Amen.

Believe Christ—And Live!

> *"These are written that ye might believe that Jesus is the Christ, the Son of God, and that, believing, ye might have life through His name."*
>
> SAINT JOHN 20:31

Lord of Eternal Life:

We praise Thee, Father, because Thou hast given us the Scriptures, in which the everlasting truth is clearly revealed. Particularly do we thank Thee for Thy grace in granting us the glorious Gospel of Thy Son Jesus Christ. Without Scripture and without the Savior we should be hopelessly lost, but with the Bible and through reliance on the pardon purchased by Jesus we are saved eternally. Keep us from regarding our blessed Redeemer with anything less than the fervor of a living faith! Constantly remind us of the unfathomable compassion with which He loved us and gave Himself for us while we were yet in our sins. When doubt of our salvation or despair over our transgressions would seize us, heavenly Father, send us Thy Spirit to banish fear and increase our trust! Keep us humble, reverent, and courageous, even when the tide of warfare seems to turn against us! In Thy time and according to Thy gracious purpose, let bloodshed cease and peace prevail! Until the last shot is fired, watch over Thy children wherever they may be in the turmoil of this struggle and fortify with the strength of Thy presence the lives of all who trust Thee! Grant us this mercy, for we plead in our Savior's name! Amen.

ONE of the most thrilling rescue stories of the present war comes from Norfolk, Virginia. At a religious meeting in that city a young American sailor who had been at Pearl Harbor gave this testimony: "My ship was torpedoed; four other men and myself were on a small life raft out on the ocean for over thirty-two hours. I had my New Testament in my pocket. I had hardly read from it before, but surely did read from it on the raft. . . . Three of the men made fun of me for reading, but the fourth said, 'Read on, Buddy! Read it out loud, so I can hear!' I read and prayed that God would have mercy on me, a poor, helpless sinner, and save me from a watery grave. Nightfall came, and one by one the three men who scoffed and laughed at me slipped from the life raft, out into dark eternity. This left but two of us, so we prayed that if God would spare our lives, we would live for the Lord Jesus Christ. After what seemed an eternity, a light came out of the darkness, . . . a searchlight from a United States destroyer. . . . Then and there . . . I knew that my sins were forgiven. Ever since that hour I have been living for Christ."

God rescued that sailor; and some of you, adrift on life's sea, tossed about by the waves of adversity, can likewise find deliverance from sin, sorrow, destruction, if only, with all your heart, you take God at His Word and trust His promises in Christ. Too many, however, like those three scoffing sailors on the raft, ridicule the Bible; and unless you stop rejecting His Word and His grace, you likewise will drop off into the darkness of eternal death. There is no other guide to spiritual safety besides our Bible, no other Savior in addition to Jesus, no other escape from the consequence of sin than through faith in His atoning blood and redeeming death. Therefore, today, on Universal Bible Sunday, may God give you — especially the uncertain, the doubting, the scoffing, the self-confident — a firm faith in the Bible's greatest promise:

BELIEVE CHRIST — AND LIVE!

Saint John's inspired words (chapter twenty, verse thirty-one) offer you this pledge: *"These are written that ye might believe that Jesus is the Christ, the Son of God, and that, believing, ye might have life through His name."*

I

THE FAITH WHICH GOD'S WORD DEMANDS

Saint John does not stop to debate or argue the Bible's assertions, and neither should we. He heard Jesus pray, *"Thy Word is truth,"* and that settled any uncertainty for him, just as we should unreservedly acclaim Scripture the unfailing Word of life, in at Genesis and out at Revelation, the Almighty's divinely inspired, errorless, marvelously protected record of our salvation.

Some of you, however, are prejudiced against the Scriptures. You heard a brilliant infidel attack the Bible, an unbelieving college professor direct his sarcasm against its pages, or a blasphemous atheist completely denounce it. Without taking time to investigate Holy Writ, you joined those who put question marks behind its promises and otherwise belittle its utterances. Yet many of those who most vehemently attack God's Book do not know the Sacred Volume. American and British agnostics have often confessed that they either had no copy of the Scripture they sought to destroy or that they had never read it completely. Are you making the same mistake? Why not be fair and at least give the Bible a chance to prove its heavenly origin and its divine power by a careful, personal, unbiased study of its record?

Keep in mind, too, that many who sought to discredit the Bible, once they studiously investigated its truth, were led to drop their hostility and, convinced of Scriptural truth, acknowledge Jesus Christ as the Savior!

BELIEVE CHRIST — AND LIVE! **115**

Alexander Hamilton, Lord Lyttleton, Sir Gilbert West, General Lew Wallace, Sir William Ramsey, Professor Paul Elmer More, Lord Rochester, Giovanni Pappini, Professor Henry Drummond, Professor George Romanes, Thomas Jay Hudson, Felix Mendelssohn, John Stuart Mill — these and many more made a right-about-face from unbelief to reverent faith. May the Holy Spirit today touch the hearts of you who have kept your distance from the Bible and convince you of its heavenly might!

It is helpful, likewise, to know that many claims repeatedly raised against the Bible have been altogether disproved. One hundred years ago, in December, 1842, the task of uncovering the ruined, long-buried cities of Assyria and Babylonia began, when Paul Emil Botta, French consul at Mosul, dug into one of the huge mounds which the dust and debris of twenty-five centuries had heaped over Nineveh, the largest, proudest city of its day. The recovery of these ancient, devastated nations has helped emphasize the Bible's absolute, divine truth. Just at a time when, particularly in Germany, higher critics were denouncing the Scriptures as unhistorical, untrue, unreliable, the very stones of these fallen empires cried out in defense of Holy Writ. For example, enemies of the Bible used to say that Sargon, mentioned in Isaiah twenty, was a fictitious character. They maintained this attack until 1842, when Botta, in his first excavations, discovered the palace, the annals, the pictures, of the very Sargon whom unbelief had boldly, but mistakenly, denied historical existence. They used to say that Moses could not have written his five books because he lived before people knew how to write; but they do not repeat that erroneous claim now, since archaeology has unmistakably shown that long centuries before Moses men inscribed their thoughts into clay and stone. On the table

before me today is part of an inscription, secured in Iraq
by one of my students, written 500 years before Moses.
Critics used to claim that Nineveh never fell, as the sacred
writers predicted it would; but they do not reaffirm that
now, because in 1924 a tablet was deciphered containing
an account of the city's capture — a record in remarkable
agreement with Old Testament prophecy. They used to
say, in a hundred other overconfident assertions, that
Holy Writ had been proved misleading and mistaken;
but no modern critic will repeat the attacks of 1842; for
a hundred years of excavation have shed new, welcome
light on many assailed Bible passages and strikingly supported their accuracy.

We in this broadcast believe that Holy Writ, as the
true Word of God, cannot successfully be charged with
error. Annually we have challenged unbelievers in our
audience to produce from it a single statement that can
be proved false. We reissue that challenge today. In past
years, though this message every week reaches many
skeptics and atheists, we have received no charge that
could be substantiated. Instead, only the restatement of
ancient attacks rejected so often that they should have
been dropped long ago! Our Christian faith, far from
being accepted only by third- or fourth-rate minds, has
been acclaimed by recognized leaders in human affairs, endorsed and exalted by scholars of international
fame and by first-rank scientists. Mark that, you college students who are tempted to question or contradict
Scripture!

The Bible is not simply true, accurate, honest; it is
not only excellent when viewed from the point of literature and morals; above all it is a saving Book, because
it teaches what no other volume can offer: the truth about
our Lord and Savior. Pointedly does Saint John declare

in our text, *"These"* (the many miracles he has reported)
*"are written that ye might believe that Jesus is the Christ,
the Son of God."* His whole purpose, he says, in recording
marvelous incidents throughout our blessed Redeemer's
life, is to prove that He should not be classified merely
as a man among men; but that He is infinitely higher than
all earthly leaders, all supermen and saints; that He is,
in Heaven's own truth, *"the Son of God,"* with divine
power and resources at His disposal. Twice the great
God said of Jesus, *"This is My beloved Son."* In many
places Jesus asserts that He is God's Son. Hundreds
of passages in both Testaments similarly acclaim Him.
Scores of startling miracles gloriously prove His divine
Sonship. Therefore the Jesus whom the Bible and this
broadcast give you, in distinction from the Jesus preached
this morning from many pulpits where He was acknowledged as a great man, but only a man; the Christ who
alone can help fumbling, faltering, falling mankind; the
Savior who holds out certain solution for your problems
and assured relief for your afflictions, *is* the Son of God,
almighty in His power, unlimited in His understanding,
unrestricted by time or space, unhindered by any human
weakness, as He comes to you with pardon. Will you not
agree that for our distressed day — when human props
have collapsed, when human plans for peace and progress
lie shattered, when human proposals for safeguarding
the future provoke deep-rooted suspicion — we need divine direction and superhuman assurance? Are you not
ready to admit that the difficulties in your own life are
beyond men's counsel and consolation; that your heart,
crying out for a deliverer, asks, *"Oh, that I knew where
I might find Him!"* the Source of all my help? Thank
Heaven today, that question is eternally answered by
Jesus! In Him you have your God, whose power can

rescue you in every affliction, whose knowledge foresees each path you take and leads you with loving-kindness, whose presence daily accompanies you, so that you need never be without His sustaining companionship! If you are fighting life's battle alone — and losing; if you struggle against evil only in your own strength — and suffer defeat; if you find yourself crushed beneath the avalanche of sorrows that no human rescuers can ever remove, believe the Bible! Believe God! Believe Christ! Believe the *"many infallible proofs"!* Believe the true, unimpeachable witnesses who, pointing to Him, declare, "He is our God"!

All this is inseparably tied up with the second great Bible truth by which we declare that Jesus is not only divine, with the Father and the Spirit our one and true Lord of lords, but also that He is, as Saint John likewise states, *"the Christ."* Do you know the real, blessed meaning of the six lettered name *Christ?* (Regrettably this is so frequently misused in profanity and so lightly regarded even by those called Christians that the eternity of love and the measureless compassion it contains remain unrecognized.) Listen carefully, then, as I explain this name of everlasting blessing! *Christ* means the One Anointed of God, the promised Messiah, the long-foretold Deliverer who, moved by fathomless mercy, left His eternal glory to become, as the Christmas message proclaims, a helpless mite of a babe in Bethlehem's manger, to live years of service and sacrifice on this sin-scarred earth, and then, in the startling climax of His indescribable self-sacrifice, to lay down His life in suffering the penalty of all mankind's iniquity. To understand what *Christ* really means for your soul, you must first see yourself hopelessly lost in sin, separated from the Father by the evil of your transgression, unable with all you have and are, with everything you can earn, to purchase pardon and release even from a solitary violation of the divine Law. You must see yourself rejected by the Almighty, in whose sight no sinner can stand, continually ruled by the lustful, covetous longings of an evil heart. You must find yourself banished from heaven, consigned to hell. But then this name above all names, Jesus, *the Christ*, can have new and personal meaning for you, when you believe assuredly that He took from you the curse of your sin, even though it cost Him His life; that He removed hell's clutching grip on your soul, even though He had to be nailed to the cross to gain the victory; that He paid once and entirely the price required to redeem you from eternal death, even if He had to endure indescribable agony in becoming your Substitute and your Salvation. That Christ — and may every one of you say, "*My* Christ, *my* Redeemer, *my* Ransom, *my* Substitute on the cross, *my* Savior from sin" — is the center of the Bible, the fulfillment of startling prophecies which predict His birth, death, and resurrection centuries before He went to the cross; the climax message of the New Testament and its thousands of radiant passages.

My fellow redeemed, is Christ the sole and sacred glory of *your* faith in this morally upside-down world — on the one hand with millions of men bent on killing, and on the other with millions spending and squandering, living in drunkenness and debauch, impurity and vice, as though there were no war and American men were not being sacrificed daily? If anything or anyone has kept you from proclaiming Him your Redeemer, cut yourself loose today from all soul-destroying influences! Make this a glorious Christmas season! Cause joy in heaven and on earth by declaring with a contrite, yet faith-filled heart: "O Jesus, my Prophet, Priest, and King,

Thou art my Friend, my Sustainer, my Guide; but, above all, Thou art the Son of God and the Christ, my Lord and my Redeemer! I am weak and sinful, but Thou art almighty, and Thy blood can cleanse me. I am not worthy even to approach Thee, but Thou art full of grace and plenteous mercy. I have only a faltering faith. Yet, dear Jesus, '*I believe. Help Thou mine unbelief*!' Strengthen me! Keep me with Thee and bless me eternally!"

II

THE BLESSING WHICH GOD'S WORD PROMISES

When Christ is thus acclaimed in sincerity and devotion, you have a gift of grace so radiant that eternity will not be long enough to exhaust its marvelous mercy. Saint John promises us that, when we truly believe in Jesus, we shall have "*life through His name.*" Because on the cross He paid for all our transgressions, we have no sin in God's sight and have therefore been completely freed from the terrors of the grave. "*Christ . . . hath abolished death and brought life and immortality to light.*" Think of it, believe it, exult in it, praise God for it! Christ gives those who are His a hallowed dwelling in His Father's house, an unending home in paradise! After earth's turmoil, heaven with its rest; after death, everlasting joy; after the repulsive vices in this life, heaven with its sinlessness and purity, its beholding and worshiping Christ, instead of the cursing and blasphemy here below; heaven with its higher knowledge, in place of our errors and limited understanding; its light and beauty, in place of the grime and gloom in this war-racked world; heaven and its reunion with those beloved ones who died in the faith, instead of parting and farewells; heaven, where we shall be like Jesus, after an existence during which in our sins we have been altogether unlike Him — that heaven Christ offers everyone of you! God grant you will not turn away indifferently from the most blessed gift which even the Almighty's grace can grant!

The life which our text promises is not, however, reserved exclusively for paradise. As soon as you acclaim Jesus your Savior, you are reborn, a new creature, and even here in this world you begin that blessed, God-directed, everlasting existence. Therefore believe Christ— and live joyfully, despite the weight of your affliction! Through Jesus your sufferings are hallowed. Every sorrow is the evidence of the merciful Father's compassion, for *"whom"* He *"loveth He chasteneth."* With this unquestioning faith in divine guidance an Illinois mother who has lost five children at birth could tell us in a letter last week that she still trusts her Savior. That is why an Ohio friend could write that though he has been in bed for forty-eight years and apparently must suffer until God calls him home, he still glorifies his Savior.

Believe Christ — and live courageously, for with Jesus as your Redeemer, you face no hardship or danger alone. Never forget that, you men in the armed forces! More than everything else you need the strengthening Savior. Keep close to Him, you, the weak and uncertain who make too many compromises with unbelief and refuse to protest when His name and His truth are attacked! In connection with the Boston fire a newspaper told the remarkable story of a woman who, leaving that night club with her friends in protest against a dirty song featured by one of the entertainers, was hardly out of the building when it was turned into a blazing inferno. If you give Him your heart, He will plant within it a resistance to temptation and evil which, under God, can help save your soul from destruction.

Believe Christ — and live in Christlike service! This greedy, self-destroying world cries out for men and women who, following in the Savior's footsteps, will extend the guiding hand of love and sympathy to suffering mankind. And where, if not in Jesus, can we discover the perfect example of devotion to the needs of others? By putting His *"new commandment," "that ye love one another,"* into action, many of you can find new happiness. Princess Eugenia of Sweden, a humble believer, spent most of her income on various charities. When the Island of Gottland was sorely pressed for a hospital to serve the poor, she, constrained by Jesus' love, sold her crown diamonds and with the proceeds built a home for incurables. There one of the patients seemed peculiarly unapproachable, and the princess, in her own words, "prayed much for her." One day, after long intercession and tireless testimony, as Eugenia approached her bed, the sick woman broke her icy unbelief, saying, "I thank God that *'the blood of Jesus Christ, His Son, cleanseth us from all sin,'* and that means me." Even as she spoke, the tears streamed down her cheeks, and "in those tears," wrote the Swedish noblewoman, "I saw my diamonds again." In the joy of salvation which the Savior permits you to bring into others' lives, you, too, can discern everything you have ever given for Him.

Believe Christ — and live victoriously! With the Son of God enthroned in your heart, doubt will not secure a permanent foothold on your soul. Adversity's storms can never demolish your faith, for it is built on a Rock. Even war cannot destroy your calm of soul, for its peace is sealed with Jesus' blood. As long as you have Him, you will not be uncertain of your salvation; for it is offered you by His pure grace, as our text emphasizes when it declares that, *"believing, ye might have life,"* and have it *"through His name."* You require, not your own good resolutions or intentions, your money or merit, but faith in the Savior's mercy vouchsafed by His name. You need only believe the thousands of golden truths in Scripture. As you focus your eyes on the cross, declare, "All these pledges of mercy, these assurances of victory over sin and temptation, these guarantees of triumph over death and hell, all the offers of eternal life, are mine, as definitely as though my name were inscribed on every message"!

What is it, then, that our age needs with particular force if not a return to the reverent regard and the serious study of the Scriptures, a new understanding of the Bible's promise, "Believe Christ — and live"? Therefore take your Bible! Read it reverently and devotedly, with concentration of thought and consecration of mind! As I recall a friend in Cambridge, Massachusetts, who out of love for Holy Writ spent five years in learning the Hebrew and the Greek languages so that he could delve more fully into the depths of divine promise, and who, together with his wife, has read God's Word from cover to cover more than sixty times, I plead with you, Resolve that, the Holy Spirit strengthening you, you will read through the entire Bible, starting today! If you need directions and guidance for Scripture readings, we shall be happy to supply them. Get right with God; now, in the only way you can, through faith in the Christ promised by His errorless truth!

Read the Bible in your family circles! More than two thirds of all domestic troubles could be avoided, I think, if disturbed households had time, interest, love, for Scripture.

Read the Bible in your churches! If the entire laity of Christian congregations were enrolled in Bible classes, we could witness the mightiest upswing Christianity has ever experienced in this country. Much of the pulpit disloyalty to Jesus would be banished, and many more churches could become spiritual forces for the help of individuals and for the strengthening of national morale.

Have your children study Holy Writ daily, if at all possible, in the Christian day schools that I regularly endorse because they can bring eternal salvation to your boys and girls!

In short, my fellow countrymen and fellow Christians, let us, each one of us, individually, dedicate ourselves to this program: The Bible for my world! The Bible for my country! The Bible for my church! The Bible for my home! The Bible, with Christ and His promise of life eternal, for my soul, now and to all eternity! Amen.

Christ is Coming!

"Lo, I come; in the volume of the Book it is written of Me."
PSALM 40:7

Blessed Lord Jesus:

Receive our joyful thanks that on the first Christmas Thou, our Lord and Savior, didst come into this sin-cursed world as a helpless Babe to begin the task of our redemption, which was to end on the cross at Calvary! Thou wast born to die for us in the eternal deliverance of our souls from sin and everlasting destruction; O blessed Christ Child, continue to come to us through Thy Word and Sacraments! Help us believingly ponder the miracle of Thine incarnation, as did Mary, joyfully acclaim Thee, as did the shepherds, reverently worship Thee, as did the Magi! Turn many from sin to Thy salvation, and, O Jesus, may it be Thy will to grant us peace with a victory which will fully please Thee and soon end this bloody struggle! Watch over our young men in the armed forces! Strengthen them to resist evil and trust Thee alone! Give them the full Christmas blessing! Come to all of us now through a Spirit-filled Advent into our hearts and homes, O Christ, and help us come, penitently but radiantly, to Thee, our only Redeemer! Amen.

A DISTRACTED Delaware woman writes me that a military plane carrying her son in Alaska, long overdue, has been reported "presumably lost" in the frozen wilderness. Yet her mother heart clings to the hope that he is still alive; and she asks us to join her in beseeching God that, if it be His will, her boy may soon be found. As you sit in the warm comfort of your homes, busy with happy Christmas preparation, say a prayer for that Christian lad, who at this moment may be fighting paralyzing cold or facing the fury of a polar blizzard!

May God mercifully grant him the rescue which saved another Arctic traveler! One day while journeying in Greenland with a sledge and dog team, Peter Frenchen missed the trail blazed by his Eskimo guides. For hours he pushed on as best he could; when darkness fell, early, as it does after those short northern days, he had strayed onto treacherous, thin ice. Lost in vast, crushing stillness and frozen blackness, he cried out with all his might until his hoarse throat was silenced; but the sole answer was the echo of his screaming. He could only wait, hope, try to keep himself from falling into fatal sleep and freezing to death. The night wore on, and his terror increased. Suddenly — he could hardly believe his ears — he seemed to hear a distant call: "I am coming! I am coming!" Minutes that seemed like ages passed. Then he heard the voice again and — this time there was no mistake — it sounded clearer and nearer as its promise rang through the night: "I am coming! I am coming!" Can you imagine what joy surged in his heart every time thereafter the cry was repeated, always louder and closer, until finally his rescuer, an old Eskimo companion, did come? Just as he arrived, the first rays of the Arctic sun began to streak the horizon, ushering in the day of joy, Christmas, and with it safety, light, life, happiness.

Many of you, like Peter Frenchen, have lost the way; only for you the dangers and sorrows are incomparably greater, since you have turned aside from the one road to your Savior. You may not realize that you are lost. Indeed, you may actually boast that now at last, with the largest income you have ever enjoyed, you have really found life; but the hour is approaching, the midnight of judgment, the heavy blackness of suffering, which some of you experience even now, when you, too, will scream yourselves hoarse as you plead in vain for rescue. Oh, may every one of you lost in the night of sin, affliction, doubt, unbelief, today hear the welcome voice, not of a human guide, but a heavenly Deliverer — Jesus, your Christ, your Redeemer, your God, repeating His age-old promise: "I am coming! I am coming!" With the dawn of Christmas may your faith-filled heart exult, "Jesus, my Redeemer, has come and saved me"!

Because I am hoping, praying, for a right Christmas in your home as you make room for the Holy Child, my message for today sounds the Advent call,

CHRIST IS COMING!

the pointed promise of Psalm forty, verse seven, *"Lo, I come; in the volume of the Book it is written of Me."*

I

"CHRIST IS COMING!" WAS THE CRY BEFORE THE FIRST CHRISTMAS

How marvelous these words, in which David, a thousand years before the first Christmas, envisions his Savior as declaring, *"Lo, I come"!* Yet long centuries before David, yes, from the very moment sin entered the world to curse man and drive him from the Paradise which God Himself had planted at Eden, the Almighty had promised the woman's Seed, who would break hell's clutching hold on men's souls. Well does Jesus say in our text, *"In the volume of the Book it is written of Me,"* for the whole Old Testament foretells His coming into the flesh. The first book of the Bible also predicts that this death-destroying Redeemer will be the Seed of Abraham, Isaac, Jacob, descended from the tribe of Judah, yet of such superhuman power that nations shall be gathered submissively before Him. The first great poet of the Bible, David, by divine inspiration records that the Father said to this promised Deliverer, *"Thou art My Son; this day have I begotten Thee."* The greatest of prophets,

Isaiah, foresees the miracle of His birth, when He whom *"the . . . heaven of heavens cannot contain"* will be born of a virgin. It is even foretold that *"His name shall be called Wonderful, Counselor, The Mighty God, The Everlasting Father, The Prince of Peace."* The place of His birth is recorded in advance by Micah, who, singling out Bethlehem, *"little among the thousands"* of villages *"of Judah,"* predicted, *"Out of thee shall He come forth unto Me that is to be Ruler in Israel; whose goings forth have been from of old, from everlasting."* Daniel foretells the time of His coming. Jeremiah and Hosea record the startling events following His birth: the flight into Egypt and the massacre of innocent children. In its glorious climax the Old Testament thus previews the purpose of His birth: He is to bear *"our griefs"* and carry *"our sorrows."* He is to be *"wounded for our transgressions, . . . bruised for our iniquities."* From the first pages of the Old Covenant until the last, when Zechariah cries out, *"Behold, thy King cometh unto thee,"* and Malachi exults, *"The Lord, whom ye seek, shall suddenly come to His Temple,"* the Savior's assurance: "I am coming! I am coming!" brought strength, comfort, joy, to believing hearts. Even in the pagan world men held a dim, uncertain anticipation that a mighty Rescuer of the race was coming. The Latin poet Vergil, who died only nineteen years before Christ came, declares his expectation that a Deliverer would soon be born, who would usher in a golden age. Truly that greedy, sin-encrusted era needed deliverance. It was a world in which Sumerians, Egyptians, Babylonians, Assyrians, Persians, Greeks, Romans, had in turn enslaved, tortured, destroyed their fellow men. It was a disillusioned period, in which human dreams of happiness were suddenly shattered; a lustful century, in which purity and decency were ridiculed; and although deeply religious, with ten thousand gods and goddesses, lavish temples and elaborate worship, unnumbered altars and uncounted idols, it was an age of dread fear, cringing superstition, spiritual hopelessness. Only God's own people had hope — because in their believing hearts this promise constantly resounded: "I am coming! I am coming!"

On the first Christmas—O glorious day!—Christ came; and He appeared to fulfill those ancient prophecies concerning the place, time, purpose of His virgin birth. His nativity at Bethlehem, therefore, should be sufficient to make any person accept the entire Bible; for where, among the thousands of books written by men, is there a single volume that can do what the Old Testament does when it foresees, five hundred, a thousand, almost fifteen hundred years in advance the incarnation at David's city? Today fear-weighted people, especially in our national capital at Washington, cause fortunetellers, crystal-gazers to work overtime; but be sure of this: No man can unlock the future. God alone can foretell accurately, and as a matter of record only His inspired Scripture has consistently forecast the truth. Skeptics and unbelievers ought to believe Scripture if only because of its fulfilled prophecy. You believers, children of God, should find strength in the assurance that, if Christ kept His pledge: "I am coming! I am coming!" and in the "fullness of the time" came, then certainly He will carry out every one of His blood-sealed promises to you. I cannot blame you if you put a question mark behind human assertions. Some of you trusted your best friends, but they lied, cheated, stole your business; or you paid dearly for impressively sealed stocks and bonds of great corporations which have failed to meet their obligation of repayment. Others among you have built your hopes on the assurances of politicians and statesmen, only to find their utterances empty, windy phrases; you relied upon your children's word, but they broke it; you put your confidence in the sacred marriage vow now severed by cruel unfaithfulness. Do not let this embitter your heart against Jesus, for the first Christmas proves that He keeps His word! He came as He had promised; and He will come to you as His Word declares.

When the Old Testament ended and the New Testament began at Bethlehem, the Christ child had been born of the Virgin Mary for one marvelous, merciful, magnificent purpose. He did not leave His heavenly throne to found an earthly empire, for He forbade His disciples to take the sword even in defense of His life. Jesus did not introduce an age of ease, comfort, power, and prestige. On the contrary, He said, *"If any man will come after Me, let him deny himself, and take up his cross daily and follow Me!"* He did not come to consort with the mighty and devote His time to the political interests of self-righteous leaders. Instead, He pledged: *"I am . . . come to call . . . sinners to repentance."* He was not born to bring universal peace among nations, for He warned, *"I came not to send peace, but a sword"* — the persecution, the violence that those who confess Christ must endure at the hands of evil men. He came, not to enjoy the honor and acclaim which was rightfully His; rather does He tell us, *"The Son of Man came not to be ministered unto but to minister and to give His life a ransom for many."* Truly, *"this is a faithful saying and worthy of all acceptation, that Christ Jesus came into the world to save sinners."* He came to offer Himself as a living, dying sacrifice in atoning for the transgressions of all mankind. He came, a Mediator between Heaven and earth, to restore lost men to their God. Therefore He appeared as *"the Light of the world,"* to banish darkness; as the Hope of the world, to plant joy into the hearts of despondent men and weeping women. He came with the victory by which His followers are *"more than conquerors"* in life's struggles. And because He came, the earth was changed, history was altered, our calendar began anew. He was born nineteen centuries ago, but His grace has not lost its power as the years have slipped into history. He was cradled in a manger, though His influence has been stamped on every great, good movement since that day. He never traveled far, with the exception of His flight into Egypt and His trips north to the shores of Tyre and Sidon — a distance of about two hundred miles separated these points — yet His Gospel has advanced to the ends of the earth. His mother and foster-father were Jewish, but His love has brought men and women of every nation, race, color, and clime to their knees before His cross. Jesus never wrote a book, nor do we read that He ever attended school. However, He gave the impulse to the best of modern enlightenment; more volumes have been written about Him than about a thousand of history's mightiest figures. He came for men cold in their cruelty, to bring hundreds of millions the warmth of His compassion; for mankind hard in its hatred, to redeem sinners and put love in the hearts of His believers; for a world groaning in its misery, to make the sorrowing and tear-stained raise their heads happily and sing, "Joy to the World, the Lord *is* come!"

II

"CHRIST IS COMING" SHOULD BE THE CRY BEFORE THIS CHRISTMAS

Praise His eternal mercy! Though Jesus no longer walks earth's pathways, He still comes to us, as it is written of Him in *"the volume of the Book."* Every time a picture or a greeting card portrays His love (What a shame that on this hundredth anniversary of the Christmas cards so many feature irreverence, hatred, anything except the Christ who gave this day His name!), every time you hear a carol praise the new-born Savior, He comes to you, asking entrance into your heart, promising Heaven's blessing for your life.

You may feel yourself lost in the darkness of many and grievous transgressions, but the Savior of whom it is written, *"He appeared to put away sin by the sacrifice of Himself,"* now calls to you: "I am coming! I am coming to *you* with the promise of pardon for all your sins." Do not regard Christmas only as a holiday on which you can stay home from work! Do not let fancy wrapping paper and evergreen decorations, burned up after New Year's, mean more to you than God's everlasting love and His unspeakable grace in His Son! Do not let the quickly tarnished tinsel and the fragile ornaments take more of your interest than the worship of Jesus Himself! Find time even during this holiday rush to learn in a personal, unmistakable way that the Redeemer was born for you! Let Christmas Day be Christ's and yours in the mystic union of faith and love!

Are you suffering under life's many sorrows? Jesus calls, "I am coming; I am coming with comfort, strength, and help." He knows the anguish you must bear, for He suffered far more than all mankind has endured. When friends asked a young woman whose life was slowly ebbing away whether she suffered much, she admitted that she did; "but," she added, pointing to her hand, "there is no nail there; He had the nails, I have the peace." Touching her brow, she said, "There are no thorns there; He had the thorns, I have the peace." Laying her hand on her side, she concluded, "There is no spear there; He had the spear, but I have the peace."

Are you poor and unnoticed? The Christ Child was, too. In one of the Pacific Coast race tracks, where the Japanese evacuees were temporarily placed, a believing Japanese, forced to live in a reconstructed stable, wrote: "On the wall of my stall hangs a picture of Mary and the Christ Child. He was born in a stall, and so, I guess, He must feel at home here. That makes us feel so much better." You, too, will feel a new upsurge of joy if in your anguish you answer Jesus' call, "I am coming, I am coming to you," with the prayer: "O Lord Jesus, come to me now! Strengthen my faith! Deepen my trust! Turn these sorrows into joy! Make all this torture work together for good because I love Thee!" As the apostles sang in the midnight of their imprisonment, so, no matter how completely you feel yourself encircled by darkness or how eagerly hatred seeks to control your thoughts, you likewise can find courage in faith and song.

Hardly six days remain before the anniversary of the Savior's birth, and during these Jesus cries out with con- stantly renewed love, "I am coming, I am coming." The question of life-and-death importance for you is this: Will you open your heart, so that He can bring you pardon and hope? Some years ago, when Ibrahim Pascha, Egyptian general, was to make an impressive entrance into Jerusalem, laborers smoothed the way along which he would travel. Heavy stones were removed from the road and the holes filled. A large banner proclaimed, "The Pascha is coming"; and from all sides the cry arose: "The Pascha is coming! Remove the stones!" That was the picture Isaiah had when, beholding the Savior's ad- vent, he appealed, *"Prepare ye the way of the Lord!"* For you this means that every barrier, obstacle, hindrance, which keeps Christ from your soul must be completely removed, so that He, the Lord of Love and Prince of

Peace, can come into your heart. This Gospel broadcast, on the Sunday before Christmas, has the one definite appeal: it asks you in the name of Bethlehem's Babe: Give Him the control of your souls and bodies! Beseech Him to remove the impurities, stubbornness, pride, lust, covetousness, doubt, unbelief, disobedience to God, neglect of His Word! Accept the greatest Christmas Gift Heaven itself can give: the indwelling of Jesus and His Spirit, which grants you hope and strength, courage and joy!

Let me emphasize, as the birthday of our divine Lord approaches, that there is no other source of salvation for you, except faith in the coming King. False Christs, lying, deceitful Messiahs roam over the earth today; but before you give them your allegiance, recall the disasters their falsehoods have provoked! A century after Jesus was nailed to the cross, an impostor named Ben Chochbha announced that he was the promised Deliverer. Mobs flocked to him, and it is claimed that he was able to capture 980 Judean towns and villages; but three hundred thousand of his fellow countrymen were slain on fields of battle; many more died of plague or famine; finally the false Christ himself was slain. Even more disastrous are the spiritual consequences of trusting men and human deceptions. God Himself knows of no eternal help for you except in Jesus, for *"there is none other name under heaven given among men whereby we must be saved"* but Christ's holy, precious name.

Your Redeemer is coming — will you greet Him in faith and welcome Him in love? When Christmas dawns on this war-torn world, will you be for the Savior or against Him? Will you young folks celebrate His birthday in a series of wild parties even though American lives are lost hourly in the struggles of this widening war, or will you be in a true church of Christ, joining your hearts and voices with joyous worshipers in the new-born Savior's praise? Will your home be so overoccupied with holiday preparations that after crowded days and sleep-robbed nights the Infant Jesus will find even less room in your house than at the Bethlehem inn? On the blessed day when inner peace and complete gladness should reign in every household, will joy be banished from your family circle by bitter quarrel, brutal drunkenness, blasphemous cursing?

III

"CHRIST IS COMING!" MUST ALWAYS BE THE CRY

This cry, "Christ is coming," which the believers raised during long centuries before the first Christmas, should constantly surge through our souls and leap from our lips; for the same Savior who entered the world as a humble mite of humanity will come again, not to suffer at the hands of His enemies and die on the cross of shame, but in almighty power and heavenly majesty, to judge the quick and the dead. This, too, is written *"in the volume of the Book";* indeed, few truths of our entire faith are more frequently expressed than the promise of His second advent. Do you realize that in the New Testament alone 318 passages, no fewer than one of every twenty-five verses, speak of Jesus' return, as it is mentioned in every New Testament book except three of the smaller epistles?

No doubt should remain: Christ is coming. Listen, as over the bloodshed and brutality of a world in war Jesus cries, "I am coming"! Through all of man's blasphemy, the taunting of atheists, the lies of false prophets, who sneer, *"Where is the promise of His coming?"* our Lord repeats, "I am coming." Amid the persecution which His Church sustains, amid the sufferings which believers endure for His sake, the Savior repeats the promise of deliverance, "I am coming." More definitely than thousands of millions who have preceded us, we are close to that blessed but awful day of His return. *"The time is short."*

Behold the startling fulfillment of the signs to precede His coming for judgment and deliverance! Here are only a few: War! At no time in previous history has bloodshed been as widespread as now. Famine! Over in Honan Province in China, hunger-crazed mothers are trying to sell baby daughters for twenty Chinese dollars, a single dollar in our currency; and if there are no buyers, the children are often thrown away and left to die. Think of Greece, where "many of the children are like skeletons," Belgium, where 60 per cent of the school children have no breakfast! Earthquakes! From various, widely removed parts of the world come ominous reports of tremors. *"Men shall be lovers of their own selves, covetous, boasters, proud, blasphemers, disobedient to parents, unthankful, unholy"* — eight signs that describe our generation, the age which has produced dictators, leaders swollen with pride, and has seen more disobedience on the part of children to parental or governmental authority than we have ever before known in this country. In the last days, men shall have *"a form of godliness,"* but deny *"the power thereof."* How true of our time with its mighty church buildings, its million-dollar congregations and their unbelief; its overpretentious, costly rituals, from which the plain Jesus, clothed in His workman's garb, would turn in sorrow! Great apostasy, falling from faith, will mark the beginning of the end; and if the true Christian churches in the United States could compute the number of people lost this year, when many have proved themselves *"lovers of pleasure more than lovers of God,"* the total would be appalling.

Masses of Americans do not discern these and a score of other signs. They have not returned penitently to God in Christ. From the State of Washington a listener writes: "I am a shipyard worker. The cursing, swearing, obscenity here are unspeakable. Sixteen-year-old boys learn to blaspheme and outdo their elders. I could not possibly paint the picture too dark. A shipyard is an average cross section of our nation. Can we win a war with this situation? Will God stand this blasphemy forever? I am afraid for our beloved country." Many other letters come to my desk showing that multitudes in the United States scoff at the thought of Christ's return. I beseech you: Believe that Jesus is coming soon! Prepare yourself now for His advent! He is coming, the sacred Volume warns, *"suddenly."* It will be too late if you postpone accepting His grace until He comes. You must receive Him now. Set your house in order before He returns! My fellow redeemed, come out of the Sodoms and Gomorrahs of this world to be rescued by Jesus!

Beloved, as the Advent and Christmas cry rings out, "Jesus is coming," how will He find you? God grant that, even though the lights of hope have gone out in vast areas of this sin-darkened world, the lamp of your faith will burn ever brighter; and as Christ now calls to you through this broadcast, "I am coming," may you, penitent but confident, sin-conscious but grace-assured, beholding Christ, your Redeemer from ruin, your Savior from sin, your Pardon from eternal punishment, pray in joy and triumph, "Oh, come, Lord Jesus, come quickly!" Amen.

No Room for Christ,
Yet Room for Us!

"There was no room for them in the inn."
SAINT LUKE 2:7

"Yet there is room."
SAINT LUKE 14:22

Blessed Savior of Bethlehem:

Angels sang their praise at Thy birth. How, then, can we with unclean lips, living in an impure world, worthily exalt Thee on this happy day commemorating Thine advent into the flesh! Nevertheless, receive our praise, precious Savior, weak and imperfect as it is; help us daily grow in grace so that we may constantly direct our thoughts to the heaven from which Thou didst come and which, through Thee and in Thy time, we shall enter! Bring the peace of which the celestial host caroled, the harmony beween Thy Father and His redeemed children, into many hearts throughout the world! In the greatest Christmas gift that even Thou canst bestow, grant multitudes the assurance of salvation through faith in Thine incarnation, atonement, and resurrection! Millions of Thy children are embattled in various parts of the world. Grant them a glimpse of Thy soul-peace and lead them closer to Thee this Christmas! In Thy forgiving Spirit we also intercede for our enemies, pleading that they may be brought to a penitent understanding of Thy truth and grace! If it please Thee, let this be the last wartime Christmas, blessed Savior! Let the earth re-echo with praise for Thy mercy and songs of Thy love! Precious Jesus, as Thou wast born in Bethlehem, by Thy Holy Spirit be born in us today! We ask this newness of life, the true Christmas gift, by Thy endless compassion. Amen.

Two years ago, when the Germans invaded the Low Countries, the officials of a small Belgian community prepared to flee. Their village church contained

138

a famous Van Dyck painting of Christ, and to save this treasure, the burgomaster and his wife loaded it on a truck and started for Southern France. During their whole hazardous journey they found no welcome for the priceless painting of the Savior, no roof under which the masterpiece could be sheltered. Because the weather was cold and stormy, they used its large frame and canvas as a shelter from rain and wind, until, months later, it was safely housed.

As I wish every one of you not a merry Christmas (for who, considering the American lives lost hourly in the war, the souls constantly endangered in the present conflict, can be merry in a carnal, careless way?) but a blessed, Christ-centered Christmas in your soul and family circle, I remind you that this Belgian incident represents on a small scale the startling contradiction continuously in progress since the first Christmas. Millions have closed the door of their hearts and homes to Jesus; yet in His unfathomable love He still stretches forth His hands with the invitation of love *"Come unto Me!"* The striking contrast of nineteen centuries is summarized in this mystery of mercy and misbelief:

NO ROOM FOR CHRIST, YET ROOM FOR US!

the double truth of our Christmas text: first, the words of Saint Luke, chapter two, verse seven, *"There was no room for them in the inn";* and then the Savior's pledge of peace, Saint Luke, chapter fourteen, verse twenty-two, *"Yet there is room."*

I

SINFUL MEN REFUSE TO RECEIVE THE SINLESS CHRIST CHILD

Before the war the newspapers described a $5,000 crib made for a baby born into one of Europe's royal families. Five thousand dollars' worth of carving, metal work, studded jewels, and artistry—all for a human child! Yet, when Jesus, sinless and stainless, born of a virgin by a marvelous miracle, came into the world, His parents had not even a plain cot on which He could lie. They laid Him in a manger, the feeding trough of animals. You have seen that manger glorified on Christmas postcards as an ornate bed, bright with dazzling colors, pictured in a pillared, vaulted room. Famous painters have reproduced it as a substantial piece of furniture, not unlike the little crib in which perhaps you were cradled, and have depicted worshiping angels and celestial musicians hovering about it. But how utterly different the poverty of the Savior's birth! Most of you cannot imagine the conditions in that stable where the King of kings came into this world. His birthplace was probably a cave dug into a hill outside the inn, a stable for beasts of burden; a dirty, smelly place that few American communities would tolerate.

Why was the Lord of glory born an outcast? Our text explains, *"There was no room for them in the inn,"* and no willingness to accommodate them, we may add. It was every man for himself in those days, and men before women, particularly women with children. We may assume that, if *"there was no room . . . in the inn,"* probably no resting place in the "little town" was available on that Christmas Eve. Modern Bethlehem has only 8,000 inhabitants; in the Savior's day it may have been only one-tenth as large. Who among the villagers would be interested and warmhearted enough to shelter a couple that expected a baby within a few hours? Who would bother with them when it would be so much more convenient to rent space to others in the crowd registering for the census? Mary and Joseph may have had friends or even relatives in Bethlehem, but apparently all doors were barred to them. The priests, the Levites, the scribes, the Pharisees, the businessmen, the traders, the workmen, the shrewd housewives — all those *"of the house and lineage of David"* who had come to Bethlehem at the decree of Caesar Augustus and his governor — never dreamed that they could have accepted the most startling opportunity for service mortal man has ever known, the privilege of providing quarters for the promised Christ Child, the Redeemer of mankind. If they saw Mary and Joseph, they doubtless raised their proud heads higher, the more disdainfully to look down on the couple that had come from despised Galilee at such an inappropriate time.

The whole Christmas story, despite its Palestinian setting and its distance in time, has modern and American counterparts. We read that all the people had enrolled for taxation, and we begin to compute our new taxes, the highest in American history, levied for the year drawing to its close, with more people than ever before making returns. As we see Mary and Joseph on the road, traveling from Nazareth to Bethlehem, we think of the tremendous military and industrial movements in the United States that have made many of you journey far and often, that today station you soldiers and defense workers away from home. Recalling the crowded conditions in Bethlehem, we survey the many overcrowded American communities, where some of you now hear this Christmas message in cramped quarters, trailer camps, furnished rooms. When you find the Holy Family surrounded by unsympathetic people, you will be inclined to draw comparisons with the fact that you, too, are a stranger in a strange place, that no one has paid attention to you, except those who can make money through your patronage. Yet it seems to me that the most striking similarity

between the first Christmas and this anniversary is the
rejection of Jesus. Multitudes still have no room for Him.
Before we begin to denounce the unfriendly citizens of
David's City, we should admit that masses in America,
had Mary and Joseph come to their homes this morning,
would have refused to welcome them. More than half
our population has heard of Christ's merciful love; millions celebrate the day of His birth intensively and speak
His name in holiday greetings; yet consistently, year after
year, they have closed their hearts to Him, saying in effect, "There is 'no room' in my shriveled, hate-filled, care-
crowded soul for that Child in the manger."

With all the modern cries for tolerance, too many
show the bigotry of Bethlehem. There is still *"no room"*
for Christ's love; else why would this generation bleed its
best power away in a second World War? *"No room"* for
His humility; else why would half of this earth hear Him
say, *"Blessed are the peacemakers,"* but be forced to follow Nietzsche as he cries out in contradiction, "Blessed
are the war makers"? *"No room"* for His holy Word in
modern culture, where experts would train our children
without reverence for God and faith in His Bible! *"No
room"* for our Lord's creed of self-denial, when certain
modern magazines feature page after page, picture after
picture, paragraph after paragraph of profanity and in-
decency, but not a single sentence regarding this ageless
message, *"Unto you is born this day in the city of David
a Savior, which is Christ the Lord"!* *"No room"* for the
promise of His cross and His blood, when more Americans reject Him than ever before; when theological pro-
fessors, contradicting the holy angel's anthem, *"He shall
save His people from their sins,"* deny that the Child in
the manger is our Immanuel, our God-with-us; when
many American churches do not once open their doors

on Christmas Day! *"No room"* for the Nativity mercy, which promises us that we are saved through humble, penitent, trusting faith in the Babe of Bethlehem as our Lord and our Redeemer, while great religious bodies deny this center and climax of our faith, *"By grace are ye saved"!*

A pointed, personal issue confronts you: Jesus, the Christ Child of Christmas, in this moment seeks entrance into your heart. Will you turn away from Him because your soul is saturated with the driving desire for money? Fresh in our minds is the account of a merchant-marine sailor who had secured a thousand dollars, perhaps more money than he had ever owned in his life, a sum so impressive that his heart was closely attached to this treasure, carefully stored in his locker. His ship was torpedoed, and after he was rescued, he admitted that in those perilous hours he had never even thought of his thousand dollars. — In the crisis moments of life, if you have rejected Jesus, you have lost more than money can ever buy. You have sacrificed your soul's salvation. This is Christ's warning, *"He that believeth not shall be damned."* The Christmas appeal, above eating and drinking, giving and receiving, visiting and being visited, lighting and decorating, the plea that comes from the very manger of the Christ Child, asks you: "Make room for Jesus! Grant Him entrance into your heart! Welcome Him into your home!"

II

THE SINLESS CHRIST CHILD ALWAYS WELCOMES SINFUL MEN

Although *"there was no room"* for Christ at Bethlehem's inn *"yet there is room,"* as the second part of our festival text explains — room for you in His heart of love, in His Kingdom of Grace, in His Father's heavenly mansions. At His manger crib *"there is room"* for every sinner, especially the desperate and downtrodden, including those of you who write me tear-stained letters declaring that the transgressions of the past rise up to disturb you, waking or sleeping. When you come to Jesus in faith and He comes to you in His mercy, He removes the curse of your sin. He washes away its stain. The fire of His devotion burns away your iniquity. The power of His presence purifies your heart and strengthens your life. Take courage and believe on this Christmas Day that nothing can keep you from Bethlehem and the forgiveness in the newborn Savior but your own impenitence, your refusal to accept the Christ Child's promise of full, free, and final pardon!

At the manger *"there is room"* for all, regardless of race restrictions or color classifications. *"There is room"* aplenty for friend and foe, since the Infant Jesus is the world's Savior. He was born and He died so that all men, regardless of how completely they may be segregated into opposing groups, might be saved. During the First World War, Christmas came to a Russian war prison camp in Siberia. Up to that time it had been the scene of homesickness, misery, hatred, and despair. Suicide had been frequent. But when the prisoners and their guards gathered in the half-underground barracks for the Christmas celebration, the leader arose to say, "There is one song all can sing tonight, 'Silent Night, Holy Night.'" They sang it — the guards and the prisoners, each man in his own language. When they were finished, the Russian commander's eyes filled with tears as he told the captives, "Tonight is the first time in more than a year that I have been able to forget you and I are supposed to be enemies." If you, too, will acclaim Bethlehem's Babe in faith and trust, your hatred will shrivel away, and in new joy you will be able to worship the Savior who commanded, *"Love your enemies!"*

"There is room" at Bethlehem for the poor, unnoticed, unacclaimed, just as the Savior's birth was first announced to the shepherds, lowly laborers. Joseph Mohr, who wrote the beloved lines of "Silent Night, Holy Night," lived a humble, unpretentious life. He died within twelve miles of the place where he was born; yet his Christmas carol has sung its way around the world. And the Christ whose *"strength is made perfect in weakness"* can likewise save you for important purposes, no matter how little attention the world pays you. Indeed, the plain and underprivileged have always been especially welcomed by His mercy.

"There is room" at the manger for those who feel themselves lonely, forsaken; particularly for the families in which a son has laid down his life for the nation's defense. How hard the Christmas festivities seem to you when contrasted with the sorrow burdening your heart almost to the breaking! This anniversary of your Savior's birth has graciously dawned for *you*, to give you the Heaven-granted assurance that through the Christ Child *"your sorrow shall be turned into joy."* Before this day ends, select some quiet spot and read Saint Luke's story of the Nativity! Read it aloud! Read it prayerfully! It contains only 412 words, and it will take only a few moments. While you read, be fortified by believing that all this is written to show you that the Savior's promise, *"Yet there is room,"* holds assuredly for you, in the love that knows no limit, the grace that recognizes no bounds.

Often in the history of these last nineteen centuries Christmas has been a time of mighty conversion. Today, when God uses this radio to offer you *"His unspeakable*

Gift," His own incarnate Son, picture the blessings which come with this Gift — the washing away of your sins, the salvation of your soul, the defeat of death, the assurance of heaven, the reunion with your loved ones in the realms of celestial glory; all these blessings which Saint Paul lists as *"the fruit of the Spirit": "love, joy, peace, long-suffering, gentleness, goodness, faith, meekness, temperance"!* Then, as the Christ Child appeals for room in your heart, asking, *"Where is the guest chamber?"* answer with the trusting faith of Martin Luther's Christmas carol:

> Ah, dearest Jesus, holy Child,
> Make Thee a bed, soft, undefiled,
> Within my heart, that it may be
> A quiet chamber kept for Thee!

Do not be satisfied with a second-best, shoddy welcome! Years ago in a Scotch village an old lady stepped from a pony carriage, walked to a workman's cottage, and politely asked for a glass of water. Only reluctantly the housewife agreed, showing her displeasure by bringing the water in a cracked cup. After the visitor had gone, a neighbor ran over to exclaim, "Do you know who that old lady was?" You can imagine her dismay to be told, "She was Queen Victoria!" That cracked cup is still held in high esteem, though it should be a sign of perpetual reproach. Let our welcome to Jesus be genuine, wholehearted, soul-sincere! Earth's Savior, heaven's King, has come to you! Give Him the best you have, the best you are, and the best you can be by His grace! While we cannot receive Him in the flesh, yet He promises concerning our charities, *"Inasmuch as ye have done it unto one of the least of these My brethren, ye have done it unto Me."* Before this holy day is over, resolve to share what God has given you with your poor, suffering, destitute fellow men!

Especially, however, may we, having received Jesus and made room for His redeeming love, bring the message of His grace to others! If you feel that the circle of your influence is too small for your testimony to bless many, remember, His Word never returns void! Church papers tell us of an American missionary who spent last Christmas in jail, imprisoned by the Japanese. The bars and barricades could not restrain his spirit, and on that holiday morning through the prison stillness he whistled "Silent Night," "Oh, Come, All Ye Faithful," and other carols, until the guard demanded that he stop. Yet the next day one of the prisoners whom he happened to pass braved the wrath of the prison officials by whispering to the missionary, "Thank you for Christmas!" And if your testimony to the Savior rings clear, wherever you may be, you can strengthen and fortify the faith of others.

When the trans-Atlantic cable was completed, the first message flashed from continent to continent by the marvel of that invention ended with the angels' chorus at Bethlehem, *"Glory to God in the highest, and on earth peace, good will toward men!"* By the greater marvel of the radio, may this same message now speed its way over all natural boundaries of mountains, rivers, lakes, seas, and find room in your heart! From shore to shore let us unite in exulting, *"Glory to God in the highest, and on earth peace, good will toward men,"* all through the Christ Child for whom *"there was no room"* at His birth, but through whom, by the rebirth of faith, we find eternal room! God grant every one of you this Christmas blessing! Amen!

Hold Tight to Christmas!

"Mary kept all these things and pondered them in her heart."
SAINT LUKE 2:19

O God, Unchanging and Unending:

At the approach of another year's end, help us realize how much closer we are to eternity and how entirely we depend for our life, and particularly for our salvation, on Thy compassion toward us in Christ Jesus! For His sake and by the cleansing power of His holy, precious blood forgive our iniquities committed during the passing year! As we review our many sins and confess that daily we have broken Thy holy Law, we know that we have deserved nothing but condemnation; yet we have the confidence that through our Savior every transgression has been removed as far as the east is from the west. Bring this assurance into many hearts today! Strengthen especially the men and women in America's armed service! Nothing is impossible with Thee, our God. Therefore we humbly ask, let this be the last year of the war! Through faith in the Christ Child banish our fears, encourage us in afflictions, deliver us from doubt, but always and everywhere keep us close to Thee! We plead in Jesus' blessed name. Amen.

THIS last Sunday in December reminds us in the increasing rush of time that we are all a milestone closer to the grave, twelve months, which we can never again regain and relive, nearer eternity. Only a few more Christmases for most of you, no more for some of you, and life, with all its unrealized hopes and unfulfilled ambitions, will be over! We are living in the fastest tempo history has known; therefore we are under the heaviest pressure. Hurry and swiftness are the watchwords of this speed-it-up generation, with the result that our whole

148

existence is being snatched away more rapidly than we realize.

With this high tension, increased during war's emergencies (when ships, formerly made in many months, are now launched after a few days; when mighty military camps with a total area larger than some of our entire States spring up almost overnight); with this amazing rapidity, comes the danger that we too quickly dismiss eternal truths from our minds. Here it is only the second day after the anniversary of our Savior's birth, and thousands of people throughout the country are busily at work in department stores, removing all signs of Christmas. In our homes, after a short week or two, the outward evidences of this radiant day will similarly disappear, and in too many hearts the magnificence of the Nativity mercy will be lost.

Added to this is the growing indifference by which the blessings of the Savior's birth are carelessly taken for granted. Some people drive over the bridge at Niagara Falls and seldom look at that mighty spectacle, one of the world's wonders. They have seen it too often to be thrilled by its grandeur. A transcontinental passenger, traveling by train through the Rocky Mountains, writes that everyone in the car was visibly moved by the magnificent panorama, except one woman, who hardly raised her eyes from her book. Later she explained: "This is the thirteenth time I have crossed the mountains. The first time I could not keep the tears from rolling down my cheeks, so impressed was I. But now I have known it so well that I frequently go through the whole range with scarcely a glance out of the window." Similarly, as Christmas follows Christmas, many of you think that you know the whole story, because you have heard it so often, when in truth you can never begin to exhaust the treasures of its grace. The most deep-rooted enemy of American Christianity in our time is not the brazen atheist who boldly brandishes his blasphemy, for only *"the fool hath said . . ., There is no God";* not the sarcastic Modernist who often preaches only to a handful of people; not the down-with-religion Communist who threatens to destroy our churches, for God laughs at this bombastic boasting. As menacing as all these opponents of our faith may be, the most dangerous enemies of the Redeemer's Gospel are the easy-going, self-confident Americans within the churches and without who hear Heaven's invitation and then quickly dismiss it from their minds to live and act as though there were no Savior, no Christmas with its message, *"God"* is *"manifest in the flesh."* These, I repeat, are the most dangerous foes because they are counted by the millions.

Now to all of you who are hurrying madly through life, with no time for the Holy Child, no heart-and-soul interest in the promise of His redemption, I say, in His name and with the plea that involves your salvation, your blessed eternity, your promise of heaven,

"HOLD TIGHT TO CHRISTMAS!"

Celebrate the Savior's birthday every day! Take as your example our Lord's mother, of whom it is written that after the first Christmas had come and gone, after the shepherds had worshiped and departed, *"Mary kept all these things and pondered them in her heart"!* (Saint Luke, chapter two, verse nineteen.)

I

CONSTANTLY KEEP THE CHRISTMAS TRUTH!

How noble and outstanding the Virgin Mary was! While we dare not endorse the error of some who have made her almost equal to God Himself, called her, in effect, the promised deliverer of the human race, we must not descend to the other extreme which regards her only as an average Palestinian mother. Twice, in the words of angels and men, does the Bible call her *"blessed . . . among women."* We dare not detract from that or go beyond it. She who bore our Lord Jesus should be an example of excellency for all women.

Therefore we plead: Women of America, follow Mary! Remember that God has made you, the wives, mothers, daughters, of this country the guardians of much that is best and highest. If you fail us, the loss will be irreparable. The forces of hell are working in unbroken shifts, using the emergencies of war for a systematic attack on Christian womanhood. Too often their unholy assaults have been successful. Think of the girls lined up at tavern bars, elbow to elbow with men! Recall the startling increase in drunkenness among women! Hear the reports of growing profanity in large industrial plants! Behold the evidence of shocking immorality, cunningly practiced in the name of patriotism, and then ask God to give you a constant vision of Christmas and the glorious heights to which womanhood was exalted when Mary became the mother of the world's Savior!

Especially, however, should we all follow Mary in her faith. She knew more about the birth of Christ than any other person on earth; and unfalteringly she trusted the Almighty. It is recorded of her in Scripture, *"Blessed is she that believed."* There were mysteries for Mary at the manger, promises she could hardly understand. The angel had told her that her Babe was to be the Son of God; yet He came into the world amid abject poverty, and the first to adore Him were not priests or churchmen, but lowly shepherds. She had been assured that her

Child would "*save His people from their sins*" and that
His coming brought "*good tidings of great joy*" for "*all
people*"; still was her Son not born an outcast? Only once
in the whole marvelous story of her motherhood did she
inquire, "*How shall this be?*"

We need that same trusting faith. I shall not argue or
debate with you at length questions concerning the incarnation, the virgin birth, Christ's two natures, and
other truths which surpass our powers of understanding;
I simply ask you to approach the whole Christmas record
with an unbiased mind and permit facts to convince you.
Daniel Webster and Rufus Choate were once the opposing counsels in a famous trial where the point of con-
tention was the resemblance of two car wheels. Any
open-minded person would have said that the wheels
were essentially the same, made from one model. Nevertheless, Choate in a long, intricate oration, filled with
technicalities and complicated arguments, sought to convince the members of the jury that they ought to overrule
the verdict of their own eyes and decide that the wheels
were different. When Webster arose in reply, he pointed
to the wheels and said: "Gentlemen of the jury, there
they are. Look at them!" Those six words completely
shattered Choate's elaborate argument. Similarly, to you
who have been uncertain as to the truth of the Christmas
story; to you college men and women with questioning
minds; to you light seekers who have been misled by
some boisterous, blaring infidel; to every doubter I say,
pointing to the evidences of Christ's truths in the world
about us: "There they are. Look at them: Hellholes of
heathendom transformed into model communities; sav-
ages become servants of God; cannibals changed into
confessors of Jesus; sinners remade into saints; drunkards

reborn into decent men and women! There it is. Look at it; the whole Christian Church! A thousand times the Savior's enemies have sworn that they would destroy His kingdom, but a thousand times they have been defeated. Repeatedly infidels have boasted that Christianity had been wiped out for all time. Today it is stronger than ever."

Do not insist that modern research and culture have disproved our faith. Scientists, even the greatest of them, can be wrong. Most of you have heard of Sir Isaac Newton, often called the prince of scientists. It is claimed that when that great man of learning came to grips with a practical issue of life, the problem of enabling his cats to enter the barn, he did not hesitate to cut two holes in the door, a large hole for the large cat, and a small hole for the small cat! Now, if scientific leaders make such mistakes in the trivialities of life, why should we be concerned about their denials of divine truth?

Always keep in mind, too, that many outstanding leaders in human thought have declared themselves humble and sincere followers of the Savior. Listen to testimonies like these, not from uncultured circles but from American universities, and not from any insignificant instructor, but from presidents and deans, men chosen for leadership because of their exceptional qualifications: President Thompson, Ohio State University: "The Christian hope, a living hope, begotten in us by the resurrection of Jesus Christ, satisfies, inspires, and comforts. . . . I am a Christian because the Gospel of Jesus Christ . . . brings me a satisfying message for the life that now is and a sure hope for that which is to come"! President Burton, Smith College: "In His infinite patience with sinners, in His divine forgiveness for those who harmed Him, in His terrible suffering and death, Jesus . . . says there is a God that hates sin, that this God is our Father, and that we are His children"! President Wheeler, University of California: "The Bible must be read more and studied more and taken more deeply into the life of every Christian. We cannot do without it. It is the heart of our faith"! Dean Rogers, University of Michigan: "I heartily accept the Bible as the Word of God and sincerely believe Jesus Christ is the Savior of men"! President Wayland of Brown University: "I place no dependence on anything but the righteousness and death of Jesus Christ"! President Finley, Princeton University: "I triumph through Christ"! President Cyrus Northrop of Minnesota University: "I shall uphold Christianity as the religion which is to save the world"! If these and many other heads of outstanding universities have followed Mary's simple and trusting faith, what keeps you from kneeling humbly before the new-born Rescuer of the race?

Mary did not merely listen to the Christmas message and then forget it. We read in plain, one-syllable words, that after Jesus was born she *"kept all these things,"* the startling promises concerning the Holy Child, *"in her heart."* We likewise must hold tight to the Christmas blessing even after the evergreen and decorations have been removed. The benedictions of our Savior's birth are far too great to be restricted by the short span of twenty-four hours. You cannot put the Atlantic into a drinking glass; even less can you crowd the glories of His incarnation into a single day. When Paula, a fifth-century Christian, came to Bethlehem, she knelt at the reputed site of the manger and exclaimed: "I see the divine Infant wrapped in His swaddling clothes. I hear my Lord crying in His cradle." Then, quoting in Latin, Greek, and Hebrew, as the verses came to her mind, she recalled all the prophetic passages which dealt with His coming and concluded: "Have I, a miserable sinner, been permitted to kiss the cradle where my Savior uttered His first cry? Have I been counted worthy to offer my prayers in this cave, where the Virgin Mary brought forth my Lord? Here shall be my rest, for it is the country of my Lord. Here will I dwell, since my Savior chose it." While it is neither possible nor advisable for you now to make a pilgrimage to Palestine, by faith you can constantly keep close to the Christ Child. Accept Him as your Redeemer now! Take Him with you tomorrow when you go to work, when you march or drill, when you who must travel begin your journey! Let every day re-echo the rejoicing of the first Christmas: *"Fear not; for, behold, I bring you good tidings of great joy, which shall be to all people. For unto you is born this day in the city of David a Savior, which is Christ the Lord"!*

On this last Sunday of a year which not only reminds us of our steady approach either to hell or — God grant it! — to heaven, but which also serves as a time for spiritual inventory, look deep down into your souls! Many of you, I know, will admit that, unlike Mary, you have not kept the Christmas truth. You have lost the greatest treasure you can ever own. You had God-fearing parents. They taught you to believe that Jesus came to save you. You prayed to Him, and for years you trusted Him. Then something tragic happened. Usually it was prosperity, with pleasure seeking, luxurious living, the quick, easy making of money that crowded Him from your life; and though many of you seem successful in the sight of man, you are bankrupt in the eyes of the Almighty, because you have not kept Christ. Before it is too late — and think of the sudden deaths during the past days:

boulders hurtling down a Pennsylvania hill to destroy almost all the passengers in a large bus; a family, driving to Christmas exercises in a public school, killed in a crash with an onrushing train; a commanding general in Africa shot down by an assassin's bullet — these and hundreds of other deaths, without mentioning the heroic sacrifices on the field of battle, appeal to you personally: "Delay not! Delay not! Come to the infant Redeemer contritely, confessing your sins, trusting Him completely! He will forgive, restore and strengthen you to keep His glorious Gospel." This week a letter from Texas told me that a man who grew up in the shadow of our Seminary and who was once ardent in the faith but for more than twenty-five years without Jesus and against Him has now been reclaimed for the Lord by the power of the Holy Spirit using this mission of the air. May the same Comforter now speak living words of invitation and appeal into many hearts throughout this land — into your soul, even if you have turned from Jesus thirty-five, forty-five, fifty-five or more years ago! Come back to the manger during this radiant Christmas season with the holy resolve that, God's Spirit sustaining you, you will guard every assurance of the Savior's love as your priceless possession! Keep Christ in your family circle! Fathers, think of Mary, a weak woman with outstanding strength of devotion; and before the old year closes, resolve with Joshua, "As for me and my house, we will serve the Lord"! Keep the Gospel in your churches! Keep Christ on the air! Battle determinately against every sinister, un-American, anti-Christian movement that would bar broadcasts like our Bringing Christ to the Nations in a day when our boys are shedding their blood to preserve the freedom of religion!

II

CONSTANTLY PONDER THE CHRISTMAS BLESSING!

Mary not only *"kept all these things"* as a person treasures a costly jewel or a rare painting, but we know that she also *"pondered them in her heart."* Constantly her thoughts dwelt on the angel's promise that her son was God's Son, a King whose rule would know no end. He would be called *"Jesus,"* the wonderful name which means "Savior." Household duties, of course, demanded much of her time. Her Child needed her motherly care. There were no servants in Joseph's humble home. Mary did all the cooking and baking, the cleaning and mending, the spinning and weaving. She never neglected her domestic tasks; yet she found time constantly to reflect on divine mercy. Not a day passed at Bethlehem, on the difficult flight into Egypt and the hazardous return journey, in the Nazareth household, without having her thoughts wing their way back to that first Christmas.

Here, too, Mary is a model for all Christian wives and mothers. Ten times as many women work in war industry today as a year ago; and while we pay tribute to their patriotism, this change brings acute problems to religious and home life. We read of children, locked in a room, burned to death while their parents worked at a defense plant. Much more widespread is the increase of domestic trouble owing to the mother's absence from the family. No wife should unnecessarily take the place of an unmarried worker; the Government must do more to provide adequate practical help and direction for the children of defense workers. How tragic to win the war on the battle front but lose it on the home front! The mother who keeps her house tidy, sees to it that her husband has warm, well-cooked meals when he comes home from work, keeps her children clean, their clothing neat and mended, their manners courteous and polite, their souls turned to the Lord Jesus, and still takes time, like Mary, to ponder the promise of divine love, is rendering a service to American morale which, although often unrecognized and unapplauded, is as necessary as any uniformed service to which women are admitted.

God give us all much more of that pondering spirit, for too often people refuse to consider personally, seriously, unbiasedly, the claims of Christ on their souls! You may smile indulgently at the Scotch woman who, too poor ever to have seen any paper money, received letters from her soldier son containing bank notes, which she thought were simply pretty pictures. But are not many of you guilty of far more serious misunderstandings? You received many Christmas greeting cards, some of them, I feel sure, with pictures of Bethlehem's Babe and words of Scripture. Did you take time to ponder the meaning of that Child, to read and believe those passages? They are divine promissory notes, these Bible truths, which pledge, *"God so loved the world that He gave His only begotten Son, that whosoever believeth in Him should not perish, but have everlasting life."* The bank of heaven always keeps its pledge; yet they meant nothing to you.

What do you suppose helped Mary daily recall the remarkable happenings of the first Christmas? She was no superwoman, she was flesh and blood as you are; and with God's help you can do what she did. Continually she thought of the Lord Jesus because she had the Christ Child with her day and night. She herself nursed that holy Infant. Her own hands bathed and clothed Him. She sang Him to sleep with her own lullabies. She cuddled Him to her breast, fondled Him with her arms, kissed Him with her lips. Her precious Babe was constantly before her to remind her every moment of God's marvelous mercy. You, too, can keep the Savior before you in the repeated promises of His Word. Within the covers of your Scripture is the whole story of salvation told so plainly that even a child can find its way to heaven. Read it! Ponder it!

As the old year hastens on to its end, may you who have not lived it with Jesus realize that you have had time for yourself but not for Christ; time for your body but not for your soul; time for amusement but not for spiritual growth; time for sin but not for grace; time for falsehood but not for truth; time for Satan but not for the Savior; time to cause others untold suffering but not to bring them happiness; time to read unclean stories and lust-laden magazines but not to read the Word of God and clean, constructive literature; time to drive your soul to hell but no time to find the one way to heaven in the Christ Child. Before these twelve months run out into the unchangeable past of all history, I plead with you: For your soul's salvation take time, blessed time, to behold that Babe long and lovingly! Ask yourself: "Who is this Child of Bethlehem, and what does He mean to me?" Out of the miracle and the mercy of divine love comes the answer "He is your God, the almighty Lord of the universe, who loved you with the divine affection that made Him come into the world to take your place in fulfilling the divine Law you have broken, to become your Substitute in removing the curse of death, your Ransom in paying the debt of sin you by yourself could never pay." — Repeat the questions: "Who is this Holy Child? What is He to me?" And the divine Word replies, "He is your Savior, whose unlimited, unconditioned, unpurchasable pardon and peace are granted you without payment or price, freely and forever." — Inquire again: "Who is this cradled Child? What does He mean to me?" And divine truth responds, "He is your Friend, who helps when human friends give way, whose love kindles the warmth of comfort, the hope of deliverance, the assurance of heavenly joy in all life's heaviness and sorrow." — Put the pointed question once more, "Who is this Child, predicted by prophets and proclaimed by angels?" O my fellow redeemed, as the embers of the dying year burn in their last brightness, listen closely, every one of you, my countrymen at home and abroad, you men and women in the armed forces who hear these messages on the firing lines of the Pacific, in the lonely outposts of the Aleutians, on the bleak Alaskan frontiers, in remote sections of our own country, in Canada, Mexico, the West Indies, South America, the British Isles, and in other distant places — this Child is your Ransom from ruin, your resistance to temptation, your Path to purity, your Promise of a new and better life on this earth, your Pledge of resurrection glory in heaven! Keep Him, and He will keep you, through life's fleeting years and death's darkness, safe for a radiant eternity. We ask this old and new year's blessing confidently, for we plead in His blessed name. Amen.

A New Heart for the
New Year

> "*Create in me a clean heart, O God, and renew a right spirit within me!*"
> PSALM 51:10

O God, Truly Our Help in the Past, Assuredly Our Hope for the Future:

On this first Sunday of the new year we come before Thee in our Savior's name to beseech Thy guidance and protection during the trying days ahead for our country, our churches, our homes, and ourselves. We have not gone this way before, and we need Jesus every hour to pardon our sins and to walk by our side. We need the Holy Spirit to remove our fears, destroy our doubts, and grant us divine comfort. We need Thee, heavenly Father, to defend us against all evil by day and night. If we have to face the coming twelve months alone, meet the terror of war in our own strength, fight the evil without Thy support, O God of glory, grace, and majesty, we will indeed be helpless and pitiable. Therefore come to us and bring us to Thee! Call many to Christ through the preaching of Thy pure Word, and for the new year grant us all new hearts, new consecrated lives, new faith, new courage! Hear us and help us every day for the Savior's sake! Amen.

EVERY day during the new year, until the Almighty answers our prayers, we should constantly plead: "O God of all mercy, put an end to the war! Stop this bloodshed, so that our men and women in the armed forces may return from India, Africa, the South Sea Islands, the Aleutians, from the sixty-five countries to which our troops have been transported! O God of all power, who didst send Thy Son to lay down His life for our redemption, grant us a just, equitable, righteous peace, with the triumph of truth and the defeat of evil, the restoration of liberty and the freedom to worship Thee! O triune God give us a victory that will not provoke further bloodshed, but bring the nations more closely together! We ask it, according to Thy will, in Jesus' name."

Not everyone will join in this prayer, of course. Some will continue to forget the power of intercession. Others will refuse to petition peace because they want more war. They have larger incomes than ever before. Why should they wish this sudden prosperity checked? Why, indeed, unless they could hear the wounded scream in agony, see bodies torn with shrapnel, visit hospitals filled with sufferers who have lost sight or limbs! Still others will reject this pleading for peace because they deny the existence of the Almighty and ridicule the mere mention of Christian prayer.

This we-don't-need-God spirit has produced a boastful overconfidence which leaves the Lord entirely out of the country's future. In its December issue a year ago a national magazine printed predictions for the twelve months just closed, written not by amateurs but by acclaimed radio commentators, military experts, public figures. Even a few days before hostilities were declared, not one of them definitely foresaw war with Japan. Several boasted emphatically that, should Japan attack us, it would be completely wiped out within a short time. Today, as we witness the complete failure of these expert prophecies which left God out of their reckoning, we ought to understand that, while no man can foretell what will happen during the months ahead, if we are to enjoy true peace, real blessing for ourselves and our country, we must have God on our side; and if the Lord is to rule national life, as well as individual hearts and homes during the new year, ours must be a repentant, trusting faith in Jesus. We must turn from our sins to His salvation; we must come before our heavenly Father in the Savior's name with clean hearts, the *"right spirit"* of reverent trust, and new, Christ-dedicated lives. If we would meet courageously any adversity this twelvemonth may bring; if we would triumph over the temptation that its victory and prosperity may produce; if we would find comfort for suffering and confidence in calamity, let this be our plea and our assurance:

A NEW HEART FOR THE NEW YEAR!

May we, as David in our text (Psalm fifty-one, verse ten), refusing to rely on ourselves, turn to Heaven and plead, *"Create in me a clean heart, O God, and renew a right spirit within me!"*

I

WE NEED A NEW HEART

This prayer was prompted by David's remorse over a deep crime. He had taken the wife of one of his officers, Uriah, and then by devilish design had sent him to a battle front where he was sure to be killed. — What a pointed warning every one of us should find in David's planned murder! If the sweet singer of Israel, the king close to God, the ruler with whom the Almighty spoke repeatedly, the prophet who foresaw the Savior's crucifixion and resurrection, could descend to the depths of such wickedness, treachery, and lust, how can we, with our evil natures and desires, boast that it is impossible for us to fall into iniquity and crime? Do you think that because of your church membership you are above committing a terrifying transgression? Do you feel confident because you are a minister of God and wear clerical robes that the destructive passions smoldering in your breast cannot break forth in consuming flame? *"Let him that thinketh he standeth take heed lest he fall!"* On the other hand, what sustaining comfort to know that, since David, home-breaker and murderer, could be forgiven and restored to divine grace, you, too, can have the positive assurance, *"Though your sins be as scarlet, they shall be white as snow; though they be red like crimson, they shall be as wool"*!

For this pardon you must follow the Psalmist's penitent faith. He knows and admits that his old heart, crowded with sinful longings, impure impulses, is foul and filthy. He makes no attempt to justify, explain, or excuse his crime. He does not claim that the king can do no wrong or that, as ruler of Israel, he is above the law. No; in penitent prayer he turns to God and pleads, *"Create in me a clean heart, O God, and renew a right spirit within me!"*

If only every one of us were guided by the same realization of our personal iniquities and sin's sordid, destructive power! Instead our perverse age has popularized, glorified, even glamorized the transgressions of the divine Law. Public entertainment — look at your newspapers! — applauds impurity. Men and women of many matrimonial ventures can become the idols of millions. An authoress who smuggles a soldier from camp is arrested; but the same woman, whose books can take decency from the hearts of young readers, is rewarded with huge royalties and wide acclaim. The Bible warns us that abusing God's name is a heavy sin, which provokes divine vengeance; yet our puffed-up generation regards profanity as a sign of red-blooded manhood. A New York daily, often considered the outstanding newspaper in our country, declares itself ready to print the profanity of a high Government official or Army commander, provided it is not too violent — as if the cursing of men in prominent positions were not far more dangerous than others' misuse of the divine name! Again, the Scriptures ask children to obey their parents and those in authority; yet many distinguished, eagerly heard educators and sociologists ridicule the Biblical command and insist that boys and girls follow their own whims, be permitted to grow up without discipline! What a heavy payment our country must now make in retribution! Juvenile crime is more serious and widespread than ever before. Kansas City, for example, records an increase of 107 per cent in the seventeen-year-old class! Yet when young offenders are haled before court, they are often dismissed with the instruction to read *Huckleberry Finn!*

At a time when the most widely attended plays are frequently the dirtiest and the most popular novels often the most suggestive, we can understand that the public denunciation of sin is the weakest. Indeed, by systematic falsehood, sin is disguised as attractive, alluring. Here are some of these vicious untruths: Lie Number One: "Why not enjoy life?" young people, and especially military men, are asked. "You do not know what will happen to you. Why not take a final fling and squeeze every drop of pleasure from the little of life that may remain?" But what of the accusing, torturing conscience, the searing memories of sin, the injury and suffering it brings others? Lie Number Two: "No one will ever find out." Yet God's eyes behold everything. They pierce your flesh and bone to search the secret thoughts in your heart. Lie Number Three: "You can get by and escape consequences." So the gangsters killed in Chicago last week thought, when several months ago they shot their way out of prison.

If the FBI's long arm recaptures convicts, can you elude the arm of divine vengeance? Lie Number Four: "Sin is not serious. In fact, it often brings a reward." However, sin never pays, but the unforgiven sinner always pays.

Sin has burdened the whole world. Early missionaries to the New Hebrides noticed that native women, leaving their homes to draw water or work on plantations, bore heavy, pressing loads on their backs. Inquiry revealed that they carried with them their household valuables, including even the chickens, lest these be stolen during their absence. Similarly, sin has brought suspicion and hardship throughout the world. It has set nation against nation, for every war, including the present conflict, comes as divine visitation. Sin has produced untold sorrow, reverses, and punishment, for God warns, *"I will punish the world for their evil, and the wicked for their iniquity!"* His judgment never fails. Sin has changed man, made in the Creator's image, holy and righteous, into a creature of unholiness and unrighteousness. It curses his labor with opposition, disappointment, and exhaustion. It causes sickness, disease, and finally death. It has filled him with evil and made him incapable of any good thought or helpful action. It has split homes, torn husbands and wives apart, separated parents from children. It has divided Christ's Church into scores of opposing groups. Above all, sin, unremoved, closes the gates to heaven. The Bible decrees, *"Know ye not that the unrighteous shall not inherit the kingdom of God?"* Whatever men say of sin; however they seek to excuse, disguise, minimize, or exalt it, God's true Word declares: First, *"All have sinned."* Second, *"The soul that sinneth, it shall die."* The Almighty is so holy that no one with unforgiven transgressions can ever stand before His throne. If we would approach the Lord of heaven, our unclean hearts must be changed and cleansed. Our evil, destructive spirit must be made new and right. Therefore David pleads, *"Create in me a clean heart, O God, and renew a right spirit within me!"*

With the same emphasis on inner renewal Jesus declares, *"Ye must be born again."* He wants more than a mending, patching, repairing of our old iniquitous lives. His Word demands, *"Put off . . . the old man . . . and . . . put on the new man!"* Though we were born in sin, we must be reborn to righteousness. That means more than living a polite, outwardly honorable life which, as far as men can see, avoids *"the lust of the flesh,"* spurns drunkenness, contributes to charities, and heaps up virtues. You can do all this and much more, and yet remain outside God's kingdom. If your hope of eternity is built only on such respectability; if you forget your secret faults; if you refuse to admit that your whole existence is marred by many and deep-rooted sins, that your mind produces unclean thoughts, your heart often beats with hateful, greedy impulses, you are still far from the kingdom of God. You must have a *"new heart." "Ye must be born again."* Suppose you had an apple tree that yielded wild, stunted, sour fruit; would you be satisfied with painting the bark white, spraying the foliage, pruning the tree, watering it regularly? You could do this every day as long as the tree lived, and it would still grow the same disagreeable fruit. In only one way can you make the tree produce a good harvest: graft a new twig from a good apple tree. Similarly, God must graft new life into us.

Neither is it sufficient, if we would be saved for eternity, that we are merely convinced of our sins; that we realize and confess our repeated transgressions of God's Law. Judas knew the enormity of his betrayal better than anyone else, but he ended in despair, a suicide. Since his day scoffers have found themselves in terrifying agony when the full realization of their folly dawned on them. Sir Francis Newport, who had received early religious training, only later to become an infidel, exclaimed on his deathbed: "Whence this war in my heart? . . . Do I assert that there is no hell, while I feel one in my own bosom? Am I certain that there is no after retribution, when I feel a present judgment? . . . Wretch that I am, whither shall I fly from my heart? What will become of me?" — That is the question many of you should ask yourselves, "What will become of me unless my heart is changed and I am 'born again' into spiritual newness?"

Hear David's plea once more, *"Create in me a clean heart, O God, and renew a right spirit within me!"* to understand that the change which brings you to the Lord, the conversion which saves you from death and hell, starts with your innermost life! Realize what Jesus meant when He directed, *"Cleanse first that which is within the cup!"* Attending divine services, holding church offices, singing in the choir, leading young people's organizations — as commendable as all this is — will not insure you a place in heaven. You need a *"new heart"!* *"Ye must be born again."* Family advantages, the love of a God-fearing husband or wife, the guidance of believing fathers and mothers, church papers, Christian art in the home — who will deny the good these can accomplish? Yet alone they are no guarantee that God will receive you. A Christian wife cannot redeem an infidel husband. Believing parents cannot rescue their unbelieving children. You yourself must have a *"new heart."* *"Ye must be born again."*

Do you object: "I have been baptized. What more

do I need?" — You can destroy baptismal blessing by rebellion against the Lord, by cruelty toward your fellow men, by sin against yourself. Baptism without faith is no pledge of pardon. Do you insist: "I pray. What more do I need?" — Jesus Himself warns, *"Not every one that saith unto Me, Lord, Lord, shall enter into the kingdom of heaven."* People all over the earth today are praying hard and long, but in the wrong way, without hope of answer. — Do you try to justify yourself by claiming: "I read the Bible. What more do I need?" Not every one who studies the Scriptures will be saved. Bible critics who have devoted their lifework to finding fault with Holy Writ have examined its pages with greater intensity than most of you know. If you are to be acceptable in God's sight, you must have a new, *"clean heart." "Ye must be born again."* Do not fall into the serious error which tells our military men that, if they die in battle, no matter what they believe, they will find quick entrance into heaven! A United States general sent a message to American mothers who had lost their sons, promising them that God would take these dead warriors to Himself. It is a clear violation of our Christian faith to assert that anyone can be saved by dying in defense of his country. That is Mohammedanism, but not Christianity. The Scriptures declare with the same force to you men in the armed services as to us civilians, *"Ye must be born again."*

Throughout the new year and all your days on earth keep this vital, life-or-death, heaven-or-hell alternative clearly and constantly in mind! For your rescue from sin, you need more than what men call "a good life." High intention and New Year's resolutions are not sufficient. Bravery and patriotism; membership in a Sunday school, Bible class, or church; confirmation and church rituals, are not enough. Religious emotions and enthusiasm are not enough. Morning and evening prayers — all these are not enough. — They can be glorious gifts of God and privileges of faith; but if they are contradicted by unbelief, unforgiven sin, they only make the charges against you at the bar of divine justice the more serious. First and foremost you need to be cleansed completely, re-created spiritually. You must have a *"new heart." "Ye must be born again."*

II

CHRIST CAN GIVE US A NEW HEART

Now, if *"a master of Israel"* acquainted with the Scripture once asked Jesus, *"How can a man be born when he is old?"* doubtless the question you are waiting to ask is, "How can I secure this *'clean heart,'* this *'right spirit'?"* Surgery, particularly during this generation, has performed remarkable heart operations, and doctors now know more about this vital organ than ever before. But no scalpel can cut deeply enough to remove sin. No cardiac specialist can cleanse the heart from the stain of inherited and committed wrong.

Nor is there hope in learning. When we witness the irreligion and immorality produced by modern theories of education; when we find college men behind penitentiary bars, titled university graduates master minds of crime, we realize that our culture, although it can mold the mind, cannot change the heart. New York City has seen a wide rebellion within the public-school system. Instructors were seriously injured, their eyes blackened, their faces scratched by the pupils. A few were more brutally assaulted. One was murdered by a pupil. This may be only the beginning of what we can expect on a far wider scale when more of the atheistic-Communistic revolt against law and order sickers down to our elementary and high-school youth, in fulfillment of those prophecies concerning the last times: "Many will be *'disobedient to parents.'* Many will be *'ever learning, and never able to come to the knowledge of the truth.'*"

Is there any assurance for this age in evolution, the claim that men are perpetually raising themselves to higher levels, that civilization is marching on to greater self-improvement? No other generation in American history has beheld the folly of that delusion as clearly as we. True, we have made progress in engineering and aeronautics, transportation and communication, but not in holiness, brotherly love, international understanding, and racial harmony. We have discovered multiplied means of making life easier and more comfortable, but no human methods for moral progress or spiritual betterment. Despite roseate claims to the contrary, the world is not growing better. It is becoming worse. With increasing insistence its depravity calls upon the Lord to return and put an end to the disorder which makes men, at the zenith of their achievement, drop lower than the beasts. Even jungle animals know when to stop fighting; but one World War has not been sufficient for our haughty age. This theory of man's brute ancestry (taught to many of your sons and daughters in tax-supported schools), the fallacy which makes us creatures of chance, mere human animals, as all errors, holds out no hope whatever for a *"clean heart"* and a new, *"right spirit."*

To secure that inner change, which no man, not even the most learned and virtuous can give us; to receive the blessing which no angel, not even the mightiest archangel can bestow; to be born again with a *"new heart,"* we must turn, with David, to the Lord. As the Psalmist prays, *"Create in me a clean heart, O God,"* so we, too, must push aside all questions and doubts, every false thought of our own merit or moral achievements, and approach the Almighty in these opening days of the new year, beseeching Him, with whom *"nothing shall be impossible,"* for a *"new heart"* and a reborn spiritual life. King David could foresee only dimly, at the distance of a thousand years, the glorious means by which the Lord would grant him that newness. How much more blessed are we who in faith can stand beneath our Savior's cross to learn this marvelous power of His atoning love, *"He died for all"!* The sins that burden your life, keep you from heaven, and sentence you to hell; the iniquity which neither you nor anyone else can ever remove — these transgressions in their immeasurable vastness, Jesus removed from you, Himself bore their entire guilt and endured their eternal punishment at Calvary. For you He fulfilled to the last letter God's Law, which you daily break, paid the penalty of your sins, and restored you to your heavenly Father.

Whatever else the new year may bestow on you — money, praise, recognition — if it does not bring you faith in the sin-bearing Redeemer, it will leave you poor and pitiable. Whatever you suffer under the multitude of trials the coming months may heap upon you, if you have Jesus, the Burden-bearer, the Sorrow-sharer, you are strong and rich in spirit. On this first Lord's Day of the new twelvemonth I beg of you, in the name of Him who can crown this year with a mighty benediction for you, accept your Savior now!

God has not only redeemed us through Christ, His Spirit also grants us a glorious rebirth. The Almighty has done everything *for* us by granting us Jesus; He has done everything *in* us by giving us a new heart. Hear it once more: our conversion and regeneration is all the Lord's work. He sent the Savior. He puts trust in that Redeemer into our hearts. He changes our lives through this faith.

From the very moment that Jesus takes control of your life, you are reborn in Him. His inviolable truth pledges, *"If any man be in Christ, he is a new creature: old things are passed away; behold, all things are become new."* You who without the Savior are slaves of sin, with Him can become liberated children of God. Now you are under divine wrath; but in Jesus you come under divine grace. Talk about the startling changes of our age! They are not to be compared with the marvels of this new birth. Debate the possibility of miracles! Is anything more striking than the conversion by which God's enemies become His friends, blasphemers learn to sing His praise? Of course this is no change into absolute perfection; for as long as we live in a world of sin, we will never be completely free from its taint. We can, however, join John Newton, marvelously brought from ruin to redemption, in declaring: "I am not what I ought to be. I am not what I want to be. I am not what I hope to be in another world. Still I am not what I once used to be, and by the grace of God I am what I am," namely, one of Christ's redeemed, with a new loathing of sin, a new desire to follow Jesus and turn from wicked men, a new courage to face life's uncertainties, a new joy when afflictions crush me, a new zeal to fight evil and resist temptation, a new freedom from doubt and fear, a new devotion to humanity, a new interest in home and finally, a new fervor to contribute to the nation the exalting righteousness it needs in this harassed hour, altogether a completely new and eternally blessed existence!

O pray Jesus today for that renewed spirit, the *"clean heart,"* the second birth, the regenerated life, because He Himself has unmistakably warned us, *"Except a man be born of water and of the Spirit, he cannot enter into the kingdom of God"!* If David had not turned to God with this prayer and trusted the coming Messiah to restore and recreate him, he would have been lost forever, even though he was a powerful king and once served the Lord with a holy zeal. No matter who you are, how high your position, how wholeheartedly you once took part in the Lord's work, if you have fallen from grace and remain estranged from God, you cannot see *"the kingdom of God,"* let alone enter it. There is no other way to heaven than Christ's way, and He says, *"Ye must be born again."*

It would be blessed indeed, particularly during days of stress and nights of worry like these, if masses in our country would turn to the Lord Jesus! Diplomats and statesmen argue for this or that new order, when in truth the only real newness any people can have or need is a spiritual rebirth. As experts outline the conditions of peace before the war is won, we ought to remind ourselves that, unless Christ's Spirit has its place at the conference tables, nothing is more certain than that a struggle of even greater scope can follow the present international conflict as soon as the belligerents have recuperated. The only guarantee against the early outbreak of World War III, under God's grace, is the *"clean heart"* and the *"right spirit"* for which David prayed three thousand years ago. Missionary history shows that, whenever countries have accepted the Christian religion and its people have been led by Jesus' ideals, an entirely new life has dawned, with a high morality instead of widespread ruin, education in place of ignorance, progress rather than superstition. On one of the Samoan Islands, Pentecost Sunday, 1862, more than five thousand natives, warriors and chiefs were gathered with King George, their ruler. Practically all these thousands had been born as heathen, many of them even cannibals, but on that day they pledged themselves to the Lord Jesus. From that time heathendom, polygamy, cannibalism, witchcraft were doomed, and the islands, utterly changed, became model communities, governed by the love of God. How marvelous if in our own beloved country, the most richly blessed of nations, our gratitude to Christ would be shown by millions' turning to the Savior in humble faith! The benedictions of peace and prosperity that were ours when America, young and fervent in its trust, clung closely to the Redeemer could be restored. — Do you love your country and want to contribute to its moral and spiritual strength? Above all, do you seek courage for life and strength for death, the assurance of your salvation and the pledge of heaven? Then repeat David's prayer and ask the Lord today for that rebirth in Christ's redemptive love! Because Jesus promises this blessing through faith in His Word and by the cleansing of baptism, I invite those who have never been baptized to receive this *"washing of regeneration."* The Savior Himself declared, *"He that believeth and is baptized shall be saved."* His Word assures us, *"Baptism doth also now save us."* Scripture calls out, *"Arise and be baptized and wash away thy sins!"* Let us send you a Christian pastor, one in the mighty army of my co-workers, who will instruct you and your household for the blessings of church membership!

What a glorious year this can be for you through that radiant rebirth! With Christ you will have light during the darkest hours. For the most grievous sins you will find forgiveness in His blood. Amid the deepest sorrows the Holy Spirit will put a song of gladness on your lips. If death enters the family circle, you can look beyond the grave to life. If this year is the last for you on earth, it will be the first for you in heaven. Therefore, my beloved, God wants me to ask pointedly: "Are you truly *'born again'*? Have you a *'clean heart'* and *'a right spirit'*?" Do not side-step or postpone the answer! Do not surrender to despair, as though your sins were too scarlet! Do not let doubt dominate your spirit! Come to the mercy seat! Kneel humbly but fervently before Jesus! Repeat David's plea, *"Create in me a clean heart, O God, and renew a right spirit within me!"* and from the love that never makes a mistake, never spurns a penitent sinner, never bars or excludes, comes the answer written in God's own Word, but positively penned for you, the promise of the great and glorious Creator, Redeemer, Sustainer, the word that now would wing its way into your soul, *"A new heart also will I give you!"* Believe that and be saved! Amen!

The Strongest Secret Weapon, Christian Prayer!

> *"When thou prayest, enter into thy closet, and when thou hast shut thy door, pray to thy Father which is in secret; and thy Father, which seeth in secret, shall reward thee openly."*
>
> SAINT MATTHEW 6:6

God of All Grace:

Help us believe firmly that despite our sins we can always and everywhere approach Thee through prayer in Christ's name and assuredly find blessed answer according to Thy will! Forgive us, for the Savior's sake our neglect of communing with Thee, our insincerity and hypocrisy, as well as our many other disloyalties! Cancel and remove them all, merciful God, because we trust in the atoning death of Thy Son, our Redeemer! Bring many to that saving confidence, particularly the men and women of our fighting forces, who take our places on the battle lines! Let the promise of peace strengthen their hearts! Show them what a heavenly Deliverer Jesus is, what a privilege they can have in carrying all their needs to Him through fervent pleading! Make us a repentant, prayerful people! Bless this day particularly those who sorrow because of their transgressions or stagger under heavy burdens! Without Thee, O Triune God, we can do nothing. With Thee hope and heaven are ours. Come to us, then, and bless us for Jesus' sake! Amen.

Ever since the beginning of the Second World War we have read repeated predictions of a secret weapon. Three years ago Hitler boasted that he had a startling means of defeating his enemies, but we have failed to witness any proof of its existence. The French proudly announced that they had undisclosed guns, which would blast their foes into retreat; yet their country collapsed despite this much-vaunted artillery. In our own nation an air-force officer recently told mechanical engineers that our secret planes are "enough to make the angels gasp." But angels do not gasp. If they did, it would be to express dismay at such irreverence. Our cause is ill served by such flippancy.

Nor is America's secret weapon our sense of humor, as a full-page newspaper advertisement proclaims, glorifying comic strips and asserting that, as long as our people can laugh, we shall be victorious. You parents ought to realize, however, that not much laughter is afforded by some of these comic pages, which reveal to your children the technique of crime, the language of the underworld. Besides, merriment will never win the war. Victory will truly take tears and sweat and blood.

Yet there *is* a powerful secret weapon, and everyone of us can wield it in our country's defense as well as for the defeat of any dark force. Captain Rickenbacker found it. Describing his twenty-three days on a raft in the Pacific, he wrote: "We organized little prayer meetings in the evening and morning. . . . Frankly and humbly we prayed for deliverance. Pangs of hunger showed up, and we prayed for food. . . . Within an hour after the prayer meeting a sea gull came in and landed on my head . . . and we had food." Mrs. Ethel Bell, adrift with her two children for nineteen days on the South Atlantic, used that secret weapon. She stated: "Every morning and as the sun set, the children and I would sing hymns and say our prayers. We never doubted that our prayers for rescue would be answered." And they were rescued. Ruth Straub, of the Army Nurses Corps, reported that Bataan's brave defenders discovered courageous strength in this secret weapon. Her diary revealed: "There is not an atheist on Bataan. When the bombs come, every one lies on the ground and prays aloud, regardless of who is around." Private Hollinger, who with five companions staggered through harrowing days and terrifying nights in a Solomon Island jungle, knew that secret weapon. He exclaimed: "We just prayed evening and morning. Believe me, we did a lot of praying." And they were saved. Similarly, for the defeat of formidable foes mobilized against our souls, for the strengthening of our hopes, for the protection of our nation, we, too, have a marvelous, superhuman, divine power in

THE STRONGEST SECRET WEAPON, CHRISTIAN PRAYER!

For this victorious promise we turn to Christ's own words in Saint Matthew, chapter six, verse six: *"When thou prayest, enter into thy closet, and when thou hast shut thy door, pray to thy Father which is in secret; and thy Father, which seeth in secret, shall reward thee openly."*

I

THE NATURE OF THIS PRAYER

Note that Jesus devotes no time to prove that His followers must beseech divine help! To Him prayer is as necessary for the spiritual life as breath is for our physical life, the sun for bodily growth, or water for the development of plants and trees. If your spiritual stature is stunted; if you suffer one punishing blow after the other; if cherished plans collapse in a sudden moment, may the trouble not be this, that you are pushing God to one side, trying to carve your own career, rejecting prayer as unmanly? How foolish and fatal, particularly in times of war — this proud, boastful claim that you do not need the Almighty! How puny and helpless men are, with all their vaunted strength, when God's ice and His snow storms put proud battalions to rout, when the angry ocean crushes mighty battleships! You need not argue the necessity of supplication with most men on the firing line. A national news magazine reports, "The closer you get to the front, the more you pray to God." On the brighter side of the present scene is the fact that never before has prayer been mentioned in our newspapers with as frequent approval as now in World War II. It is, therefore, of surpassing importance that we know without question or doubt how rightly to invoke the help we need.

For this direction we must turn — not to human teachers, men who promise that, if we wish long and intensely enough, we shall surely receive what we want; to scientists who have studied the habits of semicivilized people and advance theories of prayer evolution; to Modernists with their own individual anti-Scriptural theories of intercession. For the true assurance of answer we must come to the Lord Jesus Christ. He is our God. He never makes a mistake. Think of it — in a score of passages Jesus gives us prayer instruction! And more! He not only taught us how to come before God, He also put His teaching into practice. Well do we sing, "Learn of Jesus Christ to pray!" for no one has ever pleaded with the power and blessing that mark our Lord's supplication.

The Savior's first great prayer lesson, and one that lies at the base of our text today, asks us to direct our entreaties only to the true God: to His Father, to Himself, to the sanctifying Holy Spirit. It is of no import in what language men speak their entreaties, how eloquent or simple, how long or short, how loud or soft their supplications. It matters nothing where they plead, whether at work or at worship, in church or at home, on journeys or in sickbeds. If prayer is to be answered, it must come before the Creator who gave us our existence, the Savior who redeemed us, the Sanctifier who preserves us — the triune God revealed in Sacred Scripture. When it was recently announced that Emperor Hirohito knelt before the shrine of his ancestress, the sun goddess, Amaterasu, to inform her of the war's progress and beseech her aid in victory, millions in America laughed at the very thought of a fictitious, heathen goddess helping our enemies. Yet multitudes within our own boundaries make a similar mistake. Either their pleas are directed to an entirely unknown being as they cry out, "O God, whoever, wherever, and whatever thou art!" or they address a supreme spirit, a mind of the ages, an architect of the universe, in such a way that they clearly reject the one God; or they send their supplications to human beings who have died and passed into the next world. But all the while the Lord clearly instructs us, *"Call upon* ME!"

Christ's second lesson in intercession, and again one which underlies our text, emphasizes that every request to God should be made in Jesus' name. This means far more, of course, than merely to close your supplication with the phrase, "This we ask in Jesus' name." You must have the firm conviction which recognizes that you, in your sins, cannot come before the Lord in His holiness; that, while human names designate those who *"have sinned and come short of the glory of God,"* "Jesus" is the name of your Redeemer, who by shedding His blood and dying the death of all sinners on the cross completely cleansed you of all guilt, took away the curse and eternal punishment of your iniquities, and through faith makes you spotless and stainless in His heavenly Father's sight. Therefore, if you are Christ's, God will receive you when you approach Him in prayer. My fellow redeemed, in this solemn moment He wants me to ask you whether you thus know Jesus as your Savior. You need Him more than anyone else. What can we do to help you realize that without Him you are lost completely, lost hopelessly, lost forever, but that with Christ you have forgiveness, life, and salvation? Is there any aid we or the thousands of pastors working shoulder to shoulder with us can offer, so that you will learn more of Jesus and with His assistance tear yourself loose from sin's entanglement? When David Rittenhouse, Pennsylvania astronomer, measured immense planets, he found that a small silk thread stretched across the large lens of his telescope could cover even a star of the first magnitude. Are you kept from beholding Jesus' magnificent mercy because some secret or favorite sin, which you regard as small and inconsequential, is obscuring Christ's radiant love? Ask the Spirit to help you remove anything that prevents you from seeing your salvation! How wonderful beyond words, when your iniquities are taken away, to have a new start in life and daily to behold Jesus as He gives you His limitless grace *"without money and without price,"* without condition or credential!

If you have that faith, nothing can prevent you from approaching Christ. No man-made barrier, no decree of dictators, no prison walls, no pronouncement of proud churches, no feeling of your own unworthiness, no racial prejudices, no consciousness of the most terrifying iniquity need keep you from praying to the Lord.

It is to be regretted that public prayers sometimes ignore Christ as though He never lived and died for our sins. Altogether too frequently that name above all names, at which *"every knee should bow,"* is deliberately omitted to please people who hate the Savior. But if we

sidestep Jesus, can we blame Him if He sidesteps us?
Thank God, many of our soldiers show outstanding loyalty! The Cleveland *Press* tells the story of Richard
Gourley, an eighteen-year-old marine from that city,
wounded in a bloody Guadalcanal battle, who declares:
"We pray, and we don't just say, 'Our Father who art in
heaven.' We pray like this, 'Jesus Christ, help us!' " The
whole country should have that young marine's spirit.
Some of you need it with double urgency. How long before you will accept the Savior? Will it be necessary that
you face enemy fire by day and bombing by night?
Must you be torn from your self-confidence by the crash
of affliction? May you realize the curse of sin and then,
turning to Jesus and His grace, understand this loving
promise, *"Whatsoever ye shall ask the Father in My
name, He will give it you"!*

Because we pray in Jesus' name, we must plead humbly, penitently, with the contrite spirit of the publican
who, hardly daring to raise his eyes to the Lord, could
only beg, *"God be merciful to me a sinner!"* In our petitions we must become nothing, but Christ everything.
We should say to God, *"We are the clay, and Thou our
Potter."* We should look to Jesus, as did John the Baptist,
and resolve, *"He must increase, but I must decrease."*

When we pray in the Savior's name, we must plead
in the spirit of reconciliation and forgiveness. We cannot
ask God to remit our offenses if we, in turn, refuse to
pardon those who injured us. You parents who have banished your children because they made a serious misstep;
you church members who refuse to speak to fellow Christians because they have hurt you, listen: Do not expect
mercy from the Lord if you continually decline to extend
compassion to others. Nor should you hope for an answer to prayer if you are living in unforgiven sin, oppress-

ing your fellow men, bringing sorrow to your husband or wife, working in an occupation that helps destroy faith. Before God will even hear you, you must be reconciled to Him through trust in Christ's redeeming love. Your sins must be removed!

Praying in the Lord's name, we ought to have time and thought for others. Too often our petitions are a series of selfish requests for money, personal advancement, pleasure. Even after God grants our requests, we are frequently too thankless or forgetful to speak a word of praise. How different another young marine on Guadalcanal! The night before a hard struggle he pleaded — and these are his very words, recorded in a letter by his chaplain: "Dear Lord, if anyone falls in battle tomorrow, may it be I, because I know Christ as my Savior and Lord. Give some of those poor fellows who do not know Christ another chance and take me, if it be Thy will, O Lord!" If only you who call yourselves Christians and know what it cost the Son of God to redeem you would show a similar passion for souls, fall on your knees and beseech salvation for others! Especially now, when millions of our young men and women are far from home, many on the front battle lines, should we ask divine guidance for these loved ones in the armed forces. We ought to revive Samuel's zeal, expressed in this assurance to the children of Israel, *"God forbid that I should sin against the Lord in ceasing to pray for you!"*

The Savior teaches another prayer lesson in our text when He directs us to enter our own *"closet"* (our room, as we would say today), close the door, and there, removed from all distraction, approach our Father *"which is in secret."* These words do not condemn public and family petitions. Rather, as the verses preceding our text show, does Jesus denounce the artificial prayers spoken for general approval, the hypocrisy which likes to *"be seen of men,"* the insincerity that thrives on formalism and outward worship, the show-Christianity which our Savior rejects in the words, *"This people draweth nigh unto Me with their mouth and honoreth Me with their lips; but their heart is far from Me."*

Instead, Jesus wants the sincerity of trusting faith. He asks us to consider prayer such a sacred privilege that, when we commune with the Father, we isolate ourselves from the rest of the world, concentrate our thoughts on God in Christ and permit nothing to distract us. Because the Lord desires not lip worship but heart worship, not empty formality but soul-deep trust, we ought to give ourselves entirely and unrestrictedly to God when we invoke His help. Let us honestly admit how many times, as we stood for prayer in church, our thoughts began to wander! We would not insult an earthly ruler with such disrespect. Why, then, should we dare show less attention and courtesy to the Almighty?

What a glorious blessing to know and feel yourself alone with God! What an unspeakable privilege to have the world recede from your thoughts, to come before Him whom angels constantly adore! Is it not deeply meaningful that practically every time Jesus is recorded as having prayed, except at meals, He knelt alone, for instance, on the mountainside near Gennesaret's shores, in Gethsemane's dark recesses? Can we not find a pointed lesson in this fact that the heroes of faith, mighty men and women of the Bible, from Moses to Saint John, often came before the Lord in private, personal, secret pleading, to pray divine benediction on their people, as well as on themselves? These things were written for our instruction. Following Christ's direction, *"Enter into thy closet, and when thou hast shut thy door, pray!"* we can experience many sweet hours of prayer in sacred solitude, but in Christ's presence, as we bring before the Mercy Throne petitions and thanksgivings for ourselves and for others. In the darkest hours of the Revolution, George Washington was seen to leave his headquarters at Valley Forge and to kneel alone, as he besought the Almighty's help for our country. During the Civil War, Abraham Lincoln declared that often when he saw no human solution to our national problems, he fell on his knees in the White House to beseech divine aid. Americans, accept the Lord as your Savior and Instructor in prayer! With the assurance of His blood-bought pardon in your soul, pray in your churches, pray in your homes, pray everywhere! But above all, make your petitions to the heavenly Father the personal outpourings of your own believing heart in the Savior's blessed name!

II

THE BLESSINGS OF THIS PRAYER

Men pay little attention, of course, to such secret, unseen intercession; and to our human understanding it may seem that the appeal of a sinner saved by Christ can exert little influence in a world apparently ruled by physical force and human might. But prayer can release the mightiest forces in the universe. It can unlock the door to an unfailing treasury of hope, strength, courage. It can help perform miracles which no scientific laboratory can achieve, as it opens the gates of heaven for the redeemed in Christ and closes the entrance to hell. It can be a means of bringing lost souls from perdition to pardon, hopeless sinners from doom to deliverance. Faith-founded, penitent, personal pleading can bind the elements of nature, miraculously avert danger, restore health even when specialists decide it is too late for healing.

Earnest entreaty in Christ's name cannot only smooth the difficulties in your life, it can also solve the nation's problems. The believer bowed low before his Savior presents the most striking contrast to the power-worshiping, control-craving forces equipped with cannon and tanks, air squadrons and army battalions, high explosives and poison gas, as they cripple, kill, and destroy; but nothing is surer than this blessed fact that the supplications of the Savior's followers, poor and persecuted as they may be, can mightily overcome a weaponed world arrayed against them.

For to whom are true prayers addressed? Not to idols made with men's hands! Not to a god who is so far off that he cannot hear! Not to weak, fallible men! Christian prayer is raised from earth to heaven, to the Creator in His marvelous omnipotence; and of Him it is written in Scripture, in history, in true believers' hearts, *"With God nothing shall be impossible."* Take every syllable of this promise on faith, my fellow redeemed! Ten Axis submarines may encircle the ship on which your son sails to the battle front, but the Almighty can swerve every torpedo aside. A hundred hostile planes may swoop down on his regiment as it marches through the Tunisian sands, but our Lord can steer every aerial bomb safely away. A thousand enemy rifles may be leveled against him on the Solomons, and a thousand bullets by God's direction can miss their mark — all because your pleadings have found acceptance at Heaven's mercy seat. Therefore I repeat: the strongest secret weapon men can ever wield is prayer in Christ's name.

See how Jesus stresses this power when He promises that, if you pray with faith and sincere devotion, *"Thy Father, which seeth in secret, shall reward thee openly"!* Don't permit yourselves even to begin doubting these words, for they are Christ's — no exaggeration, but His own exact truth! Your trust in God will be rewarded, all scoffing of atheists and unbelievers to the contrary notwithstanding. The entreaty which your heart of faith sends to the Almighty, although no man knows it, no one hears it, and many would ridicule it, will bring you unmistakable blessing.

Our Lord speaks generally when He says, *"Thy Father, which seeth in secret, shall reward thee openly."* He does not say, *"'Thy Father, which seeth in secret,'* will answer every plea of any kind you may ever utter." Often we pray blindly and ask for those things which would injure us, harm our bodies or work havoc in our spiritual life. God loves us too much to heed such requests, but instead He gives His children a real blessing, the reward of His mercy, by which our souls are brought closer to Christ. Sometimes that open reward takes the form of sorrow and suffering; but in the end, affliction can be a far greater benediction than joy or the unruffled happiness of a smooth, frictionless life, for every one of us *"must through much tribulation enter into the kingdom of God."* The burdens His heavenly wisdom permits to be imposed on us can make us more reliant on His mercy, more appreciative of His grace. Any petition for temporal, earthly, physical, bodily, family, financial help should be made according to God's will. As Jesus at Gethsemane, under the pain of indescribable anguish, declared, *"Not My will, but Thine, be done!"* so we should implore every blessing for this life according to our Father's perfect, unfailing purpose. It takes courage to ask, "O God, keep our boy across the seas unharmed, if it be Thy will!" It requires deep conviction to be able to say, "O Lord, spare the life of this baby, our only child; but Thy will be done!" Yet the more closely you walk with Jesus, the more personally you understand how gracious your heavenly Father is through the Savior, the more abundantly you will find strength in the assurance that whatever God ordains is good, that *"all things"* — and Saint Paul means *"all things,"* even disaster and death — *"work together for good to them that love God."* So trust God humbly, patiently in Christ, even though you cannot understand the mysterious way in which He moves to perform His mercies!

Keep in mind also that Jesus does not say, " *'Thy Father . . . shall reward thee'* immediately, at the place, in the time, according to the manner and under the circumstances you request." Prayer must never become dictation to the Lord. We should leave to God the way and means of His answer and confidently accept His all-knowing decision as to the where, the when, and the how of His reply as well as the why for the suffering that may intervene before His answer arrives. The time will come when, surveying Christ's marvelous dealings with us, we shall see that God's time, His place, His plan, and His degree of response are always the best.

By His divine mercy an open reward of grace will surely follow contrite, trusting prayer. Men may not recognize it, as they are often blind to God's other benedictions. Even believers may not be able to explain the Lord's public reply to their entreaties. After the fall of Hong Kong one of our Lutheran missionaries in that crown colony was about to be placed in a concentration camp with his family. He knew that the food would be insufficient and that malnutrition would be a real danger for his loved ones. He took the matter to God in fervent but secret intercession. One morning, after his devotion, the missionary, leaving his house, spied a box in the middle of the street. No one was in sight who could have lost it; so he took it to his quarters, opened it, and found that it contained many tablets of sodium, phosphorus, calcium, magnesium, iron, just what his wife and children required for the internment that followed. Through this medical aid the teeth of those in his section of the concentration camp did not turn black, and their bones did not become ricketed. He was also able to save human life through these precious chemicals. Now, how did that package happen to be there just at that time? Had it accidentally dropped from a Japanese truck? If so, why was it not claimed? We know that the box was placed there by divine direction — an open reward for secret prayer. Now, you who have spent your lifetime in sickbeds, you whose home happiness is ruined, you who have repeatedly requested that the thorn in your flesh be removed, only to find it further imbedded, may feel that God is not rewarding your prayers openly. Be patient! Give the Lord time! And always look beyond the grief and clamor of a world in sin to the glory and radiance of heaven, where the Savior will say to all who have persevered in the faith, *"Well done, thou good and faithful servant"!*

Likewise, if in any nation men humbly seek God through Christ, He will keep His word and reward them. That is illustrated in Switzerland, the country that twice preserved its liberty and independence although powerful neighboring belligerents, humanly speaking, could have crushed it into submission. The Swiss government understands the source of its blessing, and in a Call to Repentance and Prayer gives this recognition to God: "Let us remember this word of the Holy Scriptures, *'Except the Lord keep the city, the watchman waketh but in vain!'* The Lord watches with our army which stands sentry for our country. In the peace of liberty and order we have been able to sow our fields, and the Lord has blessed their fruitfulness. Therefore we appeal to you, people of Switzerland, to spend the National Day of Repentance and Prayer in quiet, reverent concentration and not to desecrate the quietness of this day by pleasure seeking and noisy entertainment. Give honor to God as a free and praying nation!" We in the United States need more of that submission to God, for we have sinned against the Almighty — sinned frequently, ungratefully, grievously! Yet here is the divine pledge, penned by the direction of God Himself: *"If My people, which are called by My name, shall humble themselves and pray and seek My face and turn from their wicked ways, then will I hear from heaven and will forgive their sin and will heal their land."* Trust that promise and find in the secret, behind-closed-door prayer of millions in America our strongest weapon for the present struggle!

Pray down God's power on our country in a real revival of true faith, which starts where every reawakening must begin, with individuals who, repentant yet reassured, come to Christ as their only Savior! My countrymen, receive Jesus as your Redeemer! May the power of prayer strengthen you, your home, your church, and your country! Let the watchword of Christianity, the appeal that promises you divine hope and our nation divine blessing, the cry that has been the clarion call of this broadcast for many years, ring out ever more clearly: "On your knees, America!" "Pray, America, pray!" Battle with this secret weapon continually, faithfully, mightily, and you will battle triumphantly! We ask this victory in Jesus' name. Amen!

Full Freedom from Fear

"Fear not, for I have redeemed thee!"
ISAIAH 43:1

O Jesus, Our Ransom and Redeemer:

As in the days of Thy earthly ministry Thou didst speak peace to Thy fear-filled disciples, so look mercifully on us, despite our weakness of faith, our readiness to surrender to doubt! Give us the conviction which challenges, "If God be for us, who can be against us?" and show us that Thou art for all who trust Thee as their atoning, sin-bearing Redeemer! Draw us ever nearer to Thee! Daily may we confess the guilt and curse of our transgressions, yet with ever deepening faith behold and believe the wondrous love of Thy life-giving death! Extend Thy rich blessings to those terrorized by life's trials, haunted by their sins, agonized by war's horrors! Send Thy Spirit to pour courage into the hearts of the men and women in our Army and Navy, especially during the hour of danger and death! O Jesus, our Savior and our God, grant us, according to Thy will, a triumph of righteousness, a true, just, and speedy peace before many more lives are taken! Hear us and help us, for our hope is in Thee! Amen.

OUR reasons for fighting this global conflict, our hopes for the postwar world have been summarized in "the Four Freedoms": freedom of speech, freedom of religion, freedom from want, freedom from fear. The first of these is not new in our country, thank God! It was written into the Constitution and has flourished throughout the United States as in no other nation. The fact that we are able to use our most widespread radio facilities and address you in behalf of our Lord Jesus Christ is a tribute to our free government and the eminently American attitude of the Mutual Broadcasting

System. With all the power and resources we have, let us battle against every attempt to regiment public opinion or restrict free expression!

The second liberty, the freedom of religion, is likewise an old privilege for us. Thank God again that we have no state church, no gestapos or commissars who control our worship or censor our preachers! Church and State are constitutionally separated. Help keep them separate, so that no denomination ever assumes control of our political affairs and no administration shows favoritism to one religious group or persecutes another!

The third liberty, however, the freedom from want, is new, as it seeks to give everyone in all the world "the right to adequate food, clothing, shelter, medical care; the right to security." No nation in history has ever been able to preserve people from poverty, unemployment, famine; and we doubt whether even a country with our resources can banish every want from the lives of its own citizens. It takes more than human ingenuity and machines to furnish food, clothing, shelter. We still need God to bless our seedtime and harvest, give increase to our flocks, and prosper our labor. If, with reliance on the Almighty, man's best thought is devoted to helping the poor, feeding the hungry, healing the sick, we should indeed invoke God's blessing on such efforts to relieve the undersupplied, the undernourished, the underprivileged.

It is the fourth liberty, however, the freedom from fear, which particularly concerns us today. The Government generously promises us security against the haunting terror that new wars will continually arise. "The use of force," we are told, "must be made less and less feasible on earth, until it finally becomes impossible," and a warless era dawns with a world-wide reduction of armaments. What a glorious picture of peace, blessed peace, always in all the earth! Yet that freedom from fear and bloodshed — often predicted in the past, but never more frequently than in these last decades of the most widespread, devastating wars — will never be fully realized. Our blessed Savior Himself, foreseeing the very days in which we live, has warned us that, as the world hastens to its end, there shall be *"wars and rumors of wars, . . . for nation shall rise against nation, and kingdom against kingdom."* Besides, some fears are even greater than war's terrors, and these cannot be removed even by a government as considerate as ours. To dispel the shadows which daily darken your soul, you must have heavenly strength. You need — and this is my message to you —

FULL FREEDOM FROM FEAR,

found only through faith in the Lord Jesus Christ and such promises of God's Word as that offered by these seven simple words of our text (Isaiah, chapter forty-three, verse one), *"Fear not, for I have redeemed thee!"*

I

WE NEED THIS FREEDOM FROM FEAR

This *"Fear not!"* of Isaiah is only one of more than a hundred Scripture passages which cry out in effect, *"Be not afraid!"* Bible critics have sought to remove some of these "Fear nots" as though they had crept in by mistake. But a hundred, or even a thousand, pledges of triumph over terror would not be too many in our fright-filled years. Think of the legions of phobias which relentlessly make men and women cringe before the thought that they will lose their most precious possessions. People fear the loss of health; and not thousands, but millions, in the United States are gripped by actual pain or the torture of imaginary disease. Again, many fear that they will lose their money, their investments, their home, their food, their work. And while in overprosperous periods like these such forebodings recede into the background, they are never completely banished from the mind. Multitudes fear the loss of their mental powers and shrink from the specter of insanity. Still others fear the loss of their good name and reputation. They cower before the thought that some evil which they thought safely hidden in the buried past will be uncovered. Unnumbered men and women are tormented because they dread the loss of love, the breakup of the family, the banishment of home happiness. Far worse, however, is the insistent voice of a guilty conscience that emphasizes God's wrath, the fear of unforgiven sins, the torture of hell. And in the most crushing combination of fear men know they are affrighted by the prospect of their own death and of facing the just, holy God. If you have never seen an unbeliever die, you have been spared one of life's worst terrors.

Some of you, of course, are completely satisfied with yourselves. You smile confidently and say: "Fear? Why should I be afraid? I have everything I need. I am not afraid of God or man. If hardship comes, I can take it. And when it is time for me to die, I will not whine or whimper. I will go with a smile on my face." But will you? Many who similarly rejected the Almighty actually became cringing cowards in their last breath. David Hume, philosopher and infidel, ranted against the Cross, ridiculed Christ, and at the same time confidently claimed that when his time for leaving life came, he would face death cheerfully. His housekeeper, who was with him to the end, asserted that when his agnostic friends visited him, he put on a brave front; but she added: "When he was alone, the scene was different. His mental agitation was so great as often to alarm me greatly. He struggled to appear composed even before me; but to one who had attended his bedside for many days and nights, who witnessed his disturbed sleep and more disturbed wakings, who frequently heard his breathings of remorse and frightful startings, it was no difficult matter to determine that all was not right within. This continued and increased until he became insensible. I hope that I may never be called upon to witness a similar scene."

Convicted murderers have sneered that they would walk to the electric chair or up the gallows stairs without assistance, since death meant nothing to them. But read Warden Lawes' account of his years at Sing Sing, in which he tells how often hardened killers had to be dragged to their execution! If you shout back into your radio that the day before yesterday in South Carolina the first woman to be executed in that State walked to the electric chair calmly, declaring, "I am ready to die," then read the full newspaper account, which tells you that she carried a Bible with her! — Despite your defiance of God and His goodness, there is a judgment which you cannot escape, a death you must die. The prouder, more overconfident, more contemptuous, your blasphemy now may be, the more appalling your despair when all the window dressing of your supposed courage disappears.

Picture to yourselves the crushing burden unrelieved fright imposes! Ask any physician to describe its consequences, and he will tell you plainly it weakens the energy of your body, lessens its resistance, interrupts its normal processes, and, if the fear habit becomes fixed, finally produces illness. Many of you have worried yourselves sick. Some of you will go to a premature grave unless you gain new confidence.

Again, worry affects the mind. It not only prevents

its victims from thinking and doing their best but also banishes calm and quiet. It undermines courage, builds imaginary barriers, makes people suspicious of their neighbors, leads them to seek sinister motives behind innocent actions, to find only gloom and pessimism in life. One of the reasons for the startling number of nervous breakdowns and cases of mental disorder is this, that too many people, refusing to trust God fully, become the victims of continued, unmitigated worry. This is tragic enough, but the spiritual burdens fear imposes are even more serious. It makes people put a question mark behind God's promises, doubt their salvation in Christ, wonder whether they have committed the unpardonable sin, and feel themselves lost forever, when in truth no one can ever be lost who trusts this plain promise of Scripture, *"Believe on the Lord Jesus Christ, and thou shalt be saved!"*

What, then, do men need? What must you have to escape these destructive forces? Money? You cannot buy peace of mind and a calm heart, even with heaped millions. When one of the financial leaders of America fell fatally sick, a Christian friend comforted him at his bedside and started to sing, "Come, ye sinners, poor and needy!" That multimillionaire, whose whispers controlled stock-exchange movements in this country and abroad, the financial leader whose wish was law for a hundred boards of directors, responded brokenly: "Yes, sing that for me! I feel poor and needy."

Can position and power grant freedom from fear, a quiet, rested mind? Before President Andrew Jackson's second term expired, the man who had risen from a log-cabin poverty to the highest position in the United States stormed out to meet a delegation, which three times had asked to see him, and cried: "Gentlemen, people envy me in this White House, and they long to get here; but I tell you that at the end of the second term I am glad to get out of it, for it is a perfect hell." The last sultan of Turkey spent $900 each night to have his bedroom guarded. In Germany Adolf Hitler rules with a sweep that even dictators rarely wield. But few people are permitted to see him privately. When high officers come for an audience, they are first searched for concealed weapons. Dictators fear death.

Can success and achievement provide a serene confidence? William Makepeace Thackeray, genial British writer, found recognition throughout the civilized world. But one day, while he sat in a Paris restaurant, he glanced to the other end of the room and wondered who the miserable wretch was whom he beheld there. He arose to investigate and found that he was looking at himself in a mirror.

Can science, culture, education free men from their sins? If learning could liberate, why are there so many suicides among the intelligentsia, such crude superstition among cultured leaders? Why the large number of nervous breakdowns and mental disorders, despite all our schools and colleges?

Can you sidestep fear by having fortunetellers reveal the future? Not one of these servants of superstition — the astrologers, the numerologists, tea-leaf readers, crystal-ball gazers, dream interpreters, palmists, graphologists, their forecasts, the dream books, the fraudulent sixth and seventh books of Moses, the rabbit's feet, the good-luck rings — can ever relieve you of your solicitude for the future. African natives converted to Christ give up their amulets and charms. A missionary to that continent states that in front of a lay preacher's hut he found rows and rows of necklaces and charms and, upon inquiring, learned that these had been placed there by the natives who had turned to Jesus and put their trust in Him. But in our enlightened country people are paying an estimated $125,000,000 a year to fortunetellers of various kinds, who ought to be banned because of the evil and sorrow they provoke.

Can you free yourself from fears by following the new creeds and mail-order religions which promise to produce supermen? They are just as dishonest as the vicious deception recently revealed, when beautifully decorated packages for the soldiers, after the contents on the top had been removed, were found to contain nothing but paper and colored straw. It is bad enough if people are thus robbed of their money, but it is far worse if men and women are defrauded spiritually by cults which offer deliverance only to substitute delusion.

Can federal laws or social programs grant release from fear? Thank God, we have a Government that says: "Don't worry about your job; we will give you employment insurance! Don't be afraid of losing your bank deposit; we will give you savings insurance! Don't be afraid of drought or blight; we will give you crop insurance!" — There are limits, however, even for the wealthiest nation. When things go wrong in your family and you fear that your home will be broken, no Congressional action can help you. If you feel some terrible hidden disease gnawing at your vitals, not even a special Presidential act can remove this terror. If you are lashed by the relentless fury of your conscience, no program by men or angels can free you from such fear. When you come face to face with death and think of the eternity in which you must stand before your God to answer for your transgressions, you need divine forgiveness and assurance.

II

CHRIST CAN GIVE US THIS FREEDOM FROM FEAR

While all human hopes of freedom from the tyranny of our fears fail, we have God's radiant assurance in our text, *"Fear not, for I have redeemed thee!"* This is likewise but one of many Scriptural promises pledging our salvation. No fewer than three dozen Old and New Testament passages proclaim in clear, clarion tones: God has redeemed us! Because this can become a glorious day of inner rebirth, if only you will stop resisting the Spirit and listen closely to God's pledge, *"I have redeemed thee,"* I ask: Postpone your after-dinner nap for a few moments! Come out of the kitchen! Lay your magazine or newspaper aside! Give these next minutes to God! To *redeem* sinners means to secure their release from punishment, to pay the ransom required for their freedom; and that, nothing less, God did for you. You were hopelessly enslaved in sin, and He made you free by His grace. You were lost in your iniquities, but His love found you. You were sentenced to everlasting death, but He secured your acquittal for life. You were condemned to hell, but He pardoned you for heaven.

How marvelous the way in which God redeemed you! No ordinary ransom could secure your release. Hear this and humble yourselves before the Almighty: He sent His only Son to save you. You parents know how hard it is to give your sons even for the nation's defense. Will you not bow thankfully before the Father's surpassing love that sent His Son Jesus not for His friends but for His enemies? No payment in money could buy you back to God, for the errorless Word explains, *"Ye were not redeemed with corruptible things, as silver and gold, . . . but with the precious blood of Christ."* Your rescue was no exchange by which you gave something to the Lord in return for your deliverance, as when captives of war are mutually released by belligerent nations. God did everything from start to finish.

While the Holy Spirit pleads with you to accept Jesus, harden not your heart! *"Behold, now is the accepted time; behold, now is the day of salvation!"* Get right with God today! Do not wait for tomorrow's uncertainties! When you receive and trust this marvelous promise of redemption, fear is defeated, then you are Christ's, He will constantly guide, guard, and protect you as His own precious redeemed. If Jesus shed His blood on the cross, took your place in suffering the punishment of your sins; if He loved you so much that He bore the burden, the curse, the guilt, the punishment of all your transgressions, can you not see that He whose mercy never changes will be close to you on every pathway of duty? The moment you accept the Lord Jesus *"even the very hairs of your head are all numbered."* Your life is not ruled by blind, cruel "fate." You are not the victim of "bad luck." "The cards are not stacked against you." Rather does everything that comes to you day after day flow from the Savior's magnificent mercy to strengthen your faith, increase your courage, and help you overcome fear. I read recently of a four-year-old child, alone, happy and undisturbed in the coach of an express train roaring at high speed through storm and night. When a passenger asked him, "Well, little man, aren't you afraid here all alone at night on this noisy train?" the youngster smiled and said, "No, my daddy is the engineer up ahead." Once in childlike faith you have been reconciled with your heavenly Father through Christ, no matter how uncertain the road of life before you may be, how black the world about you may seem, your Father is always up ahead to guide your course and guarantee your soul's safety.

Believe that through Jesus you are God-controlled; that, if necessary, your heavenly Father will draft His miracles and might to bless you! A cottage near Warsaw, Poland, is marked with an iron tablet praising the Lord's power. The villagers, explaining why it was placed there, will tell you of a God-fearing peasant named Dobry. Things had not gone well with him. His rent was long in arrears, and finally the time came when the landlord would evict him. On the evening before, as church bells called to prayer, Dobry and his family knelt to sing Paul Gerhardt's "Commit Thou All Thy Griefs and Ways into His Hands!" In the midst of the song a queer noise was heard at the window. Dobry arose, raised the glass, and saw the raven which his grandfather had once tamed and then set free. Can you imagine his surprise to find that the bird had brought him a costly ring, studded with precious stones? It proved to be the king's ring; and when Dobry returned the costly jewel to the palace, he was rewarded so generously that he could build a house of his own. To commemorate his deliverance from the fear of midwinter homelessness, the grateful man placed on his door the iron tablet, featuring the ring, the raven, and the hymn. If every American Christian family which has experienced God's glorious intervention could similarly call attention to Heaven's help, millions of homes would be marked with a tablet commemorating His divine power.

How often and how miraculously in the present war has our gracious Father not given His children the courage to declare, *"Though an host should encamp against me, my heart shall not fear: though war should rise against me, in this will I be confident"!* How vital, too, that the men and women in our nation's armed forces know the Lord Jesus and the fear-destroying faith in His mercy! Give our fighting men the best equipment money can provide, but first supply them with spiritual weapons, Baptism and the power of faith! Some of the happiest letters we receive come from soldiers, sailors, marines, airmen, who find courage in Christ's Gospel. Up on the bleak Aleutians, after one of our broadcasts, the soldiers raised $125 in a free-will offering to help expand our work. An aviator, ferrying a bomber to Africa, heard our message 20,000 feet above South American jungles and was strengthened for his dangerous task. Men on the Pacific battle front have gratefully received these broadcasts. From ships in the Atlantic, from submarines, from scores of camps, from privates and high officers, come thanks for God's Word, and at the same time repeated pleas to maintain and enlarge this radio mission, particularly for the men and women in our fighting forces.

Even when Christians meet reverses, they still have David's confidence, *"I will not be afraid of ten thousands of people that have set themselves against me."* This is not exaggeration nor mere wishful thinking. How, do you suppose, can a God-fearing wife bear a godless husband's ridicule and refuse to take recourse to divorce? How can Christians meet sudden calamity, permanent injury to their body, loss of members or senses, and, instead of groveling in fear, courageously face the future? How can believers endure wasting, destructive diseases, excruciating pain, while unbelievers often take the coward's way out in suicide? God's children have faith, and defeating fear, they can exult with Saint Paul, *"Whether we live . . . or die, we are the Lord's."*

Regrettably, many of you who know the Lord Jesus are still ruled by fear. Some of the Negroes in the Civil War days were brought north by the underground railroad, the secret journeys by which they hid in friendly homes during the daytime and under the cover of night traveled from one hospitable town to another. As soon as they reached Canada, of course, they were free. On one of the trains which drew into the Toronto station, a woman who had helped hundreds of slaves cross the border, saw a colored man still hiding in the corner, afraid that he was being pursued. She cried out in reassurance: "Joe, why are you crouching there? You are a free man on free soil! Praise the Lord, Joe!" Similarly, with Christ you have crossed the boundary from sin to grace. You are free! Praise the Lord by refusing to cringe in fear! *"Stand fast . . . in the liberty wherewith Christ hath made us free!"*

What can still put fright into your heart? The memory of your past sins? Jesus took them all away. They exist no longer. They have been forgiven and forgotten. Are you afraid because you do not feel that you have been redeemed? Martin Luther was once asked whether he felt that his sins were forgiven, and the great man of God replied, "No, I don't *feel* that they are forgiven; I *know* they are, because God says so in His Word." Your heavenly Redeemer does not say, " '*God so loved the world, that He gave His only begotten Son, that whosoever*' feeleth that he is saved '*should not perish, but have everlasting life.*' " But He does declare, *"By grace are ye saved."* That must be true!

Are you worried because the consequences of your sins may be revealed and bring you disgrace? Take it all to Christ! He will not only forgive you. He will also grant you strength to bear the results of your own folly!

Does your conscience assail you on the charge that your sins are too ruinous and repeated to be forgiven? Does the devil whisper into your heart: "There is no hope for you. You have committed the unforgivable sin"? Find courage in this sure pledge of Scripture, *"The blood of Jesus Christ, His Son, cleanseth us from all sin"!*

Do you fear that you may not be included in the Savior's grace, that the artificial restrictions men have set up may bar you? Build immovable hope on this all-embracing promise, *"Fear not, for I have redeemed* THEE!" — That includes everyone. No racial or social bar can keep you away from the Lord Jesus.

How sorely millions in our country need this courageous victory over fear! We are in the midst of trying times. Who can assuredly see the end of our difficulties? One of the cruelest of all delusions is the too frequent promise that after the war a golden age will come, the most splendid period in history, when right and truth, democracy and prosperity, will reign as never before. But the Bible warns us that in the latter times and before Christ comes to judge the quick and the dead, *"men's hearts"* shall fail *"them for fear."* Unless God is over-merciful, we must look for international upheaval and the wide spread of atheism. You cannot kill myriads of human beings, destroy hundreds of millions of dollars' worth of property, spend hundreds of billions for purposes of war, and then expect that somehow human ingenuity, statecraft and diplomacy will find a way for national and individual affairs to roll on more smoothly than ever before. Only God can avert greater suffering than this generation has already endured; yet in this world of sin and sorrow His Son, our Redeemer, looks down upon those who come to Him in humble, contrite, self-denying faith; and the heavier their burden, the louder the roar of powerful enemies, the more bitter the battle — the surer will be His comfort, the nearer His presence, the clearer His sustaining assurance. Come peace or war, health or sickness, gain or loss, prosperity or adversity, life or death itself — may the Savior's triumph over all terror constantly re-echo this victory promise in your heart, *"Fear not, for I have redeemed thee!"* Amen!

Do You Believe in Jesus Christ?

"Jesus said unto her, I am the Resurrection and the Life: he that believeth in Me, though he were dead, yet shall he live; and whosoever liveth and believeth in Me shall never die. Believest thou this? She saith unto Him, Yea, Lord; I believe that Thou art the Christ, the Son of God."

SAINT JOHN 11:25-27

Lord Jesus:

Graciously send us Thine enlightening Spirit to help us truly believe that Thou art our only but all-atoning Savior! Strengthen us to trust Thee wholly, knowing that since our sins are removed through faith in Thy life-giving death, we who love Thee are constantly under Thy guidance and protection! By Thy compassion and power Thou canst graciously provide our every need and conquer each affliction. Mercifully forgive us our doubting of Thy grace, our indifference toward Thy marvelous compassion, our lukewarmness in testifying to Thy redemption! Equip us with the courage required to acknowledge Thee before men, so that we, in turn, on the glorious day of the resurrection will be acknowledged by Thee before our heavenly Father! Direct the course of our beloved nation toward Thee! Endow the President, the Congress, those in authority, with wisdom! Shield our armed forces with Thy protecting power and send our embattled youth back to us soon with blessed, building peace! Come to us now, O Christ, and bring many to Thee through this broadcast! We ask it, believing Thy promise. Amen.

How much longer will this war last? When will the last shot be fired, the last bomb be dropped? Who is right — those who predict that victory will be ours before this year is over or those who grimly insist that we must fight through a decade of the bitterest, bloodiest battles in history? — These are the questions of the day, repeated by millions in our country. Daily they view the horrors of this conflict, cities destroyed, ships sunk by the hundreds, the very foundations of civilization attacked, our peace-time industry reorganized into a mighty system with the pointed purpose to kill, kill, kill. As they think of their dear ones on the battle fronts or on the high seas, continually confronted by the danger of death, they plead: "When will this stop? When will our sons, husbands, brothers come back? When will the all-clear signal sound over the whole world with the destruction of evil and the victory of truth, righteousness, justice?"

Only God knows. More than ever before should we penitently repeat Jehoshaphat's prayer, *"Our eyes are upon Thee,"* O Lord — not on our own vaunted greatness. More than all else we need the Almighty on our side, so that we can exult, *"If God be for us, who can be against us?"*

We must constantly keep in mind, however, for our nation, our churches, our homes, ourselves, that God is for those only who serve Him in true faith, and that a question of far greater importance even than the wondering about the war's end confronts everyone of us, soldiers and civilians, youth and the aged, the influential and the impoverished; it is a question the response to which can be a decisive factor in shaping the nation's course, in bringing courage, comfort, and conviction into your heart and life. It is, my countrymen, the question of heaven or hell, life or death—the question of all questions:

DO YOU BELIEVE IN JESUS CHRIST? —

the pointed issue raised by our Lord Himself in the text for this Sunday (Saint John, chapter eleven, verses twenty-five to twenty-seven): *"Jesus said unto her, I am the Resurrection and the Life: he that believeth in Me, though he were dead, yet shall he live; and whosoever liveth and believeth in Me shall never die. Believest thou this? She saith unto Him, Yea, Lord; I believe that Thou art the Christ, the Son of God."*

I

WHAT YOU SHOULD BELIEVE CONCERNING CHRIST

Jesus spoke these words at Bethany, a village only two short miles from Jerusalem. He was on the way to the home of Lazarus, Mary, and Martha, the dwelling where He often found peace and quiet apart from the strife and turmoil of a selfish world. Sorrow had entered this household, and the Lord was bringing reassurance and help. — When you pray to the Savior, as I know many of you do, "Come, Lord Jesus, be our Guest," and when you plead with faith and sincerity, the same heavenly Friend who entered the Bethany household will come into your family circle, no matter how difficult your problems may seem. If misunderstanding threatens to destroy the peace and joy in your home; if you feel the pinch of poverty, while others worry only over the heavy income taxes they must pay as evidence of their prosperity; if sickness has crossed your threshold; if a child of yours suffers from infantile paralysis — and, as annually, our broadcast asks you to get solidly behind the humanitarian effort now waged to help the victims of this plague; if broken marriage vows have shattered your dreams of happiness, remember that Jesus can mightily comfort you! Hard though such afflictions may be, they are far lighter than the sorrow which encircled that Bethany cottage — death. Lazarus, the friend of Jesus, the brother of Mary and Martha, had died, and Martha thought the

Savior had come too late; but she was wrong, as His miracle-working mercy proved, and it is never too late for Christ to bring you help and hope.

Christ addressed these words to Martha who had run to meet Him; and today Jesus similarly would speak to all American women. They are divinely appointed supporters of morality, home happiness, and domestic honesty — these women who never lose the power of true womanhood, who regard marriage as sacred; the mothers who, despite the sacrifices they make in defense industries, find their vital activity at home, rearing the children, which God has given them, in true faith, with full devotion to Christ and country; women, married or unmarried, young and old, who, following the example of the saintly figures on the New Testament pages, first learn *"to show piety at home"* and then find time to work for the salvation of souls and for the Church's interests. Because mothers with such faith are vital for a better nation, their high principles are being assailed with a viciousness and vehemence hitherto unknown in our country. Two courses confront every woman in the United States today: the one is followed by the pleasure-chasing, cocktail-drinking, notoriety-seeking, home-neglecting, divorce-exalting, sin-loving, Christ-denying; and the other is chosen by the Scripture-loving, home-building, sin-hating, clean-living, Christ-exalting. Women of America, as you ask yourselves pointedly, "Which path am I to take?" may God's Holy Spirit give you the devotion of Martha who ran to meet the Savior!

Once before when Jesus was a Guest in Bethany, Martha had been overbusy in preparing for His comfort and entertainment. While her sister Mary sat at the Savior's feet to catch every word of divine instruction, Martha was running between kitchen and dining room,

so to speak, in preparing the best she could for Christ.
Then our Lord reminded her that the *"one thing . . .
needful"* is not food and drink, but the hearing of God's
Word. Martha learned this lesson gratefully and quickly.
But there are many women, even in churches, who must
change their whole attitude toward the Gospel, as Martha
did. Too often people actually believe it is the prime,
outstanding work of the Church to arrange socials, meals,
teas, theatricals, and to attract people by such methods.
Correspondingly, many women think they are doing the
Lord's chief work when they spend hours over a hot
stove in preparing church suppers, waiting on tables, or
engaging in other activities designed to make money for
religious purposes, and when, as a result, they are robbed
of the time required personally to testify for Christ.
Think also of the destructive features which claim religious support. Some of you sent me church programs
showing that on last New Year's Eve, at a time when
American soldiers faced death on a dozen different battle
fronts, your congregations sponsored dances in their halls
and urged their parishioners to dance their way into this
burdened year. Recall also the public scandal of the
gambling conducted under church auspices! In New
York, where the city officials declared bingo illegal —
think of it! — some religious groups went before the legis-
lative authorities, requesting that the ban be lifted. We
need not look far afield for the reason why some churches
have lost the respect and support of the masses. — If you
are in a congregation suffering from this gambling craze,
stop this violation of God's law and man's!

Now, when Jesus, comforting Martha in her bereavement, unfolds the glorious promise which has given many
of you new hope at the side of caskets or in the cold
cemetery, He declares, *"I am the Resurrection and the*

Life: he that believeth in Me, though he were dead, yet shall he live; and whosoever liveth and believeth in Me shall never die." Then He looks directly at Martha and asks, *"Believest thou this?"* — the very question He now puts before you. Jesus wants to know how *you* stand. He does not inquire first of all: "Do the 130,000,000 in the United States believe? Do your parents believe? Do your children believe?" The important issue is, "Do *you* believe?"

You ask, "What must I believe?" and Martha gives you this glorious answer, *"Yea, Lord; I believe that Thou art . . . the Son of God."* To you, too, Jesus must be more than a great man, a good man, a gifted man; more than just a mighty leader, a miraculous leader, a martyred leader; more than a helpful teacher, a strengthening teacher, a heavenly teacher; more than a high example, a noble example, a holy example; more than godly, God-sent, godlike. He must be God Himself, God fully, God truly, God eternal, God almighty, God all-knowing. He lived as God; He thought as God; He spoke as God; He was God; He is God; He ever will be God!

Do not let anyone tell you that it matters little whether you accept Christ as God-man or only as a godly man! It makes all the difference in this world and the next. Do not be misled by the tragic fact that some denominations have sought to dethrone Him! The true Church, from Old Testament days, has been united in acclaiming Jesus one with the Father and the Spirit, *"God blessed forever."* Do not pay any attention to the unbelief of modern religious leaders who publicly reject the Savior's deity! He was worshiped as God by the angels, acclaimed God by the prophets, proclaimed as God by the Gospels, exalted as God by the Apostles, acknowledged as God even by His heavenly Father. Believe with Martha that because Jesus is *"the Son of God,"* nothing is too hard for Him! No help you may need is too difficult for Him to grant; no problem of any disturbed soul too heavy for solution by His divine power. You can trust Him, since as your God He cannot fail. You can discover daily help through Him, because as God His is *"all power . . . in heaven and in earth."* You can find guidance in Christ, since He knows the future and directs it. You can come to Him anywhere or any time, because as God He is not limited by time nor restricted by space. Let me tell you again: Jesus is more than any or all the myriads of men. He is your God.

Martha's faith went farther. When her divine Instructor looked at her and asked, *"Believest thou this?"* she also answered, *"Yea, Lord; I believe that Thou art the Christ,"* that is, God's Anointed, the promised Deliverer, the atoning Redeemer, the sin-conquering, sin-removing Savior. God grant that you, too, may say, *"Yea, Lord; I believe that Thou art the Christ"!* It is not enough to believe merely that Jesus lived a model life; for His purity serves to emphasize our impurity. It is not enough to recognize how forcefully He proclaimed the message of love, for your own heart feels too much hatred; not enough to concede that He died a noble death — millions of soldiers today are ready to lay down their lives for their fellow countrymen. You must know that Jesus, and He alone, is *"the Christ"* who was crucified — and so may everyone of you say — for "my" sins.

Believe also that Jesus saves completely, that no one is too vile to be accepted, no transgression too vicious to be remitted by the Lord of limitless love! Last week a Michigan woman wrote me in deep concern over her soul. A friend had warned her that her sins could not be pardoned, stating that if a Christian, knowing any act to be wrong, nevertheless commits it, he can never be forgiven; and she based her claim on a Bible edition and commentary which unfortunately has gained wide circulation. What a destructive denial such limiting of our Lord's all-embracing mercy! Reject every restriction of His redemption! Trust this plain promise of Scripture, *"The blood of Jesus Christ, His Son, cleanseth us from all sin"!*

Believe that Jesus saves everyone who comes to Him in faith! Nothing but your own unbelief can keep you from His love. There are no bars but your own refusal to accept His mercy. A few days ago death came to George Washington Carver, the Negro scientist whose parents were slaves and who as a boy was sold for a race horse valued at $300. Later, in his laboratory he developed more than three hundred useful products from the lowly peanut and more than two hundred by-products from the sweet potato. But the Bible meant as much to him as the laboratory, and he showed his childlike faith in the Savior by choosing as one of his favorite passages Philippians 4:13, *"I can do all things through Christ, which strengtheneth me."* I hold up Dr. Carver, Bible student, Bible teacher, Bible lover, to my colored friends as an example of the spiritual victories which can be won by those of a race often persecuted and oppressed. The words of a Sakalave tribal chief in Madagascar ring in my ears: "You see us Negroes, victims of ignorance and drunkenness; but who brought to our village the first little pieces of candy filled with liquor? The white man. Who is it that today calls us 'lazy beasts,' who mocks at our way of living? The white man. Who tells that there is no God in heaven to reign over the earth? The white man." — As I ask you in the Savior's name to forgive the cruelties inflicted by members of my race, I also invite you, whatever the color of your skin may be, to believe that Christ has compassion on every human being and often loves those most who suffer most.

Believe chiefly that Jesus saves freely; that pardon, which the combined wealth of all nations could never purchase, is granted you by pure grace, without any price or payment! This glorious compassion separates Christianity from all other creeds, as it shows that God did everything in redeeming you through Jesus. John Ruskin, British man of letters, declared: "The root of almost every schism and heresy from which the Christian Church has ever suffered has been the effort by men to earn rather than to receive their salvation, and the reason that preaching is so commonly ineffectual is that it calls upon men oftener to work for God than to behold God working for them." Ruskin is right. Among the hundreds of religions which claim men's worship, fundamentally there are only two different beliefs. The one holds that man must work for his own salvation. The other — the creed of this broadcast — exalts the Christ who by the shedding of His blood has earned salvation for us. Which will you accept?

God grant that you women may secure and safeguard Martha's faith, "Yea, Lord: I believe that Thou art the Christ, the Son of God"! Oh, that His Spirit would give you soldiers the courage of the centurion beneath the cross, "Truly, this was the Son of God"! you men, the confidence of Saint John, "This is the true God and eternal Life"! you doubters, the conviction of Thomas, "My Lord and my God"; you sin-burdened, the comfort of John the Baptist, "Behold the Lamb of God, which taketh away the sin of the world"! May that enlightening Spirit lead many this day to proclaim this deathless declaration of Martin Luther: "I believe that Jesus Christ, true God, begotten of the Father from eternity, and also true man, born of the Virgin Mary, is my Lord, who has redeemed me, a lost and condemned creature, purchased and won me from all sins, from death, and from the power of the devil, not with gold or silver, but with His holy, precious blood and with His innocent suffering and death, that I may be His own and live under Him in His kingdom and serve Him in everlasting righteousness, innocence, and blessedness, even as He is risen from the dead, lives and reigns to all eternity. This is most certainly true"!

If you have this faith, wholly, sincerely, reverently, then, whatever your denomination — Protestant or Catholic, Lutheran or Reformed, Low-Church or High-Church — you are a Christian. But if you reject Jesus, if you contradict the Gospel promises and think that you must earn your own salvation, then you may belong to a large, imposing congregation; you may hold a high, responsible position; you may be a church officer, even a clergyman, but you are not a Christian. You are still without the saving faith.

II

WHY YOU SHOULD BELIEVE IN CHRIST

No other question that can ever be directed to you has the importance, the weight in time and eternity, the urgency of this, "Do you believe in Jesus Christ?" With that faith comes the answer to the problem which has always disturbed human hearts, the removal of the fear which from the cradle days of history has made men cringe in fright — the terror of death. When Jesus, our God and our Savior, declares, *"I am the Resurrection and the Life: he that believeth in Me, though he were dead, yet shall he live; and whosoever liveth and believeth in Me shall never die,"* He who can never deceive nor speak an unfulfilled promise, gives you the personal, glorious assurance that, though you must die, through Christ you will not remain in the grave. For the Christian what men call death is only the beginning of a new, incomparably greater life in eternity with Jesus.

Therefore, when He who proved His power over the grave by raising lifeless Lazarus and at Easter by bursting from His own tomb assures you, *"I am the Resurrection and the Life,"* believe with your whole heart that through Him there is a life to come and decay is not the Christian's final destiny. Though the time will surely come when you draw your last breath, when your body, cold, motionless, rigid, dead, begins to decompose, nevertheless by God's might and as a believer you will be awakened in a radiant, heavenly body, perfect and painless, without flaws or faults, without marred or missing members, without any taint of disease or weakness in age.

What a sustaining comfort in this pledge! How assuredly it ought to make death easy, welcome, a glorious triumph, instead of the screaming and cursing terror it often is for unbelievers! Some of you are living your very last days. Your physicians have given you at most a week or two longer on earth. Because you have Christ, you will be indescribably better off next Sunday, if God takes you during this week. Then you will be free from all suffering; you will worship with angels and archangels; you will meet your loved ones who have preceded you in faith.

The more rabidly infidels argue against this sacred truth, the more firmly you should believe it! These words of Jesus Himself, *"I am the Resurrection and the Life,"* are the highest truth. Christ is not only your life-restoring God and Savior; He is the *only* God, the one Mediator between heaven and earth, the sole Assurance of life beyond the grave. Listen to Him as He instructs especially you who may think that a dozen roads lead to a blessed eternity, a hundred different paths to Paradise above! He does not say, "I am One of the ways to the resurrection and the life." He does not say, "He that believeth on Me or anyone else shall never die." But He does say: *"I am the Way, the Truth, and the Life; no man cometh unto the Father but by Me."* He does say, *"If ye believe not that I am He, ye shall die in your sins."* His Word clearly declares, *"Neither is there salvation in any other, for there is none other name under heaven given among men whereby we must be saved."* No doubt remains! Jesus is your only Savior! — Do you believe this?

III

HOW YOU SHOULD BELIEVE IN CHRIST

I pray God that you not only accept it, but also acclaim it with the confidence of Martha, who, casting all misgivings aside, declared in exultant, confident faith, *"Yea, Lord; I believe"!*

We need much more of this *"Yea, Lord; I believe"* conviction, especially because in an age of widespread falsehood and poisoned propaganda we are told that educated people no longer accept the Bible or regard Jesus as a divine, personal Savior. There are men who deliberately spend their entire lifetime in the futile attempt to "expose" Christianity. Organizations have been established for the unholy and blasphemous purpose of discrediting the Gospel. How can anyone find happiness in tearing down the faith by which men live and die? Aside from the terrible sin of denying Christ, I would not be an atheist or a modernist because of the cruelty of robbing others of their trust, of kicking the crutch from beneath a crippled world.

How absurd the claim that the Christian truth and scientific truth are at swords' points! The other day our newspapers reported the death of two outstanding scientists: The one was Nikola Tesla, an eminent leader in American electrical research. Editors called him "the father of radio and modern generation and transmission systems." His inventions and discoveries as listed in *Who's Who* are astonishing in their number as in their variety and stupendous achievement. Without Nikola Tesla the radio might never have been perfected; and the projects on which he was working when he died, particularly the transmission of power without wires, place him in the front ranks of America's outstanding scientists. We ask, Was Nikola Tesla an atheist, like some of the small minds that sneer and snarl at the Bible? No! His father was a servant of God. Nikola was reared in the faith of the Serbian Orthodox Church, and he remained true to it. His priest informs me that he was indeed a Christian, that he believed the Bible, accepted the Lord Jesus, and that he showed his love for the Savior through generous support of the Serbian missions in this country.

The other scientist mentioned on the same page, Dr. Howard A. Kelly of Johns Hopkins University, was an internationally recognized medical authority. He was made an honorary fellow by the universities of Edinburgh, Glasgow, Dublin, London, Paris, Rome, Bucharest, Vienna, Kiev, Lima — perhaps the most widely known American surgeon and gynecologist. Now, did Dr. Howard Kelly show the anti-Bible, anti-God attitude which mark some physicians? He regularly spent from one to four hours a day reading his Bible. He wrote vigorous, convincing books and articles in behalf of his Savior. He never missed an opportunity of testifying to Christ. Though he died a few days ago, yet he lives and speaks to all doubters today as I repeat his words: "I am sure that the Bible is the Word of God, with an assurance greater than all other convictions." "Above . . . logical deductions from philosophical and scientific premises I place the clear light of truth shining from the pages of the Bible."

Many other outstanding scientists, leaders of the leaders, have been courageous, confessing Christians. The American culture of the past had room and recognition for *"the fear of the Lord"* as *"the beginning of wisdom."* In 1860 246 colleges and universities flourished in the United States, and all but seventeen were directed by the churches. Of 1,700 colleges and universities today hardly one third are under religious control, and many of the rest tolerate opposition to Christ. A Yale professor reported that not one of his forty students could tell exactly who Judas Iscariot was. Another teacher there declared that a senior insisted he had never even heard of Moses. A Radcliffe girl asked her teacher: "What are the Ten Commandments? I see them referred to so often in Chaucer's *Canterbury Tales.*" The dean of Columbia University, in his last annual report, asserts that there is "a shocking degree of religious illiteracy among college students." To protest against all this and to put more of Jesus into our education, we must stand behind Christian, church-supported colleges. Their path will become increasingly difficult during this age before us, but their part in promoting the nation's spiritual welfare will be more vital than ever, since only by a return to the sincere, simple faith, based on the Bible and culminating in the Savior, can the masses in our country, especially our youth, find assurance for the future. If we can assist you in suggesting Christian schools for your sons or daughters, please write us! We shall be happy to counsel you.

Now, when you ask, "How can I have Martha's firm

faith?" I answer: You must meet the Savior as she did. You must read His words of encouragement and strength in the Bible, the deathless record of His life and death for your salvation. The deep-rooted trouble with many of you who oppose the Redeemer is this, that you have never actually sat down systematically to study the Word of His truth. If you would, the Holy Spirit could give you the grace He extended to Dr. David Nelson, a physician in the United States Army. He came from a Christian home, but through his college training he began to regard God's Word as false and Christ's Gospel as superstition. Yet one day the thought came to him, "Why don't you deal fairly with the Scriptures?" He did two things: He carefully re-examined the writings of Voltaire, Hume, and other skeptics, noting their inaccuracies, their unfairness, their dishonesty. At the same time, however, he began to study the Scriptures, and as he read he was brought to the full, unreserved knowledge of the Lord Jesus Christ. In gratitude he wrote a striking book against infidelity, which has been circulated in more than 100,000 copies. May the Spirit touch many of you today, so that you begin delving into Scripture personally, privately, and with your family!

Every day you live in unbelief adds to the peril of your soul. Who knows how long it will be before you stand at the tribunal of eternity? — One of our Lutheran chaplains, cited twice for his bravery on the Aleutian Islands, told me that for weeks he had instructed a young man in the Christian religion. The young convert was so eager to confess his Savior publicly that he wanted to be baptized in a church; yet late one night he knocked on the chaplain's door. He had walked thirteen miles through the desolate tundra country to be baptized immediately. He could not wait any longer, and there, after midnight, in the presence of several Christian soldiers he was baptized. A few hours later he returned to his lonely post. Before that day drew to its close, the Japanese attacked, and the young man was killed. Within less than twenty-four hours he was received into the Church Militant on earth and the Church Triumphant in heaven. If within the next twenty-four hours you are summoned from life, will you be blessed by this magnificent assurance, *"I am the Resurrection and the Life: he that believeth in Me, though he were dead, yet shall he live"*? That depends on the answer to the question which Jesus Himself now puts before you: *"'Believest thou this?' 'Believest thou'* that I am thy God and Savior, thy Ransom and Redemption, thy Pardon and Peace, thy Resurrection and Life?" God grant that now from the four quarters of this country, from beyond its borders, in Canada to the north and Mexico to the south, from the islands and from the ships of the seas to the east and the west, there may come — in a mighty harmony of trusting faith — this confident, triumphant answer, *"'Yea, Lord,'* with all my heart, with all my soul, and with all my might *'I believe that Thou art the Christ, the Son of God'!"* Amen!

Is Yours a Faith-Filled Family?

> "There was a certain man in Caesarea called
> Cornelius, a centurion of the band called the
> Italian Band, a devout man and one that feared
> God with all his house, which gave much alms
> to the people and prayed to God alway. . . .
> Then Peter opened his mouth and said, . . . Who-
> soever believeth in Him [Christ] shall receive
> remission of sins. While Peter yet spake these
> words, the Holy Ghost fell on all them which
> heard the Word."
>
> ACTS 10:1, 2, 34, 43, 44

God, Our Creator and Sustainer:

*For the homes and families of this nation we ask not wealth,
luxury, comforts, but a firm trust in the sure mercies of the
Lord Jesus, Thy Son, our God and Savior. Strengthen parents
and children, entire households, with His abiding presence!
Enlighten them by Thy Spirit individually to believe that
through Christ all their sins have been washed away; that, as
in the days of His flesh He entered the homes of His countrymen bringing help and courage, so today He is eager to come
into every home with His unfailing promise of peace. Support our American families with this trust when many forces
arise to destroy the sanctity of the Christian household!
Mercifully protect the homeless and the distressed! Guard our
fighting men and women, far from their families, close to
danger and death! O God of all power, as we ask in every
broadcast, so we plead today: May they soon return to their
homes and loved ones, with the triumph of truth and the
pledge of honest peace! We ask this according to Thy gracious will and in the Redeemer's precious name. Amen.*

Most of you are familiar with the fact that
of our forty-eight States Nevada has the laxest divorce
laws. The indifference to the sacredness of marriage

which its statutes have helped produce may be seen in the attitude of a Reno judge — during twelve years he granted 20,000 divorces — who invites: "Come to Reno! Get a divorce! Try again for the prize in the matrimonial lottery and keep on trying until you find true love!"

People who cannot have their nuptial vows legally broken in their own communities because of stricter laws may travel to any Nevada city, establish residence in a hotel, tourist camp, or boarding house, and after six weeks secure a divorce in hearings which sometimes last only two minutes. Now the question repeatedly asked, "Are Nevada decrees legal outside its borders?" was recently answered by the Supreme Court of the United States in a six-to-two verdict which ruled that the whole country must recognize Nevada divorces. This is one of the most dangerous decisions the high tribunal has ever made. We agree entirely with a dissenting justice who warned that the Supreme Court action "repeals the divorce law of all the States and substitutes that of Nevada." Today American home life should be most firmly founded, with husband and wife completely devoted to each other, children zealously safeguarded, wedded life "for better or for worse" "until death do you part" exalted as the ideal of every young couple. It is therefore disheartening to see that our highest judicial authority can give an opinion which will be construed as official approval of easy, quick divorce. If the Vichy government put an end to lax marriage laws in France; if the divorce orgy has been drastically reduced in Soviet Russia, should not our nation, which has ranked notoriously with these two countries as leaders in this scandalous home-breaking, strain every effort to protect the solidarity of the family and the sanctity of wedlock, particularly during emergencies like these? Because America's welfare calls for saner, stricter domestic laws; because God's Word protests against the present debauch; because the family is one of the foundation units in our national defense and victory, it is indeed overtragic that a single State can drag down the marriage standards of the whole land. On the same principle which the Supreme Court has now recognized, any other State, driven by the lure of making money through marital misfortunes, may pass legislation granting a divorce after six days' residence and have this made binding for the entire country!

It is vitally important now that uniform marriage laws be enacted for the whole United States. A bill to this end, soon to be introduced in Congress, deserves every citizen's support, provided, of course, it does not contradict God's law. But new legislation will not solve America's home difficulties. We need the *"clean heart"* and the *"right spirit"* for which David prayed, and which comes through personal faith in the Lord Jesus Christ and the renewing power of His Holy Spirit. The most potent antidote to the poison of domestic trouble is Christian home life, which welcomes Christ's sustaining presence and seeks His guidance in household worship, Scripture reading, prayer.

To impress on everyone of you, married or unmarried, believing or unbelieving, happy or unhappy, that this Savior is the one divine Source of help and hope for you and your home, I ask you pointedly in His name,

IS YOURS A FAITH-FILLED FAMILY?

This question is suggested by the remarkable story in the tenth chapter of Acts [verses one, two, thirty-four, forty-three, and forty-four], from which these words have been chosen as our text: *"There was a certain man in Caesarea called Cornelius, a centurion of the band called the*

Italian Band, a devout man and one that feared God with all his house, which gave much alms to the people and prayed to God alway. . . . Then Peter opened his mouth and said, . . . Whosoever believeth in Him [Christ] *shall receive remission of sins. While Peter yet spake these words, the Holy Ghost fell on all them which heard the Word."*

I

YOUR FAMILY SHOULD BE FILLED WITH FAITH IN CHRIST

The text takes us to Caesarea, a heathen city on the Mediterranean coast north of Judea. It was a thriving, modern community with palaces and theaters, commercial concerns and banks, markets and industries, yet with all the corruption and vice crowded into every ancient metropolis under Roman rule. Self-respecting Israelites generally stayed away from Caesarea; it was among the last localities in which one would look for the startling miracle of divine mercy which this tenth chapter of Acts records. God often chooses unpretentious places to demonstrate His power or manifest His love. Some of history's leaders grew up in remote, unassuming localities. Luther, God-blessed Reformer of the Church, was born in a mining town; George Washington, fearless father of this country, in a Virginia hamlet; Abraham Lincoln, liberator of an enslaved race, near a Kentucky crossroads. If God wants you for His glorious purposes, no spot is too distant or notorious to prevent Him from finding, using, and exalting you. Even in this moment the Almighty, who sees and knows all, is beholding you, wherever you are, however unfavorable or discouraging your surroundings may be. Lord of love that He is, His thoughts for you are plans of mercy.

In that pagan metropolis God chose one house to be marvelously honored by His grace — the home of Cornelius. We know nothing of his nationality or personal history up to this time except that he was not an Israelite, but a Gentile who was the leader of Italian troops stationed in Caesarea. We do know that in the godless, sin-filled city he was *"devout, . . . one that feared God."* Here was a man not a member of the chosen race, far from the Temple at Jerusalem, and in the service of the hated Roman conqueror. Yet somehow, perhaps through a friend's urging — and on the great Judgment Day the person who helped bring Cornelius to the Lord will be received with exceeding joy — he had learned to know the one true God and to spurn the heathen idols. — Christians of America, with similar mission opportunities before everyone of you, put these questions to yourselves: "Am I helping to bring people to Christ? Are my life and my testimony drawing men to their Savior?" A Memphis woman telephoned four thousand people urging them to tune to our broadcast; a Chicago friend mails hundreds of letters for the same purpose. Have you ever invited anyone to listen in? Will you not make it your objective personally to direct at least one soul to this Gospel message every week? We shall gladly send you announcement leaflets and helpful literature upon request. Keep clearly in mind what the Bible says of those who lead others to faith, *"They that turn many to righteousness,"* shall shine *"as the stars forever and ever"*! Can you think of a greater glory than this heavenly radiance?

We should also find a timely lesson in the fact that Cornelius, a reverent, God-fearing man, was a soldier, a commander of one hundred troops. Some believe it impossible to remain a Christian while serving under arms. They emphasize the cursing, unbelief, blasphemy, cruelty, which often mark army life, and God knows how true this indictment sometimes is. You men in the armed forces who write me of the temptations confronting you or the obstacles besetting you if you want to keep your radio tuned to our mission of the air, realize fully how easy it is to forget God while on military duty, how close the danger of disregarding your parents' instruction, rejecting Bible truth, and taking a fling at what some call "life," but what actually may be spiritual death! Yet many military men, like Cornelius, have a strong faith. I think of a Pacific Coast commanding officer who for years has set aside the time of this radio mission for regular communion with God; a colonel in the Carolinas who prays fervently for the Holy Spirit's blessing on our message; a Kansas private who writes, "I have my dial turned to your hour, and I am sure that before long the entire barracks will be listening to your 'Bringing Christ to the Nations' services." There must be sincere Christians in our armed forces, if a young soldier from London instructs his parents in Iowa to contribute twenty-five dollars of his salary each month to our mission of the air; if officers and privates in the American and Canadian forces, with a generosity proportionately greater than that of civilians, regularly send a large part of their pay for the maintenance of this radio crusade. The best morale-building agency for America's Army and Navy is the Gospel of Jesus Christ. For this I ask your prayers, interest, and support. The most we can do in bringing Christ's message to our military camps throughout the world will fall far short of paying our debt to these soldiers who risk their lives for us.

Our text also records that Cornelius *"prayed to God alway."* How many men are there in the United States today of whom it can likewise be said that they pray *"to*

God alway"? How many within the churches who pray
"*to God alway*"? Most people, even in Christian circles,
rush through their petitions in the morning and the evening and think their prayer duties are thus fulfilled.
Masses are too preoccupied, self-sufficient, or indifferent
to know the real blessing of fervent intercession. Before
this war is over, some of you who haughtily claim that
kneeling before the Almighty is weak and womanish will
be driven to your knees when you realize your utter helplessness without Him. You business executives need the
guiding, sustaining power of communion with God. You
are making more money than you thought possible a few
years ago, but some of you likewise are more disturbed
and distracted than ever before. A successful sales di-
rector told me that he had stacks of unfilled orders and
had to avoid buyers, who were eager to purchase anything he could sell and in any amount he could supply.
Yet he confessed that he was not happy. Only closeness
to Christ can put real joy into life.

Especially noteworthy is the interest Cornelius took
in his home. We read that he "*feared God with all his
house.*" He knew that as a father, despite his military affairs, he had a definite responsibility toward his family.
His wife, his children, the servants in the household, all
were under his spiritual guidance. Contrariwise, some of
you fathers do not care where your boys or girls were
last night, where they will be tonight. You have never
spoken to them about their souls. You have given them
money, education, protection, and a certain kind of love,
but you have withheld the most important gift a father
can bestow — direction and guidance to heaven. I should
think you would be afraid to face eternity, because you
have not only steadfastly refused to bring your children
to Jesus, but you have constantly kept them from their

Savior by your own bad example of unbelief. Your little ones have looked up to you; yet by your disinterestedness in Church, their minds were molded against the Christian faith. What will you say on that great day of appearing before the Lord, when Christ will ask, "Where are the sons and daughters I gave you?" What will you answer when your children, your own flesh and blood, point an accusing finger at you and declare: "Father, you never told us of God's truth; you never took us to church; you never went yourself. You led us astray." Fathers of America, recall the terrifying sentence of woe Jesus pronounced on all who give such offense; and before it is too late, turn to Christ! Give up everything which keeps you from serving as God's representative in your own home! Keep first things forever first! The foremost of your responsibilities, after you yourself have come to your Savior, is not, as blessed as this is, that you help evangelize dark Africa, support missions among the Eskimos, but that you bring your own household to the Redeemer. Scripture declares, *"Learn first to show piety at home!"*

Cornelius also knew how vital it was that the whole family share this faith. The text reminds us that "ALL *his house*" feared God. There was no mixture of belief and unbelief in that home. It was no house divided against itself; parents, children, servants — all could plead together, give thanks together, sing hymns together, worship together, adore one God in the same trust. Such singleness of faith is the strongest pledge of home happiness; yet often in the excitement of today's war, young people after overhasty courtships have a quick wedding ceremony performed by a justice of the peace (A bill before the Missouri legislature would enable every notary public to solemnize marriage. It ought to be crushed.) and in altogether too many instances completely disregard the questions of religion and the necessity of agreement in faith. Listening to some of these professional counselors on questions of love, marriage, and home life, you will gain the impression that religion plays no great part in marital happiness, while physical questions, social adjustments are the vital issues! Nevertheless experience, not theory, reminds us that the greatest inner blessings of family life rest on those households, rich or poor, highly cultured or simple, in which father, mother, sisters, brothers belong to the same true Christian Church and have one undying hope of salvation in the crucified, risen Savior. Because of the heartaches your letters reveal, I cannot let a broadcasting season pass without raising my voice to warn against the dangers lurking in marriages between children of God and unbelievers, Christians and Jews, Protestants and Catholics, members of opposing churches. Do not think you are an exception to the tragic results which frequently come from mixed marriages! For the most important earthly relationship you need the most powerful spiritual influence for good; and that, I tell you in Jesus' name, is the unity of true faith shared by the whole family, as by the entire house of Cornelius.

If I could speak to you personally and ask, "Is yours a faith-filled family?" many would answer, "No; ours is a strife-filled home, crowded with quarreling and bickering, marked by hatred instead of self-sacrificing love." This week I received a letter from an Illinois woman in which she told how she made life unbearable for her husband, brought discord into the home, and wished her husband dead. Now that he has died, she is tortured with remorse. Often that quarrelsome, contentious spirit goes farther. It resorts to brute force; husbands beat their wives, whom they have pledged to love and honor; at times — oh, the horror of this! — such hatred ends in murder. — Now, if you feel that love is vanishing from your home, as quarrels and nagging increase, follow Cornelius by turning to God in your family and by invoking His help through constant prayer! When you truly trust Christ and agree that He is to be the Head of your house, the deathless devotion with which He gave Himself for sin-burdened mankind will show itself in your family by a willingness to bear and forbear, to practice self-denial and self-sacrifice. Before the sin of selfishness strikes wounds which can never be healed on earth, before the separate lives some of you married folks are now living (you have your own amusements and pastimes; you share very few confidences; one goes this way and the other that) become permanently disrupted, give yourselves wholly to Christ! Bring your entire household to the Savior!

If I were to ask others among you, "Is yours a faith-filled home?" tears would come into your eyes as some of you would answer, "No; ours is a sorrow-filled home." During the ten years of our broadcast I have never before received so many letters that start in this way: "My husband was a good man until about a year ago. Then he began to drink and go out with other women." If you could read the stacks of letters — of course, they are kept strictly confidential — which deal with alcoholism, you would agree it is one of the worst scourges of present-day life. The modern tavern in many ways is certainly no improvement over the old saloon, for these drinking places which have sprung up in large numbers and attract many women can be far greater menaces. If it should be the burden of your family that the father, a grown son or daughter, or — may God forbid it! — even the mother comes home drunk, what should you do? What must you do, if not, following Cornelius, pray constantly, beseeching God for His almighty aid? Though slavery to alcohol is a strong curse, the Lord is far stronger. He has helped men who have listened to our program break the bonds of this terrible tyranny. Kneeling before their radios, they have pledged themselves to stop drinking, and they have kept that pledge. He can help you if this is your besetting weakness.

Other homes are marked by deep-rooted grief caused by pain, sickness, and suffering. A California listener writes that through a physician's carelessness her baby was born a spastic, without control of its members, because a large part of its brain was torn. While repeated operations have shown some improvement, according to the verdict of specialists the child is doomed to a lifetime of abnormality. Yet that mother is learning to love Christ, and therefore she loves that poor, handicapped child, caring for it by day and night. The Lord will sustain her, just as He will support those families burdened with life-long sickness, invalidism, and injury if only they put their whole trust in Him.

There is no domestic affliction in which God cannot aid. If your sons or daughters have disgraced your name, reliance on Christ can lead you to forgive and help them. If you are in danger of losing your home or your hard-earned savings, you can have the assurance of divine guidance; but to secure that blessing, let the spirit of Cornelius rule your household! You can face the cruelest personal anguish life can offer: broken marriage vows, desertion; you can meet the deepest sorrow known to the race: the death of a beloved one on the battle front or the home front; still you can defeat rankling resentment and despair. If you would have that benediction, it must be said of you and your family, as it is written of Cornelius, *"He . . . feared God with all his house . . . and prayed to God alway."*

II

YOUR FAMILY CAN BE FAITH-FILLED THROUGH CHRIST

None of you should ever question the truth that the Christ of all compassion will come to bless your home, no matter how large or small, how approved or despised, how happy or sorrow-filled. Keep clearly in mind that Cornelius was a Gentile; and up to this time, months after Jesus had been crucified, had arisen and ascended into heaven, no messenger of His Gospel had ever crossed the threshold of a pagan home! That, it was thought, would make them unclean. The Apostles had reserved the message of salvation for their own countrymen. One day, however, Cornelius received a vision from the Lord, directing him to send for Peter. About the same time God instructed Peter to visit Cornelius, and in this way the Apostle for the first time in his life entered a Gentile dwelling. What a marvelous day that was! If only we knew its exact date, we ought to celebrate it each year! If only we knew the spot where Cornelius' house stood in Caesarea, we ought to mark it with a tablet indicating that at this place began the promise of the Gospel's reach into every home.

True, some churches deliberately teach that the Lord of love, limiting His mercy, offers it only to a select few, while He has damned the others in advance without giving them a chance to be saved. This is a shocking denial of the universal, world-wide compassion to which Scripture repeatedly testifies. It is likewise true that some congregations cater to the upper classes and show little interest in the common people and the underprivileged. How directly this contradicts our Lord, whose life constantly illustrates an opposite tendency! Again, it is equally evident that many people think themselves too poor, unnoticed, unlearned, sinful, to have and hold the promises of Gospel grace; yet the account of Peter's visit to Cornelius' home is God's own restatement of His Son's pledge, *"Behold, I stand at the door and knock; if any man hear My voice and open the door, I will come in to him and will sup with him, and he with Me."* The high and mighty may never come to your door. The self-righteous and self-esteeming may frequently pass your house by. Friends and relatives may keep their distance. Jesus, however, will never neglect or spurn you. The Savior who invited Himself into the despised home of the outcast publican Zacchaeus, who banished doubt when He abode with the Emmaus disciples, who brought comfort as He lingered with Mary and Martha at Bethany, who gave life when death entered another centurion's household at Capernaum, who repeatedly came with healing into the rooms of the sick and suffering, is the Christ for everyone, the Redeemer for every home, the almighty God for every family.

See how easily yours can be a faith-filled home! Cornelius received the Lord's command and obeyed it. If you follow God's instructions, obey His Word in marriage regulations; if you refuse to reject parenthood and instead welcome your babies as the precious miracles of divine love; if you teach these children the heavenly truth and give them Christian education; if you let the Word of God *"dwell in you richly"* and make time, the most valuable moments in the whole day, for the whole family to approach God in prayer and praise; and if all this is based on personal faith in Jesus, no power on earth can keep the Savior from your household.

This trust in Christ is the keystone in the arch of home blessing and hope. Therefore Peter brought Cornelius the message which every Christian pastor should bring the families in his congregation — not a discussion of the war or the weather, but the appeal for the acceptance of the Redeemer's love. The climax of that first sermon preached in a Gentile house was the whole Gospel in these nine Spirit-sent words, *"Whosoever believeth in Him [Christ] shall receive remission of sins."* Put this truth into American family life; let parents and children learn to receive and revere Jesus — God and Man, God and Savior, God and Lord; let the full, unrestricted promise of the blood and the cross, the death and the atonement at Calvary, convert all within the household to the faith which I pray will be yours, namely, that by trusting Christ, your sins — your many, repeated, degrading, damning sins — are removed completely; let this victorious confidence fill every family, and the new day of inner joy, spiritual strength and moral power will dawn for the American home!

We read, *"While Peter yet spake these words, the Holy Ghost fell on all them which heard the Word."* If you will listen to the Lord, the same renewing, enlightening, purifying Spirit can fortify your families, so that, faith-filled, they also become Spirit-filled, endowed with God's power. When Cornelius and those gathered with him heard the Apostle's appeal (note that Cornelius did what you should do: he invited others to his home; he wanted the message to reach as many as possible), all of them, young and old, were baptized. And all of you should receive this *"washing of regeneration,"* for no one less than Christ Himself — remember, you who belittle the Sacrament! — declared, *"He that believeth and is baptized shall be saved."*

In that Savior's name I beseech you to follow the plan and pattern which brought Cornelius such joy: First, pray to the Father continually for guidance! Pray with your

whole family! Second, obey God's Word unfailingly!
Third, welcome the messenger of His mercy, the prophet
of His peace! Be sure, however, that he brings the whole,
genuine Gospel! Don't criticize the Church! Don't speak
caustically of its work because you may have had some
personal disappointment! Instead look to the Savior and
His true Church for help and hope! Let us send you
a servant of God who will do what Peter did for that
family in Caesarea: show you the way to Jesus, bring
you and yours to baptism and membership in the Church!
What greater gift can God Himself give you on this earth
than these blessings of a faith-filled family?

Such Christ-dedicated homes can be centers of earth's
highest happiness, the foundation for the nation's strongest defense, the means of the Kingdom's greatest growth,
the source of strength and support during the troubled
days ahead, when American home life may be attacked
with a fury hitherto unknown. These faith-filled households, however, are more. They are the very foregleams
of our eternal home, where the whole family that worshiped Christ on earth will be reunited to adore Him in
the endless glories of heaven. Work and pray ceaselessly
that everyone in your household will be saved for this
glory! Constantly keep this hallowed, better country in
mind! High on the dome of the Capitol in Washington
is the figure of Liberty, symbolizing the freedom which
reigns on our shores. That statue was made by Hiram
Powers, who for thirty years lived in Europe, far away
from America, his native land. When asked how he could
produce this and other intensely American masterpieces,
like the Massachusetts Puritan, the California Pioneer,
although for many years he had not touched our shores,
Powers answered: "I have never been out of touch with

America. I have eaten and slept in Italy for thirty-odd years, but I have never been anywhere but in the United States." As he lived physically in Europe, but mentally in America, so may we here on earth mold, carve, sculpture our family happiness by focusing our thoughts on the celestial homeland, its reunion with our loved ones in faith and — glory of glories! — with our blessed Savior. Above all else for which we may ever ask or hope, O Christ, bring everyone of us into that heavenly home! Amen!

Faith's Glorious Discovery: Victory Close at Hand!

> "Benhadad, king of Syria, gathered all his host and went up and besieged Samaria. And there was a great famine in Samaria. . . . And there were four leprous men at the entering in of the gate. . . . And when they were come to the uttermost part of the camp of Syria, behold, there was no man there. For the Lord had made the host of the Syrians to hear a noise of chariots and a noise of horses, even the noise of a great host. . . . Wherefore they arose and fled in the twilight. . . . When these lepers came to the uttermost part of the camp, they went into one tent and did eat and drink, and carried thence silver and gold and raiment and went and hid it; and came again and entered into another tent, and carried thence also and went and hid it. Then they said one to another . . . Come that we may go and tell the king's household."
>
> 2 KINGS 6:24, 25; 7:3, 5-9

Gracious, Glorious God:

*M*ay Thy Spirit strengthen us to realize at all times that through faith in the Lord Jesus Christ, Thou art close to us with Thy love, Thy strength, Thy blessing! When life's sorrows are heaped on us; when doubt of the Savior's mercy assails us or temptations assault us, fortify our faith, so that with absolute certainty we know how Jesus defeated every enemy of our soul! By His atoning death He conquered sin, hell, and the grave. Grant that our trust in the atoning Savior increase daily and, O Father of all truth, bring us constantly closer to our ever-blessed Redeemer! Show our men and women on the far-flung battle lines how near Christ can be to them in each

238

harassed hour, if only with unquestioning faith they cling to His promise "Lo, I am with you alway"! Graciously protect our country! Lead America to repentance and trust! Bless us according to Thy will with a true victory that can soon stop war's horrors! Hear us for Jesus' sake! Amen.

An Ontario friend sends us the remarkable story of a settler in Western Canada who had purchased a new farm, much of which was still covered with swamp and brush. Soon after he took over the property, he went hunting and was rambling through the wilderness, when nightfall overtook him. Confident that he could find his way home, he started out, despite the darkness, through treacherous marshlands and untracked forests. Morning came. His clothes were soaked and torn, his face and hands scratched and bleeding; worst of all, he was lost. That entire day and the following night he continued to battle his way frantically through the undergrowth. Aching, exhausted, half starved, he was seized by the desperate fear that he would die in the wilderness. Resting on a log for a few agonized moments, he suddenly heard a rooster crow; and rarely, I suppose, has that barnyard song been more welcome. He knew that he was close to a farm, and with new courage he headed in the direction from which the sound had come. Before long he stumbled from the thicket into a large clearing — which proved to be his own property. Only a few hundred rods from his own farmland, he had concluded that he was lost, beyond hope of rescue.

Most of you have read similar stories, accounts of fugitives in hiding for years even though they had been pardoned; battles fought by armies unaware that peace had been declared; sailors in the South Atlantic who almost died of thirst, not realizing that their rafts were floating in the fresh water the Amazon River sends far out into the ocean; soldiers hiding in fear of the enemy when in reality they were safe behind their own lines; families living in poverty while an immense pool of oil remained untapped beneath their scrubby acres. Yet of all instances in which terror-stricken men have overlooked the help close beside them, the Bible story chosen as our text is the most startling; for it shows an entire army, a capital, famished when food almost beyond measure was within easy reach. Because too many of you similarly suffer in spiritual weakness when God's strength is heaped high around you, because your faith is starved though He has placed soul nourishment right before you, I pray God that in the battle of life you will make

FAITH'S GLORIOUS DISCOVERY: VICTORY
CLOSE AT HAND!

For this assurance we turn to the words of Second Kings, chapters six and seven, and read in selected verses: *"Benhadad, king of Syria, gathered all his host and went up and besieged Samaria. And there was a great famine in Samaria. . . . And there were four leprous men at the entering in of the gate. . . . And when they were come to the uttermost part of the camp of Syria, behold, there was no man there. For the Lord had made the host of the Syrians to hear a noise of chariots and a noise of horses, even the noise of a great host. . . . Wherefore they arose and fled in the twilight. . . . When these lepers came to the uttermost part of the camp, they went into one tent and did eat and drink, and carried thence silver and gold and raiment and went and hid it; and came again and entered into another tent, and carried thence also and went and hid it. Then they said one to another . . ., Come that we may go and tell the king's household."*

I

DISCOVER THE GLORIOUS VICTORY CHRIST HAS WON!

The powerful Syrian army under Benhadad, their king, had besieged the city of Samaria. So tightly were the Israelites locked in their capital that their food supply was completely cut off. Before long a horrifying famine began. An ass's head sold for eighty pieces of silver — a fortune in those days. Garbage was literally worth its weight in precious metal. A mother cooked her own child and ate it.

I hope that none of you will object: "This is ancient history; it could not happen here!" Are you positive? Ten years ago who would have believed that horse meat would be sold on open markets in America and food restricted in a country as productive as ours? While everyone of us would willingly have two, three, four meatless days each week, provided our armed forces are well supplied, it may not be out of place now to recall that only a few years ago 6,200,000 pigs were destroyed in the United States in a few months under a false philosophy of scarcity that stands condemned by God's Word. In 1935 7,750,000 bags of coffee — over a billion pounds — were destroyed within a single month. Can there be any connection between this and the fact that bacon and coffee are at a premium today? In the light of what we now know, would it not have been a hundred times better to follow the Savior's own example in conserving food, to have processed pork and coffee instead of wasting it? Two million tons of corn — enough to keep thousands of starving children alive in Greece — were destroyed. In Los Angeles alone 200,000 quarts of milk regularly were dumped into the water; yet in China baby girls are being sold because their parents have no milk to give them.

Mountains of oranges were piled up to decay; apples, cherries, strawberries, remained unpicked; vast acreages of vegetables rotted in the ground. We systematically deprived ourselves of the divine bounty; and now we are driven to rationing, as though God Himself would say, "O America, I blessed you as no other nation on the face of the earth, but you spurned My bounty, you wasted My gifts; so I have permitted some of My blessings to be withdrawn, and instead of lavish overflow, your food will be measured to you."

Now, though the siege in our text was so dreadful that it left the capital half crazed with hunger, actually there was food in abundance for all. While the Syrian armies, haughty in their assurance of victory, were securely encamped about the city, the Lord came out against them; and so almighty is He that the multiplied battalions of Benhadad's trained warriors could not resist Him. We read that God *made the host of the Syrians to hear a noise of chariots and a noise of horses, even the noise of a great host.* In their dismay the besieging Syrians thought, *"Lo, the king of Israel hath hired against us the kings of the Hittites and the kings of the Egyptians to come upon us."* Panic spread through the regiments; such fear and confusion reigned that they *"arose and fled in the twilight and left their tents and their horses and their asses, even the camp as it was, and fled for their life."* The Almighty required no men, armies, battle strategy, to put those formidable foes to flight — only a few sounds: the noise of chariots and armies that never existed.

Similarly the Lord can end this war today. His power in nature can liquidate the strongest armies. His ocean kept Xerxes back and defeated that proud tyrant; His winds blew the haughty Spanish Armada to its doom; His cold and ice routed Napoleon; His snowflakes, drift upon drift, pushed Hitler's shock troops back from the Volga. Will you not believe that the Lord of hosts could destroy the whole Japanese fleet from the Aleutians to New Guinea with a single blast of His hurricane or that a single earthquake could level Tokio? Again and again in the Old Testament records we read accounts of such majestic triumphs over the opponents of God's people. His power is not weakened since those days; but to secure His blessing, we must come contritely before Him, confessing all our sins, national and individual. The Nazis and Nipponese are not the only enemies of the United States. Within our own borders we have America's inner adversaries, for whose rejection of the Almighty, repudiation of Christ, and ridicule of the Bible this war may be prolonged. The Lord is not blind, that He cannot behold the entrenched godlessness on our shores. He is not indifferent, that He closes His eyes to wickedness in high or low places. He is not deaf, that He fails to hear the taunting attacks on His Son, His Church, His Word. License and lust, carnival and carousal, cursing and swearing, perjury and scandal, luxury and indulgence, nudity and nastiness, half-filled church buildings but overcrowded dance halls, card playing in parish houses and little praying in the members' homes — these lamentable conditions can extend the war beyond the coming summer, fall, winter, into the next year, and even beyond.

As we see this remarkable contrast — on the one hand, the people of Samaria cowering in fear, dying of starvation, and on the other hand, the Syrian armies running in reckless flight, leaving the deserted camp filled with food — let us find a far more serious parallel in the lives of those besieged by worries and fears, the distressed and desperate who are spiritually starved even though food for their soul is placed right before them. Masses of discouraged men and women feel that they have been defeated at every turn; yet the Bible, God's help particularly for the downcast and downtrodden, often remains unread, its counsel neglected. Here are the unhappy, strife-torn homes; and while the power of Christ-centered prayer is within immediate reach of every family in the United States, yet most of these families never kneel to implore inner peace and blessing. Here are souls burdened with loneliness, lack of love and companionship, and though the Savior is close at hand with the promise *"Lo, I am with you alway, even unto the end of the world,"* still He is never acknowledged and welcomed. Here are the legions of men and women tortured by shadowy specters of the future; but most of them daily pass true churches of God where the Redeemer's blood-bought promises could put confidence and assurance into their hearts. Here are the doubting, disturbed minds, groping for light and truth, whose questions believing teachers are ready to answer; yet too often preference is given to Christ-denying counselors. Here, in the largest group of all, are those who are enslaved by sin and driven by their conscience; every time they hear a message like this, centered on the Lord Jesus, every time they see a cross, every time their thoughts revert to the crucifixion at Golgotha, their heavenly Father, who is *"a God at hand . . . and not a God afar off,"* wants to be close to them, through His Holy Spirit, as He offers complete cleansing from their transgressions. However, in their blindness they turn away from the atoning blood and begin the hopeless treadmill task of trying to earn their admission into heaven.

For your peace of mind, joy of life, assurance of heaven, stop this overlooking Christ, passing Him by, neglecting Him! He is your God, and nothing is too hard for Him. He is your Redeemer, and no sin is too vile or vicious to be removed by His pardoning love. He is your Friend, and if you remain faithful to Him, no power can destroy His love of you. He is your Guide, and no way that you take is unknown to Him. Any opposing leader must direct you to destruction, but Jesus always chooses the right road, the right destination. He is your King, and He can protect you in every danger. Earthly rulers are often so distant or secluded that their subjects can rarely approach them; but our Savior — O marvelous mercy! — is so close that everyone of His faithful finds His help at hand for every need.

If you have never known the full heavenly blessing He offers you; if you hardly hear or use His holy name except in profanity and have only a vague, uncertain notion as to who Jesus really is; if you once acknowledged Him, but have forgotten Him in your poverty or wealth; if you now ask, "What can Jesus do for me?" listen carefully, listen prayerfully: Christ, God's Son and the Virgin's, was defeated at Calvary to give you victory, nailed to the cross to assure you of the crown, crucified to give you life! By accepting, believing, trusting Him as your Redeemer the enemies of your soul will be put to flight, as were the Syrian armies besieging Samaria. In Jesus you have victory over your sins, since you are washed and cleansed by His purifying blood. Through faith you will reject temptation, since the Holy Spirit will strengthen you to resist. You are above surrendering in despair to sorrow and suffering, because you can thank God for afflictions, which come from His mercy. You can defeat your all too human flesh and blood, with its unholy desires and cowardly fears, since by accepting Jesus you are *"born again"* with a new determination to subdue evil. You can successfully repel this cruel, hostile world of war and hatred that continually opposes Him, for the Bible definitely pledges, *"This is the victory that over-cometh the world, even our faith."* You can put hell and its power to flight, for by His crucifixion and resurrection Jesus broke Satan's dominion forever. You can conquer death, *"the last enemy,"* for at the Savior's open grave, assured of your own resurrection, you can exult: *"O Death, where is thy sting? O Grave, where is thy victory? . . . Thanks be to God, which giveth us the victory through our Lord Jesus Christ!"*

In short, when you place yourself at Calvary beneath the Redeemer's cross and raise your hand in an oath of allegiance, proclaiming valiantly: "Thou, O Christ, art mine, and I am Thine. With Thy help I will serve Thee in soul, mind, and body," the super victory of the ages is yours. You can join Saint Paul in challenging: *"Who shall separate us from the love of Christ? shall tribulation or distress or persecution or famine or naked-ness or peril or sword? . . . Nay; in all these things we are* MORE THAN CONQUERORS *through Him that loved us."* — This, dearly redeemed fellow sinners, the guarantee of God's guidance for this life, the assurance of everything you need for heaven, is close at hand. I plead with you in the Savior's name, "Claim your victory!"

II

DISCOVER THE GLORIOUS VICTORY CHRIST HAS WON *FOR YOU!*

The besieged people of Samaria were to learn of their rescue in a most remarkable way. Our text tells us of four lepers outside the gate, who because of their dread disease were banned from the city and, since they were Israelites, could expect nothing but death from the encircling Syrians. In the torment of hunger they argued that, if they had no hope of escaping death, they could lose little by entering the enemies' camp and appealing for a few crusts of bread. Stealthily they make their way toward the Syrian encampment. They come to the sentry's outpost, but these frontline guards are missing. They advance to the outer tent rows; these are empty. They hurry past the supply houses, the officers' quarters; not a sound is to be heard. They rush to the center of the camp; not a soul is in sight. Instead, on all sides, marks of confusion and flight! It soon dawns on the bewildered minds of these four lepers that the enemy has been thrown into panic-stricken retreat.

As the first Israelites to discover the victory were lepers, social outcasts, living in vile, isolated places and crying, "Unclean! Unclean!" when anyone approached them, so by God's grace the promise of eternal triumph is often first revealed and most joyfully accepted by the lowly, oppressed, persecuted. This emphasizes the truth that there is room in God's kingdom for everyone, especially the burdened and underprivileged. A man wrote me last week to ask why American churches are not more interested in poor people, and I want to answer by saying that true churches of Christ have always been vitally concerned about the destitute. In fact, the early Church was made up of poor people, slaves, outcasts, and, thank God, a sprinkling of the mighty, the wealthy, the learned. Since those beginnings Scriptural churches have always been eager to reach the suffering masses. The danger hour arrives when congregations become rich and socially influential; when, as some of you write from your own experiences, they look askance at the cheaper clothes, the lower financial rating, the humbler social position. Such discrimination is as contrary to Jesus as black midnight to brightest noon and can lend support to the Communist charges (and, make no mistake about it, these will be raised with increasing hatred during the adjustment of the postwar period!) claiming that Christianity is capitalistic, opposed to the workingman.

When the starved lepers discover that the camp is deserted, a scene of intense interest follows. First of all they find food beyond measure and imagination — good food, fresh food, clean food, life-saving food. These sufferers who had eked out a miserable existence, living almost literally from the garbage dumps of the city, now have their choice of meat, fruit, and vegetables. Hardly is their hunger satisfied, when they begin to discover silver, gold, jewels, more than they can collect. The text pictures them as running from one tent to the other. They spy a large chest left behind in the flight. They break the lock and there, wide-eyed and amazed, behold gold bars, silver chains, a handful of rubies, a box of pearls, an ornament studded with emeralds, engraved bracelets, heavy onyx seal rings. Swiftly they bury these treasures and rush to another tent, to find an even larger chest, perhaps the paymaster's, filled with Syrian shekels of gold and silver; and these lepers who had lost everything in life — health, money, happiness — now fill their hands with coins and let them trickle through their fingers. This money they also carry away to a secret hiding place. They speed into another tent, uncover a complete wardrobe of costly garments — crimson and purple, silk and wool, woven with gold, studded with jewels; they tear the filthy rags from their bodies and clothe themselves in resplendent robes, such as they have never worn before. What a startling change! On the morning of that day the lepers are destitute, in dirty rags and starving. In the evening the choicest Syrian foods are heaped before them; they are fabulously rich; they are robed in the best cloth Damascus weavers can produce.

An even more amazing change awaits you when you discover the glorious victory that is yours by faith in the Lord Jesus. You find a joy you never before could believe possible. Your sins are forgiven, your conscience quieted; you have peace with God through the blood of His Son, peace with your fellow men, peace with your own heart. That is why some of you have written me, as an Illinois listener did last week: "You cannot imagine the happiness which has come into our home since my husband has become a Christian and joined the Church. Ours is a new family. We have a joy and a closeness to Jesus we never knew before." That is why many of you have sent letters to explain you are really reborn creatures in Christ, that *old things are passed away*," since you have accepted Him. Like the lepers, you were hunted and haunted, desperate and downcast, doomed to spiritual death — until you discovered the glorious Gospel grace; and then a new existence, with hope, blessing, and the pledge of salvation, really began. You, the children of God, who have this victory in Christ, will join with me as I ask every unconverted sinner in this audience to give himself wholly to his Savior and in return enjoy the best, truest, happiest life.

Recall the overflowing measure of food, precious metal, and treasures those lepers discovered, since you may well find in this a picture, weak and insufficient, of course, of the overabundant soul blessings daily assured you through the Lord Jesus! Even if we have transgressed the divine Law frequently; if we have repeated the same sin against better knowledge, the supply of His saving grace is so boundless that, when we truly repent, He will remove all our iniquities. You may think, in short-sighted misunderstanding of the full Gospel grace, that you have suffered too many, deep, and permanent sorrows ever again to experience real joy; yet, if you will stop limiting His mercy, you will not only discover, "Earth hath no sorrow that Heaven cannot heal"; you will also experience the fulfillment of His promise *"As thy days, so shall thy strength be."*

Find a pointed parallel also in the glorious truth that, as those lepers obtained an overflowing measure of gold, silver, jewels, costly clothing, without earning or paying for their abundance, so the Bread of Life and the Living Water are yours by mercy, not merit. The Evangelist of the Old Testament cries out, *"Ho, everyone that thirsteth, come ye to the waters; and he that hath no money, come ye, buy, and eat; yea, come, buy wine and milk without money and without price!"* The robes of righteousness in which you must stand before the all-holy Judge of Eternity are beyond purchase; yet, because they are given you by grace, through faith, you can exult:

> Jesus, Thy blood and righteousness
> My beauty are, my glorious dress!

The lepers found the whole camp cleared of the Syrians; for God had given Israel a final, complete triumph. In a vastly greater victory Christ has vanquished our enemies, now and for eternity. His Gospel does not teach us that Jesus only partially overcame our adversaries and we must finish the task. The Bible knows of no fractional freedom by which our Lord went only a portion of the way in securing our deliverance and we must go the rest. We are not told, " *'Behold the Lamb of God,'* which has begun to take *'away the sin of the world,'* " so that we must now carry on, earning our own pardon or having someone else, living or dead, secure it for us. This destructive error contradicts the heart and essence of our Christian faith. When the Son of God, crucified at Calvary, moaned out into the darkness enshrouding that scene of murder, *"It is finished,"* the divine plan for the emancipation of the race was indeed completed, so that no man, saint, angel, or archangel can add anything to the redemption by Jesus. Sin, hell, and death are forever vanquished in His eternal victory. For this reason the Bible assures us, *"There is . . . now no condemnation to them which are in Christ Jesus."* Therefore it promises the believers, *"Sin shall not have dominion over you."*

Once more, then, I lay before you in Jesus' name this alternative: On the one hand, reject Christ, who is close beside you; refuse to believe the Gospel which you have now heard; turn away from the Lord's mercy which this message brings into your home, placed, as it were, right in front of you — and you spurn the Son of God; you forfeit His guarantee of joy in this life and of everlasting radiance in heaven! On the other hand, accept Jesus; trust Him humbly but wholly as your own all-powerful Redeemer; return to Him in contrite repentance if you have willfully strayed from His outstretched arms — and as those lepers found vast supplies, immeasurable riches, so your soul will discover in the Savior, before you in this vital moment of glorious deliverance, that every hostile force assailing your soul is defeated forever by His sure, blood-bought salvation! God grant that you will not make the tragic mistake of refusing His magnificent mercies which are nearer to you even than the radio bringing this plea! Are you sure — and I am asking not only the men and women under arms, but also you civilians in the uncertainty of present-day life — are you sure that the Lord of love will ever again be as close to you as He is now, that this personal appeal to accept Him will ever be repeated? If you do not come to Jesus in this world, you cannot approach Him in the next. There is no second chance.

Many of you are the Lord's, and I remind you that, after those lepers had made sure that some of the treasure was theirs, they ran back to the besieged city to bring the famished and dying the news of the victorious deliverance. In a much higher degree, you, grateful for your blessings in Christ, deeply desirous of showing your thanks to Him who endured the shame and unspeakable agony of the cross, will likewise want to hasten out into this baffled, besieged world to bring men, famished for the truth, dying in spiritual ignorance, the message: "Your foes are in flight! Victory now is yours in Jesus!" Testify to the Savior who has broken the siege of evil in your life!

Will you not help this mighty mission of the air, spreading the message of Christ's mercy to all men, by giving us the pledge of your prayers and your gifts? During the past weeks God's grace has permitted us to add sixteen new stations in the Argentine, a chain of seven powerful outlets in Chile, a strong network of nine transmitters in Cuba and nine in Peru — forty-one new or replaced stations in Latin America — a mighty step forward in our spiritual Good Neighbor Policy. As amazing as this increase seems when we compare it with the small start we made ten seasons ago, it is hardly more than the beginning. It is our purpose to secure every available and suitable station throughout the world for the spread of the eternal Gospel. With your help and by our heavenly Father's promise we will succeed, because we have the sacred objective to proclaim the redeeming Christ, the atoning Lord of love, the resurrected Son of God; to help men and women come out from the siege imposed by their sins and sorrows, discover Jesus, and declare that He is theirs by faith, theirs freely, theirs completely, theirs assuredly. God help us in this privilege and task for our Savior's sake! Amen!

Why Must We Suffer?

"Whom the Lord loveth He chasteneth."
HEBREWS 12:6

O God, Triune, True, and Eternal:

*A*mid the sorrows of this heavy hour, teach us by Thy Spirit to approach our blessed Savior with all our burdens and worries, assured that He can and will help us! So increase our confidence in Christ, His power to save us to the uttermost and His divine love for our sin-bound souls, that we accept adversity without protest or despair, convinced that "the sufferings of this present time are not worthy to be compared with the glory which shall be revealed in us" when we come home to Thee in heaven! Comfort especially all Thy children suffering from the agonies of war: the imprisoned, the starving, the oppressed, the wounded, the dying! In their darkest hours help them believe that through Jesus, the sin-atoning Redeemer, their sorrow shall be turned to joy! Fervently we beseech Thee, O God of wisdom, power, and love: turn this war into peace; direct the course of the nation's leaders along the pathways of righteousness, guard our armed forces, bring many in this broad land to repentance and faith! Hear us for Jesus' sake, since our only help is in Him! Amen.

Why does God permit this war to continue? How can He see millions killed or crippled for life without calling a halt to world-wide bloodshed and brutality? Where is the power — if the Lord is almighty — that can stop all the misery and cruelty with which our age has been cursed? Who can explain why, on the one hand, God is good, merciful, gracious, compassionate and, why on the other hand, every day men and women are crushed by agonies almost beyond their endurance?

These are the questions of our disturbed day, asked

not only by atheists and enemies of religion who contend that human suffering proves there can be no loving Deity, but also by bewildered believers, who, staggering under the burden of anguish, cry out, "Why must I bear this misery? How can God lay all this suffering on me?"

Do not imagine for a moment, my afflicted friends, that you alone are troubled by the mystery of suffering. One of the earliest books in the Bible, the record of Job, deals with this difficulty. You feel the war's hardships; but has anyone in our audience sustained losses as large as Job's, when treacherous enemies captured his men, all his herds and flocks? Perhaps you have received a notification from Washington that your son was killed in action; Job lost seven sons and three daughters in a single day. Others among you are stricken by sickness, groaning in pain; Job suffered from a form of leprosy that made his body a mass of boils and sores — the worst torture in this life Satan himself could devise. Family trouble has crossed many of your thresholds; misunderstanding between husband and wife may have marred your home happiness; yet, when Job, lying on an ash heap, scratching the inflamed, ulcerous surfaces of his body with a potsherd, cries desperately for help, his wife, who above all people should have brought comfort, taunted him for his trust in the Lord and cruelly sneered, *"Curse God and die!"* Then, when he found no human explanation of his agonies, Job turned to his Maker, asking, *"Show me wherefore Thou contendest with me!"* (chapter ten, verse two). That old, but ever new question,

WHY MUST WE SUFFER?

Why this war? Why our personal pains? Why this great grief in our hearts? we shall answer with a word from

Holy Scripture, the strengthening assurance in Hebrews, chapter twelve, verse six, *"Whom the Lord loveth He chasteneth."*

I

CHRISTIANS, UNLIKE UNBELIEVERS, DO NOT SUFFER
BECAUSE GOD IS ANGRY WITH THEM

When Job sought the reason for his torture, he approached God. Only through the Almighty and His revealed truth can we, too, solve the enigma of pain. Our schools, our highly praised culture, our scientific research, are unable to explain sorrow. If godless education fails dismally — as it often does — in producing even outwardly good, clean, constructive lives; if a college president is imprisoned because of a serious crime; if a Chicago psychologist reveals that intelligence does not help avoid lawbreaking, how can we expect human reason to solve this inner problem of suffering?

Yet, in their blindness, men reject divine guidance to insist that everything in life comes from chance, cruel or kind. Fate, they declare, smiles on some people, and they have an easy, rich, untroubled existence. Fate frowns on others, and they are beset with unnumbered difficulties. It is all a matter of luck. A man has no more control over his career, they tell us, than a blade of grass that may be trodden down in a moment, a leaf blown by the wind, a twig thrown into the river. Since we are only creatures of accident, they conclude, why not press every drop out of pleasure while we can and have our full fling before tomorrow comes — and death with it? What a shocking mistake! How completely it fails in every crisis! We read recently of a marine en route to the Pacific battle front who talked atheism all the way from the United States to the Solomon Islands. No God could regulate human affairs, he told his shipmates; there was no hereafter which they should fear, no Savior, no inspired Bible, no Judgment to keep them from following their lusts and desires. Under fire in Guadalcanal, however, that boisterous denier of Christ meekly told his chaplain, "If this keeps up, I will be thinking the way you do." The rejection of the Almighty, the ridicule of Jesus, when put to the test of trial and affliction, always collapse. No matter how loudly scoffers may boast that they have defeated sorrow, when confronted by death, they are often overcome by terror. They know there is a God. Their conscience gives them no rest. They realize that they must stand before the bar of eternal justice. It was to help such men in their last hours that a prisoner in the Ohio State Penitentiary at Columbus requested our *"Fear not, for I have redeemed thee!"* wall motto, for the room where murderers, condemned to the electric chair, eat their last meal.

Other skeptics have gone to the opposite extreme and declared that men suffer because they are weak. Learn to be hard, cruel, ruthless, they urge us. Smash all opposition! Away with sympathy, kindness, and mercy! Down with love! Might makes right! Don't be a weakling, be a superman! That is the delusion of Europe's dictators and the cause of immeasurable misery. May it be totally wiped off the earth!

If we now turn with Job from human failure to sacred truth and ask God in His Word why we endure pain, we must recognize that our text, *"Whom the Lord loveth He chasteneth,"* implies a difference in the suffering inflicted on Christ's disciples and on God's enemies. You need not search long or deeply in the Scriptures to learn why unbelievers meet reverses and anguish. They are under divine wrath; their sorrow is the punishment for their sins.

If you put the question, What is the reason for this world war? I answer, This conflict is a punishment for every unbeliever. If you continue, Why does God not stop this bloodshed today? the explanation again is this: In the sight of our almighty and all-holy Lord men have not yet paid sufficient penalty for their wickedness. Divine wisdom has permitted our country to be attacked because too many Americans have been God-less, Christ-less, faithless. God gave us more churches than most other nations. Yet more than 55 per cent of our citizens have no membership in any congregation. On an average Sunday more than half of those who call themselves believers are not found in their houses of worship. Many who do attend hear a denial of God's truth, the rejection of our Savior's atonement, an attack on the hope of the resurrection. God gave the United States stalwart Christian schools founded on firm faith with loyalty to Jesus, their Cornerstone; but human reason has dethroned sacred revelation in many of these classrooms. The Lord gave us homes, the best history has known; but we have gone further than most other nations in permitting them to be broken. Can you not see, therefore, that the visitation of this struggle cries out with bleeding emphasis to every unbeliever in the country: "Repent! Get right with God!"? Before winning the war and winning the peace, we must win divine favor.

Some of you may be smiling in a superior, cynical way at this plea for a return to the Almighty; many of our soldiers in the fields do not favor such ridicule. A chaplain in the Aleutians told me that his men read God's Word and give themselves to prayer, since they realize how quickly they may face death. A young lieutenant who has met the enemy face to face writes: "I plead: Tell America to pray! This war will not end until nations and peoples have paid in blood and tears for thrusting Christ out of their hearts and countries. Tell them to send Bibles and more Bibles!" He continues, "You complacent, bridge-playing, cocktail-drinking mothers, why don't you teach your son about God instead of handing him a cigarette and dance program? Get down on your knees and ask God to forgive your sins and then pray for the Army! Pray! Pray! Pray! And you preachers" (he refers to the Christ-denying moralists, book reviewers, news commentators, Modernists and Sadducees, in the American pulpits), "why don't you teach the people to pray? Only repentance for sins can stop the shellings and the killing." He adds, "I would like to have this letter broadcast over every radio in America." We have done our part in complying with his request, because we are completely convinced that the Church's mission for our land in this hour must be the continued appeal for contrition and return to God.

Therefore to every unbeliever I say pointedly: If you have met reverses more crushing than you have ever known; if you must endure grief and hardship heavier than you have ever been forced to carry, do not try to console yourself with the vain hope that your fortune will change and your difficulties will soon disappear! Why clench your fist against the Almighty and boast that you will conquer your calamities? Without the Lord Jesus you are beaten before you start, doomed to perpetual defeat. Stop resigning yourself to bitterness or despair; rather be honest, fair, open enough to hear what God says about the sorrows encircling your life! Admit that you are paying for your own stubborn rebellion against the Lord, that even now you are beginning to experience the tenor of God's everlasting wrath! If everything has gone wrong in your life, do not attack God, blame luck or chance, censure your family or your friends! Accuse yourself; and as the Spirit now urges you to cease your resistance, approach Christ, plead fervently, "O *'God, be merciful to me, a sinner,'* an unbeliever, a blasphemer, a scoffer! Forgive me for Jesus' sake!"

That prayer and the faith behind it will help give you the second, the strengthening answer to our question "Why must we suffer?" — the assurance which only those blessed by Christ can ever have. When you believe that the Son of God is your Redeemer and realize that without the Savior you are hopelessly, eternally, irrevocably lost, rejected by the great and glorious Lord of eternal justice, damned to hell, and then, when you take these glorious passages, *"God so loved the world that He gave His only begotten Son, that whosoever believeth in Him should not perish, but have everlasting life";* or, Christ *"loved"* us *"and gave Himself for"* us; or, *"He was wounded for our transgressions, He was bruised for our iniquities,"* and you apply their comfort so completely to yourself that you can say, " *'God so loved'* me *'that He gave His only begotten Son'* "; and, again, "Christ *'loved'* me, *'and gave Himself for'* me"; and again, " *'He was wounded for'* my *'transgressions, He was bruised for'* my *'iniquities'* "; when you find the central power of the Christian faith in the Savior's becoming your Substitute, suffering for your sins, paying their penalty, serving the sentence of their guilt — then, by the joy of this inner conviction you know you are God's. Christ has removed every barrier between you and your heavenly Father. All the dark-red stains of many sins which could send your soul to hell have been washed away by His holy, precious blood. You are convinced that notwithstanding the accusing voice of conscience, the fears of your own doubtings, the contradictions of unbelieving men, you are saved completely, eternally.

When I assure you that God loves you and because you are Christ's He will not punish you in His anger, this does not mean, of course, that Christians will not suffer. Indeed, as a group, they have always endured much more of the world's hostility and carried a larger burden of agony than most unbelievers. The Apostle's ultimatum, once addressed to the believers, still holds true, *"We must through much tribulation enter into the kingdom of God."* In the years ahead Christians may be tried as never before. But when God's Word strengthens believers with the pledge, *"There is therefore now no condemnation to them which are in Christ Jesus,"* it also tells them that they will no longer be punished for their sins, since our Lord — praise be His matchless mercy! — paid the full penalty, completely atoned for every transgression, removed the curse of all evil from our lives. Jesus (and you can find His name in the New Testament more than seven hundred times, to give you more than seven hundred assurances of your salvation) Christ (and you can find that name likewise more than 350 times, to give you more than 350 promises that He is your anointed, long-promised Redeemer from ruin), the blessed Savior, promises you in His unbreakable Word that, because you are His, the changing events which crowd into your life come from your heavenly Father's love, His mercy, His all-seeing wisdom, His tender devotion to your soul's salvation. Beneath the cross you are persuaded — although you can never fully understand and this contradicts everything men may try to tell you — that God permits sickness, loss, sorrow, pain, a hundred kinds of suffering, to overtake you because He loves you. *"All things"* — and we must refuse to restrict Scripture — *"all things"*: sickbeds and sorrow, loneliness and opposition, accident and mental anguish, disaster and even death itself, *"work together for good to them that love God."* Therefore our text assures us, *"Whom the Lord loveth He chasteneth."*

II

CHRISTIANS, THROUGH CHRIST, SUFFER BECAUSE GOD LOVES THEM

See how this promise proves itself in the individual Christian's life! Here is a man, for instance, who, like many of you, enjoyed the blessing of a pious home and the guidance of devout parents. Years ago life was a struggle for him; but the Lord was good, granted him success and a comfortable income. Hardly had the first rays of prosperity begun to shine on Him, when he made the mistake of which every one of us in our proud self-esteem is guilty: he began to think that he himself was responsible for these blessings, that the little church where he had worshiped was too small and unnoticed, too narrow and strict, because it proclaimed the old Gospel of grace, insisted that besides Jesus Christ *"there is none other name under heaven given among men whereby we must be saved."* Gradually he neglected his private prayer; his family no longer found time to join in reading the Bible and in winging their petitions to the Throne of Mercy. Now, because God loved that man and had chosen him as His own, the Almighty had to prevent him from ruining his soul. You ought to see clearly, then, that when this man, in deadly danger of forfeiting heaven, began to lose his money, health, family happiness, this visitation came from divine grace, not anger, from the Lord who says, "I chasten you because I love you."

The hardships of this war have come to many of you who are Christ's for the same remedial purpose: to call you closer to God. When the Nazis bombed Coventry, the local cathedral was demolished. Yet the bombs which fell on the ancient structure tore the plaster from its walls, revealing two pictures of Jesus, more than four hundred years old. They had been painted on the original cathedral walls but had been covered with plaster at the time the building was enlarged and improved, thus remaining concealed until the raid. Similarly in our lives it often requires disaster to blast away the covering with which, particularly when financial success enlarges and improves our prosperity, we shut out the Savior.

Again, when the Bible declares, *"Whom the Lord loveth He chasteneth,"* we are assured that through the present conflict our heavenly Father speaks earnestly to His Christians, urging them to recognize His love even more deeply, to cling more closely to Jesus, to redeem the time more carefully. The war, by the Holy Spirit's guidance, is bringing thousands of our fighting men nearer to God. A veteran marine sergeant from Cleveland, who fought through to the victory at Guadalcanal, asks, "Do the marines pray?" and then answers, "They pray unashamedly, and often aloud." He tells of one boy in his outfit who wrote home to his parents: "You had a hard time making me go to church when I was at home. Well, you won't when I get back."

It is to be regretted deeply, however, that masses in the United States stubbornly, willfully, continuously, reject the lesson this war would teach. Unlike our fighting men, they have not seen bloody battles. Instead of risk, danger and loss, the conflict has brought them unequalled income, undreamed-of prosperity. In the month remaining before March 15 they are much concerned about what they owe the Government; yet in their narrow, selfish, ungrateful way they do not even consider the tremendous debt of gratitude they owe the Lord for permitting them to enjoy these blessings and the Christ for giving Himself as their redemption. I shudder to think of the penalty to be paid by those who, when God speaks to them, shut their eyes, close their ears, and refuse to heed the correcting, warning appeal for repentance. I pray that the Almighty will use this World War as a purging fire and send His cleansing Spirit into the souls of heroic Christian men and women who with new and undaunted courage will proclaim the Gospel, *"the power of God unto salvation."*

A celebrated physicist has said that if 2 per cent of the people in any country believe in a project completely, cling to it despite all opposition, work for it without interruption, insist on it without compromise, they will eventually win the whole country for their program. While we realize from Scripture that also in our country *"many are called, but few are chosen,"* we know just as assuredly that, if 2 per cent of our Christians — that means about 2,600,000 — would throw themselves body and soul into the task and sacred privilege of evangelizing America; if they would demand that their pulpits resound with messages of courage and faith in the Savior's redemption; if they would live Christ and preach Christ; if with the restless zeal and tireless energy men show for political and social projects, they would give up all for Jesus, with the glorious conviction of ultimate victory, then an electrifying religious awakening would begin in the United States, and the sufferings of war, by the miracle of divine mercy, could be turned into the profit of spiritual peace. Only a small, salt-of-the-earth group, under divine grace, is required to bring multitudes of troubled hearts and lives this amazing message of the Savior's love: *"Your sorrow shall be turned into joy."* Fellow worshipers, I ask now in that Redeemer's name: Will you who know *"the grace of the Lord Jesus Christ"* be among those who with the Spirit's blessing can help build the faith triumphant over trials in the hearts of your countrymen? God grant that here and now you resolve, "I will!"

We find comfort in this truth, *"Whom the Lord loveth He chasteneth,"* when we also believe that the Almighty permits suffering in order to make us realize His power and prepare us through affliction for higher responsibilities, increased blessings. One day Nathaniel Hawthorne came home with the sad news that he had been discharged from his position at the Salem Custom House. It seemed that his life was ruined. However, this loss was a disguised blessing. For now, with his wife's help, he could devote himself entirely to writing. He might have stayed at the Custom House for the rest of his life and remained an obscure official. But through that loss he gained international renown. Trust God in your own life, convinced that He who takes away what you regard as necessary for happiness can compensate you a hundredfold!

Perhaps by the marvels of Jesus' mercy you are being prepared for triumph through trials. Some supposed treasure to which your heart was firmly attached has been torn from your tight grasp, only to grant you superior boon and blessing. Job experienced that truth. The Lord gave him ten children to take the place of those who had been killed; and He restored doubly everything else the afflicted patriarch had lost in war. — The Almighty's helping hand is not shortened today. He is the same God with whom *"nothing shall be impossible"* to those who call Him Father in Christ.

Again, we know that *"whom the Lord loveth He chasteneth"* to create sympathy and increase brotherly love. Even Christians who have received Jesus' *"new com-mandment,"* *"Love one another!"* and who should reflect their Savior's devotion still have so much of the old Adam, the selfish, human nature within them, that they are not always considerate of their suffering fellow men and grumble too easily over life's small inconveniences. Some people are deeply dissatisfied with the rationing of shoes although they have more than an adequate supply. I wish they could hear the story of Mama Tumpwa in the Belgian Congo, a leper, but a firm believer in the Lord Jesus. The dread disease has already eaten away her toes and is fast destroying her feet. She has no shoes at all, and in her poverty she uses scraps of discarded rubber as knee pads, with which she literally crawls each Sunday to the mission to hear her Savior's promises. When they ask her, "Mama Tumpwa, how do you feel today?" she answers with the optimism of Christian courage, "A little bit well." God often permits us to endure agonies which others also bear so that we will know the intensity of their pain and comfort them in their misery. And what can more directly help heal war's wounds and promote a feeling of brotherhood among all sufferers, despite their differences in race and nationality, than this feeling of Christian sympathy which flows from the love of Jesus?

Because the believer finds in trial and tribulation proof positive of his Father's love, you should ask the Holy Spirit for a faith which bows submissively before the divine will and refuses to charge God with cruelty! The Seminary gardener this week began his spring pruning on our campus, and huge piles of branches have already been cut off. The shrubs and trees thus thinned out seem to shiver in the February cold. Not thoughtlessness or cruelty, but a deep interest in the proper growth and spread of the foliage prompts this pruning.

In a similar way, Jesus says, we must be purged by critical, contrary forces, so that we may bring forth more and better fruit. Tens of thousands of operations were performed in this country alone during the last week, but can the surgeons who removed diseased parts of the body and performed amputations reasonably be branded as heartless because their patients suffered pain? Why, then, accuse God of cruelty, when He cuts from our lives everything that endangers our souls?

Trust the Lord even though you wonder why particularly those who are Christ's seem to suffer the most! Henri Neil Reichelt, the son of a pastor in New Milford, New Jersey, was a seaman on the cruiser *Juneau*. In one of his last letters to his parents Henri wrote, "When the decks are cleared and the *Juneau* swings into action, every man from Captain Swenson down to the youngest blue-jacket prays, and, if he can, reads a Bible verse or glances into his book of prayer." Yet the *Juneau*, with its praying captain and praying crew, was sunk off Guadalcanal in November; and Henri Reichelt, that God-fearing young man, was one of those whom it carried to their death. We ask, "Why?" and Jesus tells us, "*What I do thou knowest not now: but thou shalt know hereafter*"; His Word assures us: "*My thoughts are not your thoughts, neither are your ways My ways, saith the Lord. For as the heavens are higher than the earth, so are My ways higher than your ways and My thoughts than your thoughts!*" Some day, in the radiance of that higher, fuller, better knowledge, we shall receive the answer to the repeated *why's*. I can promise you on the basis of God's unbreakable truth that we shall discover divine healing in every hurt, spiritual remedy in each reverse; that, if we suffered with Christ on earth, we shall reign with Him in heaven. Wait "*patiently for the Lord*"! Wait joyfully even amid heartbreaking sorrows! His deliverance is sure. No sorrow can ever overshadow you which will not end in God's right time and in His good way.

Men and women of mighty faith who found advantage in affliction have been able to join the Apostle Paul and rejoice in their infirmities. It takes the highest trust to enjoy that triumph over suffering. I read recently of a woman left alone by her husband in the heart of the Zulu country many miles from the nearest white settler. One day she saw a hideously painted savage peeping in the window. With a scream she bolted the door, locked the shutters, reached for her rifle and threatened to shoot him. He refused to go; after a while he managed to thrust a white envelope under the door. Suspicious, the woman grasped it only to find a letter entrusted by her husband to this Zulu messenger, whom he had selected to bring her word from him. You can understand, then, how, during the lonely weeks that followed, the pioneer woman, though terrorized by that fiercely marked savage, would still look eagerly for his return, since he would bring loving greetings from her beloved husband. In much the same way we recoil at the approach of affliction; yet, as soon as we rise to the heights of victorious faith and know that this is the way our Father chooses in expressing His devotion to us, we can welcome the hardest blows as evidences of His deepest affection.

Is not this the answer you need for the age-old question, "Why must we suffer?" — the assurance that once you have Jesus, you are chastened because God loves you as His preciously redeemed, protects you as the apple of His eye? Is not this Savior the help you need with increasing urgency during these turmoil days, when some of you have already faced the fierce fires of affliction, disaster, even death in your family circles, and when all of you must be prepared to meet tremendous personal and national issues?

May God give you Christ and lead you to give yourselves, wholly, contritely, trustingly to Him! As the Redeemer now appeals to you, the burdened, the afflicted, the sick, the lonely, the bereaved, the helpless, *"Come unto Me, all ye that labor and are heavy laden, and I will give you rest!"* may the Holy Spirit fill your heart with that victorious faith by which, contrite yet confident, you join in this answer:

> Just as I am, poor, wretched, blind;
>   Sight, riches, healing of the mind,
> Yea, all I need, in Thee to find,
>   O Lamb of God, I come, I come.

Amen

Softly the Savior Calls

> *"A great and strong wind rent the mountains and brake in pieces the rocks before the Lord, but the Lord was not in the wind; and after the wind an earthquake, but the Lord was not in the earthquake; and after the earthquake a fire, but the Lord was not in the fire; and after the fire a still small voice. And it was so, when Elijah heard it, that he wrapped his face in his mantle and went out and stood in the entering in of the cave."*
>
> 1 KINGS 19:11-13

O God, Our Faithful Father:

Send us Thy holy, enlightening, purifying Spirit, through whom we may now hear Christ's gentle voice pleading that we accept Him as our only Savior, spurn temptation, find comfort and courage in Scripture's promises! Show us again that because we have cleansing in Jesus' blood, salvation in His atonement, life in His death, we can trust Him wholly in every need of soul or body; that the Holy Spirit's voice within our Bibles and within us, through faith, is the only guide we need for earth and heaven! In their danger and loneliness speak comfortingly to our men and women in the armed forces, and above the roar of battle let them hear the pledge of the Redeemer's presence for all who believe! Spread Thy Gospel mightily throughout the world and use it as a divine means for ending this conflict, granting us the triumph of truth and all men on earth the blessings of a righteous peace! Hear us, O Father, as in Jesus' name we pledge ourselves anew to hear and heed the Spirit's voice within us! Amen.

As the nation pauses to honor George Washington's memory, Americans should recall our first President not only as a soldier, a statesman, an executive of outstanding achievement, but, above all, as a humble follower of Jesus. Washington's loyalty to his Redeemer was greater even than his heroic devotion to his country. He recognized how completely the welfare of the colonies required divine blessing and understood in a personal, powerful way that the only true God, without whom we could never win, but with whom we could never lose, was the God of the Bible, revealed to men in the Lord Jesus, the Redeemer of the world. Openly Washington confessed that faith. As a young man of twenty he copied reverent prayers centering in Christ's atonement. Until his death he did not shrink from giving loyal testimony. It was not flattery but absolute truth when his funeral orator proclaimed: "Let the deist reflect on this and realize that Washington, the savior of his country, did not disdain to adore and acknowledge the great Savior, whom deists and infidels affect to disdain and despise."

Christ-centered faith sustained our country's father in the dark hours of the Revolution, when American men in arms, paid in paper money, could hardly buy a full meal with a month's wages; when 1,300 soldiers set out to secure their rights from Congress at the point of the bayonet; when bloody footprints at Valley Forge marked the pathway of suffering. Washington had to contend with the personal ambition of his officers, the divided interests of the colonies, the menace of mutiny in his armies, the lack of financial support. Yet whenever he became disheartened, he took his heavy problems to God. Alone, far from his headquarters, he knelt humbly to implore guidance in Jesus' name. The Lord answered him. The quiet, but unmistakable voice of the Almighty gave him both the assurance of his own salvation and the pledge of power for his cause.

Thank God, the same Savior who spoke to Washington in those difficult days will speak to every one of us, especially the discouraged or distracted, and call us to faith and fortitude. Though we sin frequently, the merciful, compassionate Redeemer will speak to every penitent heart. For Scripture gives us this blessed assurance:

SOFTLY THE SAVIOR CALLS

To appreciate this grace more fully and to understand that our Lord comes to us not in loud and mighty movements, but gently, personally, in His Word and through His Spirit, let us learn and apply the lesson presented by our text (First Kings, chapter nineteen, verses eleven to thirteen): *"A great and strong wind rent the mountains and brake in pieces the rocks before the Lord, but the Lord was not in the wind; and after the wind an earthquake, but the Lord was not in the earthquake; and after the earthquake a fire, but the Lord was not in the fire; and after the fire a still small voice. And it was so, when Elijah heard it, that he wrapped his face in his mantle and went out and stood in the entering in of the cave."*

I

CHRIST CALLS AND COMFORTS US — NOT IN A TERRIFYING, DESTRUCTIVE VOICE

Even stalwart heroes of faith can become discouraged and disheartened, as the story of Elijah's flight shows. After God had answered his prayer on Mount Carmel by sending fire to consume his sacrifice, together with the altar, the zealous prophet thought that Israel would penitently return to Jehovah, that the tyranny of Ahab and his wicked wife Jezebel would be destroyed forever. He soon learned the discouraging fact that the masses in one moment can cry, as they did at Carmel, *"The Lord, He is the God; the Lord, He is the God!"* yet in the next bow at heathen shrines. He also experienced the fearful attempts at vengeance by a spurned, frustrated woman; for

Jezebel had sworn with a heavy oath that she would kill Elijah. Because her agents were stationed throughout the country, he had to escape quickly, secretly. He hurried across the border from Samaria into Judah, and still he was not safe. Hardly resting to regain his strength, he sped on to Beersheba, the southern edge of civilization; but he dared not stop even here. Headlong he plunged into the stony wilderness, constantly assailed by bitterness, reproaching the Almighty for the persecution now heaped on him. So this was the pay for his loyalty to Jehovah! This was the reward for the unflinching defense of his God! He told himself that his work had failed completely, that nobody besides himself believed in the Lord of hosts. Banished from his homeland like a hunted, haunted creature there in the desert, he wanted to die on the spot and end the disgrace, the despair of it all. The Almighty spurned his plea for death; instead, He miraculously strengthened the prophet; and as soon as his strength revived, he resumed his flight. If he must live, so he concluded, he would remain exiled from his fellow men to endure his persecution alone, unseen. Farther he plunged into the rocky, waterless waste, through the heat and blister of forty days, through the cold and darkness of forty nights, until he made his uncharted way down death-filled ravines and over dizzy heights to Horeb, where 550 years before Jehovah had appeared to Moses. There on the lonely boulder-strewn mountain he found a cave and hid himself in its dark recesses. As we see his form disappear into the shadows of that rocky dungeon, we ask ourselves: "Is this fugitive from God and man the same Elijah who on Mount Carmel challenged powerful enemies without flinching? Can this be the hero who in other crisis moments readily faced death in championing God's cause? *'How are the mighty fallen!'*"

We might doubt that men of Elijah's fearlessness could run away and surrender to bitterness, were it not for the fact that the same tragedy is repeated, in principle, today. The only difference is that now many people do not wait until their lives are threatened before they become discouraged; they lose heart at the first ruffling of their feelings. Men and women in this audience, I am sure, have left their church because they felt God had failed them when they lost their business, their home, their health; and all the while the Lord was planning to strengthen their faith. Some of you, your letters reveal, are staying away from divine services, leading resentful, secluded lives, because of a petty slight, a personal rebuff you think you received in the ladies' aid society, the choir, or the congregational meeting. You are going to show that you can get along quite well without them, though the selfish, revengeful hatred within you is shriveling your spirit every day you live, increasing the eternal danger to your soul. Before we criticize Elijah, hidden in Horeb's cave, let us be honest enough to admit: if we American Christians had to suffer only a small portion of the hatred heaped against that man of God, most of us would be far more resentful, louder in accusing our heavenly Father!

In the marvel of His compassion the Lord approached disheartened Elijah. The Creator who strewed the stars and planets across the expanse of space, the God who directed the course of the centuries through history's mighty upheavals, that supreme Ruler of the nations shows His love for an impatient, fear-weighted prophet. Build your hope on this truth that our heavenly Father, before whom angels shield their faces, still deals with individual, sinful men! Because Jesus Christ, true Lord and true Savior, came to "*seek and to save that which was lost,"* believe that He will come to you, whoever and wherever you are! You, too, may be far out on life's barest desert; you may shun your friends or be shunned by them; you may have outlived your beloved one, even your children, and exist friendless, alone; but through faith in the Redeemer the same God who found and comforted His bewildered prophet in the cave at Horeb will bring you hope and consolation. No one is beyond His reach, because no one is beyond His love. As this broadcast comes to you, the lonely, separated from your families by stubborn sin and selfishness; as the miracle of radio sends this message through heavy granite walls and steel bars to you in prison cells, may it show you that the Lord has found you, that His message of comfort in this moment is directed individually, pointedly to you! A few years ago a foreign correspondent told how the Prince of Wales inspected a small British hospital for hopelessly disabled victims of the First World War. He went from one cot to the other, shook hands with the men who had given more for their country than you and I can realize. Before leaving, the Prince asked the head nurse: "I was informed that there were thirty-six men here, but I have met only twenty-nine. Where are the rest?" He was told the others were so hideously disfigured that most visitors were unable to stand the shock of seeing them. He insisted on visiting them and was led into a small room to behold the wrecked bodies of men, some with features so ghastly and shocking that they had to be veiled. To them likewise the royal visitor gave what comfort he could. As he turned to leave, he counted the beds and said to the nurse, "I have seen only six men here. Where is the seventh?" Falteringly she explained: the seventh man's disfigurement was so horrifying that absolutely no one except a few hospital authorities ever went near his bed. He had a room for himself and would not leave it until carried out a corpse. "Your Highness," the nurse concluded, "please don't ask to see *him!*" The Prince did ask, and a few moments later he stood beside the maimed, misshapen form of what had once been a man, but now was an indescribable, living horror. For a moment the heir to Britain's throne paused to take hold of himself; his face was white and grim; his eyes twitched; tears rolled down his cheeks; suddenly he bent over and kissed that shunned, broken body. — Rarely do earthly rulers show this interest in sufferers and outcasts, but such seeking of the utterly destitute is the Savior's exceptionless mission of mercy. *"They that be whole,"* He says, *"need not a physician,"* as He comforts the sick and sorrowful, the disheartened and distressed, the lonely and forsaken. While the visit from the Prince of Wales could momentarily cheer those sufferers, Christ, the Prince of Peace, offers forgiveness, light, strength, salvation, eternal life. No worldly power, human might, influence of wealth or position can grant the sinner the rich blessing God gives him through the Savior.

How did the Lord come to Elijah? We read in the text that after he had entered the cave *"a great and strong wind rent the mountains and brake in pieces the rocks before the Lord."* A screaming, devastating hurricane, such as the prophet or any other man had never seen before, lifted huge granite boulders and sent them flying through space, as though they were grains of dust. Yet we read, *"The Lord was not in the wind."* Almost immediately after the wind subsided, the earth began to tremble, the fastnesses of the mountain shook, the ground rose and fell as the billows of the sea; but *"the Lord was not in the earthquake."* Hardly had these tremors stopped, when the hiss and the roar of fire swept over the heights;

yet when the red flames died out, the prophet knew that *the Lord was not in the fire.*" All nature had been tremendously convulsed, overwhelming forces loosed; still God had not spoken to him by these powerful demonstrations. Elijah's bitterness and discouragement were not removed; his soul remained untouched; he went back into his cave.

Millions in our day see a world filled with hurricanes of horror. They feel the foundations of civilization shaking, and they retreat farther into the darkness of their doubts. What will bring them out? War? Dictators build grandiose schemes, entice their fellow men into the bleeding and brutality by which empires are to be created; but God is not in their plans. The Almighty is no war lord who revels in slaughter and delights in anguish. He is the Lord of love in Christ. Do not listen to the people who tell you that the heavenly Father uses this conflict to make a better earth with bloodshed banished! The dream of a strifeless world is ruled out by God's inerrant Word. In our twentieth enlightened century, "war has reached a total eight times greater than in all previous centuries," says Harvard's Professor Sorokin. What reason is there to hope for improvement in the future? We should defend our country with all possible energy and resources, working and praying for an early, righteous victory. But let us be clear on this: war itself cannot save a single soul!

Some want to lead mankind out of its darkness by establishing an entirely new postwar world. We hear of mighty international movements by which America is to help hold the other countries in check. Before we police the world, we ought to evangelize the world. Before we tell others what they are to do, we ought first of all put our own house in order. The control of the world by the

United States, a League of Nations, an entirely new social order—these mighty programs alone will never lead mankind out of its darkness. We will thank heaven if men all over the earth enjoy the four freedoms: freedom of speech and worship, freedom from want and fear. First of all, however, they need the four spiritual freedoms: freedom of conscience, freedom from sin, hell, and death.

Others maintain that the world must be saved by social upheavals, the fire and hurricane of godless Communism. It is claimed by a Congressional committee that even officials in responsible positions at Washington advocate this overthrow of Americanism and Christianity. If this is true, they ought to be removed from office at once; for God is not in this atheistic destruction.

Still others demand a tremendous spiritual movement, a return to religion; but they do not specify which religion. Any kind of creed is certainly not enough. We like the positive conviction by which Sir George Hume, member of the British Parliament, declares: "What is needed above everything is a return to the Lord Jesus Christ, not merely as the example of a perfect man, but as the Savior, the only means by which we may be pleasing to God." The cry of this hour is not for powerful religious federations and superorganizations; not for large, wealthy, socially important churches; not for intellectually brilliant pulpit orators; not for costly vestment and ecclesiastical parade; above all, not for recourse to the sword, lighting the fires of persecution, drafting the powers of the State to punish those of a different religious persuasion. As we recall the streams of martyr blood that have flowed throughout these nineteen centuries, all the cruelty imposed by so-called Christian nations on people of the black race, the horrors suffered by the Jews under Nazi rule, we ought to understand clearly that God is not in any movement, no matter how large, which is built on persecution and oppression, that He is doubly against all tyranny operating in the name of His Son, the loving Savior.

II

CHRIST CALLS US IN "THE STILL SMALL VOICE"

After the three convulsions of nature had subsided, the prophet heard a *"still small voice."* To many it would have been merely a passing sound, a whisper; but to that man of God it was, at last, the assurance that the Lord Himself had come. As soon as Elijah heard it, *"he wrapped his face in his mantle and went out and stood in the entering in of the cave."* That *"still small voice"* produced such reverence that he shielded his countenance from beholding his Lord, such obedience and comfort that it took him from the black recesses of the cave to its entrance, ready to hear and follow divine instruction.

Throughout the centuries the Almighty has led men out of sin's night through the astonishing *"still small voice."* When in the fullness of time the climax of history dawned, and God sent His only-begotten Son to become the Mediator between heaven and earth, the Atonement for the sins of all the world, Jesus appeared, not as a resplendent conqueror with armored battalions, but as a helpless, outcast Baby. He was born not in a world capital but in a humble town of a few hundred souls. He lived not in a stately palace but in a laborer's hut. He worked not particularly with the high and mighty but among the lowly and exploited outcast. He spoke without pomp and circumstance, without fanfare or flourish. Only once is it recorded that He cried with a loud voice — when He hung suspended on the cross, suffering in His own holy body the punishment for the iniquities of the whole hostile race, paying with His own

life for His enemies' transgressions. After they had crucified Him, they thought that the *"still small voice"* had
been silenced forever. During the entire first century not
a single Latin writer even mentions Jesus. When His
name begins to appear in the second century, the heathen
authors refer to Him grudgingly, sarcastically. Yet by the
miracle of God's grace that *"still small voice"* becomes
the means of drawing men from darkness to light, from
sin to salvation, from social misery to the liberties which
are ours in the United States today. Write this down as
one of the assured facts of history: the Savior's quiet voice
that the ancient world despised and modern skeptics
reject has brought humanity the blessings it enjoys!

Inestimably more important, however, is the truth that
Jesus' *"still small voice"* offers the sinner His salvation,
the lost soul its way to life and heaven. Every time you
hear the story of your redemption through Christ's substitutionary self-sacrifice; every time you behold Christ
nailed to that instrument of death, suffering in your
stead and in your behalf, that *"still small voice"* pleads
within you. God Himself speaks to you, beseeching you
to be reconciled with Him by accepting the Savior's love.
Every time you are led by that Spirit to tune in our message — and remember, no man hears the Gospel simply
by chance — Christ Himself appeals to you through the
Holy Spirit, entreating you to believe in Him, so that
the blood which dripped from His lacerated head, His
pierced hand, His riven side, may not be shed in vain
for you. The *"still small voice"* of God's Son, the Redeemer of your soul, now, in these moments, comes to
you with the highest and holiest message that can ever
make its way into your soul. You may try to ignore it;
you may stamp your feet, clench your hands, grit your
teeth in stubborn unbelief; your hand may be ready to
dial another station, but all the while the Savior is speak-

ing to you. To avoid rejection by God, banishment from heaven and punishment in hell itself, for your own salvation, listen: "Softly and tenderly Jesus is calling"!

Pleadingly He would say to you: "Why have you so often pushed away My outstretched arms? Why are you crucifying Me anew with your willful wickedness? Why do you doubt and deny? Why do you delay and postpone? Come to Me, My dearly redeemed, for whom I shed My lifeblood, for whom I died the death of all deaths! Come to Me, for I have loved you *with an everlasting love.* I have pardon and peace, redemption and rest, for your weary, sin-sick souls. I have joy and life, heaven and eternity, for you! O come, come *now,* come trustingly, come triumphantly!"

Drop everything when that voice pleads! Thousands are now praying with me that the Spirit will help you. Answer: "O Christ of Calvary's cross, I have heard Thy *'still small voice'* of heavenly love and power speak to my soul. And because Thou didst give Thyself for me, I give myself to Thee." — That is all you must do to become a child of God. No initiation, no ceremony, no fee! No possibility of discrimination or rejection, for He promises, *"Him that cometh to Me I will in no wise cast out!"* But you ask, "How can I come?" How did the jailer at Philippi come? The Apostle Paul told him, *"Believe on the Lord Jesus Christ, and thou shalt be saved!"* He believed and by his faith came to the Savior. How did Cornelius, the soldier at Caesarea, come to Christ? He heard Peter say, *"Whosoever believeth in Him* [Jesus] *shall receive remission of sins."* How has anyone accepted the Redeemer since that first Good Friday when the crucified thief looked up to behold Jesus, his King and the Lord of the heavenly paradise? How did the "ten thousand times ten thousand," the ransomed saints in white, accept the

Savior? By joining a congregation? By signing their names to the church roster? By raising their hand at a revival? By stepping forward to shake the preacher's hand? You can do all that and yet remain far from Christ. First of all you must answer the *"still small voice"* by declaring: "Lord, I believe with all my heart that I am saved not by my own good works or good intentions, not by the virtues and merits of parents or pastor, saints or angels — but by grace, through faith in Thy sin-destroying self-sacrifice on the cross. O Jesus, I trust Thee wholly." If today, before your radio in your own home, on the train, in an automobile, or wherever these words reach you, you hear the Savior's soft and tender voice and answer it in this way, you are Christ's.

Then, of course, you will want to learn more of His marvelous mercy. You will hear Him say, *"Be baptized,"* and you will want this *"washing of regeneration."* You will hear Him say, *"Where two or three are gathered together in My name, there am I in the midst of them,"* and you will be eager to stand shoulder to shoulder with other believers in the true Church. Our broadcast and a nation-wide system of Gospel-preaching congregations behind it offer you this help, freely, gladly, thankfully. Will you not, while this *"still small voice"* speaks within you, write to tell us that you want to come closer to Jesus?

To hear and heed Christ's gentle voice, you must meet Him in the words of Spirit, truth, and life found in your Bible, the passages of golden promise penned for all the world, but written particularly for you. More than ever Scripture must assume a decisive position in American lives. The Government is placing a New Testament into lifeboats and rubber rafts, because the experiences of this war have shown that men from torpedoed ships want God's unfailing Word. Why wait for crushing catastrophes to read the Scriptures? The Bible should occupy an honored, prominent place in each home. It should be the Book of all books in every American life; for it is through this sacred, errorless, divinely inspired, eternal Volume that the Father, the Son, and the Spirit speak to us in the *"still small voice."* Therefore read and revere your Bible! Ponder and memorize its pledges! Hear it expounded by true teachers who can rightly divide the divine Word! Don't waste your time on human and fallible theories of prophecy! Don't become involved in any side issues, but delve deeply and directly into the heart of the sacred Book to find Him to whom the inspired writers, from Moses to Saint John, testify with one accord: Jesus Christ, the gracious God, the incarnate Son of the Highest, the Atonement for sin, your Friend in the needs of soul and body!

The gentle voice of Jesus will help you resist temptation. When you have grasped your Savior in faith and made Him your own in soul-deep trust, you not only have the highest Example of perfection, sinless and stainless, but you are also *"born again"* into a new, pure, clean, noble life in which you begin to hate evil, to love good. When temptations arise, as they will, this *"still small voice"* guides you to say, "Get thee behind me, Satan, in the name of the Lord Jesus!" The reason some of you have fallen into heavy sin, denied your Savior, even allied yourselves with the enemies of His cross is plainly this, that, though your Lord's *"still small voice"* pleaded: *"Fight the good fight of faith!"* *"Keep thyself pure!"* *"Resist the devil!"* *"Watch and pray!"* you spurned His appeal. You listened to the world rather than Christ. You followed the devil instead of your Redeemer.

When the Almighty's *"still small voice"* spoke to Elijah at the opening of that cave, He granted him heavenly assurance. The Prophet had thought that he was the only believer left in Israel, but God declared, *"I have left Me seven thousand in Israel, all the knees which have not bowed unto Baal."* When you follow Christ's direction, you, too, will have 7,000 times as much help as you had without Him. The victory will be yours. By the Savior's promise you can count on the resources of heaven, the vigilance of angel guardians, the protection of the Savior-Companion, no matter where you may be. Through Christ, you can face emergency, opposition, danger, death itself, with confidence in your heart because the *"still small voice"* whispers to your soul, *"Fear not; for I have redeemed thee, I have called thee by thy name; thou art Mine!"*

Is not this the spiritual strength we need for our distracted day? Christians who follow the *"still small voice"* have no room for pessimism and cannot be defeated. Whenever they feel that the forces of unbelief have gained the upper hand, let them read these chapters in First Kings again to learn that finally Elijah was victorious; Ahab and Jezebel, destroyed. Translating this truth into the practical issues of our modern life we can confidently face the hardest trials and deepest sorrow these problem years may bring if we meet them in Christ. With joy in our hearts and a song on our lips we should repel the conspiracy of wicked men and hell's agents by this cry of confidence: *"If God be for us, who can be against us? He that spared not His own Son, but delivered Him up for us all, how shall He not with Him also freely give us all things?"* We need no earthly weapons with which to fight the Spirit's battle, for every Christian has *"the sword of the Spirit, which is the Word of God."* Bibles can win greater battles than armored divisions. Every Christian home has the power of family prayer in the Redeemer's name, and American households on their knees in prayer can help win more startling victories than air armadas. Every Christian church has the glorious

Gospel, and when this is preached fearlessly, without human addition or restriction, it is mightier in our nation's defense than motorized battalions. Every true disciple of the Lord has the example of his Savior's self-denial and service of love, even for those who persecute him. Because God has promised His aid *"not by might, nor by power, but by My Spirit,"* Christian meekness can triumph over human brutality. When a brawny Highland sergeant in an Egyptian garrison was asked how he came to Jesus, he explained that his company had one outstanding Christian soldier who was humility itself. One night, after the company returned wet, tired, and muddy, that young disciple knelt in prayer. Filled with the sort of cruelty we can hardly grasp, the sergeant took off his boots, heavy with mud, and threw them at the kneeling man, striking him on the head. The soldier rose and retired. The next morning the sergeant found his shoes beautifully polished at the foot of his bed. "That was his reply to me," he said, "and it just broke my heart. I was saved that day." How true the Savior's words, *"The meek,"* the Christians of the *"still small voice," "shall inherit the earth"!* The victory is always theirs.

Forward, onward, upward, then, you, God's children, who love the Lord Jesus and are guided by His pleading grace, His sustaining love, His deathless devotion, His strengthening power! The eternal triumph, the salvation of your souls, is yours in Christ; for as sure as He is your great and glorious God, your resurrected Redeemer, your living Intercessor at the Father's right hand, and the coming Judge of the quick and the dead, just so surely His *"still small voice,"* fatally ignored and spurned by many, will become the hallowed voice of eternity, to grant those loyal unto death the welcome and blessing, *"Well done, thou good and faithful servant!"* O God, keep us all for that glory, through Christ! Amen.

Jesus, Still the Storms of Life!

> *"There arose a great storm of wind, and the waves beat into the ship, so that it was now full. And He [Jesus] was in the hinder part of the ship, asleep on a pillow; and they awake Him and say unto Him, Master, carest Thou not that we perish? And He arose and rebuked the wind and said unto the sea, Peace, be still! And the wind ceased, and there was a great calm."*
>
> SAINT MARK 4:37-39

O Christ, Who Didst Quiet the Raging Sea:

*B*ring the calm of Thy forgiving love into our storm-tossed lives by removing our sins — many, repeated, grievous though they are! We ask this humbly, but confidently, because we believe in the cleansing power of Thy blood shed for us at Calvary. As once Thou didst still the wind and waves at Galilee, so, we earnestly beseech Thee, say: "Peace! Be Still!" to the turbulence of fear and worry in our hearts! Bid the tumult and terror of this war-racked world cease! Show us in every affliction that Thou, as our God and Savior, canst give us peace and joy! Bless our beloved nation and draw it closer to Thee in repentant trust! Shield our dear ones in the armed forces! They have left all to defend our country and need Thy constant presence. Turn the unconverted to faith in Thee and keep Thy followers in Thy divine protection! Particularly do we intercede today for the United States Navy and all those in peril on the sea. O Christ, let them be strong in body, clean in word, pure in mind, fervent in faith, and unswerving in loyalty to Thee! Send them home to us soon, O Jesus, with peace and a righteous victory! We ask this according to Thy will. Amen.

ABOUT eighty years ago an English clergyman named Whiting was sailing through the Mediterranean when a terrifying storm broke. With a fury the passengers had never before witnessed, the winds became a shrieking hurricane, and the towering waves threatened to crush the helpless craft. Since it was impossible to launch life boats, the passengers felt doomed, for no ship, not even the strongest, could withstand such wind or weather. Whiting, however, continued in heart-deep prayer, and by divine mercy the storm lost its power, and the ship was able to make port. This remarkable rescue might have been forgotten, had not Whiting, deeply grateful to God, penned the hymn, "For Those in Peril on the Sea," also called, "Eternal Father, Strong to Save." American naval men regard this as their most beloved hymn. At the close of each divine service in the Annapolis Naval Academy, the entire congregation kneels to sing this sacred song, and the custom of concluding worship with this prayer has spread to many ships at sea. Few other fighting forces show the deep devotion to the Lord Jesus contained in this second stanza:

> O Savior, whose almighty word
> The winds and waves submissive heard,
> Who walked'st on the foaming deep
> And calm amidst its rage didst sleep:
> Oh, hear us when we cry to Thee
> For those in peril on the sea!

As I thank Commander Green and Chaplain Calhoun for the privilege of originating this broadcast here in the United States Naval Air Station at Lambert Field, Missouri, I tell you men and women of our armed forces, especially in the Navy, that you need the guidance and encouragement these stanzas can bring you. If daily, with humble, trusting reliance on Jesus, you sincerely repeat the words of "Eternal Father, Strong to Save," He can give you calm and quiet for every storm-tossed moment.

All of us — soldiers, sailors, civilians, defense workers, parents, children, young and old — should realize that in perilous times like these, surrounded as we are by the worries of war and burdened by uncertainty concerning tomorrow, the course of many lives may well be pictured as an ocean journey. We begin with great hopes; but in a flash the storm clouds gather, the smooth sea is tossed into angry, destructive waves. Before we are aware of it, we find ourselves close to disaster, physically or spiritually. In these survive-or-perish moments, when we are beyond human help, may we be given the grace to behold our Savior and pray,

JESUS, STILL THE STORMS OF LIFE!

As our merciful, majestic God He can grant us calm and quiet even during life's most turbulent tempest. To prove His mighty power, our text for this Sunday (Saint Mark, chapter four, verses thirty-seven to thirty-nine) declares: *"There arose a great storm of wind, and the waves beat into the ship, so that it was now full. And He* [Jesus] *was in the hinder part of the ship, asleep on a pillow; and they awake Him and say unto Him, Master, carest Thou not that we perish? And He arose and rebuked the wind and said unto the sea, Peace, be still! And the wind ceased, and there was a great calm."*

I

STORMS WILL BREAK UPON US: WE CANNOT CONQUER THEM ALONE

The scene of this miracle is the Sea of Galilee; and the time, our Lord's first ministry to the forsaken, despised people in that northern territory. Jesus had come through a crowded but blessed day. In the morning He had spoken the first of His parables and, standing on the prow of a boat, had taught the multitudes precious truths concerning the kingdom of heaven. All that afternoon He continued His divine instruction as the eager throng remained to hear this unparalleled Teacher. What a wonderful privilege for these underprivileged, oppressed Galileans to see Christ and catch every word of divine wisdom that fell from His lips! Yet what a task even for our Savior to preach hour after hour all through the sultry afternoon with the intense, personally directed appeal which marked His instruction! No effort was too arduous for Him if only it would kindle faith within the heart of a single hearer! In His tireless, self-sacrificing energy, servants of Christ should find an example and a challenge. More than ever Gospel messengers should be ready, if necessary, to wear themselves out in bringing the promises of His mercy to sin-stricken souls.

When evening came, Jesus asked His disciples to sail across to the eastern shores of Galilee. Probably He needed complete rest away from the pressing throng, just as you should have quiet moments with your God in sweet hours of prayer, when you appear alone in your Redeemer's name before the Lord of heaven and earth. The reason some of you have gone backward in your zeal for Christ may be traced to the fact that you have been so overbusy with cares and worries, so overcrowded with your business and social contacts that you have not been able to follow the Savior's instructions, *"Thou, when thou prayest, enter into thy closet, and when thou hast shut thy door, pray to thy Father which is in secret!"*

In connection with this journey across the lake, Matthew tells us that three men stepped out of the throng, desiring to become Christ's disciples. Although their motives were wrong and their understanding faulty, our Lord took time to hear and correct them. The one, a scribe, exclaimed with overconfidence, *"Lord, I will follow Thee whithersoever Thou goest,"* only to hear

Jesus, emphasizing that discipleship would bring neither money nor position nor authority, declare pointedly, *"The foxes have holes, and the birds of the air have nests; but the Son of Man hath not where to lay His head."* In His name I am pledged to tell you who write me of your wish to enter the ministry, and you older folks who inquire about joining the Church: while I rejoice and thank God for your good intentions, never before in this country has discipleship brought with it the necessity of bearing the cross as in these years, when despite all outward emphasis on religion there is a deep-rooted, growing hatred for the message of His cleansing blood and life-giving death at Calvary. The second would-be disciple was a man who wanted to bury his father before casting his lot with Christ; and probably because Jesus knew that, if he went home, he would never become a real believer, the Lord warned him against going back and directed, *"Follow Me!"* Today the Son of God repeats these words to you who feel you should confess Him your Lord, yet are continually postponing the most blessed privilege a man can ever have. Who knows in this uncertain age whether you will not hesitate and excuse yourself once too often and never have another chance of accepting your royal Redeemer? Now, while the Spirit pleads with you to be reconciled with God, is the best time for you to say: "O Jesus, I will turn away no longer. With the help of Thy Spirit I will follow Thee through life and death itself into eternal glory."

The third inquirer, impressed with the Savior's message, seemed eager to join Him; but first of all he, too, wanted to return to bid his friends farewell. Pointedly our Lord told him, *"No man, having put his hand to the plow, and looking back, is fit for the kingdom of God."* Today He would send many of you that same warning, because you are turning back to the attractions and enticements of your old life. For the sake of your blood-bought souls go forward with Jesus! Forget the allurement and enticement of the past and *"press toward the mark for the prize of the high calling of God in Christ Jesus"*!

Finally, after these delays, the ship got under way; and only a few moments later, it seems, the Savior, weary and worn after an exhausting day, was fast asleep in the stern, His head, which could have worn the crown of all earthly authority, resting on the helmsman's bench, His tired body stretched out on the bottom of the boat. As we pause to behold Him before whom angels in their glory shield their faces, what marvelous love we are privileged to witness! He whose heavy eyes have quickly closed is more than a self-sacrificing leader, preacher, teacher. He is our God; Sovereign of the air, land, sea; Ruler of the universe; Lord of lords, eternal, all-knowing, omnipotent.

Do you object: "Explain how Jesus can be the Sovereign of heaven and still be overcome by this deep sleep. Prove that He is our God." I cannot explain the superhuman mystery of this marvelous truth that Christ is both divine and human; but I do not need to prove it, for in a few moments it was demonstrated beyond all question, when even the forces of nature obeyed Him. Throughout His ministry, by stupendous miracles which only He could perform; by His atoning death, in which He offered Himself as the Ransom for all human sin; by His resurrection from the dead, our Lord gave convincing evidence that, far more than a great man, even the greatest of men, He was — believe it for your soul's salvation! — very God of very God.

While we cannot analyze this mystery which even angels do not fully fathom, in the slumbering Jesus we

see the Savior, the evidence of Heaven's strongest love.
Why, we ask ourselves, did He whose throne is in the
celestial realms condescend to become one of us? Why
did He leave His eternal glories to live among men who
hated and persecuted Him, to die on the cross between
two criminals? The answer can be found only in that endless compassion for your soul by which He took upon
Himself the reality, the penalty, the totality, of all your
sins, fully paid their guilt, and at Calvary completely
earned the ransom by which you can be forever freed
from sin and Satan, death and damnation.

It was not long after Jesus closed His eyes in much
needed rest, when suddenly a terrifying tempest broke
over the Sea of Galilee. This was an inland lake, 600 feet
below sea level; and as the cold winds from near-by
mountains swooped down to its surface, they churned its
waters into seething madness. Breaking high over the
sides, *"the waves beat into the ship, so that it was . . .
full"* of water. A few moments before, the disciples had
been serene, secure; now they were frightened for their
lives — so quickly did disaster descend upon them.

With the same speed adversity can overtake us. Who
knows what message of sorrow may come into our homes
before this day draws to its close? With American armed
forces in many corners of the earth, confronting trained
and desperate enemies, death is close to millions of our
countrymen. Let us face the facts and understand that
hard, crushing grief may come to us, entirely unheralded!
Not an alarmist, but a member of Congress, asserts that
the United States will suffer at least 1,000,000 casualties
this year. If this be true — though we pray: "O God, stop
this war! Save these young lives!" — almost 1,000,000
American homes will endure bitter afflictions. Because

our Secretary of War has predicted that the struggle will end, not this year, but one or two years hence, will you not agree with me when I say that we must be prepared for distressing reports of disaster?

Where, then, can we find courage, guidance, strength? If we look only to ourselves, our own resources, scientific progress, and widely applauded programs, which have no room for the Almighty, then indeed we shall be like those disciples on Galilee. They were seasoned fishermen, acquainted with the treachery of the lake; yet the storm was too much for them; they were pitifully powerless against the raging elements. Today, too, we pride ourselves on knowing all the answers to our multiplied problems; yet, when a crisis comes, how weak and weary we often are! As we listen to the boasting of warlords — and regrettably some of this taunting bravado is heard within our borders — we realize that altogether too many would banish God and win this war without Him or even against Him. What is human strength compared with God's? How puny is our brain power when at the height of man's intelligence we have not been able to prevent nations from attacking each other in history's most widespread war! How unreliable our scientific power when even mechanical wonders sometimes fail to function! A few days ago in Seattle a giant bomber, the final word in aircraft thus far, driven by a reputable test pilot, crashed, causing a score of deaths; and no one knows why. — Above all, however, how frail and fragile, hopeless and helpless, are our souls apart from God! How utterly impossible for us to purchase peace of mind, courage and contentment! How completely helpless we all are when the storms of sorrow break over us and our homes; when sickness, accident, suffering, knock at our doors; when disaster and bereavement cross our thresholds!

II

ONLY CHRIST CAN CALM OUR STORM-TOSSED LIFE

With the cry recorded in Saint Matthew, *"Lord, save us; we perish!"* the disciples turned to Jesus for help. Where in this upside-down world can we discover deliverance if not in the same Savior whose invitation remains unchanged through the centuries, *"Come unto Me, all ye that labor and are heavy laden, and I will give you rest"?* The one spiritual blessing which can accrue from years of bloodshed may be this, that the losses of war finally make many Americans understand that they cannot carry on successfully without Christ. Some of you are so overconfident that the Almighty has to take away every human prop, remove all earthly means of your rescue, to show you that without God life cannot be worth the living nor death worth the dying. How blessed, then, after you have been crushed and humbled, to have the Holy Spirit capture your cold heart, direct you to Christ as your only Hope, and make you kneel before Him to cry out, *"Lord, save us; we perish!"* If you have been overtaken by soul sorrow and mental anguish too deep for human consolation; if in all the world you can discover no escape from your misery; if you feel that another heartache added to your burden will make you collapse, then cling to Jesus, and find in Him Heaven's unfailing help.

At first the desperate disciples were shocked to learn that our Lord continued to sleep soundly; for they could not understand how, with destruction close at hand, the Savior would slumber on. As Saint Mark tells the story, *"they awake Him and say unto Him, Master, carest Thou not that we perish?"* They made a grave mistake: they forgot that the Almighty was in their ship, that without His permission no disaster could overwhelm them.

Before they blame these followers of the Savior too severely, people should confess how frequently they think Jesus is asleep; how readily they conclude that He is absolutely unconcerned about the tragedies of the present age. The war spreads, more soldiers are killed on its widely separated battlefields; and in their small faith, men charge the Savior with slumbering! They see evil throughout the world, as atheism and blatant blasphemy persecute Christ's humble followers. The open denial of His atonement, the rejection of His redeeming, cleansing blood, secure control of churches, often entire denominations, and people lament: "God must be sleeping! He does not care what happens."

In the narrower spheres of your lives, particularly during heavy hours of affliction, you, too, assert all too hastily that the Lord's eyes are closed to the welfare of His own. Cutting cruelties are heaped on you; you are slandered; you suffer unjustly; and in this misery you complain that God knows nothing of your affliction. Your plans for the future collapse although you are God's children; yet boasting infidels are crowned with increasing success. You have cried yourself hoarse, pleading with God to make your husband stop drinking, breaking his marriage vows, blaspheming; yet there seems to be no answer. — After thirteen years of married life your heavenly Father gives you a beautiful, healthy child; but in a terror-filled moment it accidentally falls and dies — a personal tragedy one of your letters described. As one blow follows the other, your faith wavers; you complain that Christ must be asleep, otherwise He would be aware of your anguish and offer His help.

Just as Jesus could not have slept on and permitted His disciples to perish, so He will never slumber when perils threaten to destroy your soul. Because He gave

Himself for you into Calvary's bitter bleeding and dark dying, you, purchased by the highest price recorded in history — His own blood — are so precious in His sight that every moment, waking and sleeping, you are under His constant, vigilant protection, by which, if necessary, angel guards will always defend you. I cannot promise, nor can anyone else (no matter how loudly self-appointed false prophets, preachers of lies, contradict this), that, when you accept the Lord Jesus, you will be showered with earthly advantages, material blessings, better business, larger incomes, the assurance of safety during this war. In the Redeemer's name and by His own pledge I can, however, promise you, by day and night, in prosperity and adversity, during peace and war, at home and abroad, the Savior will never close His eyes to your real needs as long as you remain faithful to Him, He will ceaselessly protect you in every danger, marvelously turn your afflictions into inner strengthening, and finally change your sorrow into joy. Here is the truth for the battle front and the home front: When you are utterly weak and helpless, if you but acclaim Christ your own Redeemer, the full brilliance of His grace will break upon you. As you become nothing, Jesus will be everything. My fellow redeemed, lock this promise in your heart, and with the Savior's help keep it safe and secure forever! The time will come — it is close at hand for many of you — when you will want this pledge of His power more than all else on earth.

See how mightily our Lord proved His faithfulness and His divine strength on turbulent Galilee! Hardly had He been awakened, when *"He arose and rebuked the wind and said unto the sea, Peace, be still"*; and because He is God, because wind and wave follow His command, the surging of the sea subsided, the mountainous billows disappeared, the howling storm vanished, the crisis was safely past. Another miracle, stupendous beyond description, had been enacted before the disciples' eyes. If this marvel was witnessed and attested by the men in the ship who exclaimed, *"What manner of man is this, that even the wind and the sea obey Him?"* certainly modern unbelief, at a distance of 1900 years, has no right to question this full, final truth. Christ, the Son of God and the Savior of the world, quieted those angry waves.

Instead of doubting, we should rather find comfort in His ability to still present-day storms of life. Be clear on this: the Lord of the Galilean Sea can quiet the uproar and turbulence of our bleeding age! In His unlimited strength, as our glorious God, Jesus, facing the storm of world strife and the raging floods of hatred, could repeat those three words, *"Peace, be still!"* and we would have peace today. One word from Him and our enemies would be defeated forever. One command from His all-conquering might, and the slaughter of the world's strongest and healthiest young men would cease. One rebuke from His omnipotence, and there would be no more bombing and blasting, no more submarine sinkings and torpedo destruction, no more death and drowning in this war. One divine decree by Him, and our American youth could prepare to return to their homes and the occupations of blessed peace.

Why, then, does Christ not stop this conflict? Because He knows that the world is not ready for peace! Iniquity has not been punished enough; Christians have not been sufficiently chastened and purified. Too many people in the United States still doubt His power, still reject His redeeming love. Last Monday night President Roosevelt told us that we have no Joshua in this struggle, before whom our enemies' walls will miraculously crumble. The President was right. We must fight this war the hard way, pay the full price. America has no Joshua today, and the enemy resistance is not broken, because we have refused to do what God's people did in Joshua's age. We have not gone back to the faith of our fathers. We have not humbled ourselves before the Almighty. We have not repented as did the Israelites under Joshua. Yet we can have more than a Joshua in Jesus. Every day of this war, could the full story be told, witnesses the absolute proof of the Savior's unlimited might. A book just published tells the thrilling rescue of Mrs. Alice Bell, missionary to Africa, and her four children, whose ship was torpedoed in the South Atlantic and who, together with fourteen men, was adrift twenty days on a raft, eight by ten feet, so small and crowded that they could not lie down for rest. They were never dry. The sun scorched them by day, and the cold chilled them by night. Huge sharks continually followed them. They had little food and less water. Some of the men died and were buried at sea, but during those three weeks of torture Jesus sustained that Christian worker and her children. When they reached the hospital in Barbados, the nurses and doctors declared their rescue "as great a miracle as the feeding of the five thousand in the New Testament." After the war thousands will thankfully recall that in life-or-death moments, when all hope in human help had vanished, God marvelously brought deliverance.

Storm-tossed Galilee was stilled when the disciples prayed and their pleading was answered. Storm-tossed America can be stilled if, according to God's will, we employ the power of faith-filled intercession. Millions in the United States are neglecting that secret but successful weapon. For the sake of a God-pleasing victory, to save the lives of our youth, who will be spared if this war is stopped soon, let believers everywhere pray as never before! Every church throughout the land should be open constantly to welcome multitudes who would plead personally and persistently for peace. Every family in the land should be united in fervent intercession. Every Christian should follow the Apostle's injunction and be found *"praying always with all prayer."* Every American, no matter how he may have laughed at the thought of kneeling before God, should use this emergency to learn the lessons of prayer — and that means first to confess the Lord Jesus Christ his Savior.

The disciples in that tempest-tossed boat show skeptics and unbelievers how to pray. As those men on storm-gripped Galilee turned to Christ, so your only hope is in His loving willingness and His power to answer every true petition. As they went directly to Jesus, without anyone else to plead for them, so, despite your total sins and weaknesses, you can have free access to the Throne of Mercy. As they counted themselves nothing, doomed without the Savior, so you, too, must confess that, since the best you can offer is worthless in God's sight, you should come humbly, trusting in Christ's merit. As the disciples' intercession was heard, so every supplication you speak in Jesus' name will be answered in His chosen manner and time, if it be for your soul's salvation. — What better can we do, then, while the nation's defenders prepare to sacrifice themselves, if necessary, than to maintain a prayer front and to make this our cry: "Pray, America, pray! Pray repeatedly! Pray earnestly! Pray penitently! Pray in Christ's name, relying on His promise!"

We are told that, after the winds stopped, *"there was a great calm"*; and if you hear and heed the Savior, the peace and consolation of an even more marvelous calm will bless you. How we thrilled a few days ago when we read of a serious operation performed not by a surgeon in a sterilized hospital room but by a pharmacist's mate in the crowded quarters of a submarine, beneath the ocean off the Japanese shore! What gave the young afflicted sailor calm and confidence in that critical period when his life hung on a slender thread? An officer on the submarine reports, "He got the most consolation out of the first verse of the Forty-sixth Psalm, *God is our Refuge and Strength.*" One of the Navy fliers at Guadalcanal, whose exploits were recently featured in a nation-wide news broadcast, is a member of our Church. This young lieutenant, attacking a Japanese Zero squadron, was forced down when his motors failed at 10,000 feet. He hit the water with a terrific impact that left him unconscious. He would have drowned, for he had not unfastened the safety belt which tied him to the sinking plane; yet, regaining consciousness, he found himself afloat. "The hand of God must have unfastened the safety belt," he later wrote his parents. There he was in shark-infested waters, about a mile and a half from a Japanese battleship and five destroyers, and another mile and a half from a little island which, he thought, had been captured by the enemy. He was marvelously rescued, however, by friendly natives. Thanking God for his deliverance, he sent word home: "Let me tell you, Mom and Dad, I pray plenty over here. So does everyone else, for that matter. While I am taking off and flying to interception, I sing, 'A Mighty Fortress Is Our God,' and among other things the Twenty-third Psalm and the Ninety-first Psalm. It helps a lot. I think I will come out of this O. K. However, if I should meet some mishap, you may be confident of the fact that I went as a child of God."

Everyone of you can have the same calm confidence with which to face danger, even death itself, if only you take Christ into the ship of your life and pray,

> Jesus, Savior, pilot me
> Over life's tempestuous sea!

If that Redeemer is at the helm to direct your course, He will bring you safely through every storm into the haven of heaven. As we repeat the prayer of our message, "O Jesus, still the storms of life!" may every one of us — you men of the sea and the air, you soldiers who cross the ocean to distant battle fronts, we who stay at home — add to that appeal this plea to Christ and this assurance of our faith:

> As a mother stills her child,
> Thou canst hush the ocean wild;
> Boist'rous waves obey Thy will
> When Thou say'st to them, "Be still!"
> Wondrous Sov'reign of the sea,
> Jesus, Savior, pilot me!

> When at last I near the shore
> And the fearful breakers roar
> 'Twixt me and the peaceful rest,
> Then, while leaning on Thy breast,
> May I hear Thee say to me,
> "Fear not, I will pilot thee!"

Amen

Tears Over America

"When He was come near, He beheld the city
and wept over it."
SAINT LUKE 19:41

Jesus, Lord of Love:

*O*nce *in the days of Thy humiliation Thou didst weep over
sinful, impenitent Jerusalem. The unbelief, the worldliness,
the corruption of the Temple caused tears to course down
Thy cheeks in soul-deep sorrow over the disaster which soon
would destroy that privileged but sin-laden city. Today, if
Thou wert visibly with us as in the years of Thy ministry,
Thou wouldst likewise sob over our American cities. Too
frequently we have forgotten Thy blessings; too often our
service is mouth worship; too repeatedly we have spurned
Thy mercy. O blessed Savior, enter not into judgment with us!
For the sake of Thy precious, cleansing blood forgive us!
Cast us not away, but look compassionately on us despite our
ingratitude! Make us humble and penitent! Convict us of our
utter weakness without Thee! Purify and cleanse our churches!
Grant Thy Christians throughout the country fortitude and
firmer faith! By the visitations of this war, turn the unconverted to Thee! Guide Thy young disciples who have been
called to the colors; protect them with Thy might and love!
As Thou hast put peace into the hearts of all those who receive Thee, so give the nations peace, with righteousness and
blessing! We ask this benediction, O Christ, trusting Thy
blood-bought promise. Amen.*

HAVE you ever seen a strong man weep?
Powerful lessons can be learned from the tears of great
leaders. Who can forget King David's moaning over the
death of proud, rebellious Absalom: *"O my son Absalom,
my son, my son Absalom! Would God I had died for
thee, O Absalom, my son, my son!"* Who does not feel in

this haunting lament an appeal asking American fathers to find time for their children and bring them to God before they are snatched away by death and lost forever?

Alexander, miscalled "the Great," is said to have wept because he could find no more empires to conquer. After a single victory he sold 30,000 of his captives as slaves. The world was at his feet. Yet his tears show that despite money, power, position, life without God is empty and futile.

When Peter, that rough-and-ready disciple who had cursed himself and denied Jesus, saw his Savior, bound and beaten, he wept in bitter repentance. — If you have rejected Christ, behold Him now, betrayed by your cowardice, suffering in your stead, and then sob in sorrow over your sins!

Saint Paul, the fearless Apostle, who could ride Mediterranean hurricanes without a quiver of terror, tells the believers in Ephesus that for *"the space of three years I ceased not to warn everyone night and day with tears."* What a challenge to American Christians, urging them to show their zeal for the Savior, not by bakery sales, fish fries, card or dancing parties, but by such heart-deep, self-sacrificing devotion to others that tears testify to their sacred earnestness!

When Napoleon saw the remnant of the proud army which had marched through the snow and ice of a Russian winter (the whole campaign cost him a half million lives; 90,000 died on the terrifying retreat) he broke down and sobbed. Here was the confident war lord who boasted that he did not need God to conquer Europe! Find in Napoleon's lament a proof that the Almighty can stop this conflict overnight! — May it be soon, heavenly Father!

Yes, vital present-day lessons are to be learned from

the tears of history's leaders; but the strongest warning and appeal come from the tears of the mightiest Figure in all history — Jesus Christ, Son of God and Savior of the world. Three times the Scriptures record that Jesus wept: first, at the tomb of Lazarus, where He proved Himself a compassionate Lord, moved by the suffering of friends; and last, in the Garden of Gethsemane, where at the beginning of His never-to-be-measured agony in atoning for the world's sins (so the Epistle to the Hebrews testifies) He *"offered up prayers and supplications with strong crying and tears."* Only five days before that groaning in Gethsemane, Jesus, about to enter Jerusalem, had also wept; for Saint Luke records in our text (chapter nineteen, verse forty-one), *"When He was come near, He beheld the city and wept over it."* This is the Savior's grief to which I call your attention as I show you His

TEARS OVER AMERICA

May God's Holy Spirit bless these words and throughout the land bring sinners to their weeping Redeemer!

I

THEY ARE TEARS OF SORROW FOR OUR SINS

The Jerusalem of our Savior's day was far more glorious than it is today. Even pagan writers paid their tribute to its brilliance. A Latin author calls it "one of the world's wonders." People were so blinded by its radiance as it reflected the Palestinian sun that they had to turn their eyes away; so Josephus, the Jewish historian, tells us. Yet when our Lord, at the head of a large throng preparing to enter Jerusalem, stopped on Mount Olivet's heights to look toward the majestic city, there was no awe or admiration in His gaze. Instead, He stood silent. His lips quivered; His eyes filled; tears coursed down His cheeks.

Why was Jesus, about to hold His victorious entry into Jerusalem, in the moment of His greatest earthly triumph, so moved by the sight of His country's capital? To find the answer, let us stand in spirit with Him on the crest of Olivet to see what He beheld in the panorama before Him. Perhaps He was at a point where His first glance would single out the Temple, a magnificent structure, on which architects and laborers had toiled for fifty years and were still not finished — a colossal sanctuary of white and red marble, gilded roofs, dazzling courts, stately pillars, nine gates covered with gold and silver — altogether an imposing monument to God. Yet that grandeur left Jesus untouched, for He was inexpressibly saddened by the hollow mockery, shocking insincerity, cold formality, to be found in that house of the Highest. With His mind's eye He could see the money changers, the sellers of the sacrificial animals, and others who piled up profits in the name of religion. He remembered the multitudes who bought doves or lambs, the wealthy who purchased steers or bullocks and thought that by such offerings they could be cleansed from their sins even though their hearts were far from God and they refused to repent. He could almost hear the loud chanting of the Pharisees, who threw their shoulders back, raised their heads high in their self-esteem, and intoned, *"God, I thank Thee, that I am not as other men are, extortioners, unjust, adulterers, or even as this publican."* Because the Savior saw masses ruined, in spite of this outward worship, cursed because of their hypocrisy, His eyes were wet with tears.

If Jesus were with us today, He would undoubtedly weep over America's spiritual life. We have congregations that count their real estate and resources in millions, some of them in tens of millions! Yet that alone means nothing to Christ. The United States likewise is crowded with churches which forget the divine command, *"Thou shalt love the Lord, thy God, with all thy heart and with all thy soul and with all thy strength and with all thy mind,"* and which, instead of this inner, heart-centered, soul-deep worship of God, permit head and lip worship to creep in, formalism and ceremonies to receive far too much attention. The plain preaching of the Gospel, without which no man can be redeemed, is pushed into the background. Ask the average American: "How do you expect to be saved? What is your hope of heaven?" and you will find first that many of our countrymen do not want to be saved, since they think they do not need to be; and you will also learn that of those who believe in the hereafter, the majority actually like to think themselves so good, so much better than others, that God will welcome them with open arms — when they ought to understand that without the Lord Jesus they are lost forever; that their hearts are filled with greed, lust, hatred, their lives marked with secret and disguised sin. Because millions in this nation, founded by Christian pioneers, blessed above all other people on earth through religious freedom, have forgotten their God, neglected their privileges, spurned their blessings, rejected their Savior, we can find Him on Olivet, grief-gripped not only for Jerusalem's Temple, but for churches in the United States that are more concerned about money raising than soul-winning, more intent on gaining popular applause than divine approval. As we hear Christ repeat His warning, *"This people draweth nigh unto Me with their mouth and honoreth Me with their lips; but their heart is far from Me,"* may God give us the spiritual insight required to understand that, if America is to come closer to the Almighty, this rededication must start in the churches; that the groups called Christian must receive a transfusion of firm, unquestioning, self-denying trust. To stop the tears of Christ, we must go back to the Bible, back to the blessed Savior, back to the blood of His atonement, back to justification by faith, and faith alone.

From Olivet the Savior could likewise see the palace of Caiaphas, the high priest. He wore the sacred robes and the breastplate inscribed, *"Holiness to the Lord."* He occupied the highest position in Old Testament worship. He alone could enter the Holy of Holies on the solemn Day of Atonement. Yet that high priest, who should have been closest to God, was an unbeliever, a murderer at heart, a sworn enemy of Jesus, and long ago he had begun to plot the crucifixion. He was surrounded by many Sadducees, who openly attacked Scripture, denied the hope of the resurrection, claimed that life was ruled by chance, that death ended everything. These men, politicians, perjurers, bold unbelievers in priestly apparel, were responsible for their country's downfall. It was true, then, as now, that

> When nations are to perish in their sins,
> 'Tis in the Church the leprosy begins.

Would not the same Savior who broke into sobs over the treachery of these priestly traitors raise His voice in lament if He were with us today to behold the unbelief in the ranks of the American clergy? The war has not yet brought a real revival of true Christian faith in America. Modernists, deniers of the free and final atonement by the Lord Jesus, are still in control of many congregations and of some denominations. Twentieth-century Sadducees sit securely in high places. Pulpit politicians, who heedlessly step over the line separating Church and State, are on the increase. For political reasons, ministers of the Gospel, in direct contradiction to Christ's Spirit, have decried the sending of food to Europe's starving children. The number of those who teach and preach that Jesus, God's Son and Mary's, our Lord and Savior, our Ransom and Redeemer, our Atonement and Reconciliation to the Father, is the only but heaven-blessed Hope for every sinner, does not increase with rapid strides. Yet, because an unbelieving, Christ-debasing, Bible-ridiculing clergy can bring disaster on the nation, the appeal in this crisis to every servant of God must be: *"Preach the Word!" "Call . . . sinners to repentance!"* Proclaim the Gospel with all its comforting and sustaining love! — Believing American homes must help in safeguarding the Savior's truth. A national magazine presents a survey, taken among "a faithfully balanced cross section of high school students," which reveals that almost half of the young people do not attend church regularly. Is there any connection between this startling fact and the F. B. I. report which showed an increase last year of more than 55 per cent in the arrests of girls under twenty-one? Ask yourself pointedly, "Would Jesus weep over conditions in my home?" If you know that He would, implore Him to enter your household now and bring your entire family to His unfailing grace!

Prominent on Jerusalem's skyline were the palaces of the governing officials, imposing structures with high towers: the castle of King Herod, the residence of Pontius Pilate, the other government buildings; and Jesus could detect the corruption, deceit, iniquity, practiced within their pretentious walls. He wept as He contrasted with the hideous doom soon to break over the city the happy, blessed days its people might have enjoyed, had God-fearing, honest men conducted public affairs. — While we ought to thank the Almighty daily for the marvelous benediction He has given us in a free, representative government, no one should be blind to the fact that graft, bribery, corruption, have sometimes flourished in the high government places; that public officials, judges, federal officers, have at times been convicted of dishonesty. The fault for much of this is on your shoulders, Christians of America. You have not prayed hard enough for your country. You have not worked zealously enough. You have refused to vote and spurned every opportunity to run for office.

From the crest of Mount Olivet Christ could behold the fortress of Antonia, headquarters of the Roman army that held Jerusalem in control. Not far from the barracks was the amusement zone, the pleasure areas, the dark corners of vice, the taverns with their cursing, slobbering drunkards, all the enticements to evil which the sensual ancient world knew. As the Savior's eyes swept over that lofty-towered fortress, He could have thought of the young legionaries who went on day after day without knowing God, living in the cold cruelty and the sin which marked military life. His tears may well have dropped for those soldiers, as for all the sorrows and heartaches that war, the result of sin and unbelief, had brought upon the royal capital. If Jesus today would stand on a high hill overlooking American cities, His eyes would overflow as He would think of the spiritual dangers confronting our soldiers and sailors — multitudes without Christ — still unprepared for eternity, all of them facing insistent and repeated temptations, deliberately created for them. To you men in the nation's armed forces I express this public regret that we have not more vigorously helped you fight profanity, which according to plain Scripture statements, incurs God's wrath. I deplore the type of entertainment offered you by some communities, where nastiness and filth systematically attack you, where unprincipled, avaricious individuals try to make money from you, our defenders. A mother who is certainly entitled to be heard, because her only son lies buried on Guadalcanal, writes to protest against the amusements offered our soldiers. I join her. With all our power and resources we should stand by these young men spiritually and help them prepare to meet their God. This is not the hour for carnival, when American blood daily trickles into the Tunisian sands, when American lives are crushed out in air disasters, when the sons and support of American families are drowned on the high seas.

Again, as the Savior's eyes scanned Jerusalem, they would have alighted on its cultural quarters, the residences of its intellectuals, the scribes, the teachers of the people, those too proud to accept the lowly Christ, perverted minds which used their God-given talents to blaspheme the Lord. His tears were shed for them, and today they would fall, too, for the American intelligentsia that can only sneer at Jesus. Most of you churchgoers have absolutely no idea of the shocking depths to which their scurrilous insults can descend. Listen to these lines, spawned by hell itself, entitled, "Good-by, Christ!":

> Listen, Christ,
> You did all right in your day, I reckon —
> But that day's gone now.
> They ghosted you up a swell story, too.
> Called it the Bible —
> But it's dead now.
>
> Good-by,
> Christ Jesus Lord God Jehovah;
> Beat it on away from here now.
> Make way for a new guy with no religion at all —
> A real guy named
> Marx Communist Lenin Peasant Stalin Worker Me —

I thought long and prayerfully before deciding to read these lines publicly; but most of you must be stirred into action. Remember, these are the words not of an amateur writer but of a man who won the Harmon Gold Award for Literature, the Guggenheim Award for Creative Literary Work, and the Rosenwald Fellowship!

Jesus wept over Jerusalem because He knew the appalling price it would pay for rebelling against God. He predicts, *"Thine enemies . . . shall lay thee even with the ground, and thy children with thee, and they shall not leave in thee one stone upon another because thou knewest not the time of thy visitation."* The disaster Jesus foresaw came within less than fifty years, when in the siege and capture of the city, which makes some of the massacres in this World War seem small, 1,100,000 men perished and 97,000 people (the children and grandchildren of those to whom the Savior spoke) were led away captive, and so many of the citizens sold into servitude that no one would buy any more slaves. It was a shocking devastation; yet incomparably worse was the eternal destruction of souls which could have been saved through faith in Christ.

"Be not deceived; God is not mocked," is the warning America should read in Jerusalem's ruins. If up to this time you have insolently risen up against your Redeemer, turned your back on His arms nailed to the cross but stretched wide in invitation to welcome you, then, with all the life-and-death earnestness of this warning, I tell you that on Olivet Jesus was weeping for you, shedding divine tears because, if you continue to reject His ransom for your sin, you must pay in eternity for every unforgiven wrong, every unremoved transgression! Look at the Christ of sorrows once more! He weeps for you, knowing the peace, pardon, hope, and happiness you

have lost without Him; the heavenly home, the seeing Him face to face in the blessed eternity you have spurned, the pain and horror of hell which you, sin-blinded, have chosen. Is your heart stone, that you are not moved by your sorrowing Savior, the Lord of heaven and earth, the God of all might, mourning over your preciously bought but carelessly lost soul? It was too late for masses in Jerusalem to repent and return to God. But, thanks to the Savior's marvelous mercy, it is not too late for you to throw off your stubborn resistance to Jesus and fall on your knees in contrite sorrow over your sins. You unbelieving husbands, unfaithful wives, ungrateful children, you blasphemers and scoffers; you, the self-satisfied and self-righteous; you who are sending your souls to hell by living in sin, helping destroy the morals and the faith of others — there is still time for you to kneel before the compassionate Christ and say: "What a fool I have been to reject my soul's salvation! Now I have found You at last, my all-forgiving Redeemer. You do not need to weep any more for me! O Jesus, dry your tears! Wash me! Cleanse me! Purify me through faith!" When you come to the Lord of limitless love with that faith, His face, once stained with tears, will be wreathed in heavenly happiness. The lips which once pronounced the woe over Jerusalem will tell you, *Him that cometh to Me I will in no wise cast out.*

There is time for every one of you, but not so much time that you dare continue to postpone and delay accepting grace. *"Now is the day of salvation."* You may not be with us next Sunday to hear another appeal for return to your heavenly Father. A week ago, while speaking to the men in the United States Naval Air Station at Lambert Field, Saint Louis, I warned the cadets against the "speed and suddenness with which adversity may overtake us in these darkened days of war," and I asked them, in these very words, "Who knows what message of sorrow may come into our homes before this day draws to its close?" A few hours later two of those young fliers met sudden death in the first air collision at the training station. So quickly and unexpectedly, by God's inscrutable will, was the truth of that warning proved! Some of you may never have another opportunity to hear that Christ loved you despite your sins, died on the cross as your Substitute. Now, while heaven is still open for you, while Jesus pleads with you, while the Spirit urges you, wherever you are, accept Him! Say, "He is mine, and I am His for time and eternity!"

The nation needs men and women with that trust. The first line of America's defense is faith in the Savior. The strongest weapon against enemies from within and without is the power of God through Christ. To have the promise of that strength, millions in America must repent. They must return to God. They must acclaim their crucified Lord of love!

II

THEY ARE TEARS OF DIVINE LOVE AND SYMPATHY

Besides the stern warning we must find in Christ's tears heavenly comfort, the consolation we need particularly during times of war and upheaval. The Savior sees our afflictions and is deeply moved by our sorrows. The Redeemer is not like the sleeping Buddha in one of China's famous temples, a monstrous figure lying on his side with closed eyes, slumbering on, indifferent to his people's woes. Jesus is not like the Modernists' god, a vague, indefinite force, so far removed that He is not concerned with this world. Our precious Lord is not so majestic and omnipotent that He does not stoop or stop to help us. By the miracle of His mercy, none can be too lowly, unnoticed, poor, for His gracious interest. On the journey to Jerusalem, when He was so weighted by His suffering that even the disciples dared not disturb Him, He stopped to heal a blind beggar, enter the home of a despised publican, instruct His disciples, weep over Jerusalem.

The newspapers tell us that King George, ruler of the British Empire, daily goes to work for a few hours in a defense factory. What a remarkable example of service, when a monarch allies himself with his workers! But can you imagine any ruler going to Germany and offering his life for his enemies? The Savior did much more when He, in the words of Saint Paul, *"took upon Him the form of a servant and was made in the likeness of men; and being found in fashion as a man, He humbled Himself and became obedient unto death, even the death of the cross."* Because He lived as a true man, save for sin, among men stained with sin, no one else in the world knows human needs as personally as Christ. No affliction with which you may be tormented was foreign to Him. Every hard, bitter road along which you drag yourself He has trodden. Whatever your path of grief, you are always following in the footsteps of the agonized Redeemer, and in comparison with the suffering He endured, yours, even in its worst and crushing torture, is only trivial. Are you poor? Jesus felt the pangs of poverty. He had not *"where to lay His head."* Are you overworked and worn out? Jesus can feel for you, because He was often at the point of exhaustion, overweary in fulfilling His ministry of love. Do you parents whose only sons have been called to the colors complain that you are lonely and forsaken? Are some of you men and women in the service depressed by grim loneliness?

Think of your Lord suffering in the Garden, alone in His heartbreaking agony! Picture Him on the cross, forsaken by God and man, and realize that He knows more deeply than you the pangs of lingering loneliness! Are you maliciously attacked and slandered? Recall the false witnesses, the perjurers, the paid spies, who sought to destroy Christ, and believe that His heart beats in sympathy for you! Are you ministers loyal to the Redeemer, suffering the disfavor of the higher-ups in your church organization? You need not explain this persecution to Christ. He knows from His own bleeding experience what it means to be cursed and condemned by the highest religious authorities. Are you sick, an invalid of many years, gripped by increasing pain? You can have unfailing consolation in Jesus, who knows anguish inestimably greater than the worst you can stand; for in His own body He bore *our griefs and carried our sorrows.* Are you at death's door? Has the doctor said that your days are not only numbered, but that soon — perhaps within a week, even before nightfall — they will be over? Then during these last moments of your earthly suffering I tell you in the name of our blessed Redeemer who died at Calvary and whose body was laid into the grave that He knows more definitely what death means than anyone can ever explain. The tears which Christ wept at Jerusalem are a proof of His sympathizing love in every grief you must endure, any pressing burden you must carry. When life seems too hard, when you feel too depressed to face another day, think of the tears flowing down your Savior's cheeks; believe with all your heart that He was suffering in tender devotion to you — and then sing:

> What a Friend we have in Jesus,
> All our sins and griefs to bear!
> What a privilege to carry
> Everything to God in prayer!

These tears, however, are also evidence of the Redeemer's divine yearning to help and deliver you. You have not only a weeping Christ, but a bleeding Christ, a dying Christ, a crucified Christ. Human tears often mean little; some people can cry for the slightest cause; but Jesus proved His sacred earnestness when in the highest and holiest example of self-sacrifice He, the mighty and majestic God, bowed His head into death's death at Calvary. My fellow sinners and fellow redeemed, behold Him suspended between earth and heaven; and as you see those tears of love give way to the suffering of love, ask God's Spirit for the repentant faith by which you proclaim: This Christ of nail-crushed hands and feet, the Christ of wounded brow and riven side, the Christ of bleeding back and buffeted face, the Christ of anguish and thirst, the Christ of derision and Godforsakenness is my loving, compassionate, all-merciful Savior!

When we thus discover the sympathy in His tears, we have Heaven's own assurance that we need not weep endlessly and disconsolately over the sins and sorrows crowded into our lives. Then we have the inner conviction that because Jesus loves us with this tear-filled devotion, He will not only forgive us, but He will help us meet adversity, triumph over temptation, find strength in weakness, and turn the gloom of affliction into inner glory, the storms and turbulence of life into the calm and quiet of assured faith. The years before us may test us severely. Despite the cruel promises that America is on the threshold of a postwar period filled with prosperity and advantage such as our people have never known, we must not lose sight of the decisive fact that war has always burdened the succeeding generations and that, the wider the conflict, the heavier the sufferings in the aftermath. This is the most destructive struggle in all history. The price we must pay for it will be higher than for any previous conflict. We may witness terrifying up-heavals in our own country. Our own liberties may be drastically restricted. Men with un-American and un-christian principles may seize control of this land, but whatever comes — and believers of all denominations, children and parents in every believing household, should daily be on their knees, asking God to avert these trag-edies! — we will find comfort, sympathy, guidance, when we think of the Savior's tears and His blood drops at Golgotha. With this vision constantly before our eyes, we shall be prepared for hardship or, what may prove far more difficult, the ease and warmth of luxury and artificial prosperity.

You can see, then, that Jesus, weeping in warning and wondrous love, is the Savior for whom our sin-racked age cries with special pleading. The Christ who could mourn for His enemies should be the Example and the Power for America today. It took Madame Chiang Kai-shek, whose husband is generalissimo of a heathen na-tion, to remind us that in the Savior's spirit we must be ready to forgive our foes. I ask all real, confessing Chris-tians throughout the land to pray regularly and re-peatedly not only for victory and a quick end to this war, if it be God's will, but with the same determination to intercede for the people of Germany, Italy, and Japan, pleading especially that the cause of His Son's kingdom may be advanced among them, that they may learn to know and cherish the memory of Jesus, weeping for the men who would soon condemn Him to the cross. Is not this the Redeemer whom with all our resources and energies we must bring to the ends of the earth, also through the challenging, penetrating means of the radio?

Our only hope is in Him. Human methods to save the world from itself are doomed to defeat, if they banish Christ. Some time ago Count Alfred D. Pierre Court left

$2,000,000 to his native city, Rouen, France, for the express purpose of propagating giants. He wanted to raise a physically superior race that could lift humanity out of its woes. The trustees of his fund searched all over the world to secure men and women of large stature and unusual strength. The effort failed. The only people who can ever help mankind are the spiritual giants, the reborn children of God, whose love mirrors the devotion of that weeping Savior. Therefore listen closely as the Lenten invitation resounds, *"Behold, we go up to Jerusalem, and the Son of Man shall be betrayed unto the chief priests and unto the scribes, and they shall condemn Him to death and shall deliver Him to the Gentiles, to mock and to scourge and to crucify Him; and the third day He shall rise again"!* That Lenten call comes in a crisis such as this nation has never seen, and in a personal appeal to everyone of you, telling you now that for your soul it is either Christ or chaos, either heaven or hell, either life everlasting or death never-ending. As you see the tears of sorrow and sympathy stream down the Savior's face for you, will you, can you, dare you turn away from the only Redeemer you can ever have and say, "These tears mean nothing to me"? God forbid! May you rather feel the tears of deep repentance and joyful faith well into your eyes as you, a weeping sinner, come to the weeping Redeemer for pardon, purity, and peace! The holy angels will swell the anthems of heavenly praise if now in your innermost heart you accept God's Son. Rededicate yourself to Him! The Savior's tears for you will give way to gladness. My beloved, preciously redeemed, will you not make the compassionate Christ your own now and forever? Our heavenly Father grant above all else that in this moment thousands of you may say with inner conviction, "God helping me, I will!" Amen.

Father, Forgive Them— and Us!

> *"Then said Jesus, Father, forgive them; for they know not what they do!"*
> SAINT LUKE 23:34

Our Father:

*A*s Thy beloved Son, our only Savior, pleaded for His enemies in the agony of the crucifixion, so, with firm faith in the Christ of Calvary we now intercede for those who hate us, our personal and national adversaries. Father, "nothing shall be impossible" with Thee; therefore, we beseech Thee to bring all those who oppose us to the cross, so that they witness Heaven's highest compassion, heed the appeal for repentance, and find the assurance of their redemption through faith in the crucified Redeemer. If Jesus loved us while we, His enemies, were yet in our sins; if He gave Himself into that painful, shameful death to atone for those who blasphemed Him, how can we hate our fellow men and refuse to forgive, even as we have been forgiven? Show Thy mercy to our military men and women throughout the world! Restore many listed as missing! Heal the wounded! Cheer the captives! Comfort the dying! Again, O Father, we ask: Give us a true, triumphant peace soon! We pray according to Thy will and in Jesus' holy name. Amen.

LAST week the United States ambassador to Russia issued an amazing indictment. In effect he asserted that, although our country has shipped the Soviet armies large supplies of airplanes, tanks, cannon, ammunition, raw materials, and food, this fact is being systematically withheld from the Russian people, who do not know the extent of our help nor appreciate the aid we have sent.

318

Serious, nation-wide concern was shown over this statement. But why, I ask you, are we not more vitally agitated by the spiritual ignorance in our own country, according to which men and women, beholding the Savior's cross, do not believe that it represents the greatest source of national and individual help? Why have some American churches hushed the message of the groaning agony at Golgotha? Before we accuse the Russians of ingratitude to men, should we not plead guilty of our own ingratitude to God?

Because it is either Christ or continued crisis, either the Savior's cross or men's double cross; because America needs spiritual security before social security, I shall devote every message in this Lenten season to the central, vital heart of our true Christian faith, the cross of the Lord Jesus. I ask everyone of you not only to meet with us each Lord's day in this mighty mission of the air, but also to direct others, the uncounted self-righteous sinners, the afflicted, sorrow-burdened friends, to the crucified Christ of all compassion. Begin with us, then, this afternoon! Stand in spirit at Calvary's crest to hear Jesus plead (Saint Luke, chapter twenty-three, verse thirty-four), *"Father, forgive them; for they know not what they do!"* and to echo:

"FATHER, FORGIVE THEM — AND US!"

May the Holy Spirit bless this message and bring many souls to their only Savior!

I

THE MARVELOUS MERCY IN CHRIST'S PRAYER,
"FATHER, FORGIVE THEM!"

These words, the first spoken from the cross, form a prayer. Jesus might have shrieked in agony; He might have screamed in protest against the hellish injustice that had sentenced Him to death. Instead, during His first moments on that tree of torture He prayed. On the last day of His earthly life our Savior maintained the regular communion with God which had marked every previous day, and which had made Him spend long hours, often the entire night, pleading with His heavenly Father. If only we would follow Christ in esteeming and applying the power of fervent prayer! War's multiplied perils should constantly bring us down on our knees before God; yet too many in the United States have no interest in intercession, no understanding of its necessity and blessing. We may have to suffer far more than the worst we have experienced in the past before we fully realize our utter dependence on the Almighty and the merciful privilege which is ours in humbly petitioning His grace. Prayer can prevail when every earthly hope collapses. Dominic Izzi, United States Navy gunner, will testify to this truth. With two other companions, he spent eighty-three days in a small raft on the open sea. What kept him alive during almost three months, when the raft drifted twenty-two hundred miles? Was it his will power, his own strength, his good luck? Ask him! He replies, "I prayed daily, and I knew that God was with me all the way."

Jesus prays to His Father; and if your pleas are to be heard, they must be directed to the one God, who can and will reply to His children. As throughout His life, so in His death Jesus reveals to the world who the true and eternal God is — not Allah, the god of the Mohammedans; not Zeus, the god of the Greeks; not Jupiter, the god of the Romans; not Asshur, the god of Assyrians; not Marduk, the god of the Babylonians; not Brahma, Vishnu, Siva, the Hindu gods; not Buddha, worshiped by millions in China and the Far East; not Ahura Mazda or Ahariman, the gods of Persia — all false and fraudulent. The sole Source of rescue and redemption for our age is the Father whom Jesus invoked and who together with His Son, our Savior, and the Holy Spirit, our Comforter, is the Lord of lords, the sole, supreme, triune God. He it is who made America great; and He it is to whom the nation's prayers must be directed in this crisis. Many people have read casualty listings so often that they are no longer moved by the reports of more than two thousand American soldiers fallen during a single week's Tunisian fighting, of many more American sailors lost in submarine sinkings. We are becoming so accustomed to accounts of mass killings in this war that we forget the value of a single life and the high estimate which Jesus places on an individual soul.

Besides, millions in the United States seem stolidly unconcerned about the future. Walk through the downtown streets of a typical city at night and you will find just as much revelry as before the war! While we thank God for a government which seeks to give us "security from the cradle to the grave," we need spiritual security beyond the grave. When we are promised after the war "a life of abundance unparalleled in all history," we ought to understand that, if the plans for the future leave out the Almighty and set Christian principles aside, we may face trials and afflictions unparalleled in previous history. The Vice-President of the United States felt called upon to warn our people of the possibility that Germany and Russia might become allied against us. Here are his words, "There is a great probability of Germany and Russia sooner or later making common cause." If that should happen, we must be prepared to battle world Communism, world atheism, world opposition to Christianity. My countrymen, this is only one of the disastrous dangers that may confront us. America should constantly be on its knees in penitent pleading before the Throne of Grace. The call that should resound every minute of every day is, *"Pray without ceasing!"* If you love this divinely blessed nation, beseech the Father, as did Jesus on the cross! What magnificent mercy to know that through Christ God is our merciful Father, who gives us life and sustenance, guidance and guardianship; a Father to whom we can take every trouble, who can help us when all other help fails, who *"spared not His own Son, but delivered Him up for us all"!*

How astonishing also that in this first prayer on the cross — only ten words — Jesus did not plead for Himself! By contrast, think of our petitions, in which we often ask: "God, give me this! God, give me that!" and rarely take time to voice a word of sincere thanks for His unnumbered blessings on soul and body! It was refreshing to read this recognition in General MacArthur's order of the day following the victory at New Guinea: "To God Almighty I give thanks for that guidance which has brought us to this success in our great crusade. His is the honor, the power, and the glory forever. Amen."

True, there was abundant reason for Christ to think of Himself. He had come through a sleepless night of horror. He had been betrayed by one of His disciples and deserted by the rest. He had been beaten, bruised, spit upon, by His own countrymen. He had been scourged, crowned with thorns, by the Roman soldiers and made to carry His cross until He collapsed under its weight. And now, perhaps as He spoke this prayer, heavy nails were being hammered through the flesh and bones of His hands and feet. How terrifying the agonies of that crucifixion! How crushing, beyond the physical pain, the soul anguish such as earth and heaven had not witnessed otherwise. There, on those rugged, gory beams He bore

in His own holy body the burden of all transgressions
that curse the entire human race; yet — O marvelous
mercy! — He pleads not for Himself; forgetting the torture of His soul, He prays for others.

For whom particularly did Jesus intercede? Not for
His mother, who stood, bewildered and hopeless, beneath
the cross; not for the godly women who had traveled to
Calvary, hoping to perform some last, lingering service of
love; not for His disciples who, despite their declarations
of loyalty, had proved cringing cowards. He had knelt
for them and all the faithful only a few hours before in
His majestic high-priestly prayer. It is easy to plead for
those who love us — a mother for her son, a wife for her
husband, a pastor for his flock; but here Jesus intercedes
for the soldiers who are crucifying Him. Was there ever
love like this? Recall, by contrast, the hatred of Tamer-
lane, Oriental conqueror, said to have made a pyramid of
90,000 human heads on the ruins of Baghdad! Genghis
Khan killed more than 18,000,000 human beings in China
alone. Review the hatred practiced in the name of religion! When Mohammed was wounded in battle at
Ohod, he cried in resentment and rage: "Let the wrath
of Allah burn against the men that have besprinkled the
face of his apostle with blood! Let not the year pass
over them alive!" And within the twelve months they
were all killed. Again on Easter Monday, 1282, during the
joyful festival of the Savior's resurrection, when the ves-
per bells rang throughout Sicily, 8,000 French men,
women, children were cut down in a religious war. Yet,
at Calvary, Jesus, suffering in the vilest miscarriage of
justice, appeals for His enemies and pleads not merely
that their penalty be reduced, not that the Lord instead
of striking them dead on the spot, would grant them some
consideration; but by the highest, deepest, widest love

even God could show, He begs that they be entirely forgiven, completely pardoned, their sins altogether removed, the charge of murder wholly canceled. We call it noteworthy clemency today when a governor commutes the death sentence of a guilty criminal to life imprisonment; how much greater is the Savior's total mercy which, in those terrifying moments when His enemies were crucifying Him, pleaded that their sins, their guilt, punishment, curse, and doom to hell, be absolutely and finally removed. — Was there ever love like this?

We may be assured, however, that Jesus' prayer, *"Father, forgive them!"* was spoken not only for those Roman crucifiers; He was pleading with the earnestness of unquenchable love also for the high priests, scribes, Pharisees, those proud, unbending, hate-filled clerical killers, who conspired to destroy Him. He was approaching His Father in behalf of the Jerusalem politicians who had agreed that He, the innocent, spotless Son of God, should be delivered into death. He was raising His voice for the blood-thirsty mob howling at Him in derision, shaking their heads in mockery, taunting Him in His suffering. From that high altar where Jesus was being sacrificed as the final offering for the sins of the world, He appealed for all who had despised and rejected Him, for every sinner in the ages yet to come. Above all, however — and this is the personal message of the Lenten season, the warning and comfort of Christ's cross — He pleaded, *"Father, forgive them!"* because He was thinking of you and your transgressions, because even the agony of the crucifixion could not make Him forget you nor keep Him from beseeching His Father to remove your iniquities.

You cannot understand the real meaning of the crucifixion unless you know and confess that your sins sent

Jesus to Calvary; that your guilt made Him suffer agony, unfathomable and indescribable. You will forfeit His grace; you will let the eternal salvation of your preciously bought soul slip away unless you are convinced that, when Jesus prayed, *"Father, forgive them!"* He was reminding Himself of your utter helplessness and hopelessness without Him, and beseeching His Father that your iniquities might be forgiven, your disloyalty, hatred of the truth, rebellion against the Almighty, canceled and removed forever. Many moving appeals have been made before the bars of human justice in behalf of prisoners condemned by their own confession; but never again will earth or heaven witness that most powerful and penetrating petition with which Jesus began His death plea, *"Father, forgive them!"*

Christ did far more than pray for you. In His matchless mercy and endless grace He died to seal your pardon with His blood. Amazing grace: the sinless Savior crucified for sin-filled mankind; the pure and holy Redeemer suffering for an impure and vicious race; the glorious Son of God offered as a living and dying sacrifice for all the selfish sons of men; the almighty Lord of lords slain for His depraved, degenerate creatures; Jesus Christ delivered into death for you!

Today we see many examples of heroic devotion. Millions of American young men under arms risk their lives in defending our country. Oh, that we genuinely appreciated what they are doing for us, that we could understand the sorrows surging through the hearts of America's gold-star parents! Our admiration goes out to a chaplain from Newark, Father John P. Washington, whose transport was torpedoed in the North Atlantic. He drowned after giving his lifebelt to save a soldier who had none. We are deeply moved by the love of a Brooklyn father who last week lost his life attempting to rescue his son from a burning house. These men each died to save one person; Christ died to save the world. These heroes gave their lives for a friend or a dear one; the Savior was crucified for His enemies. The chaplain and the Brooklyn father went to their doom attempting to rescue men's bodies for this life; Jesus went to Calvary to rescue souls for eternity. Here at Golgotha, then, is complete compassion, the removal and canceling of all our sins. Here is guaranteed grace, no wishful thinking, no "perhaps," no "if" or "maybe," but assured certainty. "*I am persuaded,*" we can exult with Saint Paul, "*that neither death, nor life, nor angels, nor principalities, nor powers, nor things present, nor things to come, nor height, nor depth, nor any other creature shall be able to separate us from the love of God which is in Christ Jesus our Lord.*" Here is the full forgiveness, without payment, without intercession or introduction by saints, the magnificent mercy that receives you just as you are, with all your sins and shortcomings. Therefore, repent and rely on the Savior! Here on the cross, towering over the skull-shaped hill, is positive pardon for you, all-embracing atonement for your transgressions, all-sustaining love for your life's sorrows.

Note this added mercy: Jesus pleads that His murderers may be forgiven because "*they know not what they do.*" Plainly He indicates that the Roman soldiers nailing Him to the cross did not realize they were killing the Prince of Life. Many in that hate-swollen crowd, even some of the priests and higher-ups in the political circles of Jerusalem, did not recognize the terrifying crime in which they had involved themselves; and Jesus had compassion on their shocking, damning lack of knowledge. — Ask any attorney, and he will tell you that ignorance of human law is no excuse. If you exceed the speed limit, it will not help you to say, "I didn't know I was driving too fast." If you neglect to pay your federal income taxes, the Government will not listen to your plea, "I did not know I had to make a return." If you are eligible to register for military service, no one will even consider this excuse, "I did not know I should report." But at the cross men learn that Christ, as always, has more mercy than we have. Only He could pray, only He and His have ever interceded, only He and His faithful will ever plead, *"Father, forgive them; for they know not what they do!"*

II

THE URGENT NECESSITY THAT WE PRAY, "FATHER, FORGIVE THEM — AND US!"

Now, we will do well to add to the Savior's prayer and plead, *"'Father, forgive them'* — and us!" for too many people, without Christ or against His cross, similarly do not know what they are doing. Some of you are entirely ignorant of the destruction and disaster your rejection of the Redeemer can cause. You *"know not what"* you do, you the religiously indifferent, who keep your distance from the church and think Sunday only a holiday; but you are not only starving your own souls, you are undermining the foundations of the nation. General Henri Giraud recently ascribed the downfall of France, in part at least, to the neglect of the Lord's day. You *"know not what"* you do, you enemies of the home: attorneys who make money by easy and quick divorce; judges whose decrees split the family after plain collusion; club women and agitators who are working for the public distribution and open teaching of birth-control methods; physicians who aid impurity; husbands and wives who secretly break your marriage vows — you not only disregard God's Law but also weaken American family life and help to increase national guilt. You *"know not what"* you do, you hypocrites who in the name of patriotism are trying to make money from soldiers and sailors; you tavern keepers, who ply them with drink; you frauds and cheats who advertise large, attractive packages for our service men but stuff them two-thirds full of straw and paper. You are not only defrauding the country's defenders; you are also undermining their morale, working hand in hand with the enemy. You *"know not what"* you do, you Modernists who question God's Word, misinterpret it, and finally deny it in sermons delivered from pulpits built by true believers in Christ's atonement and the resurrection. You are not only guilty of deceit; you are also blind leaders of the blind. Far more, many of you refuse to accept the redemption in Christ; not knowing what you do, you are endangering your own preciously bought souls, toying with your eternal destiny, daily drawing closer to the brink of hell. For the guarantee of heaven, will you not come to Calvary and pray, " *'Father, forgive them'* — and us, for often we *'know not what'* we do"?

Some of you are purposely blaspheming the Lord, deliberately sneering at Jesus, willfully living in sin, determinately rebelling against the Almighty. To you I can only say, "May God have mercy on your souls!" Jesus was not praying for you, *"Father forgive them; for they know not what they do!"* You *know* what you are doing. Yet, despite your avowed wickedness, Christ, whose grace is new every morning, whose forgiveness is never withheld from any penitent sinner, however vile, offers you atonement, if only before your heart is altogether hardened, you humbly, contritely, accept Him as your Redeemer! No matter how terrifying your rebellion against the Savior, He died for you.

No forgiveness is complete until it is accepted. Even the United States Supreme Court has ruled: if a prisoner refuses to agree to a pardon, he is not released. The blessings of redemption are not yours until you believe in Jesus. So that Christ will not have been crucified in vain for you, I ask you: Come to the cross! Accept your Redeemer! Be cleansed in His blood! Find life through His death! Crushed by the weight of your sins, stand at grim Golgotha to pray, "*Father, forgive*" me! and from Heaven itself will come the assurance that your sins — every one of them — have been canceled at Calvary for eternity!

Because we have received mercy, we must show mercy. In this age of personal hatred, class hatred, religious hatred, national hatred, we hear Jesus say, "*Love your enemies; bless them that curse you; do good to them that hate you; and pray for them which despitefully use you and persecute you!*" If we would be Christ's, we must try to put this command into practice. We are not worthy disciples of the loving Lord unless we ourselves radiate forgiveness and compassion. True, forgiving charity starts at home, in our family circles. Some of you are living in households split apart by long-nourished grudges. Brother is estranged from sister; parents have banished their own children; as unbelievable as this is, husband and wife are often practical enemies, working at cross purposes, with never a kind word, never a caress. Can you, blessed as you are by the Christ who freely forgave the multitude of your heavy transgressions, wreck your own lives and the happiness of others through sustained quarrels over trivialities or through proud, selfish insistence on your rights? Now, while you behold the immeasurable mercy of your Savior crushed to the cross, give room to the resolve which the Spirit would plant within you by seeking forgiveness from those whom you have injured and granting forgiveness to those who have injured you!

There can likewise be no racial or religious, color or class prejudices among true Christians. Even a World War cannot change that statement. We dare not push religion aside for the duration to forget that Jesus specifically commanded, *"Love your enemies!"* and that on the cross He loved His murderers to the bitter end. In contradiction to Christ's compassion a high figure in American life cries out, "We must hate with every fiber of our being." A New York psychiatrist declares that, if we stop hating Germans, Japanese, and Italians, this will be "a stumbling block in our efforts to build a world in which further wars will be impossible." How utterly absurd this proposal to build a warless world with hatred! On the contrary, if passion and prejudice increase, we face a world of darkness and disaster beyond description. If during war, at the peace table, in the postwar period, we forget our Savior's holy example on the cross, who can measure the devastation and conflict which may follow? Of course, we denounce the Nazi system that has produced the hatred and persecution of the Jews; but with all our deep-rooted aversion we dare not, would we be true to Jesus, permit our hearts to be filled with bitterness and malice toward the German people. Rather must we repeat the Redeemer's appeal for His foes, *"Father, forgive them!"* and with all the means at our disposal bring them, as soon as possible, the promises of Gospel grace. I cannot forget how Russian Communists persecuted Lutheran pastors and church members. I can see those martyrs praying as they were cut down in the cold blood of mass murders; but I cannot hate the Russian people for those supercrimes. Instead, because I have pledged allegiance to the Cross, I must love them, intercede for them, and as soon as possible bring them, too, the message of full forgiveness. To this end we are seeking permission to broadcast in the U. S. S. R. After the war is over — may it be soon! — and with God helping us, we hope to enter devastated Europe with the message of spiritual reconstruction through the Savior preached in a dozen different languages. Ask God to grant us that request!

At Calvary we find two ways of life; the one is the path of might, cruelty, hatred; the other, the road of reconciliation, love, mercy. Which way will you take? Which will our bleeding, battered world follow? Before Nurse Edith Cavell faced the German firing squad in World War I, she declared "I must *die* without hating." Must we not, looking to the Lord Jesus for strength in our weakness, resolve to *live* without hating, and as we daily pray, " '*Father, forgive them!*' " add, "and us, for Jesus' sake"? God grant that every one of you will follow the example of your crucified Christ throughout a life of love — even for your enemies! We ask it by His promise. Amen.

Families of America, Cling to the Cross!

> "When Jesus, therefore, saw His mother, and the disciple standing by whom He loved, He saith unto His mother, Woman, behold thy son! Then saith He to the disciple, Behold thy mother!"
>
> SAINT JOHN 19:26, 27

O Jesus, Our Christ of Endless Compassion:

As on Thy cross of agony and shame Thou didst establish and bless a new home for Thy mother, so from the throne of Thy glory in heaven look down on the families of this nation! By Thy Spirit graciously direct parents and children to Calvary in deep contrition and with a living, trusting faith! Forgive the repeated transgressions, especially the lovelessness, strife, unfaithfulness in many households, and by the power of Thy blood remove all selfishness! Show us that without Thee we can do nothing good! We are too weak and selfish to preserve peace and mutual understanding, if Thou dost not enter our homes to bless us! Teach us, however, that no affliction of body or soul, no loss of money or treasure, no sorrow of disaster, nor even death need overwhelm us! In all these adversities we are more than conquerors through Thee and Thy limitless love! Graciously protect our military men and women who are far from their homes, daily surrounded by multiplied dangers; and, O Christ of mercy and might, grant them soon a happy home-coming in true victory and lasting peace! We plead according to Thy will and promise! Hear us, O Jesus, for our help is in Thee! Amen.

A FEW years ago, when scientists were digging in the ruins of Herculaneum, the city which, together with Pompeii, was destroyed by Mount Vesuvius' eruption in 79 A. D., they were amazed to find under the lava and ashes a cross impressed on a bedroom wall in a most beautiful ancient dwelling. Though surrounded by pagan vice and debauch, that home, the first in all history known thus to be marked, was not ashamed to show its devotion to the Lord Jesus.

Today, when far more houses are destroyed by the bombings and blastings of this world conflict than by that fire and treachery of Vesuvius, every twentieth-century household in the United States could well follow this first-century example. Of course, there is no miraculous power in the wood or the precious metals of which a cross may be made or in the costly jewels with which it may be studded. Nor is there any help for the soul in bowing before the alleged fragments of the timbers on which the Savior was nailed. It is a million times more important to understand the true meaning of Jesus' suffering and to have our homes blessed by a Christ-centered faith.

Because family life in this nation faces serious difficulties, which can be removed only by loyalty to the Crucified, I urge you: Stand once more at Calvary! Witness the Savior's deep concern for His mother's sorrows and suffering! Hear Him, as His love establishes a new home there, beneath the blood-marked cross! Ponder carefully this record of Saint John, chapter nineteen, verses twenty-six and twenty-seven: *"When Jesus, therefore, saw His mother, and the disciple standing by whom He loved, He saith unto His mother, Woman, behold thy son! Then saith He to the disciple, Behold thy mother!"* These words issue the call from Calvary:

FAMILIES OF AMERICA, CLING TO THE CROSS!

May the Holy Spirit mightily bless this message of Jesus' dying love in many sorrow-stricken, war-torn, peace-robbed homes!

I

CLINGING TO THE CROSS, PARENTS LEARN TO STAND BY THEIR CHILDREN

Who can ever know fully the anguish which surged through Mary's heart in those torturous, grief-numbed hours at Golgotha when she saw her own Son nailed to that accursed, unclean instrument of death? The Scriptures do not record that she spoke a single word during the hours of that agony, and perhaps the bleeding horror of the crucifixion left her speechless. No one knew Jesus as intimately, lovingly as His mother. How her thoughts must have raced through the thirty years in which, before His public ministry, He had been her considerate, devoted, and absolutely sinless Son! How vividly Mary must have recalled those sacred moments when her arms cradled His infant form! Yet, here at Golgotha she could not even wipe the grime, sweat, and blood from His wounded body; she could not stop the raging fever or quench the fiery thirst. She remembered that the angels had sung the promise of *"great joy"* which her Son would bring to all people. Where, she must have asked bewilderedly, could there be any joy in the appalling agony that would soon kill Him? *"He shall save His people from their sins,"* the angels had promised; but at Golgotha, Mary heard the murder-crazed crowd cry in sneering sarcasm, *"He saved others; Himself He cannot save!"* Christ, so prophecy had told her, was to be *"a Light to lighten"* the world, yet here on the skull-shaped hill of death both His countrymen and the Gentiles were united to destroy Him. Never in all human suffering has any other mother endured the horror which gripped Mary there beneath the cross.

In their cruelest punishments degenerate tyrants have made parents witness the execution of their own children.

This was the favorite penalty imposed by Caligula, the insane, satanic Roman emperor who often insisted that fathers and mothers look on while their sons writhed in agony. But love, pure and unconquerable, not force, brought Mary to the execution of her sinless Son. Gruesome though the whole crucifixion was, nothing could keep her from Jesus in His last moments. The cowardly disciples might flee and hide, but she would stand by her Son. Jesus might be ridiculed and rejected, cursed and crucified, but come hatred, come persecution to the blood, come death itself — weak, helpless woman though she was, Mary would stay with Christ and comfort Him until the end.

Mothers and fathers of America, follow Mary in standing by your children during their crisis moments! Never have they needed the encouragement of parents as intensely as now, in World War II. Eleven million of our choicest young men are to be under arms in the nation's defense before this year closes, and at least one of every three families in my audience knows what it has cost to give a son to the country. While it is neither weak nor unpatriotic to feel this loss so keenly that your eyes sometimes fill with tears, do not let self-concern dictate your emotions! Rather try to help your sons, as Mary sought to sustain Jesus!

If you truly wish to fulfill your responsibilities as fathers and mothers, work and pray that your children go out to Calvary to convince themselves that Jesus is their Savior; that, while His limitless and unrestricted love offers forgiveness, pardon, peace, and heaven itself to all men in the entire past, present, and future of history, nevertheless His cross-crowned mercy is so individual and personal that every sinner can look up to the crucified Redeemer and say: "He shed His blood to cleanse me; He was crucified to rescue me from hell. He died here, so that I might have eternal life."

We hear much of morale-building agencies. May God bless any program that can give real encouragement to our armed forces! But if you could visit our men in Pacific island foxholes, Tunisian tanks, on Aleutian airfields, or North Atlantic conveys, many would personally assure you that the highest and steadiest morale-builder is Christian faith. These men know that, when you see an enemy detachment approaching, find a torpedo steering its way toward the center of your ship, hear an aerial bomb whistling its way in your direction, you need Christ. Therefore, parents of America, strengthen your sons with the fortitude of trusting faith! It is not enough that you love them, write to them regularly, supply them with everything money can buy. They need more than devotion or letters. They must have something money cannot buy — Jesus for their hearts and their lives.

Unbelief and rejection of Christ are always destructive, but never so much as when parents who should help their children spiritually are forced to stammer hopelessly in soul ignorance. I certainly would not want to be an atheist father and have to send my son into this war with no support for its dangerous hours other than the vague hope that somehow luck or fate may be good to him. If you parents who have never brought your children to Christ — simply because you have stubbornly and selfishly resisted the Savior — want to undo the influence of your bad example, stop battling against the Almighty! Give Jesus His way in your soul! Drop your pride to confess yourselves poor, lost sinners! Ask the Lord to forgive you for Jesus' sake! Put your trust wholly, continually, sincerely, in your crucified Savior, and then — God be praised — you can do what Mary did, you can truly stand by your boy through life or, if divine wisdom decrees, through death! You can help fortify the hearts of our fighting men from Kiska to Casablanca to China. How? If you churchless and Christless listeners will accept Jesus as your Savior and then write letters like this: "Dear Son: Today Mother and I have accepted Christ. We have been blind up to this time, but now, thank God, we see the light. We are sorry that we have helped keep the Lord from you all these years, but now we beg you to welcome Him as your Redeemer!"

To help your son find Jesus a large number of Christian pastors have offered their services as Army and Navy chaplains. Records in my own Church, which has furnished some 150 spiritual leaders for our armed forces, show that in this conflict more than ever before the chaplain meets the same dangers which confront your son. As we thank every truly Christian chaplain for his self-sacrifice in behalf of Jesus, we plead with each one of them to maintain an uncompromising, unswerving devotion to the Savior and to help keep our armed forces believing and trusting the Lord of their salvation.

We cannot promise, of course, that, if you parents help bring your sons to Christ and keep them with Him, they will lead a "charmed" life, escaping danger and death. Even Mary's intense love at Calvary could not save her Son. Some of our fighting men will lose their lives; but then what blessed assurance to know that they have gone home to Jesus, that they are face to face with Him, relieved from war, wickedness, and suffering! . . . How terrifying, on the other hand, for a soldier to face the horror of death alone, without the Lord's sustaining companionship, because his own parents kept him away from this divine Companion! Believe also, however, that, if it be God's high and holy purpose, a Christian soldier can be protected, miraculously, if necessary. Recently I stated on this broadcast that the Almighty can change the course of bullets to shield His children. Some of you may have thought that exaggeration, but recently I received a letter telling of a sailor whose ship was twice torpedoed off North Africa, and who, as he took to the lifeboat, was under close, constant enemy fire. He writes: "Bullets continually grazed my legs and arms. It is a miracle of God that I was spared." Behind that miracle was a family which for two years prayed daily for his safety. If your son is Christ's, then, in life or in death, you can have the confidence by which the father of a twenty-one-year-old distinguished pilot in the South Pacific air-service wrote me: "May the Lord, if it be His will, keep Howard well and safe! But should He will it otherwise, we pray that He will give us strength and courage to travel on until we, too, shall reach the end of the road and meet again at Jesus' feet."

American parents must also stand by sons and daughters who stay at home. They, too, must battle, not so much against actual flesh-and-blood adversaries as against treacherous wickedness and alluring temptations. Here they are, these regiments of ruin mobilized against your boys and girls as never before: *Youth Enemy Number One:* loose morality. An old proverb warns: "When war breaks out, hell has to be enlarged." While we should reasonably expect that the visitations of this present struggle and the longer casualty lists would sober people, make them humble themselves under God's chastising hand, lead them to repent of their sins, we see instead worldliness on all sides. How true Jeremiah's complaint: *"Thou hast stricken them, but they have not grieved; Thou hast consumed them, but they have refused to receive correction; they have made their faces harder than a rock; they have refused to return.*" Our young people cannot escape all contact with evil forces. The laxity and looseness of immorality, the lure to live fully while you can, continually coax our young people, and too often temptation triumphs. Study the increase in teen-age lawbreakers; survey our overcrowded reformatories!

Youth Enemy Number Two: the spending, the luxury, the love of easy money. Most young people have never before handled the large sums they now receive; and the widespread extravagance they behold on all sides—$3,000 mink coats, $500 hats, $30 shoes — helps increase the love of vanity at the expense of soul growth and a clean, humble life.

Youth Enemy Number Three: lax family standards. Where, outside the churches — and not even in all of them — do any agencies emphasize marriage as a divine gift and lifelong blessing; parenthood, a sacred privilege and responsibility; motherhood, a divinely appointed power in the home rather than in business, politics, and social activities? Even the United States Supreme Court has made the lowest, easiest divorce laws granted by one of our States legal for the whole nation! Our young men and women are influenced by this collapse of family morality. Not a few of the girls who run carelessly into hasty weddings without really knowing their husbands or understanding the sacrifices wartime marriages demand are saying to themselves, "Well, if this marriage does not turn out as I expect, or if I meet someone I like better, I can always get a divorce."

Youth Enemy Number Four: sinful amusement and drink. A mere glance at the advertisements of most night clubs reveals their sordid character. Widely applauded stage productions feature the triangle relation without rebuke. The F. B. I. has branded certain public dance halls as breeding places of vice. In Saint Louis the military police have closed taverns to soldiers because they were centers of crime and disease. Drunken driving has increased 60 per cent in one of our large cities.

Youth Enemy Number Five: printed attacks on God's Word and the Christian home. Newspapers have again featured full-page advertisements of certain pamphlets, miscalled "books," published by a Kansas infidel, some of them written by perverted minds, many openly opposed to Christ and the demands of decency. I rejoice that a New Orleans friend, to present the counteracting, saving influence of the Gospel, is paying for full-page space in the largest paper of that city, so that he can bring our message to all the people in New Orleans. I earnestly invite other business men whom God has richly blessed to do the same thing in their communities. We must use the press *for* the Savior, since it is too widely abused against Him. Think of it, in a syndicated column conducted by a woman nationally known as a counselor on home questions, a nineteen-year-old Catholic young woman writes that she is in love with a Protestant married man twelve years older than she, the father of a seven-year-old child! This man plans to secure a divorce, and the girl, who states that she "can hardly wait for that glorious day," asks where she should be married. In answer, that widely heralded consultant on courtship and marriage merely suggests the wedding be performed by a justice of the peace or by some minister who does not hesitate to remarry divorced persons, but not in a single word does she warn the girl that she is helping to break a home, ruining her life, losing her soul!

Youth Enemy Number Six: anti-Christian influences. Christ-rejecting churches, often with large funds at their disposal; social-gospel churches, with much entertainment, but little soul-encouragement; sleepy, spiritually dead churches which spurn their divinely bestowed gifts; Bible-ridiculing schools, with large scholarship and endowment funds; atheist-Communist political movements, with pointed appeals to our young people — these have wrought unspeakable havoc in young lives by turning many from the Lord. The latest atrocity is offered by the Texas University student paper, in which a girl editor applauds Russian atheism and lists "religion," along with slavery and prostitution, as one of the seven sins with which men are cursed.

Youth Enemy Number Seven, the last and in many ways the worst: the indifference of parents and the breakdown of the home. Ask J. Edgar Hoover, head of the Federal Bureau of Investigation, why more girls are going wrong than ever before, and he gives this reason: "A deplorable lack of parental guidance and discipline in many homes"! Ask social workers why they are overcrowded with family case work, and they will answer that often, when father and mother both work, they are too busy or unwilling to care for the family; that far too frequently parents are separated, divorced! Ask any pastor why young people who seemed to give promise of a victorious life have forsaken Jesus, and usually he will reply that they had no reinforcement for their religion at home, that their families never took time to meet God in prayer and worship!

The order of the day, then, for the home front is: Parents, cling to the Cross and use its divine power to help your children! It is not enough that you provide them with food and shelter, educate them, lavish your affection on them. You yourself must have Christ to give them Christ. Everything else you bequeath them can be taken away; the money they inherit may endanger their soul's salvation, but the faith they have learned from you can be the imperishable assurance of their heavenly redemption.

Fathers and mothers, can you truly say, "I have stood at the Savior's cross, and my children have worshiped with me"? Do you answer, "No"? Realize then, if there is to be pardon and promise for you, you must first show sincere repentance for your sins. Then, as God's Word directs you, *"Believe on the Lord Jesus Christ, and thou shalt be saved, and thy house!"* you must accept Him as your suffering, bleeding, dying Redeemer, welcome Him into your family circle as the Head of your household, daily commune with Him in the Scriptures, constantly intercede with Him through fervent prayer, eagerly plead and work, so that the whole family — father, mother, and children — all kneel at the cross in one blessed faith and in one triumphant hope.

II

CLINGING TO THE CROSS, CHILDREN LEARN TO STAND BY THEIR PARENTS

Our text tells us that when the Savior *"saw His mother, and the disciple standing by whom He loved, He saith unto His mother, Woman, behold thy son! Then saith He to the disciple, Behold thy mother!"* The pain of soul and body which our crucified Savior endured at Calvary as He paid the full, fearful price of all iniquity, atoning for sin after sin, in the endless list of human guilt, is utterly beyond human measurement, understanding and expression; yet, when the crucified Redeemer beheld Mary, He forgot the horror and the terror our sins had laid upon Him; He provided a home for His mother, with shelter, protection, and love. How marvelous His compassion!

How striking His example and appeal, too, for American sons and daughters similarly to stand by their parents! Mary, the Savior knew, would have to face loneliness, public curiosity, persecution; and many of your parents, now or in the near future, unable to support themselves, may hover on the edge of destitution. What are you going to do? Refuse to provide for them because, as you say, you have your own worries? Send them to the poorhouse? Let them rely on state old-age pensions? Remember all that your father and mother have done for you! They gave you life; they guarded you during childhood years, provided for you until you could begin to make your own way; and if you are blessed with Christian parents, they brought you to Jesus, taught you the Savior's love, prayed for you, denied themselves so that you could enjoy advantages they never knew. Yet, in cold selfishness, many young people have forsaken their fathers and mothers. Some of the saddest letters we receive come from aged parents, seventy, eighty, or more years old, whose children have no room for them in their homes, no love for them in their hearts. How shocking that ingratitude and how terrifying its punishment! God's Word warns, *"Cursed be he that setteth light by his father or his mother!"* And again, *"The eye that mocketh at his father and despiseth to obey his mother, the ravens of the valley shall pick it out, and the young eagles shall eat it."* If you have thus sinned against your parents, fall on your knees to ask God's forgiveness! See the Savior, writhing in agony, provide for His mother's earthly needs, and resolve that with God's help you will amend and improve your sin-marked life!

Has God graciously given you parents who, like Mary, love the Savior and cling to His grace? Make it your duty to radiate their faith! Rembrandt, the world-renowned

Dutch artist, gratefully painted many pictures of his mother. Almost one hundred have been found, and in most of these she clasps a small Bible in her hands. You may not be able to immortalize your mother or father in portraits; but if you show the faith your Christian parents taught you, you will pay them a tribute more valuable in God's sight than any costly canvas. When you follow Christ's example and honor your parents, the Lord will honor you. The commandment, *"Thou shalt honor thy father and thy mother,"* is the only ordinance of the ten with a blessing — *"that it may be well with thee and thou mayest live long on the earth!"*

III

CLINGING TO THE CROSS, THE WHOLE FAMILY IS BLESSED BY CHRIST

Saint John — for he was the disciple to whom Jesus entrusted His mother — experienced the fulfillment of this promise in a long life and, despite persecutions, a good life. He was in all probability the youngest of the Twelve; but in no way was he morally or spiritually better than the others. On the contrary, before the Savior's crucifixion he shared the weaknesses of the rest. He, too, dreamed of a powerful kingdom which the Lord would establish on earth. He, too, coveted a high position of authority at the Savior's right hand. He, too, had not learned to supplant hatred with love; for when the people of a Samaritan village refused to welcome Jesus, he besought the Lord that fire from heaven might destroy them. He was a true son *"of thunder,"* who would have used force and destruction to spread the Redeemer's realm. After the crucifixion, however, John was a changed man; in his Gospel and three epistles he becomes the outstanding Apostle of love and humility, teaching that

Christ's dominion is spiritual, that it welcomes not those who resort to tumult and bloodshed but those who are *"born of water and of the Spirit."* How can we account for this startling change? We know, of course, that it was a miracle wrought by the Holy Spirit through the Word; but who brought Saint John that Word? Are we not entitled to conclude that in his home Mary confided to him the marvelous wonders which she as the Savior's mother had witnessed in the life of her divine Son — all the treasures of sacred memory she had kept in her heart since Jesus was born?

Every one of you can find the same regenerating power in your Bible, which, by its own promise, *"is able to build you up"* and strengthen your household. Is your family happiness broken by quarrel, cursing, drunkenness, unfaithfulness, waning love? You have one — but only one — hope of permanent help: God's Word, as it brings you the Gospel grace of your crucified Savior. If real understanding, true affection, mutual helpfulness have been banished from your dwelling, there is again only one way to forgiveness and unselfishness: the way to the cross, where, beholding God's Son slain in your place, you learn, believe, and trust the supreme truth of earth and heaven — *"He died for"* you. If parents and children understand the terrible curse of sin, doubly damnable, it seems, when it blasts peace and joy from the family circle; if they cling to the cross with the soul-deep assurance that *"the blood of Jesus Christ, His Son, cleanseth us from all sin";* if they practice the Savior's teachings concerning the home, invoke His presence in daily prayer, attend a true church regularly and reverently, have the children, wherever possible, enjoy the blessings of Christian day-school training, the members of that household, be it rich or poor, will enjoy the fullest blessings we can know this side of heaven.

Why, we may well ask, did Jesus entrust His mother to John, when she had close relatives, who could have given her food and shelter? Probably because these kinsfolk did not believe in the Savior, He was unwilling to entrust His mother to them. By contrast, how easily young people entrust themselves for life to unbelievers! How readily parents permit their sons or daughters to marry infidels! It takes more than money, furniture, decorations, to make the truly happy home. It takes more than even love itself. You must have Christ.

He who suffered on the cross for us can strengthen our families in any trials or sorrows. European medical annals tell of a Hungarian nobleman who lost his only child, a beautiful daughter, on the eve of her marriage. For two years he remained in a state of melancholia from which not even the efforts of specialists could free him. Then a friend suggested a new way to counteract the growing depression. The assistance of Elizabeth Mara, distinguished court singer, was secured, and unknown to the count, it was arranged that she, without being seen, would sing for him from Handel's *Messiah,* the Christ-exalting masterpiece. At first the melancholy man paid scant attention to the exquisite music. But when Elizabeth Mara sang the words, *"Behold, and see if there be any sorrow like unto My sorrow,"* and the oratorio pictured Jesus on the cross of shame and agony, the despised, rejected, sin-bearing Son of God, the count was suddenly gripped by His Savior's love. Tears gathered in his eyes, the first since the funeral of his daughter. He fell on his knees in contrite faith, and when the choir accompanying the singer joined in the "Hallelujah Chorus," his voice was blended in that hymn of praise. — The Triune God of grace promises you, parents and children, that no matter how often sorrow may cross your threshold, how heavy the weight of grief these days of war may bring, how hopeless life may seem, if you hear the crucified, sin-crushed Redeemer plead, *"Behold, and see if there be any sorrow like unto My sorrow,"* and declare: "O Jesus, truly no one could suffer as Thou didst suffer, since Thou didst take upon Thyself my sins and the guilt of all the world. O Jesus, no one could be tortured as Thou wast, for Thy soul pain on the cross grants me pardon and peace; Thy death assures me of life" — if your family is marked by that faith, the Almighty now gives you the most blessed assurance even He can grant — the promise of your glorious, heavenly home. Parents of America, children of America, come to Calvary! Cling to Christ's cross! Amen.

Thank God: Christ Stayed on the Cross!

> *"They that passed by reviled Him, wagging their heads and saying, Thou that destroyest the Temple and buildest it in three days, save Thyself! If Thou be the Son of God, come down from the cross! Likewise also the chief priests, mocking Him, with the scribes and elders, said, He saved others; Himself He cannot save. If He be the King of Israel, let Him now come down from the cross, and we will believe Him!"*
>
> SAINT MATTHEW 27:39-42

Lord Jesus, Who Didst Love Us Until the End:

How can we ever worthily thank Thee that Thou didst stay on the cross to endure unspeakable pain of body, but far greater anguish of soul, in completing the task of our redemption? O blessed Savior, with our whole heart we praise Thee that Thou didst willingly bear the crushing load of our iniquities and with Thy blood pay the fearful price demanded as our ransom from death and hell. Help us endure our sorrows and afflictions by turning to Thee, our Holy Example and Source of every comfort! We need Thy sustaining presence during every moment of these sin-darkened days, when in our human weakness we are too likely to compromise with unbelief instead of confessing Thee before men. Therefore, abide with us and bless us! Strengthen Thy followers in the armed forces to remain loyal amid all temptations to forsake Thee; and, O Jesus, Thou Prince of Peace, protect them by Thy might until — and may it be soon — Thou wilt mercifully bring them back to us with blessed victory and a triumph of truth! Hear us and help us, as Thou hast promised! Amen.

WHEN our country declared war in December, 1941, a United States Senator predicted that within six months our enemies would be destroyed. The half year elapsed, but we had to fight on. Other voices were then heard predicting the last of the conflict by the end of 1942. That year closed and we were still embattled. New prophets arose to foresee the triumph of our cause before 1943 is over; yet last week Great Britain's prime minister asserted that the struggle will last until the conclusion of 1944, or maybe 1945. Ten per cent of the Washington political and military experts, recently interviewed by a newspaper man, believe that victory will not appear on our horizon until 1946; some, not before 1951.

With so many bad guesses in the past and such uncertainty for the future, people hardly know what to believe; but every American ought to know what to do. We should be on our knees before God, constantly beseeching Him, with whom *"all things are possible,"* if it be His will, to stop this conflict now. A long struggle may mean long casualty lists, the impoverishment of the masses, the end of free government in the United States. We should humbly bow before the Almighty, confess our individual and national sins, plead for pardon in Jesus' name, resolve to remove the transgressions for which this visitation has come upon us: pride and profanity; unbelief and ridicule of the Christian religion; falsehood and false witnessing; impurity and immorality; crime and covetousness. If we want this war to end and thousands of American lives to be spared, we must not make the mistake of thinking that we ourselves can say when this bloodshed will cease. We must leave that to God and with sincere contrition plead that His might and mercy may grant us speedy victory.

Instead of repenting in sackcloth and ashes, however, millions in the United States are regaling themselves in furs and finery, luxury and lust, carnival and carousal. Multitudes have not felt God's chastening hand. They complain about the new ration schedule of two pounds of meat each week; but where in this broad, blessed country has there been any real shortage of necessities? A Congressman who investigated the restaurants in Washington reports, "Chicken dinners only half eaten; halves of good, juicy steaks left on the plates; whole bowls of peas from which only one spoonful had been taken; good desserts nibbled at and left"; and he concludes, "I believe that the waste in the District of Columbia restaurants every week would feed a thousand families in some of the occupied countries and make them fall on their knees and praise the Lord." Not only do we waste earthly blessings; the country's greatest sin is the loss of spiritual power, the neglect of Christ's blood-bought salvation.

Whatever comes, however long the war may last, the Christian — I mean the believer who looks to the cross of the Lord Jesus and to His cleansing blood for pardon, peace, and heaven's paradise — has the guaranteed assurance that these times of testing are for inner growth, for the fortifying of his faith. Today perhaps more than ever before in our country we should realize that God does not always lead His children the easy way; that their sorrows, far from being short and quick, are often long and drawn out; that sometimes they must suffer in order to gain spiritual successes. For courage in great crises, for willingness to endure agony, we turn to Christ crucified at Calvary. When He hung on the cross of shame and agony, our text (Saint Matthew, chapter twenty-seven, beginning at verse thirty-nine) tells us: *"They that passed by reviled Him, wagging their heads and saying, Thou that destroyest the Temple and buildest it in three days, save Thyself! If Thou be the Son of God, come down from the cross! Likewise also the chief priests, mocking Him, with the scribes and elders, said, He saved*

*others; Himself He cannot save. If He be the King of
Israel, let Him now come down from the cross, and we
will believe Him!"* Because the crucified Savior refused
to heed the taunting challenge *"Come down!"* we today
breathe this prayer of heart-deep gratitude:

"THANK GOD: CHRIST STAYED ON THE CROSS!"

May the comforting, enlightening Spirit of all truth now
draw you close to the dying Lord of love at Golgotha
and teach you to find joy, courage, hope, for your own
lives at Calvary!

I

THE TRAGEDY OF A CROSSLESS CHRIST

We should truly feel ashamed at being members of
the human race when we behold the Savior's countrymen
standing within the shadow of His cross and hurling
their taunting insults against the bleeding, dying Son of
God. We would suppose that no matter how misplaced
their enmity may have been before, now that their satanic
purpose had been accomplished, with Jesus nailed to the
tree of torture, they would have been satisfied and returned to their homes. No; their hatred was so fiendish
that they remained to revel in His agony. Recently the
newspapers printed the picture of a dog that kept watch
over another dog, its dead playmate. Unmistakable in
that puppy's eyes was the look of animal sorrow and
brute grief; yet these crucifiers at Calvary showed less
sympathy even than dumb, irrational creatures. We might
be inclined to regard their depravity and deep-rooted
cruelty as exceptional and entirely abnormal, if it were
not for the grim fact that within our own generation we
ourselves have witnessed the same gleeful gloating, which
made Christ's enemies drag figures and effigies of the

sinless, stainless Savior through muddy streets, led atheist societies to print dirty jokes about the Virgin Mary, urged infidel writers to feature scurrilous attacks on Scripture.

They were not restricted to one class or group, these jeering, howling throngs beneath the cross. Look at them closely, and you will find the high and the low of Jerusalem: on the one hand, priests, scribes, politicians, Sanhedrin members, influential leaders; and on the other hand, the city's dregs: criminals from its slums, wretches ruined by its vices! The common hatred of Jesus put men of opposing stations in life on the same level, just as, a few hours before He went the way of the cross, Pilate and Herod, bitter enemies until that time, were reconciled through their mutual rejection of the Savior. Even today atheists and unbelievers form similarly strange alliances. No matter how completely they may spurn each other in social life, their hatred of the Redeemer is so overpowering that they will march against Him shoulder to shoulder with people whom they otherwise shun. Inspect the roster of Reds and radicals in America, and you will see white and black, clergy and laity, capitalists and laborers, teachers and students, anarchists and socialists, Gentiles and Jews, millionaires and paupers, writers and illiterates, pacifists and warmongers. They forget their differences to present a united front against Christ.

Among these cruel critics at Calvary was a group of average, middle-class people. As we see them stick out their tongues at the Crucified, *wagging their heads* in derision, pouring out their profane ridicule, we realize that they were blind followers of blind leaders. They knew that the chief priests, the politically and socially important, had rejected Christ, and they concluded that it was smart for them to do the same thing. Why is it that some of you, after nineteen centuries, in which Christ

THANK GOD: CHRIST STAYED ON CROSS 353

has powerfully demonstrated the truth of His Gospel, are still outside the Church today? Is it not because you likewise take the word of some unbelieving teacher, infidel lecturer, agnostic writer, in preference to God's? You feel that the people whose names make news are often opposed to the Lord, their lives plainly hostile to His Gospel; and you follow them. You demand, repeating the charge voiced in the Savior's day: "Are any of the leading scientists disciples of the Lord? Are any of the intellectual geniuses Christian?" And you answer with an unqualified "No!" In all truth, however, you forget that the mightiest minds of all generations have been humble and reverent. Throw off these destructive prejudices and take time to study God's Word fairly, think for yourself, and with the Spirit's help believe for yourself!

Here, scattered throughout the morbid crowd, are the leaders in the crucifixion, the clergy that remained at Golgotha to gloat over the Savior's agony. It is bad enough when a man outside the Church is found guilty of crime; but it seems a hundred times worse when a servant of God deliberately connives with evil and murderously plans to take an innocent life. Note that the highest of the high, the chief priests, together with the scribes and the elders of the temple in Jerusalem, were the moving spirits in this supercrime. They, in the first instance, are responsible for the grief and devastation that overtook their country. They sold Jerusalem to its ruin, just as, through succeeding generations, whenever those who should be preachers and prophets of the Almighty forgot the Lord, they helped sign their nation's sentence of doom and destruction. The government refuses to draft theological students and clergymen for active warfare because it wants them to fortify the home front. However, can ministers strengthen our nation if they

Tenth Lutheran Hour   23 weaken its faith in the Bible? Can they point us to victory if they seek to defeat Christ? Can they fortify America by assisting in tearing down the mighty fortress we have in our Savior? The broadcast of this Sunday is sponsored by the students of our Concordia Theological Seminary. As I thank God for the fact that this divinity school, which during the 104 years of its existence has sent more than 6,000 ministers into mission fields on the six continents, has never had a Modernist on its faculty, never graduated a student who did not unreservedly accept the Scriptures as the inspired, inerrant Word of God and Jesus as the divine, complete Savior, I appeal to these men of Concordia, our graduates beyond the campus, yes, to every true minister of Christ, and every student of theology in the United States: Preach the Word! Preach the Law, with all its shattering, crushing power! Tell people without exception that they have *"sinned, and come short of the glory of God"!* Warn them that as far as they themselves are concerned, they are hopelessly, eternally lost in their sins! Testify that they are not strong enough, good enough, rich enough, smart enough, to make their own way into heaven, that every day they live against Christ they are destroying their own souls! But then, when the horrors of hell rise before their eyes, when the torture of unforgiven sin tears at their heart, when they realize that they are driving on to inevitable perdition, preach Christ! Preach the cross! Preach the blood! Preach the atonement! Preach justification by faith! Before God I declare that you young men who are loyal to the Gospel are, under God, the nation's and the Church's highest hope for the crisis days ahead. In the Savior's name I beseech you: "Don't let us down! Don't compromise the Redeemer! Don't surrender one iota of the blood-bought heritage, the pledge of Christ's full, unfailing redemption!"

With the same conviction I say to you men in clerical robes who have put a question mark behind the Redeemer's promise and who, if Jesus were with us today, would be under the cross like those clerical killers, your defiant denial of the Bible, your rejection of Christ's redemption, are helping to undermine the foundations of faith on which this nation has rested in the past and on which alone it can be secure for the future. You, with your veiled but violent hatred of God's Son, are the frontline enemies of the United States today, just as those Jerusalem priests were the prime factors in the destruction of their country. You, too, are not satisfied with your own sarcastic unbelief. You deliberately seek to tear others from Jesus. Someone sent me a clipping from an Omaha newspaper (I deeply appreciate this help; please give me all such assistance you can!) which told of a religious meeting in that city. Two laymen are reported as speaking. The one asserted: The Church should preach the Gospel; and the other reinforced this by declaring: The churches should stick to the preaching of the Cross. However, the newspaper reports opposition to this emphasis on the Savior; — objection — think of it! — raised by clergymen! They requested "a reinterpretation of Christ's teachings" — and you know what that means: They asked vaguely for "brotherhood" but neglected to demand the Gospel's power. How long will you consecrated laymen keep on worshiping in congregations which you and your family helped to build, but in which your Bible-grounded faith, your Christ-exalting creed, is steadily attacked from the pulpit by a man who, despite the robes he wears and the titles preceding or following his name, makes Jesus merely another human leader, a reformer, a teacher,

a prophet — anything but God's Son and the world's
Savior? How long will you devout disciples sit quietly in
your pews to hear the message of salvation by the Redeemer's blood supplanted by salvation through your
own achievement? If you really want to serve God's
kingdom and do something for your country, banish all
pulpit unbelief! Keep Christian congregations clean of
betrayal and treachery! If your church in its charter is
dedicated to support the Scriptures and the Savior but
instead is used to undermine the Bible and belittle Christ,
you have only one alternative, would you be loyal to
your Lord: You must see that those who persist in dis-
honoring Jesus are barred from your church; and if they
are not removed, you must eventually leave that congregation, hard as the parting may be!

Listen now to the taunting, cutting cries raised against
Christ at Calvary! First of all they challenge, *"Thou that
destroyest the Temple and buildest it in three days, save
Thyself!"* Viciously they twist and tear our Lord's words.
They falsify and lie. Jesus had never said that He would
rebuild Herod's temple at Jerusalem in three days. He
did say that, though the temple of His body be wrecked
(by death on the cross), yet on the third day it would be
rebuilt in the resurrection unto life, as, praise God, it was
revived. Changing God's Word has been a withering
curse during all succeeding ages. Men in Germany, England, France, Russia, and — may God forgive us! — in our
own country, gifted, talented scholars have spent long
years of university study and then devoted their lifetime
all for one evil purpose: to change the unchangeable
Word, to make Scripture say what they want and not
what God wants. Earnestly I warn you against altering
the Bible to suit yourself. Take every syllable of heavenly truth as it is written! Abraham Lincoln suggested,

take it with reason if you can, but above all take everything with faith! — When you read, *"Christ died for the ungodly,"* then reply: "God said this. Christ did it. I believe it. That settles it."

In the second place, these poison-tongued, rabble-rousing priests cry, "IF *Thou be the Son of God."* Note that they do not blame Jesus for having healed their sick, fed their hungry, comforted their bereaved! Today no one but a moron will attack Christianity because of its Sermon on the Mount. But tell men that this Sufferer on the cross is the almighty God, the Son of the heavenly Father, and immediately the finger of superior scorn will be pointed at you. You will be called a "funny-mentalist," charged with having a medieval mind. Yet it is Bible truth that Jesus, above our poor powers of understanding, is God all-powerful, all-knowing, all-merciful, without a "perhaps" or "perchance," without a "possibly" or "probably," without a "can-be" or "maybe," "could-be" or "would-be."

The cruelest of the cries at Calvary demanded, *"If Thou be the Son of God, come down from the cross!"* and again, *"If He be the King of Israel, let Him now come down from the cross, and we will believe Him!"* These people actually sought to dictate the terms under which they would accept Jesus! He had to free His hands from the nails on the crossbar, and His feet from the spikes on the beam, before they would believe Him. Many of you are making a similarly fatal mistake. You say that you will accept Christ *if* — if He gives you what you want. You are willing to agree that Jesus is your God, if He heals your sickness, brings your boy home safe from the battle front, grants you a good, easy, comfortable life. What pride, arrogance, and effrontery to state the conditions under which you are willing to receive

Jesus! Can a leaf bargain with a whirlwind? Can an insect on a railroad track argue with the onrushing express train? Can a pebble on the seashore reason with the rolling tides? You ought to crawl to Christ on your hands and knees; instead, you stand with the crucifiers and say, "I will accept You *if* —"

As these lying priests are ready to receive Christ, but not crucified, so their cruel cry, "*Let Him . . . come down from the cross, and we will believe Him!*" is revived today in American church circles. Leaders in certain denominations reject the gory cross and tell us that the picture of the Savior with His pierced hands and feet is repugnant to the modern mind. They, too, demand, "*Let Him now come down from the cross!*" Teachers in divinity schools, some of them endowed with funds gathered from the faithful, insist on human attainment instead of divine atonement and cry out, "*Let Him now come down from the cross!*" Preachers in some of the country's most influential pulpits and wealthiest congregations declare: The world needs Christ as an example, not as a substitute. They too, shout, "*Let Him now come down from the cross!*" Men want Christianity without the Crucified, religion without the redemption, belief without the blood. Keep your distance from every church that covers the cross! When the Russians invaded Finland, their planes bombed a hospital, which, according to international law, should have remained untouched by enemy fliers, since it was clearly marked with a large red cross on its roof. However, investigation revealed that in the night before the air attack, snow had fallen and covered the roof. While the cross could be seen, the wounded Finns in that hospital were safe and secure; but when it disappeared, many were killed. You see the striking similarity in our sin-marked lives. As long as we have faith in the cross of agony and redemption, our souls are under divine protection, but when that cross vanishes from our lives, we are lost.

Keep your distance, then, from creeds without the cross, from churches which refuse to recognize Calvary, from religious books ignoring the blood, from hymns that never mention the crimson-stained sign of our salvation, from prayers that spurn the Crucified's name, from clergymen who change Saint Paul's resolve to preach Christ, and Him crucified, into the brash "We preach anything but Christ, and Him crucified"! Only one creed has a cross. Judaism has a star; Mohammedanism, a crescent; Buddhism, a swastika. The ancient Assyrian religion featured an eagle; the Babylonian a sun. These are all signs of power, achievement; but the cross is the emblem of suffering and sorrow, bleeding and brutality, destruction and death. Because Christ refused to heed the taunting sneer, *"Let Him now come down!"* the cross has become the highest and holiest, the most powerful and blessed, of all symbols in your life.

You may be able to recite the list of judges, kings, and prophets; you may know names, dates, places in the Old and New Testaments; you may have memorized chapter after chapter — but if you do not understand in a personal faith what the cross means, your detailed acquaintance with Bible history will not bring you a quarter of an inch closer to your God. You may be well informed about Christ. You may be able to tell His life story from the birth at Bethlehem to the ascension from Olivet; yet, if you do not understand why Jesus went to Golgotha, you could just as well study the career of Socrates, Caesar, or Cicero; nothing of this could give you the slightest spiritual conviction.

II

THE BLESSING OF A CRUCIFIED CHRIST

To have eternal, unbreakable, victorious assurance for life and death, you must know that Jesus stayed on the cross and thank God you have a crucified Savior. When His enemies cried, *"He saved others; Himself He cannot save!"* they were right in their first claim. Jesus *"saved others";* He died to save every one of the wanton killers on Calvary's crest. He died to save His countrymen, who planned His death. He died to save the Roman rulers and their servile soldiers, who had scourged His back until it was ripped and red with His blood, pushed a crown of thorns into His head and hammered the nails through His hands and feet. Even more: the Lord Jesus — and this is the climax of my message — has saved *you,* the desperate, however frightful and vicious your sins may be. If you have never heard this supreme, sacred truth; if you have given up hope for yourself, convinced that you have transgressed God's holy Law too often to be forgiven, listen carefully: Jesus was nailed to the cross for you. He suffered on the cross for you. He stayed on that cross for you until He died and His friends removed His lifeless body. Everyone in this vast mission of the air can say: "Christ was crucified to save me. He is my Redeemer, for His mercy is wider than the world, His grace more than sufficient for a million universes like ours." Only unbelief, rejection of this limitless love, can keep your soul from being cleansed by His blood. You may spurn His salvation, but that cannot change this triumphant truth: Jesus stayed on the cross to save you from sin, its guilt, its appalling punishment. He remained on that accursed tree to redeem you from the torture of eternal death, the terror of hell. He refused to come down because He wanted to pay the whole penalty for all your transgressions and by dying in your stead leave nothing to pay or earn. When He cried, *"It is finished!"* the work of your redemption was completed. Nothing remained undone. The ransom demanded for your release was laid down before God in the only offering acceptable to the Father. Deliverance from death, the title to the prepared place in the heavenly mansions, the salvation of your soul — these indelible, precious pledges are all sealed for you by the truth that Jesus continued to suffer on the cross.

His enemies made one mistake, however. Instead of sneering, *"Himself He* CANNOT *save,"* they should have declared, *"Himself He"* WILL *"not save."* Jesus could have rescued Himself even after He had been affixed to those beams. The same almighty power which hardly twelve hours before had cast armed soldiers prostrate to the ground could have paralyzed the entire mob at Calvary. A single angel of the more than 72,000 at the Savior's beck and call could have wiped out all opposition. A mere word from His parched lips, and His enemies would have been annihilated. Jesus did not *have* to give Himself for you and me. There was nothing good and clean and noble in our lives that appealed to Him. *"All our righteousnesses"* were *"as filthy rags."* Yet He loved us despite our sins and ingratitude. I read recently of a mother who for fourteen years, day and night, attended a mentally handicapped child, constantly denying herself life's pleasures. One day she broke down and cried: "If only my child would once show that it recognized me! If only in all these years I could see a single glance of recognition and love!" That weak-minded child is a picture of human thanklessness. Masses live on year after year, decade after decade, enjoying divine bounty every moment, but never raising their sin-blinded gaze to

Christ. Yet, despite our thanklessness Jesus loved us and stayed on the cross for us. More than a dozen times before Good Friday His people had tried to destroy Him, but Jesus waited for Calvary. He willingly, lovingly, voluntarily laid down His life and in all those previous instances proved that no one could take it from Him. It was His own deliberate, determined love for you and me that made Him give Himself to the cruelty of His countrymen. He went to the cross by His own free choice.

Crucifixion is a long, excruciating, terrifying torture. If Christ had to die, He might have chosen a quick, sudden death; but He definitely selected long, lingering agony. Each moment the anguish of His raging fever heightened; yet He refused to come down. Each moment the pain of the burning, festering wounds increased; but He stayed on the cross. Each moment the parched dryness of His body mounted; still He remained riveted to those timbers of death. Each moment the crushing agony of His soul, infinitely greater than the bodily misery, grew more intense; yet, thank God, He stayed on the tree of torture to conclude the marvelous plan of your redemption!

Remember, likewise, that Jesus remained crucified so that He could fulfill the ancient promises of Sacred Scripture. Centuries before the first Good Friday, God's prophets had foreseen that He would be crucified with sinners, that His hands and feet would be pierced, that He would be mocked and derided by the very transgressors whom He had come to save, would die on the cross, His lifeless body be buried in the tomb of a rich friend, that in all this He was atoning, as Isaiah stated eleven times in his faith-filled fifty-third chapter, for our sins, suffering for our iniquities, substituting for us, dying so that we could live. There at Golgotha, by fulfilling those ancient prophecies, Jesus sealed the truth of Holy Writ in His own blood. No other sacrifice we have ever seen or can see gives us assurance for the question-marked future which awaits us, despite the glib guarantees frequently uttered by political prophets. Because the Bible assures you that *"all the promises of God in Him are yea, and in Him Amen,"* you have within the covers of your Scriptures the promise of free grace, which will be granted as positively as those Old Testament previsions were realized on Good Friday. Christ stayed on the cross until death to leave you a proved and faultless Bible, a Book which has never made a mistake and will never be convicted of error. At Calvary He gives you a volume of imperishable truth. If Scripture was found exactly accurate at the crucifixion, believe with all your heart that it will be unfailing in the small emergencies of your life! Thank God, the Savior clung to the cross and gave you the assured, errorless Scriptures!

Take courage for your own life from the fact that Jesus unflinchingly did God's will, refused to avoid the pathway of pain! Most of us do not realize that from the beginning to the end of His public ministry our Lord was constantly confronted with the temptation to substitute ease for anguish, applause for affliction, comfort for conflict. "Don't take the hard way of the cross," Satan had whispered. "Worship me, and I will give you the whole world!" "Don't go the grim, gory road to Golgotha," Peter had pleaded. "Fight your way through with the sword! Destroy your enemies!" The same appeal may come to you: "Don't take your religion and your life seriously! Why be narrow and believe that Jesus is the only Way to heaven? Why not be broad and agree that Gentile and Jew, Christian and Confucianist, student of the Bible and student of the Koran, Modernist and Mohammedan, are all headed toward the same goal? Why deny yourself? Enjoy life to the fullest and forget Scripture's Thou-shalt-not-do-this's and the Thou-shalt-not-do-that's! You young folks, why not discard the old ideals of personal purity, of keeping yourself wholly for the young man or young woman of your choice for better or for worse, until death do you part? Why do you followers of Jesus insist on living separated lives, on coming out from sin and godlessness?" These questions are repeated today with greater frequency than ever as believers are enticed from following the Savior. Perhaps American Christians must go the hard way in the years ahead. We are losing spiritual power. We are becoming soft and flabby. How many in the United States today will fight an all-out battle for Jesus, refuse to compromise, to pay the consequences of confessing Him before men? How many of our countrymen agree that resignation to suffering, under God and through Christ, is finally the best and the happiest way?

When you who love the Savior are racked by heavy anguish, don't be dismayed and discouraged! God's enemies, bloated by their own prosperity, boasting that nothing has gone wrong with them, may turn to you and taunt: "You claim that God will help you; why doesn't He? You insist that He loves you. Well, where is His devotion? Why don't you forget your religion?" Instead of discarding your faith, remember, Easter followed Good Friday; that after the crucifixion came the resurrection. The same Lord of glory is mighty in all things today. Because Jesus stayed on the cross to do His Father's will, you have the divine comfort that no matter what you may be called upon to endure, your heavenly Father in His own time and in His own way will deliver you. Your trust in Jesus will never be misplaced; and just as the empty, blood-stained cross gave way to the empty, divinely opened grave, so Christ can give you triumph after trial, victory after defeat, life after death. God grant that now across the continent, as this appeal goes to our ships on the Atlantic and our outposts in the Pacific, we may all, standing in spirit at Calvary, raise our hands in undying allegiance to the crucified Savior of all mankind and give this pledge: "We thank Thee that Thou didst not come down from the cross of shame and agony, but that Thou wast faithful unto death, so that we have the assurance of our blood-bought redemption, guidance and comfort for time, glory and majesty for eternity. O Jesus, as Thou didst remain on the cross, so we promise Thee that we will come to the cross, stay with the cross, living and dying, glorify the cross!" God help us! Amen.

The Redeemer's Robe

> *"The soldiers, when they had crucified Jesus, took His garments and made four parts, to every soldier a part; and also His coat. Now, the coat was without seam, woven from the top throughout. They said, therefore, among themselves, Let us not rend it, but cast lots for it whose it shall be, that the Scripture might be fulfilled which saith, They parted My raiment among them, and for My vesture they did cast lots. These things, therefore, the soldiers did."*
> SAINT JOHN 19:23, 24

Lord Jesus, Our Only Savior:

At Calvary those who crucified Thee took away even Thy garments, and today likewise men would strip Thee of all Thy blessings, remove Thine atoning love, deprive Thee of the glorious truth that Thou art our true and eternal God. O send us Thy Holy Spirit, who can give us the courage required to confess Thee as the only and last Hope of our decaying world! Show us more clearly every day that the call of this hour is for sincere repentance and wholehearted return to God! Grant us a soul-deep sorrow for our own sins and an immovable trust in the mercies and merits Thou didst secure for us through Thy death of unspeakable agonies on the cross! Fortify with this faith the defenders of our cause at home and abroad! Shield these young men and women against destruction and spiritual death! Let our armies and navies come home soon, precious Savior, with victory for righteousness and peace for all nations! Lead masses in our country to Thy Father and make us a humble, penitent people whose trust is only in God, whose desire is only exalting righteousness! We ask this in Thine ever-blessed name, O Jesus! Amen.

ONE of the most lavish and luxury-loving kings in history was the monarch who ruled France 250 years ago, Louis XIV. He played with gold as though it were sand. In a single building enterprise he erected Versailles Palace at a cost of $200,000,000. His outstanding extravagance, however, was showered on his own clothing. At his wedding he was arrayed in rare velvet embroidered with precious metals, covered with jewels, and prepared at a cost of over $1,000,000. As he grew older, his wild spending increased; and during public audiences he was often clad in a costume valued at more than $12,000,000.

By contrast, I ask you now to think of another King. His throne was a cross planted on a lonely hill; His diadem a crown of cutting thorns. He had no palace, for though *"the earth was His and the fullness thereof,"* He claimed not an inch of it; when He died, He was buried in a borrowed tomb. That French ruler might tax his subjects until, hungry, oppressed, barefooted, they were driven to despair; but this King, our King — may every one of you have the faith which enables you to say, "My King"! — Jesus Christ, Son of the all-merciful God and Savior of a sin-stricken world, gave His life to save and glorify His redeemed. His realm, far from collapsing, is constantly increasing in eternal triumph. While Louis was bedecked in sinful splendor, Jesus refused all robes of royalty — the ermine and crimson, the gold and silver, as well as the rare jewels and precious gems that were rightfully His. When He died He left no wardrobe, only the few articles of clothing he wore to His crucifixion. Now, as every page of Scripture is crowded with powerful messages for our unbelieving, unrepenting world, so this record can teach us all some personal lessons. Let us, then, behold the garments of Golgotha, especially

THE REDEEMER'S ROBE

and study their meaning as described in our text, Saint John, chapter nineteen, verses twenty-three and twenty-four: *"The soldiers, when they had crucified Jesus, took His garments, and made four parts, to every soldier a part; and also His coat. Now, the coat was without seam, woven from the top throughout. They said, therefore, among themselves, Let us not rend it, but cast lots for it whose it shall be, that the Scripture might be fulfilled which saith, They parted My raiment among them, and for My vesture they did cast lots. These things, therefore, the soldiers did."*

I

THE SAVIOR'S APPAREL WAS LARGELY COMMON CLOTH

To make death by crucifixion even more shameful, the victim was first stripped and then nailed to the cross. Our Lord was no exception. At Calvary He, God's Son of all glory, was crucified naked. Well might the earth have swallowed alive the degenerates who tore the clothing from the innocent, unresisting Savior. Well might a flash of lightning have flattened those blasphemers to the ground forever. Not even the few garments, the last earthly possession, could remain His. The hatred and cruelty of His enemies would rob Him of everything. So completely did Jesus permit Himself to be humiliated and disgraced when He atoned for your sins and paid their total penalty with exposure, anguish, God-forsakenness, and death!

Clothes cost relatively more in those days than now, and soldiers were accustomed to keep the apparel of every crucified criminal as a sort of ghastly payment for the execution. So the four legionaries stationed beneath the cross divided the Savior's clothing among themselves, casting lots ("throwing dice," we would say today) to see who would win this article or that piece of fabric.

It is not a pleasing scene, this picture of the soldiers beneath the cross; but as we study the Lenten account, we ought to be impressed by the fact that American men in arms throughout the world are confronted by temptations to similar sins. Those guards at Golgotha, during the six hours of the crucifixion, viciously attacked the Son of God. They did not know that they had nailed the Lord of Life to the timbers of death; and today many of our soldiers likewise do not know Jesus. An instructor in a government training school writes: "The thing that burdens me is that there are 500 pre-aviation cadets here, and I will venture to say that less than 10 per cent know Jesus. . . . From what kind of homes did these boys come? Continue to exhort mothers and fathers of our military boys to accept Jesus as their personal Savior. It is hard for boys who come from unchristian homes to realize that they need a Redeemer, and it is harder still to bring Jesus to boys whose folks played at religion. . . . Oh, tell every army chaplain who goes out that what our soldiers need is someone who can tell them of a personal Savior and show them how to find Him!"

As Pilate's soldiers hurled blasphemies at the crucified Christ, so military life still has the same tendency to make men abuse His holy, precious name! This day of national danger is the time to be prayerful, not profane, to speak with reverence, not cursing. Willful misuse of the divine name can prolong this struggle and increase our casualty lists. Soldiers of America, make David's prayer your deep petition as you ask, *"Let the words of my mouth and the meditation of my heart be acceptable in Thy sight, O Lord, my Strength and my Redeemer!"*

The company of legionaries at Calvary also tried to while away those six slow hours with wine, just as millions in America — soldiers and civilians — are trying to drink away the present hostilities. This war will never be won with whisky or at cocktail bars. Increasing drunkenness can delay the victory. Though people may smile indulgently at intoxication, God's Word warns plainly that drunkards shall not inherit the kingdom of heaven. Read 1 Corinthians 6:10 carefully!

Finally we see the soldiers gambling — another vice in present-day army life. It may sound out of place and date to call gambling a "vice," when newspapers feature it in their comic strips; when certain American cities thrive on its income; when even churches run raffles and plead for bingo; when the Government itself purchases 750,000 pairs of dice to build morale in the Army, and when a Congressman introduces a bill for a national lottery. All this cannot change the fact that gambling is a destructive evil, condemned alike by God's Law and man's. It promotes the desire to live without work, to gain at the expense of others; it has always been connected with fraud, cheating, immorality. It has caused indescribable suffering within many homes, as your letters reveal; it has left children improperly clothed and underfed, wives neglected, families burdened with misery. Christian citizens should rid their communities of all slot machines, punch boards, bingo parties; for gambling, even in its simplest forms, is the devil's device.

Though the soldiers played a sorry role at the crucifixion, one military man proved himself the exception. He was the centurion, the officer in charge who remained at Calvary — and glorified the Savior. Beholding Jesus with eyes of faith, he exclaimed, *"Truly this was the Son of God!"* What an example for many of you in the Army and Navy! A word in behalf of Christ from you may have greater power than you realize. Use that influence! Commissioned officers of our fighting forces, follow that centurion! Don't be ashamed of Jesus! Testify openly to His power and love!

As we look once more at the Redeemer's apparel strewn on the ground between the four gambling soldiers, we see that it is the common clothing of the Palestinian workman. He might have worn the choicest products of the loom; the gold of Sheba and Seba was His. Large diamonds, precious pearls were stored in the treasuries of His earth. Yet He spurned all this and chose the garb of a lowly servant. As He walked the Palestinian highways and byways, nothing in His garb attracted the multitudes. He was so unknown to the leaders that they had to secure a traitor to identify Him.

We dare not lose sight of this truth for the hard years before us. Jesus, even by His dress, showed that He was a Friend of the poor, a Companion of the afflicted; and unless God is unusually merciful to us, there will be plenty of poor and afflicted during the postwar readjustment. I cannot sufficiently warn you against the promises, sometimes made in the name of statesmanship and often in the name of religion, that, when this struggle is over, we shall enter a period of unparalleled prosperity, with money, work, food, and happiness for everyone on earth. No man knows what the future may bring; but just as assuredly, no man should dangle before the eyes of a peace-starved world unfounded hopes of wealth and progress; especially when these predictions are built on purely human specifications and advanced in entire disregard of God. Thousands may make more than the much-discussed $25,000 a year during war times, but millions in the United States have never made twenty-five dollars real profit a year. They want a Savior who understands their needs, who knows what it means to be poor; and here is Jesus whose clothes proved that He was the Man for the masses, the Man for all classes.

When rabid Communists try to inflame workers by

preaching that Christianity is capitalistic, without sympathy for laborers, that it works hand-in-glove with moneyed interests, we who love Jesus point to the Savior and demand of the atheists, "Have you ever produced one leader as humble, as poor, as *'all things to all men'* as Jesus?" Let us be on guard for the years ahead! We must follow Christ's self-denial and self-sacrifice, rejecting completely the goal of establishing wealthy, powerful congregations. For what is a church profited if it has millions of dollars in real estate and investments, while men and women are dying every second of the day without knowing the Lord? What advantage has a religious group if its legacies and investments tower into the tens of millions, yet it does not use these funds for calling sinners to repentance? The clothing of the crucified Savior appeals to us, asking Christians all over the world to emphasize the Redeemer's marvelous love in humbling Himself to become a true man among men, to live with us in poverty and privation, and to grant us the vision of service and sacrifice for our fellow men.

II

THE SAVIOR'S APPAREL WAS PREDICTED

Only one piece of the Savior's clothing was unusual, His *"coat,"* or, as we say today, His robe, which was *"without seam, woven from the top throughout."* To cut it into four pieces would destroy its value. So once more the dice rolled as the soldiers gambled for this prize.

The Gospel records do not tell us who won the robe, but according to conflicting traditions it has been preserved, wholly or partially, in various European cities, where credulous throngs bow before it. Many of these relics cannot be genuine, and to worship them is idolatrous. Do not place your reliance on anything man-made!

Put your whole trust always, completely, only, in Christ! Keep the Savior's warning in mind, *"God is a spirit; and they that worship Him must worship Him in spirit and in truth,"* not with charms and superstition! The Lord wants your crushed, repentant, trusting heart directed solely to Him.

Nor could that robe in itself exert miraculous power. A new book, Lloyd Douglas' *The Robe,* a best seller, pictures it as a marvelous garment which brought peace and healing to those who touched it. No robe in itself can ever do that. If you accept Jesus as your only but all-sufficient Savior, you need not touch anything to receive His blessing. Without rites or rituals, penances or privations, our Lord, always *"nigh unto all them . . . that call upon Him in truth,"* can mightily help you. Today, as nineteen centuries ago, He can heal you if it be His will. He can help you in any suffering or sorrow, family trouble, or business difficulty. He can richly comfort you in any affliction, grant you peace and joy instead of tears and trials; and — blessed Redeemer that He is — you can always come to Him directly, without reliance on robes or relics. He is yours by faith and faith alone.

The mention of this seamless garment is not accidental, since the very robe for which the coarse Roman soldiers gambled had been seen a thousand years before by David. Saint John says pointedly in our text that the soldiers cast lots *"that the Scripture might be fulfilled"* — and these are the prophetic words of the Twenty-second Psalm, *"They parted My raiment among them, and for My vesture they did cast lots."*

What a marvelous volume our Bible is, when in scores of similar passages it predicts such minute details centuries in advance and with absolute certainty! This fact of fulfilled prophecy alone should convince skeptics and unbelievers that the Bible is God's Word, the absolute Truth. Do you know another volume which can forecast clearly what the distant years will bring? But Scripture, because it comes from God, who plans the programs of the years, has exactly foretold the future in hundreds of passages. I challenge any one to prove that a single Biblical prediction concerning the rise and fall of ancient empires, the destruction of proud cities, the life, death, and resurrection of our Lord Jesus Christ, has ever been exposed as false.

Is not this the faultless Book for our disturbed, distracted day, when military experts are unable to foretell with assurance what will happen next year; when millions, particularly our military youth, do not know what may occur tomorrow? For assurance and guidance forget fortunetellers! Turn away from crystal-gazers! Renounce astrologers! Spurn every spiritist medium! Go back to the Bible!

Because Scripture assures us that *"all the promises of God in Him* [Christ] *are yea, and in Him amen,"* we have within the covers of Holy Writ the guarantee of comfort, which must be fulfilled as unfailingly as Old Testament predictions were realized at Calvary. If the ancient prophecies that Jesus would be crucified with sinners; that His hands and feet would be pierced; that He would be mocked and derided by the very transgressors whom He had come to save; that He would die on the cross; that His lifeless body would be buried in the tomb of a rich friend; that in all this He was atoning, as Isaiah states eleven times in his faith-filled fifty-third chapter, for our sins, suffering for our iniquities, substituting for every one of us, dying His death so that we could live in His life — if these precious pledges foretold the truth for the past, then accept the Bible confidently for your future! Trust it with all your heart! When our Lord promises, *"Come unto Me, all ye that labor and are heavy laden, and I will give you rest,"* realize that, though your life may be restless and storm-tossed, in the Savior you can assuredly find calm and quiet! When Scripture declares, *"Whosoever shall call on the name of the Lord shall be saved,"* take that glorious word, *"whosoever,"* at its full face value! Thank God that no man can ever keep you from Christ, no matter how cruelly you may be cut off from other blessings! Rejoice because your redemption is not a hit-or-miss proposition, not a vague uncertainty, nor a remote possibility, but Heaven's own truth, a reality firmer than the foundations of the world!

Are you haunted by the sorrow of war, tormented by questions concerning the safety of your beloved ones? Have you accompanied your husband or son to the railroad station during these last days to bid him a brave farewell as he left for camp, wondering whether he would ever see you again? The Bible, with its completed promise, is the Book for you; for it offers the Christ of all comfort, who consoles those who are His, *"I will not leave thee, nor forsake thee."* Since in such relatively small matters as the casting of lots for a seamless robe the Bible promises were fulfilled at Calvary, will you not believe that in the incomparably greater issues concerning your soul, which, Jesus declared, is worth more than all the world, His assurance of salvation and sustaining love will be surely realized? *"Heaven and earth shall pass away, but"* His *"Word,"* the wondrous pledge of grace, full and free, *"shall not pass away."*

What a warning also in the fact that these gambling soldiers proved the divine power and truth of Scripture! Every threat of God's punishment on unbelief will likewise be carried out. You may doubt and deny the Bible's prediction of doom for the unforgiven sinner, but *"be not deceived; God is not mocked."* The blackened ruins of ancient cities, destroyed in harmony with Bible prophecy, cry out that the Almighty will judge all unbelief; that it is impossible to escape the long reach of divine justice; that every sinner, no matter how wealthy, influential, important he may seem to be, must pay, and pay fully, here and hereafter for every unremoved transgression of Heaven's Law. If nothing has ever been able to put the fear of the Lord firmly into your heart, stop for a moment to see how exactly the Old Testament forecasts were accomplished to the letter; and then draw the conclusion that, if Scripture is faultlessly correct concerning a piece of clothing, how unquestionable must be its warnings concerning your eternity, when it thunders out this sentence upon all who reject Christ: *"The soul that sinneth, it shall die!"* *"He that believeth not shall be damned!"*

The Bible, with its fulfilled prophecy, is the one Book for these years of war and weariness; but to exert its heavenly force, it must be studied, followed as never before. Because it can mightily strengthen the nation — and we need spiritual fortifying as much as military defense — we should obey its request for a repentant nation by getting down on our knees before the Almighty in genuine sorrow over our thanklessness and pride. When Scripture asks for a godly people walking in the Lord's ways, let us work and pray that the forces of lust, the grasping of greed, the worship of might, be checked and masses be brought back to Christ, in whom is the only help they can ever know!

We need the Bible in our homes, where altogether too frequently it becomes the forgotten Book, with family devotions — may God forgive us! — falling into steady discard. Yet if home religion has decreased, assaults on domestic morality have increased. Social workers and parents write disturbed letters complaining that their daughters, fourteen, thirteen, even twelve years old, stay out until early morning in questionable company. Cases of youthful alcoholism and immorality have soared to unprecedented heights. Over in England a star performer of the British Broadcasting Corporation, a University of London professor, says the idea of man having one wife is unsatisfactory. Marriage laws ought to be altered, he suggests, so that a husband can live in polygamy with a number of wives. From now on you will hear repeated suggestions of this kind, and many will try to practice successive polygamy, indulging in one divorce after the other. Only Scripture can be an effective check against such attacks. Put the family Bible back into any home, and that household will be blessed by Christ's presence!

We want God's Word and its power for our own souls. Chaplain Willard with the United States marines on the Solomon Islands reports: "Three men in my regiment have been saved from wounds and death because they loved the Book. . . . I urge them to carry it with them into battle. One of the New Testaments stopped a Japanese twenty-five-caliber bullet which went through to the back cover. Two other Testaments prevented their owners from being seriously wounded by Japanese shrapnel." Scripture will do much more than stop bullets. It will help stop sin and the legions of hell. The Bible, through your faith in Christ, can save your soul for eternity.

III

THE SAVIOR'S APPAREL WAS BLOOD-STAINED

Look at that robe once more, and you will find it marked not by beautiful design and embroidery but by heavy blotches! What are those sodden spots, those deep stains? Their crimson color betrays them. They are Christ's dark, red blood!

Throughout history blood has been regarded as a sign of suffering; and never has this vital fluid otherwise marked such harrowing and soul-deep anguish. That scarlet dripped from Christ's thorn-cut, wounded head, from His scourged back, the same blood which spurted from His hands and feet when they were crushed to the cross, which trickled down the cross, dropped into little pools or sank into Calvary's soil — all in anguish of soul and body such as human eyes have never otherwise beheld.

Today we associate blood with crime; and again, never has any iniquity been as shocking as the injustice which made Jesus bleed. He was perfectly innocent. Even malice and perjury could invent no real charge against Him. Yet despite His utter sinlessness, His blood was spilled under the lash and on the cross in the super-crime of the ages. True, innocent people have sometimes been sentenced to death, as wrong has repeatedly triumphed over right; yet the worst miscarriage of justice is not to be compared with this gruesome murder at Golgotha. For it is not ordinary blood which stains His robe and marks His cross. Though you examine it under the microscope and find that it is human blood with the usual plasma and corpuscles, yet you must know it is the blood of Jesus Christ; and He who shed it — oh, accept this glorious truth! — is a true man, yet indescribably more: He is your God.

Blood has also become a sign of help and hope. Lives are saved by transfusion; and in the marvelous progress of medical science blood plasma has been used to preserve thousands of wounded. After the war authorities plan vast plasma banks with first-aid stations throughout the country as a means of sustaining many thousands of lives. God bless their effort, but God give us the faith to realize that the blood which stained this robe and spotted the cross can save far more than men's bodies! It can rescue our souls from ruin. In the Old Testament men sought forgiveness of their sins in the blood of sacrificial animals, slain on sacred altars, for God's Word had declared, *"It is the blood that maketh an atonement for the soul."* But Golgotha and the cross gave the world a new and final atoning blood. Because our Lord went to Calvary, because He shed His blood there for the full and free atonement of all human transgressions, we have the peerless promise of God's truth, *"The blood of Jesus Christ, His Son, cleanseth us from all sin."* Every crimson stain on that robe, every red drop oozing from the Savior's five wounds, is proof divine that God loved you, hardened and hopeless in your iniquities though you may be; loved you, sought you in your misery and anguish, even though men spurn you and friends forsake you; He planned your rescue and ransom, not by simply forgetting your sins (your heavenly Father is too holy for that), not by permitting you to work off your sentence and atone for your wrongs (since no one can pay for the enormity and multitude of his own sins), not by accepting the prayers and good works of some saint or morally superior person (for the Scripture warns, *"None of them can by any means redeem his brother nor give to God a ransom for him"*), but by providing a Savior from sin, a Substitute to bear your iniquities. By the marvel of His mercy God, our faithful, loving Father, in the sacrifice for which angels will eternally chant His praise — how our mortal minds stagger at the very thought! — sent His own Son to shed His blood and die for the redemption of all sinners. Those crimson marks on the robe, those stains on the cross, are thus a pledge to you that you are saved.

"The blood of Jesus Christ, His Son, cleanseth us from all sin." — That triumphant truth is the only hope you can ever have, and it is a positive statement. *"The blood of Jesus Christ"* is mentioned thirty-seven times in the New Testament. Remove it from the sacred record, and the race is ruined. Believe its power; teach it; preach it; exalt it; and God will mightily be with you! For as one drop of the precious blood can cleanse a world of sinners, so you alone, with faith in the atoning love, can defeat a world arrayed against you.

What, then, is the message of the Redeemer's robe for which the soldiers cast lots? What, indeed, if not God the Father's own appeal that you stop gambling with your soul, risking your salvation by postponing your acceptance of Christ? Jesus no longer wears that gory robe. In His eternal majesty He is now clothed in the radiance of dazzling purity and power. If you would see Him in that celestial beauty; if heaven is to be your home; if you want an eternity with your loved ones who have died in the Lord, then confess your sins now! Fall on your knees to cry out that you are hopelessly lost; that you are altogether unworthy; that you deserve nothing but rejection; that you plead for mercy, not merit; for redemption, not reward; for pardon, not payment; that above everything else in this world you want to be cleansed by the Savior's blood! Then from the throne of never-ending mercy He will speak peace into your soul as He declares, *"This is My blood of the New Testament, which is shed for many for the remission of sins."* Then all the filthy rags of your own unrighteousness will be gone. Your spotted garments of sin will disappear, and the Christ of Calvary will clothe you with His holiness. To that end may our constant, contrite prayer, addressed to the Savior of the blood-stained robe, ask: O Jesus, robe us forever in Thy blood-bought righteousness! Amen.

Look to the Cross!

> *"Let us lay aside every weight, and the sin which doth so easily beset us, and let us run with patience the race that is set before us, looking unto Jesus, the Author and Finisher of our faith, who for the joy that was set before Him endured the cross, despising the shame."*
>
> HEBREWS 12:1, 2

Jesus, Thou "Author and Finisher of Our Faith":

*M*ay we ever look to Thee and Thy cross for the complete pardon of our transgressions, for strength to resist temptation, for courage to live a godly life, for assurance of victory over death and hell! Because we are hopelessly lost without Thee, blessed Savior, but eternally saved with Thee, bring us, our families, our fighting forces, the millions of the spiritually dead in America to repentance and triumphant trust in Thy blood-bought power to save to the uttermost! Impress deeply into our hearts the truth that Thou hast paid the whole price of our redemption! Let this assurance of finished salvation forever comfort those who are battling for the nation's cause! Sustain our fighting forces amid all perils of body and soul! Speak peace again to the world, O Jesus, before the slaughter of human lives increases, and let Thy kingdom come into many sin-crushed lives throughout the world! We ask this by Thy mercy and might. Amen.

VICTOR HUGO, French author and an outstanding writer of the last century, was horrified by the bloodshed, crime, poverty, injustice, which he beheld on all sides. Believing that men themselves could raise their standards and ideals to lofty heights, he penned a prophecy for our day. Here it is: "In the twentieth century war will be dead. The scaffold will be dead. Hatred will be dead. Frontier boundaries will be dead. Dogmas will be dead. But man will live."

How completely false and futile every word of that prediction! "War will be dead" in the twentieth century! In 1914 a conflict began which brought 58,000,000 men under arms and sent 8,500,000 of them (more than one of every seven) to their graves — a war that cost $370,000,-000,000 (not to mention the even greater expense of this Second World War, which it provoked) and that left the nations burdened with debts ten times larger than before; a struggle which made Viscount Grey declare, "If there be another such war, civilization will never recover from it." Yet we now witness not only "another such war" but hostilities even greater in the size of their armies, the hundred billions of their expenditures.

Victor Hugo was wholly wrong, and we could dismiss his false forecast as just another mistake of an illustrious man, were it not for the tragic fact that high authorities in our country and abroad are making the same error, similarly predicting a warless world of wealth and happiness. That French author was willing to wait perhaps a century before his ideals were realized, but many present-day prophets see a new age and a new world right after the war. They go far beyond Victor Hugo in assuring everyone in the United States (some include even the whole globe) plenty of food and clothing, the right kind of housing, and suitable work. Social security "from the cradle to the grave" for everyone in a warless, wantless world—this is the pledge for the years before us.

When I call this one of the cruelest of misplaced promises, I am not concerned about financial difficulties. A Harvard professor has expressed his conviction that, when peace is declared, the postwar United States will have only one fifth the prosperity of the depression year

1929. What troubles me far more is the fact that social architects who would build our tomorrow on the grand scale systematically leave God out of their planning and have no room for Christ. Recently a high representative of our Government told the people of Chile, "Every revolution, from that begun by Christ almost two thousand years ago to the Soviet Revolution of 1917, spoke for the common man," and thus deliberately put the work of the Lord Jesus on the same level with the regime of Red bloodshed in Russia. To American Christians this borders on blasphemy, and we protest against all blueprints for a better America drawn in disregard of the Almighty. As long as our heavenly Father is eliminated or at best conceded a secondary, unimportant place, tomorrow's world need expect only continued war, deeper impoverishment of the masses, more crime and unrest.

The Christian attitude, on the contrary, asks the followers of Jesus to work for peace and prosperity; but it demands full recognition of God's supreme power. It asks not first for social security, but for soul security. It does not end with the grave, but starts anew there. It is concerned not only about the here but particularly about the hereafter. Its watchword is not, "Turn to man, to our statesmen, our scientists, our economists!" On the contrary, this is the plea of Christianity, the cry for our crisis, the invitation to every burdened soul:

LOOK TO THE CROSS!

the appeal found in the wondrous words of grace recorded in Hebrews (chapter twelve, verses one and two): *"Let us lay aside every weight, and the sin which doth so easily beset us, and let us run with patience the race that is set before us, looking unto Jesus, the Author and Finisher of our faith, who for the joy that was set before Him endured the cross, despising the shame!"*

I

LOOK TO THE CROSS FOR THE FINISHED FAITH!

Our text, picturing life as a race to be run, begins, *"Let us lay aside every weight, and the sin which doth so easily beset us,"* emphasizing at the outset that for the happy, spiritually secure existence sin must be conquered. You may have everything money can buy or human ingenuity secure; but if you are not right with God, if your transgressions remain unforgiven, be sure of this: you will never know real peace or joy! You may try to throw off the burden of your transgressions and drown your crimes in a whirl of excitement or pleasure seeking. You may try to drink yourself into forgetfulness; but when you least expect it, the remembrance of these sins will suddenly rise up to shatter your mock happiness. Your letters tell me how thirty, forty, and more years ago you violated God's law, boasting you would enjoy life to its fullest; yet now the very vices that appeared attractive prod your conscience and give you no rest.

As long as sin dominates your life, you cannot be free from fear; for no matter how calm and confident you may seem, you are constantly overshadowed by the foreboding that the evil in your past will be revealed, some secret affair brought to light and leave you exposed to friend and foe. Behind and beneath all this is the dread of death, the fear of facing God in eternity, the conviction that no one can escape the arm of divine justice. Dr. Alfred Krupp, who founded the mighty armament works at Essen, Germany, was so tormented by death's consuming horror that, it is said, he forbade his employees to mention the word in his presence. When a relative of his wife died in his home, he ran away; and when Mrs. Krupp reproved him, he became so enraged that they were separated for life. During his last illness he offered his physician a million dollars to prolong his life for ten years. Money, position, power, gave him no peace. Similarly for the highest and best in your life, you need victory over sin; your conscience must be stilled, your fears removed. You must be able to meet your God as a loving Father and not as a stern Judge with a verdict of guilt and doom. If, in this world of wickedness, men are to work together unselfishly, helping to usher in a new, happier age, they must defeat sin. No matter how men polish or disguise human nature; no matter how much outward politeness or refinement they acquire; if they are still swayed by evil, they can become more degenerate than brute beasts.

To many all this sounds quite old-fashioned at a time when sin rides high, when it is glorified in sex-ridden magazines, practiced in the name of patriotism by heedless youth, encouraged by godless education, endorsed by radical, immoral leaders, ignored even by many pulpits. The *New York Times* on its church page used about 4,000 words to print excerpts of sermons preached in New York City last Sunday; yet in all these reports the short, ugly, three-letter word "sin" does not occur once. Sometimes, of course, people do speak of sin, but for the most part they discuss not their own but someone else's sin. It is easy to condemn Hitler or Mussolini or Hirohito; it is not hard for an employer to find fault with his workers or an employee to recognize capitalists' errors. White people quickly mention the weaknesses of the colored race, and Negroes can make a long list of the white man's failings, Gentiles seldom hesitate to raise charges against Jews, and the Jews, in turn, have scores of counts on which they indict the Gentiles. But for men to recognize and confess the evil in their own actions, to turn their critical gaze away from others and focus it on their own selfishness — ah, that is a vastly different matter! We must constantly heed the Savior's warning against seeing the mote in our brother's eye, while forgetting the broad beam in our own eye! Only at the cost of our salvation can we ignore the fearful punishment of eternal death and damnation which the holy God exacts for all our unforgiven iniquity!

How, then, can we follow our text and *"lay aside every weight, and the sin which doth so easily beset us"*? By our will power, our determination to resist evil? By paying for our transgressions through a good, clean life with gifts to charity? By going to church, securing the help of Christian parents, of a believing husband or wife? By asking saints or angels to intercede for us before God, having friends and relatives pay or pray our way to heaven after we die? May God keep you from these fatal, soul-destroying errors! If you are to be saved from the slavery of sin, look neither to yourself nor to any other man or woman, dead or alive! Follow our text in *"looking unto Jesus"*! Turn to Him, not only as a sublime teacher, a heavenly friend, an outstanding hero, a courageous reformer, a mighty leader! Approach Him as your Savior, *"the Lamb of God, which taketh away the sin of the world"*! Take refuge in Him, not only for His Sermon on the Mount, but for His death on the mount; not only for His bravery in facing the masses, but for His love in dying for the masses!

Then, as you stand in spirit at Calvary's crest, you can understand why our text calls Him *"the Author and Finisher of our faith."* He is *"the Author . . . of our faith"* because He, not we, undertook the work of our salvation. We owe everything to His mercy. He found us in our sins, foul and filthy as we were; and He loved us, He washed us, He cleansed us. He saved us when we sought to escape Him, when we were *"dead in trespasses and sins,"* spiritually paralyzed, unable to find favor with God. Nothing in us could draw the Savior to us; but His boundless blessed grace, His measureless mercy, His limitless love for all sinners, began the task of our redemption; *"not that* WE *loved God,"* the Scriptures claim, *"but that He loved us"* and sent His Son to be *"the Propitiation for our sins."* The more you and I study Christ's compassion, the more His godly grace leads us to exclaim: "Why did He choose me? Why did the Lord of beauty and truth, the Sovereign of heaven, stoop to earth's grime and filth in saving my sin-tainted soul?"

That Savior — and we see it clearly at Calvary — is not only *"the Author"* but, praise God! also the *"Finisher of our faith."* Too many projects are started today but never completed. Think of the poor Polish people! When this war began, they were solemnly assured that it was started on their account, to win back their lost territory. Now, however, powerful nations seem to have concluded that not all this captured land will be restored to Poland. So it happens frequently in life. A marriage starts with pledges of happiness but ends in separation and divorce. A gifted young man begins a career with the promise of outstanding success but finishes in a penitentiary. A huge commercial enterprise, organized with the prospect of heavy returns for the stockholders, collapses in bankruptcy. Yet Jesus not only took the first steps for our salvation; He also took the last step, up the hill of the skull. He left nothing undone, nothing unpaid, nothing unfinished for our deliverance. In His dying moments He cried out, not in a weak, wavering whisper but, as the Gospels emphasize, *"with a loud voice," "It is finished."* That was the cry of victory. The anguish and the sorrow of the crucifixion were over. The divine plan for the world's redemption was drawing to its close. The whole Old Testament, with its altars and sacrifices, was giving way to the New, with Christ, Calvary's cross, the atoning blood and everything that even the just and holy God could demand for the rescue of the whole race.

"It is finished" — let this victory cry resound throughout the world! You need not — indeed cannot — earn your redemption. Do not waste your time and energies in trying to complete what Jesus has fully accomplished! *"My grace,"* He assures you, *"is sufficient for thee."* Only believe Him! Contritely confess your sins! Confidently trust His mercies!

"It is finished" — let that be your defense against doubt! You need no man-made additions to the Gospel; you can trust Christ confidently and find everything required for your redemption plainly stated in passages like this, *"Believe on the Lord Jesus Christ, and thou shalt be saved."* Why, then, should you question the eternal truth? You may have reason for being suspicious of human promises, but Jesus is the Son of God. His pledge has never failed. His assurances are sealed with His own sacred blood.

Truly Christ is the *"Finisher of our faith."* Once and for all times in your stead He fulfilled God's Law, the Old Testament prophecies, the demands of divine holiness, the eternal plan of human salvation. He has taken your iniquity away, altogether and forever. He has endured its full punishment, borne its total guilt, so that in God's sight, once you truly accept His Son, you are without sin, free from its curse, cleansed of its taint, pardoned of its guilt.

Many projects in life remain unfinished. Authors die before their books are completed. Statesmen go to the grave before their plans can be put into practice. Parents are carried to their last resting place when their children are only babies. The precious and only Savior, however, died on the cross with the heavenly pledge that not one particle in the plan of our redemption remained incomplete; that no sinner in any age or any place need ever question our Lord's death for him. Praise His holy name for this glorious grace! He might have said: "I am dying here on the cross for you. Yet before you can have the blessings of My crucifixion, you must prove that you are worthy of forgiveness. You must do your share. You must show Me that you can live a holy, pure, upright life." That would not be Jesus. The deliverance He grants is no halfway measure. He goes all the way, and He gives His mercy, not to those who think themselves worthy, noble, virtuous, but to the unworthy, the contrite sinners, who, knowing that even a lifetime of their best deeds cannot win them recognition in the Almighty's sight, kneel in sorrow and repentance over their sins and plead, "O Jesus, Thou Son of God, Thou Redeemer of the world, my Savior, have mercy upon me!"

This is God's way to salvation. It is the unchangeable way. It is the sure way. It is the only way. For here is the clear statement of Christ Himself: *"I am the Way, the Truth, and the Life; no man cometh unto the Father but by Me."* Men may ridicule this truth. Last week an Ohio woman, evidently a church member, wrote: "Why don't you get next to yourself and lay off the 'blood of Christ' stuff?" Doubtless millions in the United States feel just as she does. A magazine recently expressed surprise over a popular survey in England, much like our Gallup Poll, which revealed that only 10 per cent of the people over there are closely connected with any church. I wonder, however, whether we have any moral right to think America superior. Less than half our population claim membership in any religious group. Less than half of that half are regular attendants, and many of those worship with Christ-denying congregations. Today, when our individual and national problems are more acute than ever before, we need with absolute necessity the clear message of the final and finished atonement in the blood of the Lord Jesus. Because the Savior has commanded us to preach the Gospel; because Saint Paul was *"determined not to know anything among"* the first believers *"save Jesus Christ, and Him crucified,"* this broadcast will feature with all the strength God gives us, not war discussions, news reviews, peace plans, reconstruction programs — the country seems to have plenty of commentators, financial experts, and statesmen — but these two truths, the most vital in all the world: first, the warning that, if you refuse to accept the Savior, you are hopelessly lost; and, second, the promise that, if you receive Him, you have assured salvation, and with it, everything required to fight evil, resist temptation, lead a God-pleasing life, build your home, your community, your country, with exalting righteousness. If you do not like the Gospel and write me that the mention of the Redeemer's blood is "nauseating" to you, all I can say is, "May God have mercy on your soul!" All I can do is to plead that by divine grace, even through sorrow and disaster, you may be spiritually crushed and in your helplessness turn to your Savior!

My countrymen, Jesus is your last and only Hope. Look confidently to His cross for eternal compassion! He loves you, if no one else in all the world does; and He loves you as no one else ever can. He is *"the Author and Finisher"* of your faith, the Beginning and End of your salvation, the Start and Finish of everything good and holy in your life, your Alpha and Omega for earth and heaven. Stop resisting His grace! Stop blaspheming His name! Stop closing the gate to heaven! Welcome Him as your Savior now! Let me send you a Christian pastor to instruct you in Christ's truth!

II

LOOK TO THE CROSS FOR THE COURAGEOUS LIFE!

Our text gives us another reason for turning to the cross. We read: *"Let us lay aside every weight, . . . and let us run with patience the race that is set before us, looking unto Jesus . . . who for the joy that was set before Him endured the cross, despising the shame."* In the race called life (and how truly we hurry through our short span of years!), when Christians daily draw nearer to their heavenly home, they are often burdened by sorrows and afflictions which would prevent them from reaching their goal. Many in this audience are weighted by painful, costly, weakening sickness. Some of you can never recall a day in which you could rise from your bed, your wheel chair, your crutches, and feel the full sweep of health course through your body. Others have been crushed by family trouble: your marriage is broken; you are separated from your husband or your wife; your children have brought you disgrace; drunkenness, cursing, quarrels, have ruled your home for years. Still others have met with bankruptcy and broken hopes in business. Not a few of you are beset by spiritual problems. Satan wants you to doubt instead of believing firmly, and you are beginning to wonder whether you have committed the unpardonable sin, whether the blood of Jesus is able to cleanse the vile, horrifying thoughts which contrary to your will shape themselves in your mind. In all this torture you ask disconsolately, "How can I bear my burden?"

That is the question millions of sufferers are voicing

today and many more millions will repeat tomorrow. Believers will not find their road easy during the years ahead. A magazine published in New Jersey coldly announces that the work of Martin Luther must be undone. Does that mean that my Church is to be liquidated? In a score of ways the adversities which Jesus foresaw and foretold as signs of the last times are being fulfilled before our eyes in unbelief, persecution of the truth, apostasy within churches.

Where, then, can the afflicted, especially those who sorrow over the war, fearing that disaster or death may strike their sons on far-off battle areas, find help? Or is there no hope? Is life merely a cruel game of chance with the cards stacked against us? May God drive those evil thoughts from your mind and give you the courage to follow His Son through hardship and heartache! Let the message of these Lenten weeks impress on your mind how incomparably greater than yours was the anguish the Savior "*endured*" on the cross. He could have died in a hundred other ways, but He deliberately chose that form of death, which the ancient world reserved for those whom it would make suffer long and intensely. He could have departed from life amid splendor, as ancient kings often did, or among an invited group of friends, as Socrates did, but He purposely selected the "*shame*" of the cross, the most despised form of execution; and on the unclean, accursed tree He died between two robbers to fulfill the ancient prophecy, "*He was numbered with the transgressors.*"

How could Christ knowingly and willingly "*endure*" all this? Our text answers: It was "*for the joy that was set before Him,*" the eternal salvation of your soul and mine. Great was His agony, but even greater His love. Tears fell from His eyes; heavy groanings escaped His lips; His soul was *"exceeding sorrowful, even unto death";* yet beyond Calvary was the rejoicing in the redemption. Above Good Friday's darkness shone the beacon light of God's penetrating love.

Similarly our text directs all Christians, *"looking unto Jesus,"* to find a high and heavenly purpose in their anguish. As the agonies of the crucifixion produced the greatest blessing the race has ever known, so for our Lord's followers *"all things,"* including shattering blows, *"work together for good."* In every pain or shame with which you as a child of God are burdened, a radiant joy has been set before you, too — the knowledge that you are afflicted because God loves you and visits you, not in His anger but in His unfathomable grace, so that adversity will make you lean wholly on Jesus, trust Him without question or quiver. Here, then, is the answer to the problem of suffering only Jesus can give and only those who accept Him can receive: There is rejoicing in every reverse, power for uplift in all blows that strike us down, healing for the soul in each sickness of body, spiritual strength in physical weakness, heavenly riches in earthly loss. For that faith, my heartbroken friends, turn to the cross! As truly as the Crucified is God's Son and the world's Savior, you will realize the pledge of His word, *"Your sorrow shall be turned into joy."*

Because this broadcast, in an ever-increasing degree, is determined to direct all whom it can reach to Jesus, *"the Author and Finisher of our faith,"* our Redeemer from sin and our Example in suffering, I am privileged now to give the happiest radio announcement it has ever been my privilege to make. For years many of you have been praying that Bringing Christ to the Nations would remain on the air during the summer season. The Lutheran Laymen's League, sponsor of this radio mission, has decided that, with God's grace and your help, we will broadcast every Sunday. Particularly in soul-trying times like these, the Savior must be preached with more force and frequency than ever. Pray for us! It will cost several hundred thousand dollars to continue this work, but I have the confidence that the Lord who has mightily blessed us during the past ten years will lead you to support us, so that year after year, the evangel of everlasting redemption may be preached in Christ's name to larger masses. Thank God today for this encouraging step forward and help us reach our objective: to use every suitable and available radio transmitter throughout the world for the spread of His saving truth; to broadcast Sunday after Sunday, month after month, year after year, without interruption, this one central, saving appeal: Look to the cross for love, for life, for light! Look to Jesus, the Son of the eternal God and the Son of the lowly Virgin, for full, free, final, finished salvation! Look to Christ for strength in every sorrow, courage in every crisis! Look to the Crucified, to Him alone, to Him always — and be saved! O God, give us that cross-directed vision and victory for Thy Son's sake! Amen.

Who Is This Prince of Peace?

When He was come into Jerusalem, all the city was moved, saying, Who is this? And the multitude said, This is Jesus, the Prophet of Nazareth of Galilee. And Jesus went into the Temple of God, and cast out all them that sold and bought in the Temple, and overthrew the tables of the money-changers and the seats of them that sold doves, and said unto them, It is written, My house shall be called the house of prayer; but ye have made it a den of thieves. And the blind and the lame came to Him in the Temple; and He healed them. And when the chief priests and scribes saw the wonderful things that He did and the children crying in the Temple and saying, Hosanna to the Son of David! they were sore displeased and said unto Him, Hearest Thou what these say? And Jesus saith unto them, Yea; have ye never read, Out of the mouth of babes and sucklings Thou hast perfected praise?"

SAINT MATTHEW 21:10-16

O Lord God of Grace and Truth:

Give *us contrite, reverent hearts, so that we may worthily observe this Holy Week commemorating the torture, crucifixion, and death of Thy beloved Son, Jesus, our precious Redeemer! Take away from us every thought of pride and self-righteousness! Humble us, until we know that we are less than nothing but the crucified Savior is more than all we need for eternal life! Use this broadcast, heavenly Father, as a means of leading many to this faith! May they in sincerity and truth sing their hosannas to the Christ who would hold His holy entrance into their hearts! Let the men and women of our armed forces, in the South Pacific, North Africa, the Aleutians — wherever they are — find time and rest this day to behold the Palm Sunday Prince of Peace and join their prayers with ours, asking Thee, with whom nothing*

[395]

is impossible, to grant us blessed peace and Thy daily, divine protection! Thy will be done! Hosanna to the heavenly Savior! May He come into our hearts now! We ask it, O Father, by the promise of His atoning love. Amen.

Last week when our troops in Tunisia entered Kairouan, holy city of the Mohammedans, they were welcomed with loud, almost hysterical acclaim. Civilians, finally freed from Axis rule, lined the streets, cheered themselves hoarse, showered tanks with flowers, and vied in inviting our troops to victory dinners. Altogether it was a scene of unbounded rejoicing.

Today we think of another holy city, Jerusalem, and of an altogether different triumphal march through its streets. Along the very roads on which Babylonian battalions, Alexander's armies, Roman legions, had entered that Judean capital as crushing conquerors, we behold, on the first Palm Sunday, the most startling cavalcade the ancient city has ever witnessed, with thousands lining the way, waving palm branches, throwing their garments on the streets as carpets for the approaching Hero, shouting hosannas and hallelujahs. Were they, too, assembled to greet a mighty warrior and his victorious veterans? Not a single soldier marched in those columns; neither sword nor bow nor spear was seen; no chariot rumbled in their ranks. Instead, unarmed men, defenseless women, carefree children walked side by side. And the Leader? Never in His life did He fight on a battlefield nor seek power. On the contrary, He spurned the call to become an earthly king. He told His disciple, *"Put up again thy sword into his place, for all they that take the sword shall perish with the sword!"* He wore no shield and shiny armor; He rode on no prancing steed; He had no battle cry; instead, the promise, *"My peace I give unto you. . . . Let not your heart be troubled!"* He dealt not with violence and might, but with grace and mercy, for He was *"the Prince of Peace."*

Strangely enough, while that Palm Sunday entrance into Jerusalem — one of history's most vital processions — attracted wide attention, many of the bystanders did not know the Prince of Peace. Because millions in our own country likewise have only a faulty, incomplete understanding of His person, power, and blessing, let us ask the Palm Sunday question:

WHO IS THIS PRINCE OF PEACE?

and find the answer in Saint Matthew (chapter twenty-one, verses ten and following): *"When He was come into Jerusalem, all the city was moved, saying, Who is this? And the multitude said, This is Jesus, the Prophet of Nazareth of Galilee. And Jesus went into the Temple of God, and cast out all them that sold and bought in the Temple, and overthrew the tables of the money-changers and the seats of them that sold doves, and said unto them, It is written, My house shall be called the house of prayer; but ye have made it a den of thieves. And the blind and the lame came to Him in the Temple; and He healed them. And when the chief priests and scribes saw the wonderful things that He did and the children crying in the Temple and saying, Hosanna to the Son of David! they were sore displeased and said unto Him, Hearest Thou what these say? And Jesus saith unto them, Yea; have ye never read, Out of the mouth of babes and sucklings Thou hast perfected praise?"*

I

HE IS THE DIVINE SAVIOR

" 'Who is this' Prince of Peace?" When the Palm Sunday crowds at Jerusalem answered the question by stat-

ing, *"This is Jesus, the Prophet of Nazareth of Galilee,"*
they were right, and they were wrong: right, because
Jesus was a Prophet who did come from Nazareth in
Galilee, despised though it was; and wrong, because He
was far more. This error, the same belittling Christ and
minimizing His greatness, is repeated today. It will require only slight effort to convince even unbelievers that
Jesus was an outstanding Figure. Scoffers have often paid
Him tribute. In 1877, when Robert Ingersoll made an
extended speaking tour of the Pacific Coast, night after
night he received huge fees for blaspheming the Bible,
ridiculing our religion, heaping sarcasm on the Savior.
At Portland he met a missionary to the Chinook Indians
and began to debate with him the wisdom of devoting an
entire life to the hopeless task of teaching a vanishing
Indian tribe what he called "the questionable statements
of the Gospel." In simple, courageous answer the missionary explained the hardships of his work, but also his
joy in bringing Christ to spiritually neglected natives.
When they parted, Ingersoll, agnostic, enemy of Christ,
pressed a twenty-dollar gold piece into the missionary's
hand with the remark: "It's good work you are doing!
It's good work!"

However, to praise Jesus and exalt His work is not
enough. We must call Him more than "Master." We must
go farther than say, "He is the greatest Man in all centuries." We must go all the way and declare in firm
faith, "This Jesus, as He rides into Jerusalem, meek and
lowly, is my Lord and God, the Sovereign of my soul."

No one less than God Himself can satisfy the desires
of your soul. You need assurance above the possibility
of error. You must have a sure Word of promise and hope
which not only will make no mistake, but that has the
power, the ability, the resources, to help you through

those difficulties in which all human agencies collapse — the questionings of a disturbed soul, the accusation of many sins, the protest of an aroused conscience, the plea of your distress: "Who can show me the truth? Who can save me?" — Here in Christ is the answer, comfort, power you seek; for, as His Word testifies, as His miracles prove, He is the Lord of heaven and earth, your God of glory!

Yet this Palm Sunday Prince of Peace is more. Though His countrymen refused to see the Old Testament prophecies fulfilled in Jesus, He is the Messiah, the Christ, the anointed Redeemer, the suffering Servant of Jehovah, concerning whom Isaiah, seven centuries previously, had written, *"He was wounded for our transgressions, He was bruised for our iniquities; the chastisement of our peace was upon Him, and with His stripes we are healed."* Unless you are ready to welcome Jesus into your heart as the Son of God and the Savior who atoned for your sins, washed away their stains with His blood, paid for their guilt on the cross, you do not know Christ, though you preach Him from a pulpit.

Even if you do declare, "Jesus is the Savior," there is still this one step to take: you must be able to say, "Jesus is my Savior." On no Sunday during the entire year should you realize more personally that Christ died for you than on this Palm Sunday, when you behold Him resolutely riding into the city which in a few days will nail Him to the cross.

Recently a book appeared entitled, *Who Crucified Jesus?* It was written by a professor at Dropsie College, Philadelphia, and Yeshiva College, New York, who repeats the ancient claim that the Savior's countrymen are not responsible for His crucifixion. He insists that Pontius Pilate and the Roman authorities are to blame; that

Christ was condemned for a political crime, as a rebel against the government. All this, however, is contradicted by the record of the four Gospels and the Epistles. True, Pilate had to go through the formality of issuing the death warrant; but, humanly speaking, had it not been for the deep-rooted hatred in the hearts of the Jerusalem citizens, Jesus never would have been sent to Calvary. The Jews of His day planned His destruction long before the first Good Friday. His own priests and church officials conducted the illegal hearings, incited the masses, bought the perjured witnesses, falsely charged Jesus, and systematically sought to kill Him. His own nation's leaders blocked Pilate, who, convinced of Christ's guiltlessness, sought to liberate Him and dismiss all charges. No; history is too clear, outspoken, unmistakable: those in the first instance responsible for the Savior's death are His own countrymen.

You and I cannot understand the real meaning of the crucifixion unless we know, believe, and confess that *our* sins sent Jesus to Golgotha; that *our* transgressions helped nail Him to the cross; that *our* guilt made Him suffer agony, unfathomable and indescribable. Each one of us must gaze up to our crucified God and Savior and declare with a crushed and contrite spirit: "O Jesus, my sins brought You this unspeakable misery. My iniquities nailed You to the cross. My transgressions made You groan in agony. My wickedness made You gasp in feverish thirst. My guilt made Your head drop in death." The hymn in your heart and on your lips every week, but this week especially, should be:

> It was for me
> He died upon the tree.

With this contrite confession you will be able to receive Jesus in truth as the Prince of Peace. You will read radiant promises like this: "He '*made peace through the blood of His cross*'"; or, "*Being justified by faith, we have peace with God*"; or, once more, Jesus' own unbreakable pledge: "*Peace I leave with you, My peace I give unto you; not as the world giveth, give I unto you. Let not your heart be troubled, neither let it be afraid*"; and in a world of bursting bombs, whistling shrapnel, screaming sirens, and moaning agony you, kneeling at Calvary, can have peace, "*perfect peace*," with your God, with your own conscience, with your fellow men. More: by the Spirit's help you can bring that peace into our peace-robbed age.

II

HE IS THE CLEANSER OF HIS CHURCH

"'*Who is this*' Prince of Peace?" He also proved Himself the Cleanser of His Church. After Jesus had triumphantly entered the city, He went immediately into the Temple. What a necessary example for every one of us! Today the feeling is widespread, even in religious circles, that it is not necessary to join a true church. People think they can worship at home, outdoors, amid the marvels of unfolding nature. They can; but they must do more! When the Apostles preached the message of the crucified Savior, they founded congregations almost everywhere they traveled; and it was the Almighty's will, expressed in His own Book, that the believers should not forsake those assemblies. If Jesus customarily went to the synagogue, we ought to attend His church. He Himself said, "*Blessed are they that hear the Word of God.*" If you want the blessing of regular instruction in God's Word, the privilege of Holy Communion, and your share in extending the Savior's kingdom, join a true church! Attend regularly and support it! Radio messages like these are not enough. Your private study of Scripture is not enough. Your own devotional reading is not enough. Do what Jesus did when, soon after entering Jerusalem, without waiting for the Sabbath, He headed straight for the Temple! — On Palm Sunday years ago many of you pledged yourselves to Him and His Church, promising to remain faithful even through the pains of death. Yet today you are without Christ. What a glorious day for you to return to your Redeemer, His Church and the joy of your salvation!

Some of you say: "My Church has lost its power and blessing. The congregations in my town are worldly." Don't let that stop you! The Temple in Jesus' day was defiled with vile abominations; yet that did not keep Jesus away. We read that the meek, loving Prince of Peace *"went into the Temple of God, and cast out all them that sold and bought in the Temple, and overthrew the tables of the money-changers and the seats of them that sold doves, and said unto them, It is written, My house shall be called the house of prayer; but ye have made it a den of thieves."* When our Lord saw religious racketeers making money within God's sanctuary, profiteering for the priests, since they demanded their share of the gains; when He knew that this buying and selling was rife with fraud, lying, and dishonesty, so that *"the house of prayer"* had become *"a den of thieves,"* He was seized by holy indignation and drove every one of those temple merchants away, silencing the noise of their bargaining.

Jesus could serve as the Cleanser of His church, for He was Lord of that sanctuary. While we are in no way authorized to use force, we, too, must be ready to act in preserving our sanctuaries as houses of prayer to the true God. How tragic that many churches today similarly stand exposed for engaging in money-making projects which transgress both the civil and sacred law, feature gambling, worldly attractions, indecent shows.

All this is bad enough and calls for protest, repeated and earnest; yet even worse is the dishonesty practiced by the present-day priest, Pharisee, and Sadducee — the cunning denial of the saving Gospel, the modern misrepresentation of the cross. At the time when our country as never before needs outspoken emphasis on Christ's cleansing blood, His atoning death, His life-giving resurrection, men arise — they sound smooth and attractive, to some they sound convincing — and claim that to enter the kingdom of God, we must enter a new sphere of living, we must keep faith in ourselves, faith in the upward march of mankind. Only by living in harmony with the universe, they tell us, can our unconquerable spirit sail through today's difficulties. Not once is Christ conceded to be God. Not once are sinners told to lay their guilt on Him. Not once is the Cross preached as proof of our Savior's substitutionary suffering in our behalf.

Last week a perplexed listener in Fostoria, Michigan, sent me the summary of a radio address delivered by a man called "America's greatest Christian." Contrasting that modernist's message with ours, he wrote me: "I am convinced of this: You are a liar or else this other preacher is a liar. Either you are a fool, or he is." And he concluded: "I am miserable. I am sinful. I am helpless. Oh, that I had the peace I long for!" A few days after he sent that letter, the Holy Spirit touched his heart and he now said: "Like old Bartimaeus, at last I see. In profound and humble gratitude I thank God that in Jesus' blood my sins are forgiven and my eyes are opened. No 'upward march of mankind,' no 'moral philosophy,' no 'world understanding,' no 'faith in man's unconquerable

soul,' can ever atone for my sins that cry to high heaven.
Only Christ can, and not a mere man-made Christ who is
only a splendid example to follow, not a mere man-made
Christ who shows me how to take up my cross and earn
heaven by my picking it up, not a mere man-made Christ
who lived in harmony with the universe and showed us
how to live in communion with nature! No! No! Only
Christ who is both God and man could redeem me —
only Christ, who was crucified by my sins!" Thank God,
we say, for this enlightenment; but pray God to stop
every perverter of His truth! It was criminal for those
Jerusalem temple merchants to rob people of their money;
it is doubly damnable, however, for modern pulpit pirates
to rob hearers of their soul's salvation.

This was the second time Jesus had cleansed the
Temple. Three years previously He had similarly driven
away the profiteers; now the sanctuary had to be purged
again. Once, before our own generation, God purified the
churches in Martin Luther's mighty Reformation. That
was four centuries ago, and four hundred years is a long
time, too long for men to keep their desecrating hands
off Christ's truth. The day for another reformation has
dawned. Churches must drop the search for wealth,
power, money, pomp, privilege, and seek faith, humility,
and service. They must go all out for Christ, as the sole
but sure Savior of mankind. The pulpit must ring with
100-per-cent loyalty to Scripture, not with denial, double
talk, deception.

III

HE IS THE HELPER OF THE HELPLESS

" 'Who is this' Prince of Peace?" There in the Temple
our Lord gave us another answer, for He showed Himself
the Helper of the helpless. When the news spread that
Jesus of Nazareth had come to the Temple, large numbers of "the blind and the lame came to Him"; and though

torture, crucifixion, and death were only a few days away, the Savior, instead of remaining engrossed in the thoughts of His suffering, took time to heal everyone brought to Him.

"If only Christ were with us today to continue that healing ministry!" you, the sick and sufferers, are saying. Our Prince of Peace *is* still with us — not bodily, to lay His hands on the wounded in war, on those bruised in life's battles, but spiritually, so that, not confined to one place, He can bless His children over all the world. He who has never made a mistake nor uttered an unfulfilled promise assures us, *"Lo, I am with you alway, even unto the end of the world!"* Build your hope on that pledge! Let it comfort you! Believe that the same Jesus is personally, directly, sympathetically concerned with every sorrow which may overtake His followers! Often in the history of proud empires have the sickly, lame, disfigured, blind, been removed from the road along which the procession of a mighty king or haughty queen took its course. Only the strong, healthy, robust, were to be seen by these monarchs. How utterly different our compassionate Christ! Read the record of His Gospels, and you will see that He spent more time with the sick and bereaved than with any other group!

Believe also that the same Savior who touched those sightless eyes and made them see, laid His hands on those withered, paralyzed, broken limbs and infused them with life and strength, can still heal. Every Christian doctor throughout the land knows that often when medicine and treatment fail, the Almighty succeeds; that men and women are snatched from the edge of death by direct, divine aid. Therefore, whatever the burdens of your bodily weakness and physical pain may be; however heavy the sorrows of war's bereavement or sudden death; whenever your spiritual worries seem overpowering — and this week again brought those agonized pleas asking: "Can Jesus forgive my shocking, terrifying transgressions? Is there any hope for me with all my evil thoughts against God? Have I committed the sin against the Holy Ghost?" — take it all to Christ, and because He is your God and Savior, He will help you in every earthly sorrow! He may not heal your body, for such healing would not advance your soul's welfare; but He will always — and this is a thousand times more important — heal your soul and sanctify your suffering. He will fortify you with courage to meet the most distressing reverses, even death notices from the battle front. He will put sympathy for others into your heart. Above all, He will make the days of your affliction a time of spiritual triumph by bringing you closer to God, making you lean wholly on Christ, rely entirely on the Spirit's guidance.

Therefore on this Palm Sunday, which marks the beginning of our Lord's last week of earthly life, I appeal to you, the blind in the United States, the victims of paralysis, the 2,000,000 on the nation's sick list, the thousands of wounded who have been returned to military and naval hospitals in our country or who hear these words beyond our boundaries: in every darkened hour, when you are threatened with despair, when you deny that life is worth the agonies you have suffered, bring all your anguish to our sin-removing, grace-bestowing Christ! Did He ever refuse to receive any racked, tormented soul? His promise is, *"Him that cometh to Me I will in no wise cast out."* Approach Him now, just as you are, and the Prince of Peace will come into your life with an entrance much more blessed even than that Palm Sunday procession. He will give you heaven-sent, heaven-directed assurance, by which you can join the afflicted, persecuted Apostle in saying, *"I know that this shall turn to my salvation."*

IV

HE IS THE CHAMPION OF CHILDHOOD

"'Who is this' Palm Sunday Prince of Peace?" He is also the Champion of childhood. While Jesus was healing the sick in the Temple, the children gathered about Him and sang in happy voices, "Hosanna to the Son of David!" With childlike simplicity those boys and girls believed the Lord was truly the promised Messiah, and joyfully their praise rang through the Temple. The jealous priests and envious scribes were enraged; but when they demanded of Jesus, "Hearest Thou what these say?" He answered: "Yea; have ye never read, Out of the mouth of babes and sucklings Thou hast perfected praise?" If those proud churchmen really knew their Bible, so our Lord implied, they would have understood the Eighth Psalm's prediction that God uses even babes and nursing children for His praise and mighty purposes.

You see, then, our blessed Savior is earnestly concerned about receiving the acclaim of our American children. As the youth in Jerusalem sang, "Hosanna" — that means literally "save" us — so the youth in the United States should plead, "'Hosanna' — save us, Jesus!" Tragically, however, the average American child spends more time in clay modeling, basketry, and sand play than in the study of God's Word. A typical boy or girl in our country knows more about crime, the underworld, international spies, than about Christ. Even our high-school and college youth are woefully misinformed in religious matters. Recently 7,000 students in thirty-six colleges and universities were given a comprehensive examination in United States history. Twenty-five per cent of them did not know that Abraham Lincoln was President during the Civil War. Thomas Jefferson, the 200th anniversary of whose birth was observed last week, was called a Salvation Army worker. Alexander Hamilton was described as a watchmaker. Theodore Roosevelt was identified as the man who helped free Texas. This is dangerous ignorance. Far more appalling, however, is the lack of spiritual understanding. Our young people should know that this land was colonized quite largely by men and women who came to spread the Gospel on our shores. They should recall that America's foundation is not atheistic, agnostic, but positively Christian. They should feel that for our nation's future we need, above all, a return to God in Jesus, a reaffirmation of these early American ideals.

Instead, however, many young people are not only growing up without any understanding of the Savior, the Bible, and the Church, but their minds are also being poisoned by hideous unbelief. Last week, in Detroit, the faculty of Wayne University, a public, tax-supported school, invited an outspoken infidel — the man whose poem, "Good-by, Christ," I mentioned some time ago — to read his writings before the student body. If you parents knew the filth, the savagery, and the brutal attacks on God and His Son which this man has put into his verses, you would seriously wonder how in the name of common sense and ordinary decency educators, whose salaries are paid largely by Christian citizens, would ever dare feature such blasphemy. One of those college girls read aloud that satanic poem, "Good-by, Christ," and sneeringly told the courageous women picketing the meeting to mind their own business. Another co-ed declared publicly that she would kill her mother if she ever caught her picketing for the Bible. But here is the worst! Some of you will not want to believe this, yet I have it black on white in one of his own books: * this

---

* *The Big Sea*, by Langston Hughes (Alfred A. Knopf, 1940), page 334.

atheist, this infidel, who speaks of God having a hemor-
rhage, who mentions spitoons on church altars, received
a literary reward of $400.00 and a gold medal from the
Federated Council of Churches! Talk about the high
priests giving Judas thirty pieces of silver for betraying
his Lord!

Is it any wonder that crime, vice, and wickedness
among juveniles has reached an altogether shocking
height? J. Edgar Hoover, head of the Federal Bureau of
Investigation, reports that last year the arrests of girls
under twenty-one increased 55 per cent and immorality
jumped 104 per cent.

This neglect of children is America's most menacing
danger for the future. Our youth must be won for Christ
today if we are to stave off tomorrow's disaster. We must
return to the early Colonial ideals. They had no million-
dollar school plants, gymnasiums, cafeterias, playgrounds,
swimming pools, these pioneer settlers; indeed, they were
often thankful if they could conduct school in a log
cabin; but despite their primitive poverty they kept
Christ in culture. Let me read you this summary by an
educational expert: "Everywhere and at all times in the
Colonial period the religious element was prominent in
the schools. The Psalter and Testament were used as
textbooks, the primers were filled with religious ideas.
Every school taught the catechism." We likewise must be
ready to give our Christian children Scripture-grounded
training, for what is a nation profited if its youth can
answer quiz questions, but not soul questions; if its boys
and girls are clever and cunning, but not obedient and
truthful?

Once again, I offer our American families a practical
help. My Church conducts hundreds of Christian day
schools throughout the country, where children are taught

to sing hosannas to the coming Christ — schools noted for their sound secular training, but especially for the solid, spiritual life-foundation they build. They are open to your little ones. Let me tell you how your son or daughter can be enrolled without charge to learn daily the most sacred of all truths, the Bible record of God's love in Christ!

Before this Palm Sunday ends, I ask, "What does this Prince of Peace mean to you?" Can you begin this week, commemorating His captivity, torture, and death, with the same neglect of your Redeemer that has marked every previous week of your life? Can you hear Him cry from the cross, *"My God, My God, why hast Thou forsaken Me?"* and turn away unmoved? Are you one of those who acclaimed Jesus in momentary fervor, but disclaimed Him in some crisis, like these palm branch wavers and hosanna singers who soon became His enemies? He will return, no longer in meekness and humility, but with heavenly power to judge the world and take His children home to heaven. The signs with which He foretold His second coming are being fulfilled, particularly in widespread warfare. The world fire lighted in 1914 and again in 1939 may never be put out. World War III may soon follow if bungling diplomats keep Christ from the peace table.

When Jesus returns — or when you face Him in eternity — will you be ready to meet Him? It will be too late in the crash and flash of His coming for you to repent suddenly. Acclaim Him now! It will be too late to accept Him when you meet Him face to face in eternity's Judgment. *"It is appointed unto men once to die,"* the Savior warns, *"after this the Judgment."* Receive Him as your Redeemer now!

With all the insecurity of life today, the plea to acknowledge Jesus is direct and urgent. On Friday, Saint Louis lost one of its Christian physicians, a man in the prime of life, who without any previous warning whatever died in a few short seconds, while treating a patient. That beloved physician was prepared for his departure. Are you? Can you face the holy God if today or tomorrow death's skeletal hand reaches out for you? There is only one way by which you can remain ready — by clinging to the Lord Jesus as your own, everlasting Savior! Then, though the way of your salvation be through sorrow and searing pain, it will bring you into the radiance of the new Jerusalem! May we all be found in the sacred assembly which Saint John was privileged to behold: *"Lo, a great multitude, which no man could number, of all nations and kindreds and people and tongues stood before the throne and before the Lamb, clothed with white robes and palms in their hands; and cried with a loud voice, saying, Salvation to our God, which sitteth upon the throne, and unto the Lamb!"* Grant us, O Father, through faith in our crucified Savior, that we join the angels around that throne and sing in exalted strains, *"Amen: blessing and glory and wisdom and thanksgiving and honor and power and might be unto our God forever and ever"* through Jesus Christ! Amen.